Roads of Adventure

Also from Westphalia Press

westphaliapress.org

Roads of Adventure

by Ralph D. Paine

WESTPHALIA PRESS
An imprint of Policy Studies Organization

Westphalia Press
An imprint of Policy Studies Organization
1527 New Hampshire Ave., NW
Washington, D.C. 20036
dgutierrezs@ipsonet.org

ISBN-13: 978-1935907763
ISBN-10: 193590776X

Updated material and comments on this edition
can be found at the Westphalia Press website:
www.westphaliapress.org

ROADS OF ADVENTURE

THE AUTHOR FINDS A FOOTING WITH THE LARGE BLACK HORSE (*page 210*)

From a drawing by Rufus F. Zogbaum, who was on board of the *Gussie*. (Published in Harper's Weekly.)

ROADS OF ADVENTURE

BY

RALPH D. PAINE

Popular Edition

WITH ILLUSTRATIONS

TOVT
BIEN OV
RIEN

A full, busy youth is your only prelude to a self-contained and independent age; and the muff inevitably develops into the bore. There are not many Dr. Johnsons to set forth upon their first romantic voyage at sixty-four. If we wish to scale Mont Blanc, or visit a thieves' kitchen in the East End, or go down in a diving dress or up in a balloon, we must be about it while we are still young. . . . Youth is the time to go flashing from one end of the world to the other both in mind and body; to try the manners of different nations; to hear the chimes at midnight; to see sunrise in town and country. . . .

STEVENSON

PUBLISHERS' NOTE

Roads of Adventure, Ralph D. Paine's autobiographic narrative of his life as a Yale oarsman, filibuster, and war correspondent on sea and shore in three wars, was originally published as a large octavo in 1922. Although well received by the press and public, Mr. Paine felt that the size and price of the book kept it out of the hands of many of the thousands of readers who had found pleasure in his stories of adventure. Some months before his death he proposed to his publishers that the book be shortened by the omission of certain chapters dealing with his life in the period of peace between the time of the Boxer Rebellion and the Great War, and re-issued in smaller form at a popular price. This has now been done in strict conformity with his wishes. The book stands in the form he would have had it stand, as the final record of the most stirring episodes in a life largely devoted to war and wandering.

CONTENTS

CONTENTS

ILLUSTRATIONS

ROADS OF ADVENTURE

.

ROADS OF ADVENTURE

I

THE GREENHORN AND THE OAR

THIRTY years ago I knew a strapping six-footer of a Yale
freshman named Ralph Paine who had come from his home
in Florida to seek an education on his own resources. It was
his second attempt to gain a foothold on the campus. His
father had courageously undertaken to send him to college,
but the burden was too heavy for the income of a Presbyterian minister, and this the boy realized after three months
in the class of '93. Back he went to the drowsy, primitive
Jacksonville of those distant days and found a position as
the cub reporter of the "Times-Union" where he legged it
through the long, sweltering summer and hopefully saved his
wages of twelve dollars a week. With a small fund of his
own, therefore, he sallied north to New Haven to enter
another freshman class, determined somehow to stay there
four years.

This was in the era of Yale athletic supremacy afield and
afloat, and echoes of her prowess had thrilled his fancy, but
it was not the real incentive. He had become convinced that
it was a great thing to be a Yale man. This was the goal for
which he strove.

Whenever I go to see a boat-race over that storied, four-
mile reach of the Thames at New London, I fall to thinking
of that clumsy, rosy freshman and how his youthful destiny
came to be interwoven with the university eight and the
toiling brotherhood of the oar. And I seem to discern phantom crews come swinging down the river through the gay,
bedecked lane of yachts, and in a trailing launch the brawny,

resolute figure of the coach, "Bob" Cook, who was the master of them all and whose name is not even a memory to the present generation of youngsters.

In football and rowing there was a splendid tradition of victory almost unbroken for years. Defeat was a calamity tinged with disgrace. At personal sacrifice the great captains came back after graduation to teach the crew or the eleven, and one mentor took up the task where another had left off. There were no hired coaches. It was labor for an ideal, for the intangible values untouched by the dollar mark, and it helped to build and to preserve what was known as the Yale spirit. It made athletic endeavor a genuine part of education, the chief business of which, from my old-fashioned point of view, is to show youth how to live more worthily.

Middle age is prone to prate and preach and therefore one must steer clear of the temptation. It is better to hark back to that January day of 1891 when all would-be oarsmen were requested to muster in the gymnasium to begin the season's training. Since then rowing has been made popular, with crews by the dozen at Harvard and Yale. This is a vast improvement. In my day it was the servitude of the few, and through six months of grimly serious preparation only the university and freshman eights used the harbor. There were no races to break the monotony, seldom any spectators, and it was in no sense a pastime. To win a place in the crew and row against Harvard, this was the high honor and the great reward.

As a greenhorn I joined the crowd of aspirants for the freshman boat. The problem of self-support had not yet been solved and funds were running low, but to a lad who had sailed a boat the year round on the Florida rivers and lagoons there was no resisting the lure of the shell and the oar. For several days the freshman mob panted around the indoor running track or tugged awkwardly at the rowing machines, and then the captain of the university crew strolled over to watch the pathetic exertions. With him was a famous veteran who had come back to help get things under way.

Presently the tall captain, a superman in our sight, beckoned the six-foot freshman from Florida and told him:

"You will train with the 'varsity after this, Paine. Report to-morrow." [1]

It sounded incredible. The recollection of that bewildering moment is vivid even now. The other freshmen regarded it as sensational. The explanation was that the Yale crew happened to lack heavy, powerful men for the waist of the boat and so it was decided to hammer one of them into shape from the raw material. Behold me, then, seated as the 'varsity Number Four in that contrivance of torment called a rowing tank, with no conception of the infinitely difficult art of pulling a twelve-foot sweep, under the tutelage of two or three earnest young gentlemen who had not the slightest regard for my feelings. Daily their insults were hurled like a bombardment.

Coaches came and went, but however they might differ with respect to the merits of the other men, they were certain to agree in bawling, until they were red in the face, such cruel objurgations as these:

"*Don't* flop over on the catch, Four! Hold yourself together!"

"Shoot your hands out! For the love of heaven, wake up, you big dummy!"

"You are kicking out your slide, Paine. Can't you ever remember anything?"

"Oh, keep your head up. You sit there like a sack of meal."

"Confound you, swing those shoulders *hard!* You are behind again. Watch Number Six."

"*Don't* cock your blade. Close to the water now. Holy suffering cats, will you *ever* learn to row?"

There were perhaps forty of us in the squad before the

[1] The rule barring freshmen from 'varsity teams was not then in force.

coaches began to weed them out, several old hands who wore the magic "Y" emblazoned on their sweaters, football players of the requisite bone and muscle, men who had tried in other years and were pluckily trying again, members of former freshman crews, and spindling lads with nothing but high-stepping ambition to recommend them. Through the weeks of winter, while the river was ice-bound, we ran five or six miles every afternoon, out into the suburbs of New Haven and the countryside beyond, followed this with setting-up exercises severe enough to kill a horse, and then pulled our hearts out in the accursed tank.

In March only a dozen survivors of the squad remained, and the eight slogged away in a heavy barge on the river and harbor where the winds were biting and the spray froze on bare arms and knees. Now and then a submerged oyster stake punched a hole in the craft, and the wretched castaways swam or floundered ashore in shivering misery to gallop to the boat-house, every man with his oar upon his shoulder. Oddly enough, they liked it all and would have been nowhere else for worlds.

There was compensation in the close comradeship of the training table where men began to realize what *the crew* meant, that they were bound together in a singularly unselfish fraternity. There could be no star performers, no quest of individual glory. The eight was something with a soul of its own, like Kipling's ship that found itself.

At last the spring-time came and with it the task of learning to balance and drive the skittish, sensitive racing shell, after the sluggish barge. It was now comprehended that rowing is both an art and a science, requiring more skill than any other sport. There came a day when the shell ceased to splash and roll, when for the first time these eight men were rowing as a crew. The coxswain gave the word and the skipper of the coaching launch pulled the jingle bell for full speed ahead.

Eight blades flashed from the water so that from astern only one oar could be seen to port and to starboard. They went winging back on the recover, swiftly, then feeling for the water with tense, delicate care until, with the lightning lift of arms and shoulders they bit a clean, sharp catch while eight backs swung up as one and eight pairs of sturdy legs drove home the finish of the stroke.

Easily the oar-handles rolled in to the arching chests and then shot away again. The straight backs swayed over, the slides started to the quick jerk of the toes and then slowed down when the arms and legs were taut for the next stroke. This shifting human cargo of fourteen hundred pounds weight was stopped and started back so carefully that the long shell felt no shock and slid unchecked between strokes. Thirty times a minute these eight men combined this terrific lift and heave, this delicate finish, swift recover, and careful, deliberate slide action, even when heads were throbbing with fatigue and lungs and backs were strained and wearied until every stroke *hurt* to pull through.

A test like this over the four-mile course of New Haven harbor and there was the dawning hope that the crew might acquit itself with credit against Harvard. But there were many other days when the work went all wrong, a lifeless, unsteady shell, a set of most unhappy oarsmen who simply could not get the proper feel and *tempo* of the stroke, days when they stalked up Chapel Street from the boat-house in gloomy discouragement and glowered at each other at the supper-table while they sadly wolfed down pounds and pounds of juicy steaks or prodigious platters of scrambled eggs.

There was another heavy-weight in this crew, besides the Florida freshman. This was none other than the mighty "Pudge" Heffelfinger, giant of the football field, unsurpassed even unto this day, whose exploits have become legendary. He did not take kindly to rowing. They had virtually drafted him for the boat, and in these hours of despondency he was a particularly melancholy sight because there was so much of him. It was to be the present writer's fearsome fate to play football against this gentle warrior in the autumn of sophomore year, as guard on the second 'varsity eleven, a harrowing experience which had best be left untold. War stories are not ardently read just now.

Football was a battle in those rude, far-off days of mass formations, flying wedges, and five yards in four downs, when the spectator was seldom afforded a glimpse of the ball. It was often played in the spirit of Denny O'Neil, big and green but very willing, who waved the Yale coaches aside as he thundered:

"To hell wid your tricks an' your stratagems! Show me me man and let me at him."

It is enough to say that when in action "Pudge" Heffelfinger, six feet three in his cleated shoes and as hard as iron, was sheer devastation. During that one season of actively intermingling with him on the trampled turf, a broken nose, a telescoped neck, and a leg in a plaster cast convinced me that I had been working, in my humble way, for the cause of Yale football. It was pleasanter, on the whole, to row on a crew with Heffelfinger than to be dismembered by degrees all over the field. He was never a vicious nor an unfair player. Let us call him zealous.

This Yale crew of '91 was notable for its weight and power. At the end of a hawser it could have dragged a house from the foundations, but there was lacking a consistent harmony of action, that coördination in all circumstances which marks the finished eight. Whenever it got together it was uncommonly fast. Nobody could explain this uncertain form, why the shell should crawl and flounder on the one day and skim smoothly over the miles on the next. It was a temperamental equation, a baffling riddle.

Meanwhile the younger coaches were carrying the work

along, in a sequence of complete agreement and understanding, every one tarrying a fortnight or longer and then hastening back to his office or his factory. It made a lasting impression upon the plastic minds of youth, that these busy men should be so devoted to the service of Yale, so loyal to her traditions as to come back and coach the crew for the love of it. The association with them was immensely valuable. They were gentlemen in word and deed, and they had endured the stern test of the four-mile course in other years as captains or strokes of winning crews. They inspired admiration and respect. It was a kind of hero worship that conferred obvious benefits.[1]

These oarsmen were not so likely to pattern themselves after the members of the faculty who taught them Latin or Greek or History. These were wise and estimable scholars, but in most instances their influence extended no farther than the threshold of the recitation hall. This may have been regrettable, but it was true to human nature. It was otherwise, however, when John Rogers or Alfred Cowles or Fred Stevenson returned to coach the crew. Somehow their mission, the spirit of it, and their fine, robust personalities conveyed a sense of knightliness. Unconsciously they were teaching other things than rowing.

[1] A similar system, and as successful, existed for many years in Yale football under the leadership of Walter Camp.

II

THE DYNASTY OF "BOB" COOK

UNSEEN and in the background through the earlier months of training was the master coach, Robert J. Cook. Manager of a large newspaper property in Philadelphia, he found time to visit New Haven for a few days in the spring and later to spend the final weeks with the crew at the quarters on the Thames. His task it was to apply the finishing touches, to perfect the details which might add an inch of distance to a stroke, to find and remedy the flaws in this intricate human mechanism.

His word was law and rightly so. Rowing the Cook stroke, Yale had defeated Harvard five years in succession. His dynasty, as one might call it, was to continue much longer, and when, at length, it came to an end, Yale had lost only one race to Harvard, her dearest foe, in more than a dozen years.

To us youngsters the story of "Bob" Cook was like a romance. He had come to Yale from a Pennsylvania farm, rugged and seasoned at the plough and the pitchfork, and past twenty-one years of age. As a freshman in the spring of '72 he had wandered down to the river and the boat-house to gaze wistfully at the oarsmen. Unaccustomed to an indoor life, a winter of hard study had made him feel stale and restless. This rowing was a novelty that appealed to him. He could see no reason why he should not be given a trial.

At this time Yale boating fortunes were at a low ebb. The six-oared crews had been trounced by such smaller colleges as Bowdoin and Williams and Amherst, and nobody had any clear ideas of form or style. The crew was an exclusive organization, however, with a flavor of social caste, and lowly freshmen with hayseed in their hair were distinctly ineligible. This "Bob" Cook was the best wrestler and rough-and-tumble fighter in college, but as for admitting him to the charmed circle of the 'varsity crew, it would n't do at all. He was very curtly told to wait a year or so, and meanwhile to stay away from the boat-house.

A young man with a square jaw and a solid pair of shoulders, he had determined to break into this aristocratic company. Day after day he haunted the boat-house, and it was to be noted that none of the haughty young gentlemen appeared eager to throw him out. At length the captain lost patience and contrived a way to get rid of this nuisance of a freshman.

"Bob" Cook was told to get into a pair-oared boat. With him went the strongest and most skillful man of the crew. Each took an oar and began to pull for all he was worth. It was anticipated that this test would make a laughing-stock of the ignorant freshman. Without doubt the veteran would promptly pull him around in circles.

What the stocky young farmer lacked in experience was atoned for in muscle, wind, and courage. This was no harder than chopping down trees or pitching on a load of hay. He dug his oar into the water and laid back on it. The opponent, who set the stroke, rushed the pace to flurry him, but Cook kept time without turning a hair. The boat began to swing, but not in the direction so confidently expected by the onlookers. By main strength the freshman was winning the bout. Soon the boat was slowly describing a circle, Cook breathing easily and enjoying the exercise. It was the veteran who cried quits.

"Now will you give me a chance on the crew?" demanded this presumptuous interloper.

They would, indeed. He was invited to take a seat in the waist of the boat, but not because they wished to have him there. The captain told them to shove off and the course was laid out into the harbor. The order was given to put their backs into it for the full distance of three miles, a trial against the watch. They would kill the hayseed and so finish the business. It was a cruel ordeal for a young man who had never sat in a racing boat, who had done no training, and whose muscles were unused to this kind of exertion.

At first he caught crabs and was banged to and fro, but soon he fell into the stride and managed to chop his blade into the water and throw his weight on the handle. Forty strokes a minute and higher they pumped at that old-fashioned "donkey-engine" stroke, and three miles of it was enough to make any man gasp like a fish. "Bob" Cook was still going strong when the shell slackened headway, and he suggested another mile of it. The joke was distinctly on the other fellows. Glumly they paddled back to the boat-house and young Cook stiffly hauled himself out upon the landing stage. His wrists were already swelling and his muscles had knotted with cramps, but he addressed the group as follows:

"It was a dirty trick. And we may as well understand each other. If you refuse to give me a fair deal, I intend to whip this whole Yale crew, beginning with the captain. And you can step up right now."

Tradition has it that at least one gorgeous black eye was the sequel, but it did not decorate the stubborn visage of the embattled young farmer. Thereafter he sat in the Yale boat and no man molested him. This was a crew which had a hazy conception of the principles of rowing, notwithstanding its excellent opinion of itself, and in the annual race on the Connecticut River it was most disgracefully beaten, lagging far in the rear of Amherst, Harvard, Massachusetts Agricultural College, Bowdoin, and Williams. A worse crew had never been sent out from New Haven.

"Bob" Cook, the unterrified freshman, was elected captain for the next year, and the captain he was to be through the rest of his college course, rowing at stroke-oar. The humiliating defeat rankled. He brooded and pondered over it. College rowing in America was mostly experimental at best, and such little method as it possessed had been acquired from professional scullers. The sliding seat was still a novelty. A few crews used slides with rollers while others greased the boards with tallow and sewed leather patches on their breeches. In a hard race with a high stroke they were in danger of spontaneous combustion. It was martyrdom for sport's sake.

Young Cook returned to college from a summer on the farm and he was still considering this vital problem. What was the best way to row and where could it be learned? During the Christmas vacation he sat in his campus room reading "Tom Brown at Oxford." Here was the answer. He said to himself:

"By Jingo, that's where they know how to row. They have been at it since Hector was a pup. I am going to England somehow."

The vision was quixotic. He had no money of his own for the pilgrimage and it seemed absurd to ask for a leave of absence from college. Yale was a small place, clustered around the Old Brick Row, and its ways were very simple. The elm-shaded campus, which lived its life apart and found contentment in its own activities, regarded it as sensational when "Bob" Cook announced his intention. With trepidation he approached that benignant scholar and divine, "Prexy" Porter, and submitted his rash request. It was promptly granted.

Perhaps the worthy president had felt chagrin that his boys should be viewed as a sorry jest on the water, and I am sure that he was wise enough to grasp the real significance of this mission. It was in accordance with the doctrine of service which had won for Yale a prestige far more honorable than pretentious buildings or large endowments could possibly achieve.

Three hundred dollars was the modest budget required to finance the journey of "Bob" Cook. The legend is that the undergraduates pawned their overcoats and watches or sold their furniture to complete the amount. An interesting commentary this, when many a spoiled sophomore of to-day would never miss the three hundred dollars from a term's allowance.

In this frugal manner did "Bob" Cook set forth on his adventure, sailing for England in January. First he went to Cambridge and was hospitably welcomed by the 'varsity rowing men. They wined and dined him and took him out to follow the crews along the bank of the Cam. He rowed with them and learned all the coaches could show him. After a leisurely visit he journeyed to Oxford where he was as cordially received. Then he finished the six weeks' course of study by joining the famous crews of the London Rowing Club.

Satisfied that he had mastered the English style of rowing, he proceeded to adapt it, with acute intelligence, to fit the American college oarsman who is less mature and experienced, as a rule, than his cousins overseas. He cannot swing as far at either end of the stroke without wasted effort and needless exhaustion. The English style, somewhat shortened and with more attention paid to form and finish, was what "Bob" Cook introduced at Yale as the result of his quest. More and more influenced by his own peculiar genius, it became fixed after a few years and in its chief essentials was like the American college stroke largely in use to-day. As taught by Cook and his school of younger graduate coaches, no more soundly scientific system of rowing was ever devised in this country. Yale success afloat has been intermittent and fitful since it was discarded. At first there was opposition, often disheartening, before the "Bob" Cook system was solidly established at New Haven, but he doggedly hung on, his faith unshaken, until his ideas were brilliantly vindicated.

This was the man who snatched such time as could be spared from his large business affairs to coach this crew of ours in '91. Quiet of manner but tremendously forceful, still the rugged athlete although fifteen years out of college, he rightly regarded this avocation of his as something more than sport. He was helping to make men. With that impressive solidity of aspect he used to say such things as these from the bow of the coaching launch:

"Form makes speed, boys, but what counts is *sand*. When you are all in on the last mile, remember that the fellows in the other boat are just as groggy. It is the last ounce that wins a close race, the ounce of strength you did n't know you had in you.

". . . When you get out in the world and things go wrong, and you feel ready to quit, just stop and think that you can't go up against anything harder than the finish of a hard four-mile race."

III

"SWING, SWING TOGETHER"

FROM January until early June the daily routine of the crew was unbroken. Most of the work was done after four o'clock in the afternoon when it did not interfere with recitations or lectures. Holidays meant a grueling stretch of it and an extra session on the river in the morning. There was no burning the midnight oil to gain more study hours, for the crew men were ordered to be in bed by ten, and the rules of training were punctiliously obeyed. It was a point of honor, the spirit of the game. And yet these men stood well in their classes, better than many of those who had more leisure to loaf. Splendid physical condition kept their minds alert and their heads clear. And they were learning the indispensable habit of concentrated toil. They were mentally disciplined by the school of the oar.

In my own case there was a living to be earned besides these daily demands of the campus and the crew. It had seemed a staggering problem, but the most precious asset of youth is the sublime confidence that impossible things can be done, somehow. That year of perspiring apprenticeship as a reporter in Florida had taught me a little about the trade of getting news and writing it. This was turned to advantage. One sporting editor after another, in New York, Boston, Philadelphia, was argued into accepting Ralph Paine as a Yale correspondent who could write about athletics with an air of authority.

It was a favorable time to launch the enterprise because of Yale's commanding position in college sports. It meant grinding out an enormous amount of writing to make both ends meet because the payment was only five or eight dollars a column. On the other hand, my name was signed to much of it, as a member of the university crew, and this increased the demand. Heaven knows how the time was found to do it all, with that inexorable edict of bed at ten o'clock, but the crisis of freshman year was passed without a deficit.

And so to Ralph Paine, who could happily look forward to earning his way through Yale, there came the momentous experience of the journey from New Haven to the crew quarters on the Thames, early in June. The college assembled to send us off with exuberant cheers. Victory was expected of us. Those noisy undergraduates had never seen a Yale crew whipped. There was no other tradition in their young lives. Very trim and immaculate in white boating flannels with blue oars embroidered on the pockets, we trundled to the station in ancient hacks and sang in close harmony:

> "Jolly boating weather,
> And a harvest breeze,
> Oars on the feather,
> Shade beneath the trees,
> Swing, swing together
> With your bodies between your knees."

The Yale launch was waiting at New London to carry us up the river to Gales Ferry. To those of us who were new to the crew, it was the first glimpse of the shining stretch of river between the darkly wooded shores, with the blue and crimson flags staked to mark the four-mile course. It made one's heart flutter, but the profound thrill came when the launch passed a boat-house and a bungalow flying a crimson flag, and a row of half-naked figures, burned as dark as Indians, who were lifting a shell from the water. This was Red Top, the Harvard quarters! There is a better feeling nowadays, and the old enmity has been greatly diminished, but to us who met them on field and river so many years ago the spirit was akin to that betwixt two hostile Highland clans.

The Yale quarters at the tiny hamlet of Gales Ferry were primitive then, a farmhouse for the 'varsity crew, a low-roofed cottage for the freshmen, and a rickety shed of a boat-house for both. The place has since become an elaborately equipped colony, with a club-house and what not, and scores of oarsmen inhabit it in June. But we had no second and third eights to pit against each other for practice. The crew and two or three substitutes, this was the rowing personnel.

Nervous tension there was, and hard labor, in this last fortnight before the contest, but it was a glowing chapter of life nevertheless, and one to be wistfully recalled. The day began with a thump on the bedroom door and the shout of the darkey waiter, "Ha' pas' six, Cap'n," and then at the other doors along the hall, "Ha' pas' six, Number Sebben," and so on until the stentorian summons had aroused all hands from slumber so deep that no plummet could have sounded it.

Ten minutes later the captain was calling "All ready," and the crew tumbled out into the cool, sweet morning to stride up the country road. Through a dewy sheep pasture, along the shore, and homeward in a grassy lane they walked briskly, a mile or two, filling their lungs with pure air, limbering the muscles that had stiffened a trifle overnight, putting a razor edge on appetites for breakfast.

The barbarously rigorous training methods of an earlier generation were almost obsolete. Oarsmen were no longer compelled to muffle themselves in sweaters and run five miles on empty stomachs or to live on a diet of beef and mutton almost raw, potatoes, rice, and weak tea. There still survived, however, a stupid notion that the ration of drinking-water must be limited to three or four glasses a day, which would have been a scant allowance for a crew of ship-wrecked sailors. This was when men were sweating off six or seven pounds during an afternoon's rowing in torrid summer weather. We suffered the torments of thirst, but nobody dreamed of disobedience. Sipping a glass of water through a straw was an expedient which helped to cool a parched throat.

Morning and afternoon the crew was on the river, paddling long stretches, mile after mile at an easy gait, while the vigilant eye of "Bob" Cook found innumerable flaws. If the water was smooth, the day's work might finish with a hard pull over the upper two miles of the course while the stop-watch told the story. At least twice in the week the eight was sent over the four miles at racing speed. To loaf on the shady lawns during the intervals, to stroll together through the dusky country just before bedtime, to sing choruses at the tinkling old piano in the musty farmhouse parlor, such was the daily round of an existence which held its own peculiar satisfaction.

The one cloud of disquietude which could not be dispelled was that this Yale crew had not yet attained consistent form. Powerful, in superb condition, incessantly drilled for six months, it was never certain of itself. There was some subtle dissonance which it was beyond the intelligence of the coaches to attune. Even during these final days of toil, the crew would go out and row wretchedly and then, perhaps, astonish all beholders by an exhibition of sensational speed. In the last test over the four-mile course, we drove that shell down the river in nineteen minutes and fifty seconds which was much faster than it had ever been rowed in a race. There was a gale of wind behind us and a swift tide, but, nevertheless, it was a performance which seemed a portent of victory.

The night before the race! The tall freshman from Florida found it difficult to sleep. He closed his eyes, but his mind was tremendously active. Over and over again he counted his faults of oarsmanship which no amount of coaching had been able to erase. "Bob" Cook had told him that a man could be guilty of fifty-two different faults in pulling one stroke. In this trying hour the freshman was ready to plead guilty to all of them and several more of his own invention. If he could only remember not to kick out his slide in the race or lag on the catch, there was a bare chance that he might not disgrace himself.

In the next room "Pudge" Heffelfinger snored steadily and earnestly. This was his first boat-race, but as a football gladiator the night before the battle was no novelty in his grim career. The uneasy freshman wandered to a window and stood gazing at the starlit river. There was a murmur of voices on the lawn, and the flare of a match illumined the rugged face of "Bob" Cook. He was talking it over with two or three of the younger coaches. Their work was done. Win or lose, they could only look on. The freshman sighed. There was to be no looking on for him. Before crawling back into bed, he decided to kneel down and say his prayers all over again.

What weighed him down was the thought of the six months of preparation, half a year of striving, and all for this one supreme test of twenty minutes. Besides the rowing in the eight, there had been the many weary hours spent in a pair-oar tub in the endeavor to master some elusive detail of feathering the blade or turning the wrist. And this infinite pains and application had failed to make a finished oarsman of him. The coaches had damned him with as much gusto during this very last afternoon, when they were practicing racing starts, as when he had made his début in the tank in the gloomy basement of the gymnasium.

Thirty years later, with such wisdom as the battering school of life may have taught him, he knows that it was good for his soul as well as his body to have to try so hard to learn to do one thing. You might bluff a learned professor of Latin or get a passing mark on an examination paper by hastily cramming for it, but you could never bluff "Bob" Cook.

This race was to be rowed upstream in the forenoon, as the tide served. That last brisk walk before breakfast was a subdued affair. Vanished were the exuberant spirits, the chatter and horse-play. Later in the morning we dealt the cards or threw dice, calling it Yale against Harvard, and viewed the results with grave interest as significant omens. An hour was a year until the captain remarked:

"Well, boys, we may as well get dressed."

This eased the suspense. Down the steep bank we trudged and shifted from white flannels into the scanty blue jerseys, very brief trunks, and woolen socks. Then with gingerly care the new racing shell was lifted from the rack and, keeping step, we bore it out and let it float beside the landing stage. The launch was waiting to tow it down to the start at the railroad bridge just above New London.

On the lawn appeared old Cap'n Latham Brown, retired mariner, who owned the farmhouse and kept the grocery store. It was his custom to dye his whiskers black every Sunday morning, and through the week they faded to a dingy green. On the day of the race, however, he always gave them a special dip and put on his best black coat as well. It was his personal salute. And as usual, plump Mrs. Latham Brown flung an old shoe over the bank for luck and shouted a fervent "God bless you."

"All aboard," said the captain of the crew. "If you are licked, I want you to know that I feel every man has done his best. That's all."

We clambered into the launch and sat hunched in the cockpit, staring at the quiet, burnished river whose upper reach was deserted. Halfway down the course we beheld the unfolding of a singularly beautiful panorama, a great fleet of stately yachts, steam and sail, almost a mile of them anchored to leave a gleaming pathway of water between their ranks. They were all atwinkle with brasswork, bright with fleckless paint, gay with strings of flags. Soon the long observation train crawled into view and waited, with its thousands of partisans cheering, and the tumult came faintly to our ears on the breeze that swept in from the Sound.

It made the blood tingle, and yet this multitude of spectators seemed curiously detached and remote. They really did n't matter. All that concerned or interested us was the sight of the Harvard launch which had passed down the river a little ahead of us, and the shell that towed behind it. Floating platforms had been moored not far from the start. We climbed out upon one of them, stripped off the jerseys, and solemnly shook hands with the grizzled skipper of the launch before carefully taking our seats in the shell while the coxswain held it steady. "Bob" Cook nodded and waved his cap. He had nothing more to say.

After leaning forward to adjust the toe-straps on the stretchers with one last touch, we straightened up to look at the Harvard crew which was just paddling away from its own "float." It seemed extraordinary that this should have been our first glimpse of them close at hand. There was little to choose between the two eights in weight or height or strength, but these adversaries, naked to the waist and tanned by the sun, looked immensely formidable, like a row of young Titans. It was an illusion familiar to those who have been in similar situations.

The water was rough and choppy with a freshening wind and a swell churned up by huge excursion steamers. Had the race been rowed downstream, this erratic crew of ours might have been shaken together by rowing a mile across the river to the start in smooth water. As it was, we paddled into position while the oars splashed spray and the shell rolled wildly as the swell lifted it. From the bow of a swift yacht the referee shouted his final instructions. Harvard drifted to its stake-boat. The two coxswains bawled to this man or that to pull a stroke and swing her to port or starboard, and presently the long shells rested waiting for the word.

At the report of a pistol they leaped forward to the lunging, flurried thrusts of the first half-dozen strokes. The Yale shell lurched and tripped in the rough water. The crew was failing to find its stride. The laboring men perceived that Harvard had jumped away from them. Never mind, there were four long miles to row, and the distance made a poor start of little consequence. Twenty or thirty strokes and we should go clear of the troublesome broken water and be swinging together with the shell running on an even keel.

Such was the belief of the freshman at Number Four as he tried to remember his worst faults and to keep in time with the stroke-oar. Just in front of him swayed that long, herculean back of "Pudge" Heffelfinger. He, too, was bothered by this rolling boat which buried his oar too deep when he tried to wrench it free for the recover.

Beyond him sat the captain, George Brewster, at Number Six, gentle of manner but indomitable, who had rowed in three victorious Yale crews. Things were going badly, as he must have realized, but with faultless precision his shoulders swung up to take the time from the stroke-oar and pass it along. A quarter of a mile and the river was still ruffled by the strong wind, but it could not have demoralized a crew which had learned to pull in harmony under all conditions. The tragic comprehension had begun to dawn on us that this was one of those days when, for reasons inscrutable, we were a rotten bad Yale crew. Destiny had euchred us. We were victims of the calendar. It was no extenuation, mind you, but if the race had been rowed on that great day when we had stormed down the river inside of twenty minutes, there might have been a different story to tell.

In fiction I have often described boat-races and how the crew won and what were the glorious sensations of the heroes who left Harvard floundering astern. There is a certain honest satisfaction in telling you how one Yale crew was thoroughly and deservedly whipped because it could not row fast enough. There was anguish on the face of the little coxswain as he bobbed in the stern-sheets and implored us to hit it up for a spurt. He lied, and the Lord forgave him for it, yelling that Harvard was no more than a length ahead and we could catch her at the next half-mile flag.

Doggedly we responded to his impassioned demands for one desperate sequence of ten strokes after another, and the count ran hoarsely along the boat:

"*One — Two — Three — Four — Five —*"

But the shell did not lift and surge to this increased power. It moved with a kind of sluggish, maddening reluctance. The eight men were pulling themselves blind, but not as one man. They were struggling with a dead weight. At the end of the first mile, Harvard had long since vanished from their ken. Only the coxswain knew how far ahead was the shell with the crimson-tipped oars, and he still lied with brave and futile entreaties. This is the tragedy of such a race, that it becomes so hopeless an ordeal for a badly beaten crew, so lonely and isolated. In football there is the shock of combat to the last moment of the game, the hope of another touch-down, of turning the tide in a manner spectacular and amazing. On the baseball field a batting rally, even a home run, may snatch victory from defeat in the ninth inning. But the crew that is distanced early in the race can only row bitterly and unavailingly to the end of the four miles.

Yes, we knew we were whipped before the flag that marked the end of the first two miles was passed. No series of spurts could change the aspect of this doomed boat-race. All it amounted to was that we were rowing home to the boat-house at Gales Ferry by way of the finish flags. There was no slackening of effort. We were doing the best we could. Earlier in the race the observation train, all color and noise, had been trailing abreast of us, but now it had moved on ahead to keep pace with the winners, with the Harvard crew.

As in a trance we noted that the hordes of Yale partisans had become silent, and faintly we heard that deliberate, hateful, "rah, rah, rah," for fair Harvard, incessant, unmerciful. A kind of miracle had been vouchsafed this unfriendly cloud of witnesses. Five years of disappointment, of an increasing conviction that the "Bob" Cook stroke was invincible, and here was a Harvard crew which made no more than a practice pull of it, rowing easily, beautifully away from a boatload of Yale beef and brawn that was "Bob" Cook's own handiwork.

We eight unfortunates were bedazed, with no breath to spare for discussing the situation. Never had those half-mile flags seemed so far apart. The clamorous fleet of yachts and excursion steamers was far astern. At length, the three-mile mark slid past as we shot sidewise glances at it. And now the river was quiet and clear of traffic where the course swung in close to the western bank. It was, indeed, the lonesome finish of a long, hard journey.

"Lift it for the last half-mile, you big loafers!" piped the valiant bantam of a coxswain. "You'll catch 'em yet!"

We knew him to be a broken-hearted little liar. There would be no catching Harvard for us. But it was swing, swing together, and the shell ran better, with less of that hopeless drag and discordance. It was something like the way a Yale crew ought to be rowing. In this manner did we sweep toward the finish flags, performing the motions of a boat-race, not knowing that the victors had ceased their effort and were resting happily in their drifting shell to watch us go by. It was beyond question the great moment of their lives, thus to sit there, relaxed, bending over the idle oar-handles, and behold the Yale crew finish its mournful and solitary pilgrimage.

Dutiful to the end, like the boy on the burning deck, the coxswain called for a last ten strokes and dutifully we bent to it with a grunt and a heave. Presently we felt vast aston-

ishment at discerning the Harvard crew at ease and enjoying the spectacle. Could it be possible? The infernal race
was over! We were licked, but by how much?

"Ten lengths," somebody kindly shouted from the referee's boat.

"Ten lengths!" groaned the Yale captain.

"Oh, hell!" was the eloquent comment of "Pudge"
Heffelfinger.

Sixty feet to a boat-length! Ten lengths meant six hundred
feet! It was a scandalous drubbing, not a race but a procession, and a sore humiliation for Yale men to endure. We
were very tired, but more disgusted. A beaten crew, after
four miles of it, is presumed to display symptoms of collapse.
Fact and fiction have made this more or less traditional.
The stroke-oar may flop over in a heap while the coxswain
splashes water in his face. Some other man is seen to drop
as though he had been shot. A third hangs over the side in a
dead faint and the lovely girls on the observation train are
wrung with pity.

Not so with this Yale crew of '91. It had never done what
was expected of it. We were too sullen and sore and angry
to give an exhibition of collapsing or anything of the sort,
nor had we the smallest use for sympathy. With trailing
oars we let the shell skitter on past those jubilant Harvard
foemen who waved their hands in a friendly manner. We
found voice to salute them with a perfunctory cheer, as the
ethics of the situation demanded, and then the coxswain,
still the implacable little tyrant, yelled at us:

"Get ready, you poor fools! Nobody is going to give *you*
a ride home. Now *row!*"

Obediently, dumbly, we reached forward to grip the water
and to row another mile, across the river to our own quarters,
steadily, carefully, every man trying to mend his faults and
to keep in time. It had become like a prompting of instinct.
In silence we rowed that long stretch and rowed it well, a

silence broken by the harsh grind of the slides, the wash of water, and the beat of the oars as they rolled in the locks. Never again would these eight comrades sit in a shell together, but none of us happened to think of that. There was gloom enough without indulging in sentiment.

At the boat-house we lifted out the shell and carried it in, every man at his own outrigger, and swung it upon the rack. Then we sat in a row on a long bench, stripped to the waist, brown and hard and muscular, and the sweat ran off us in little rivers. It appeared to be difficult to find anything to say. While we sat there, the launch came alongside the wharf and "Bob" Cook jumped ashore to hasten into the boat-house. He was not an emotional man. For a long moment he stood in the doorway, gazing at those dumb, grieving athletes. He knew what it meant to them.

They were ashamed to look him in the face. I can see him now, framed in the bright sunlight of the doorway, hands in his pockets, solid, unperturbed in failure or success. To our surprise he said, with a smile:

"Don't take it so hard, boys. You can lick 'em next year."

The voice was gentle, almost fatherly. We were expecting to be scolded. This was too much, the last straw. The mighty Heffelfinger dug his fists in his eyes and blubbered that it was all his fault. In accents shaky and tearful, I exclaimed:

"T-that's w-what you g-get, Mr. Cook, for having a b-big useless d-dub of a freshman on your crew."

And there you have the moral of this chronicle of disaster. Every man took the defeat unto himself, as his own personal responsibility. There was never a thought of blaming the coaches or the "Bob" Cook stroke. If we had rowed it well, we could have won the race. We had rowed it badly and therefore we lost. There was nothing else to it. If in later years we acquired the American failing of passing the buck, it was not learned in that old boat-house at Gales Ferry.

There was to have been a triumphal return to New Haven, a brass band and a parade, fireworks and a bonfire on the campus, a banquet with speeches. The president of the Yale Navy had made all arrangements as a matter of course. He hurriedly cancelled them. After dinner together at Gales Ferry, the crew lingered until late in the afternoon. There was evidently a reluctance to mingle with the crowds in New London and the tumult of the special trains.

Ralph Paine, the freshman, remained behind, at a desk in a corner of the telegraph office. He was writing the story of the race to send to the newspapers which he served as the Yale correspondent. It was slow, difficult work. Occasionally he sniffled or wiped his eyes with a handkerchief. Having broken training, he lighted a treasured pipe, but the taste was bitter and there was no consolation in it. Particularly severe was he in his criticism of Paine at Number Four who was slow and clumsy and had failed to hold his slide under him on the catch.

Having written some two or three thousand words and filed them with a sympathetic operator who had seen the race, the freshman drifted into a train which deposited him in New Haven late in the evening. Rain was falling as he stole across the campus like a fugitive. In his foolish young noddle was the notion that the college would probably mob him at sight. Beyond doubt, all undergraduates and alumni had discerned for themselves that the big, awkward freshman in the waist of the boat had lost the race for Yale.

He dropped his luggage in his room and wandered out to find a restaurant and the comfort of a steak as big as a doormat. Timidly he slunk into a corner of Heublein's and was ministered to by a tactful old waiter of his acquaintance who had seen them take it just as hard in years gone by. And there a roisterous band of seniors and young graduates discovered this oarsman of the woeful countenance and diagnosed his symptoms. Bless their hearts, they laid violent hands upon him and dragged him along with them to that famous little place known as Mory's where they dragged the chairs to the big round table upon which one college generation after another had hacked its initials. And they put a pewter mug of musty ale in his fist and pounded him on the back and told him to buck up. He had rowed a bully good race, and Harvard had to win once in a while to make it interesting, and they would proceed to drive dull care away.

By midnight the freshman was almost persuaded that life might be worth living. He was not a complete ruin. Of course he would avoid all Yale men during the summer vacation, if he should happen to see them first, and laid away was that dream of playing tennis or swimming in the 'varsity crew jersey with the big "Y" on the chest. He desired it to be forgotten that he had rowed on the '91 crew. Was it childish to take this episode so seriously? I wonder. On the whole, I should like to see my own four sons take defeat in just this same way, anxious to try again, but blaming themselves and not circumstances.

Nothing is easier than to offer excuses. It is the most prevalent of all besetting sins. No credit to the freshman who shouldered the burden of failure in that vanquished Yale crew of thirty years ago. His comrades were of the same mind concerning each his own responsibility. "Bob" Cook had never preached it to them. It was a tradition and a very precious legacy. In the truest sense, it was *esprit de corps*.

IV

WHEN THE ODDS SEEMED HOPELESS

THE serious flaw in the college athletics of my youth was that
only the few enjoyed the benefits of the hardy physical training and mental discipline while the others looked on and
applauded. No intelligent effort was made to extend these
benefits to the average student, and this was, of course, to
overlook the chief aim and object of the sports of the campus.
It was too gladiatorial in that the chosen eleven or nine
or eight went forth to battle like the champions of feudal
Christendom. There was more or less rivalry among class
teams and crews, but it was voluntary and unorganized and
seldom received competent direction.

Valedictorians were permitted to study themselves into
early graves and the high-stand scholar was likely to be the
spindling lad with round shoulders and a poor digestion. To
play the bruising style of football then in vogue or to row a
four-mile race required strength and endurance much beyond
the average. And there was no such variety of sport as came
later and which was to include basket-ball, golf, wrestling,
swimming, gymnastics, cross-country running, all these increasing the opportunities for wholesome competition and
exercise.

Typical of the era was the situation that confronted the
Yale crew at the beginning of the season of '92, in my sophomore year. The coach of to-day would have perhaps three
hundred rowing aspirants, scores and scores of whom had
been carefully trained to handle an oar in eights, who had
enjoyed series or races among themselves or had engaged in
contests with other colleges. When we responded to the call
in midwinter, the 'varsity squad consisted of thirty men and

of these more than half were soon dismissed as hopeless. This was only one phase of a dismal set of circumstances.

The crew of the preceding year had been ingloriously beaten by Harvard. Ten lengths in four miles admits of no argument whatever. The Yale prestige of five straight victories had been knocked into a cocked hat, and Harvard men grinned discourteously whenever the famous "Bob" Cook stroke was mentioned. Of that unhappy Yale eight only two men were left as a foundation upon which to build anew.

One of these survivors was "Andy" Balliet who had pulled a mighty oar at Number Two. He was literally a squat giant of a man, standing only five feet seven, but he managed to stretch himself out and to pull as long a stroke as the six-footers in front of him. The muscles stood out on him in bunches, and no wonder, for he had toiled in the anthracite mines of Pennsylvania before achieving his dream of going to college, and this goal had been so long deferred that he was getting on toward thirty years of age when he entered the freshman class.

He was the real stuff, was old Balliet, with his bristling mustache and his hairy chest shaped like a barrel, and his serene temper. Life was hard, as he had known it, and he had learned to stand the gaff. He was really too short of stature to be an oarsman, as I say, and the exertion of swinging in an arc to match his taller comrades was tremendously exhausting, but he did it and never weakened because he was grit to the heels.

The other survivor of the '91 crew was the Ralph Paine who, rowing Number Four as a freshman, had mournfully taken it for granted that the defeat was entirely his fault. An interval of nine months had restored his cheerful outlook on life. Other college activities had diverted him from the contemplation of his own shortcomings as an oarsman and the campus did not seem to agree with his opinion that he had disgraced himself for time and eternity. Through the autumn, when not on the casualty list, he was at the 'varsity football training table.

As a sophomore he was genuinely interested in most of his studies and anxious to stand well in them.

There was also a living to be earned by writing for various newspapers. The tentative efforts of freshman year began to bloom as a campus news service, a syndicate, if you please, which was to expand and to include as many as twenty newspapers on its list, the "World" in New York, the "Press" in Philadelphia, the "Globe" in Boston, the "Tribune" in Chicago, even as far away as the "Chronicle" in San Francisco. The great discovery was that the same news could be sent, by mail or wire, to several papers in different cities. This multiplied the revenue without increasing the effort. A poor but honest classmate who pounded a typewriter as a source of income was employed to make the requisite carbon copies, and at the end of the month the checks came fluttering in from hither and yon to make a gratifying total.

The financial aspects of a college career had no more uncertainties or vicissitudes. The Paine Syndicate rolled along so prosperously that in junior year the young man was able to send his only sister off to boarding-school, on the road to college. And in his senior year he garnered an income of three thousand dollars and felt a bit reluctant to face the anticlimax of graduation and a job in a hard, cold world where campus fledglings were taken on sufferance and at salaries exceedingly small.

Even as a freshman he had been writing poems for the "Yale Literary Magazine" in competition for an election to the board of editors, which was an honor of the most ponderous and impressive dignity. When he was invited to the football training table, it seemed to be regarded as unusual for a hundred-and-ninety-pound athlete to be metrically inclined. The devastating "Pudge" Heffelfinger appeared to regard this poetic ambition as a weakness. The football season had restored his good humor. It was the jocund season of the year when he inspired in his opponents a feeling for elegies and dirges. He had rowed in that ill-fated crew of '91, but never again for him. The slavery of the oar was for those that liked it.

His literary comment at table was apt to run like this, the big white teeth gleaming like an ogre's:

"I see you did it again in the 'Lit,' Ralph. Careful, boy. If you don't swear off, I'll have to rough you at football practice to-morrow. Who ever heard of a poet that could make a hole through center?"

"Well, I am not enough of a poet to cramp my football or rowing style, Pudge," was my defense.

"And you will never be a good enough oarsman to cramp your poetic style," was the cruel retort. "Honestly, though, those last verses showed improvement. They splashed out at the finish, but I thought she ran pretty smoothly between strokes."

With these two seasoned men, then, stout Balliet and clumsy Paine, it was necessary to assemble a crew from a dearth of material. After the defeat at New London we had elected the stroke-oar as captain for the next year. It turned out to be a greater responsibility than he cared to assume, after a summer's deliberation, and he therefore resigned the position and declined to train another season. Something like demoralization was in the air. How it was surmounted and with what results makes one of the memorable stories of Yale athletic history.

It is the habit of certain self-satisfied gentlemen who affect "snappy" clothes and manners, and deal in stocks and bonds or sell the goods produced by others, to speak of "college boys" in terms of easy and lofty contempt and of their affairs as excessively juvenile. They can know nothing about playing the big game until they get out into the world and rub against the men who are really doing things. This is not altogether true. In fact, it is partly rubbish. The cities are cluttered up with bankers and business men of feeble wit and the courage of rabbits, who succeed by means of bluff and pretense and a childish bag of tricks which deceives people stupider than themselves.

Pulling that '92 Yale crew out of its difficulties and making it win was a man's-sized undertaking and it was largely accomplished by a "college boy," as I presume you would call him. This was John A. Hartwell, better known as "Josh," who had already done his full duty by Yale. He had rowed on three winning crews, one of which, in '88, had set a record for the course of twenty minutes and ten seconds, which was to stand unsurpassed for thirty years. He had played end-rush on two Yale football teams and was now a graduate student in the Yale Medical School. Absorbed in the serious business of life, which was to gain the education of a surgeon, he was done with athletics.

At a meeting of the graduate rowing committee in New York, it was agreed that "Josh" Hartwell was the only hope of averting another disaster. The system made the captain a genuine leader instead of a subordinate in the hands of a professional coach. Hartwell was stubborn, but, at length, they won him over. What persuaded him was the doctrine of duty to a cause, the high motive of allegiance. There was, of course, no financial reward in it for him and small prospect of glory. He had won all the athletic honors that Yale could confer. He was pledging himself to an uphill fight and a forlorn hope.

Lean and long and bow-legged, with a sandy thatch, a keen blue eye, and the temper of a master of men, "Josh" Hartwell fished out the faded jersey and trunks and took his seat at Number Six. He did not propose, however, to let his work in the Medical School suffer. With a diligence almost incredible he was not only one of the best crew captains that ever rowed in a Yale shell, but he also took honors in the exacting courses of his graduate school,

Soon there came another slant of good fortune. There had rowed on the crew of '90 a freshman named Sherwood Ives. In a race with the Atalanta Boat Club, over the four-mile course of New Haven harbor, Phil Allen, the Yale captain and stroke, had broken his oar. Unwilling to be a useless passenger, he had promptly jumped overboard and young Ives at Number Seven had steadily, coolly picked up the stroke, and so had driven the crippled eight to victory. He had been forbidden to row in '91 because of an irregular heart, but this slight trouble mended itself, and early in the training season we were rejoiced to learn that Ives was going to row with us.

Almost every group of young men in close association has its hero, the man whose personality has qualities commanding or arresting. This was true of "Bill" Ives, as we called him, upon whom the gods had showered all their favors, and because they loved him he was to die while still in the flower of his magnificent young manhood. He had learned to row without effort, with a consummate grace. He was held up as the perfect pattern of a Number Seven to all his college generation. Better than this, he was a very noble gentleman, strong and modest, an aristocrat who met every demand of the democracy of the campus.

There were now four old 'varsity oarsmen, including "Josh" Hartwell, and the coaches proceeded to find a new stroke-oar. At first glance you might have questioned the choice of Edson Gallaudet with his pink-and-white complexion and almost delicate aspect. By temperament he was rather a musician than an athlete. For an amateur he played the violin with unusual distinction. I am quite sure that this feeling for rhythm, the sensitive perception of the musician, helped him to become a superb stroke-oar.

There was nothing to indicate that this was to be a famous Yale crew until far into the season. In power it did not begin to compare with those vanquished strong men of '91.

Seated in the boat, we were seen to be of assorted sizes, wretchedly matched in height. Behind me, at Number Three, was Van Huyck, sturdy and broad, who was scarcely taller than "Andy" Balliet. From six feet one we ran down to five feet seven and it was against all precedent that such an odd lot could be taught to row together. And for a long time it looked as though it never could be done.

The winter passed, and the weeks of spring slipped into May. There was no more shifting men about and experimenting with substitutes. For better or for worse, this was to be the crew. The coaching system was unchanged and we rowed precisely the same style of stroke as before. We believed as implicitly in "Bob" Cook as ever. The result was up to us. One helpful factor of the equation was the tradition of victory. Tarnished the year before, we simply had to restore its wonted luster. And in "Josh" Hartwell we had a captain whose fiery ardor was like a daily hymn before battle.

When the work was ragged and exasperating and we growled under our breaths and wondered what ailed the confounded boat, he could be heard to say, and he bit off the words:

"You will row that mile over again, and you will row it *right*, understand? And if you row it like a lot of rheumatic lobsters, you'll have to do it all over again. If you don't get together, you will stay out here till dark, and I don't care a hang if you never have any supper."

And so we sweated and went hungry and swung up on the catch until this tow-headed tyrant was gracious enough to release us. We feared him and we loved him, and we knew that with every stroke he was lifting his full share of the load, his back humped a little, his long, slashing stride taking the burden from Number Seven with the precision of a watch. He joined the coaches in abusing Paine, who was less clumsy than of yore, but still the target of emphatic

A WINNING YALE CREW OF THE "BOB" COOK ERA (1892)

HARVARD WAS DEFEATED BY EIGHTEEN BOAT-LENGTHS

F. E. Olmstead (cox.), E. F. Gallaudet (stroke), S. B. Ives (No. 7), J. A. Hartwell (captain, No. 6)
A. B. Graves (No. 5), R. D. Paine (No. 4), A. L. Van Huyck (No. 3), A. J. Balliet (No. 2), F. A. Johnson (bow)

epithets and lurid exhortation. The impression conveyed was that they intended to make an oarsman of him or kill him.

The first-class golfer can never tell you how he does it. It was something like that when the '92 crew ceased to be crude and experimental and uncertain. The season was in May, as I remember, several weeks before we went to the quarters at Gales Ferry for the finish of the long training. Then all the unflagging efforts of the staff of younger coaches, and the profound wisdom of "Bob" Cook, all the self-sacrificing zeal of Captain "Josh" Hartwell, together with the spirit aroused in the men in the boat, seemed to fuse themselves into an alloy like a fine quality of steel.

It made no difference that the oarsmen were of all shapes and sizes, that in appearance they were a curious assortment of misfits. They had acquired that indefinable element, temperamental, harmonious, which had eluded the massive, well-proportioned group of athletes of the year before.

There was to be no more inconsistency of performance. What this crew had found, it never lost. And the daily task on the water ceased to resemble toil or servitude. Gone was all sense of drudgery and the bitter taste of discouragement. It was not a foolish overconfidence. Defeat had taught the lesson of humility. In the Harvard boat were six veterans of the eight which had swept past the finish flags ten lengths in front of Yale. But we knew that, barring mishaps, there would not be another holiday pageant for the crimson and the tail-end of a lamentable procession for the dark blue. At the least, there would be a *race*, four miles of it.

The awkward six-footer at Number Four, Paine by name, seemed to have mastered his worst faults. At any rate, he had been welded into unison with his seven comrades and this was the vital factor. Trained to one hundred and eighty-three pounds, he was still a bit lacking in nervous quickness, in the instantaneous application of his power,

and yet he kept the *tempo* unbroken and transmitted it to
the men behind him. Individually he was not a finished oarsman, but as one of the eight, as a cog of this delicate mechanism, he fitted into place.

It might be a brush with the freshman crew, or perhaps
the long journey of four miles out to the red buoy and the
breakwater where New Haven harbor met the Sound, and
always the eight maintained that ease and sympathetic
interplay of effort which we had vainly tried to gain and hold
in '91. Fatigue or rough water could not seriously mar it.
You could not clearly explain it. Gallaudet, the stroke-oar,
with the soul of a musician may have comprehended it better
than the rest of us could. There appeared to be no good
reason why this should be an extraordinary crew.

Thirty years after, I think of the experience with a sense
of singular gratification, and time has not dimmed its importance. This is because, with all our endeavors, we so
seldom are able really to do even one thing well.

We carried this mastery of the eight-oared shell to New
London. The word had passed among the old rowing men
that the crew was *good*. They came homing back to the farmhouse on the river-bank at Gales Ferry, warmly welcomed,
and found beds in cottages near by, and demolished the
training-table fare, yarning to us of crews and races back to
the Civil War. It was a jovial fraternity which slackened the
tension for us youngsters. "Bob" Cook's spirits were unclouded by forebodings. He seemed to regard coaching this
crew as a diversion.

He was able to give his undivided attention to those details
of form and finish which appeal to the artist. A crew that
rowed the Cook stroke well was drilled in absolute uni-
formity of motion, every back as flat as a board, heads erect,
chins up at precisely the same angle. The English university
crews slouch and swing all over the boat and are not pretty
to look at. Watermanship is their chief concern, to hit it

hard on the catch and all together, pull it through and get the oars out of the water at the same instant.

There came a day, more than a week before the Harvard race, when "Bob" Cook announced:

"I am all through with you fellows. I can't do anything more for you. After this I had better lend a hand with the freshman crew."

For once the master was satisfied with his handiwork and feared that too much fastidiousness might spoil it. We could not believe our ears. "Bob" Cook actually had no more fault to find with one of his Yale crews. And the happiest men in the boat were the two survivors of that luckless, erratic crew of '91, old Balliet and big Paine at Number Four. The younger coaches trailed after us in the swift launch and were critical as was their conscientious habit. It would never do to let us think too well of ourselves.

We did stunts with a racing shell and fairly played with it. "Let her run!" shouted the coxswain, and we sat still, raising the oars clear of the water like wings poised in flight. The shell skimmed upon an even keel, with the grace of a swallow, until the impetus died. This was more difficult than it may sound. So narrow and crank is an eight-oared shell, with only two feet of width to sixty feet of length, that without the oar-blades to steady it as they grip the water, an upset is almost inevitable. We had learned to balance it as a tight-rope walker maintains his equilibrium.

Often the pace of the stroke was varied like running up and down the musical scale. It would be dropped as low as twenty-four to the minute, and gradually pushed up until it reached thirty-eight, and so descending without a break in the rhythm of the swaying backs. What this complete accord meant was discovered when we picked up the freshman crew for a stretch of a mile or so. It was amazing to find that we simply could not help running away from them, no matter how low the stroke we rowed nor how lightly our blades were dipped. Strong and plucky lads these freshmen were and they laid into it for dear life, while we merely paddled and went through the motions. But our shell steadily slipped away from them. It was almost uncanny. They had not learned how to row together as one man. This was the secret of it.

This year the Harvard race was to be rowed downstream, late in the afternoon. We felt anxious, of course, and our hearts thumped like drums when the referee's boat blew its whistle as a summons, but we were singing "Jolly Boating Weather" when we climbed into the shell and waited to shove off from Gales Ferry. We rowed a mile to the start, across the river, swinging along at a leisurely pace, all taut and ready for the task in hand. The shell moved with its accustomed stride. Not an oar splashed the water as they bit into the catch with a noise like tearing silk. And still we wondered how we did it, these eight men of such varied physical architecture and differing temperaments.

V

THE CREW THAT COULD N'T LOSE

As we rowed so easily in the direction of the anchored stake-boats in the shade of the wooded shore, the Harvard crew came skimming across from Red Top. We let our eyes rove in swift, appraising glimpses. A Harvard blade was a trifle slow and kicked up a little ruffle of foam. A brown back swung up too late by a fraction of a second. Only an oarsman could have detected these minor flaws. To us they were revealing and significant. Unspoken was the conviction, "We 've got 'em licked."

With the race about to be contested downstream the observation train trailed its gaudy and sinuous length no more than a hundred feet from the two crews as they paddled into position. One could glance aside and recognize friends and perhaps a girl who waved a blue pennant. It was a strange sensation, after the long months of lonely training, to see this vast assemblage so close at hand.

In '91 a poor start, a bit of rough water, had demoralized the Yale crew at the very outset, and it had been unable to find itself until the race was lost beyond redemption. Here was to be disclosed an impressive difference. We were still pulling the shell around into alignment, two or three oars in the water, the others at rest, when the referee gave the word to go. Whether he misunderstood the answer of our coxswain to the query, "Are you ready, Yale?" we never knew. For my own part I was so intent on helping to swing the shell into position that I did not even hear the referee's signal.

I saw our stroke-oar sway back in a terrific heave, and "Bill" Ives and "Josh" Hartwell pick it up in the savage, hurried pace employed in starting. Behind me the other men were splashing desperately to overcome the inertia of the shell and get it under way. Down rolled a gunwale and the long outriggers slithered through the water. A few more lurching strokes and the boat flopped wildly down on the other side. The oars were waving like the legs of an agitated crab. The beginning of the race could have been no more inauspicious save in a nightmare. Oddly enough, there was not the slightest feeling of dismay, although this looked for all the world like a dismal repetition of the race of '91, with Yale floundering away from its stake-boat.

A few yards abreast of us, Harvard had been tense and ready, backs stretched forward, blades buried, shoulders squared, handles gripped in sinewy fingers. At the signal the boat had jumped away as though released by a powerful spring. The first minute of the race had not elapsed when Harvard was a clean boat-length ahead. Those eager rivals appeared to be making a practice spin of it. We saw them surging past us and still we felt neither flustered nor disheartened. The spirit of the boat was manifest in the cheery, confident voice of the coxswain:

"Steady, all. Now get together and show 'em a few things. Easy, men, easy! Don't rush it."

And the same staunch, untroubled note was in "Josh" Hartwell's words as he flung them back over his shoulder:

"Don't mind Harvard, boys! Watch your slides. Slow, now — hold 'em well under you. Keep your blades down. *Ah, there she is! You've got it! Now, heave — one — two — three — four — five!*"

Yes, by Heaven, we had it! Forgotten was the unhappy confusion of a bungled start. Magically, it seemed to us, we had settled into the familiar cadence that ran from stroke to bow. The shell rushed upon an even keel, as true as a hair, and the twelve-foot oars, tough as they were, bent to the tremendous solidity of the catch. The blades flashed out and back again without flicking the mirrored surface of the windless river. Every man was applying his strength without thought of sparing himself, and yet the effect was one of the most restrained and careful deliberation.

We were rowing as we had rowed through those days and weeks of training at New Haven and on the Thames. It had become second nature. This was a crew that simply could n't lose!

It seemed as though Harvard's lead of a boat-length was cut down in a dozen strokes. Side by side we raced a little distance and we could watch those laboring Harvard oarsmen and hear the imploring shrieks of the coxswain to spurt and hold the advantage. One by one we saw the eight men pass from our vision and drop astern, frowning faces fixed in a supreme intensity of effort, tanned arms plying to and fro like piston rods, brawny backs rocking all together. We slid away from them without raising the stroke, conscious that our boat was traveling at a terrific pace, but making no particular effort to drive it harder. It almost seemed to move of its own volition.

Harvard lagged farther and farther behind us. To a man who had rowed in a beaten crew it was a singularly joyous sight, and I knew how old Balliet felt as he pulled like a steam-engine while the sweat trickled from his bristling mustache. For us two veterans of calamity it was a gorgeous boat-ride. There would be a celebration on the Yale campus, and a banquet with speeches, and the crew men would be called up for a few impromptu remarks, and — by Jove, I was actually trying to frame something brief and witty, and here we were swinging down the river in the midst of a four-mile race with Harvard, and thirty thousand people looking on!

There was no easing up. Loafing? Not a bit of it. We were out to break the record for the course, made by the Yale crew of '88. The conditions were uncommonly favorable, smooth water, not a breath of wind, and tide and current setting strongly down the river. On this upper reach, over the first mile and a half of it, the course was staked quite close to the shore in order to make it as nearly straight-away as possible. This meant shallower water, a sluggish tide, and the danger of veering over to the eel-grass and mud-flats unless the coxswain was skilled and steady.

This was much slower water, therefore, than the last two miles which caught the full sweep of the tide in mid-channel. In spite of this we were rowing this first two miles at a record-breaking speed and ever so much faster than it had ever been rowed in a race, faster by thirty seconds, or ten boat-lengths, than the famous '88 crew had covered this same distance. A new record for the course seemed easily within our grasp.

It was the most delightful sensation imaginable because we were conscious of no fatigue or strain or agony. Poor Harvard had ceased to interest or concern us. It was merely a question of by how much we could increase the distance which steadily widened between the crews.

At two miles our lead was almost ten boat-lengths and the race had been rowed no more than halfway. This ten lengths had been the total measure of our defeat in '91. We began to feel sorry for those eight Harvard men struggling courageously, but already so far astern. Recompense was ours, with a vengeance.

Alas, for our confident hope of achieving a new four-mile record! No sooner had we swept into the wide channel and the deep water at the Navy Yard than a cool salt breeze came whistling in from the Sound. It blew dead against the shell and the wide blades of the eight oars. No matter how delicately we feathered them, this wind was holding us back. The shell was running not quite so far between strokes. It required more exertion to carry the oars back on the recover. The breeze ruffled the water, but not enough to distress us.

Refreshing was the gush of that cool wind against our bare backs and yet it caused the keenest disappointment. It meant many seconds lost on the stop-watches for each remaining mile of the journey.

And then we shot into the long, resplendent lane between the anchored yachts and this told us that the end was not far off. Cannons saluted to right and left, banging away right above our heads, as it seemed, and the startling shock of it was like touching an electric wire. The stroke was shoved higher, although there was no real need of it. In the blue haze of powder smoke we lost sight of the Harvard crew.

Soon came the call for the long, sustained spurt to finish in style. Up, up went the stroke, without a flaw, to the rate of thirty-six to the minute. Easily, harmoniously the eight men responded, oars dipping clean, heads up, backs flat, flinging into it all the strength left in reserve, yet mindful of the form and style and coördination which had become second nature.

Ah, if we could only turn back the years and row that last mile again, in the splendid exuberance of youth! The severest test of all athletic competition, they call the four-mile race, and such it is when two eights are closely matched. But to us, whom the most careful preparation had given abundant endurance, this easy victory was no physical punishment at all. Unexpectedly the coxswain yelled:

" 'Vast all! Quit rowing. You 've finished. Where the deuce are you going? Across Long Island Sound?"

We pulled another stroke through and then let the oars idly caress the water, while we drew the grateful air deep into our lungs and gazed about us. The shell wallowed in the swell kicked up by restless excursion steamers, yachts, and swarming launches. Bands were playing, thousands of people cheering. Automatically we paddled, at the coxswain's command, to hold the shell in the trough of this broken water lest it be twisted or swamped. The race was finished? Where was Harvard?

We sat in the shell and stared up the hazy course until we saw the distant oars rise and fall. Their beat was sadly irregular, like weary pinions, but those rivals of ours doughtily came on, resolved to cross the line without weakening. Almost a minute we waited before they ceased rowing and sagged over the oar-handles, beaten by eighteen boat-lengths, a quarter of a mile. To us it was a pitiful sight, and of the Yale eight, rugged old Balliet and I knew the full import of it. We had rowed on a beaten crew. None of our comrades so deeply comprehended the tragedy of it; what it meant to those exhausted Harvard men who drooped in the shell as though the very life had been drained out of them.

A long cheer for Harvard, vigorous, stentorian, and we steered through the jostling fleet of pleasure craft and halted the shell at the raft where the launch was waiting. Nimbly we scrambled from our seats, shaking hands, dealing one another mighty thumps. How fast had we rowed? Had we smashed the record of the '88 crew? What was the timekeepers' verdict? These were our clamorous questions.

"Twenty minutes, forty-eight seconds. One of the fastest races ever rowed, but the record still stands. The wind spoiled it on the last two miles. You had the record beaten to a frazzle until then."

This was not such a vital matter, after all. The day's work had been eminently satisfactory. And for many a year, whenever old Yale rowing men were foregathered, they would mention, sooner or later, this '92 crew as one of the best and fastest of those which had exemplified the teachings of "Bob" Cook when that school was in its prime. To an extraordinary degree, it was regarded as a finished product. But I cannot tell you, even now, what peculiar quality it was that won for this Yale eight its lasting distinction. Perhaps it would not be quixotic to think of it in terms of a spiritual equation. Some of us were crude and faulty oarsmen, when viewed separately, but as a crew we *blended* and became an entity.

The final scene was enacted in New Haven that same night when the campus and the town turned out to welcome us. A tally-ho coach and four horses, a noisy brass band, and bushels of fireworks were waiting at the railroad station. All in our natty white flannels we were hoisted to the upper deck of this noble chariot while a thousand admirers, young and old, the brave and the fair, marched in the wake. The pavements were thronged all the way to the campus and the air was filled with fiery balls shot from Roman candles which we dodged with nervous agility.

To be riding on top of that old tally-ho, amid the plaudits of the populace, to be twenty years old and as fit as a fiddle, with that boat-race over and done with and your heart leaping whenever you thought of it — most of life's large moments since then have seemed pallid by comparison. And I have been fortunate in finding many joyous adventures, by land and sea.

To the dinner which followed this tumultuous ovation came men of dignified station, judges, financiers, educators, leaders of business enterprise. Some of them belonged to the brotherhood of the oar and all were bound together by the ties of Yale. Tired and a little drowsy, we victors sat in a row and regarded these older guests with profound interest and even awe. They had come to do us honor, they considered our achievement as worthy of their praise.

And when, one by one, they rose to speak, they found a common theme, and it was the old, old ideal of service and sacrifice. Of their own experiences, so much wider and deeper than ours, they comprehended that we had been learning other lessons than those to be found in the textbooks and the recitation halls beneath the elms.

And when we stood all together, at the end of the evening,

the company sang the song so familiar to us young men, and we discerned that there was something more than boyish sentimentality in the words:

> " In after years should troubles rise,
>   To cloud the blue of sunny skies,
>   How bright will seem thro' memory's haze,
>   Those happy, golden, by-gone days.
>   Oh, let us strive that ever we
>   May let these words our watch-cry be,
>   Where'er upon life's sea we sail,
>   *For God, for Country, and for Yale.*"

VI

THE BITTER MEDICINE OF ADVERSITY

In the sight of a cynical younger generation, I am told, the old Yale was crude and rather stupid, blighted by the curse of Puritan traditions and wearing the fetters of the Victorian Age. Those muscular young barbarians had no feeling for culture nor were they in revolt. They even cherished quaint beliefs in religion and duty. A brilliant young Yale man of the modern era has drawn this indictment:

The bulldog is an eminently useful animal. As a drawing card, for instance, he has a far wider appeal to young prep school men than, say, Henry Adams, as a creature whose characteristics are worthy of emulation. There is much to be said in his favor. But as a symbol of the Yale of to-day he is almost as much of an anachronism as those stories in which the Yale halfback got through the entire Harvard team and was tapped for Bones. For the bulldog, no matter how admirable, how absolutely necessary certain of his qualities may be, has never been distinguished for his mentality; whereas the outstanding feature of the Yale of to-day is, I believe, the intellectual awakening of the students.

Now this book of mine, in these earlier chapters, does not pretend to reflect the many sides of college life. It has dwelt with the career of a Yale oarsman as expressing what might be called an adventurous phase and also as indicating certain deep-rooted ideals and influences that were typical of the time and the place. And yet, with this undeveloped mentality of the athlete, I could find it genuinely thrilling to sit up all night writing an essay on Thomas Hardy's novels in competition for a Townsend Prize, and winning it. And even in that bulldog era, there was enjoyment in striving for the honor of an election to the editorial board of the "Yale Lit."

One thing we had not acquired was that irreverence, so curiously infantile, which seems to mark the intellectual awakening of the campus. The critic already quoted, Donald Ogden Stewart, offers a sample of it in this spirited description: _

There are, however, in those first weeks of Freshman year, before the business of "making good" has begun, glimpses of another Yale — the Yale of careless nonchalance, of glorious drinking parties, of excited discussion about religion, the divinity of Christ, monogamy, fleeting pictures of awakening curiosity perpetually interrupted by the encroaching vision of extra-curriculum competition — lovely arpeggio passages all too often drowned by the blatant blare of calling trumpets.

For in the mind of a Freshman lie the seeds of the awakening of that intellectual curiosity which is the beginning of wisdom — curiosity about Mohammed, about socialism, about Ibsen, about sex — and all too often is this mental age of puberty postponed in the interests of success in undergraduate activities until Senior year, or in many cases indefinitely.

After all, it is along about three A.M., when Tom, stein in hand, and eyes popping, says, "This fellow Christ has ruined civilization," that the mind of youth begins to stir and there appears before him, if faintly, a glimmer of the possibilities inherent in a philosophical and æsthetic survey of the Divine Comedy in which he is to take part. And all too often is this vision suddenly cut off by an all too blue curtain.

This serves to show what a funny, old-fashioned campus it used to be, when, if a freshman had ranted, pop-eyed, "This fellow Christ has ruined civilization," he would have been spanked and put to bed as a silly young nuisance. Nor, whenever an undergraduate got drunk, did he feel compelled to make it the theme of an essay or a poem. We, too, loafed and discussed the problems of life as they appealed to the heart of youth and we were neither prigs nor plaster saints, but in our darkened Puritan fashion we harkened to the blatant blare of calling trumpets and strove with all our might to "make good." There was not so much sex and Mohammed and the futility of believing in anything.

Ralph Paine took rowing very seriously because such was

the habit and spirit of Yale. In January of his junior year the oarsmen were again summoned to begin the season's training. For '93 the omens were most propitious. In the boat were five of the men who had won that smashing victory of eighteen lengths, including Ives as captain, and Gallaudet, the stroke-oar of rare ability. The coaching system was unchanged and the merits of the "Bob" Cook stroke, when properly rowed, had been brilliantly vindicated.

Paine was shifted to Number Six, farther aft in the shell, where "Josh" Hartwell had rowed. He had reason to believe that his third year on the crew would be unvexed by discouragement. The only dubious portent was the fact that he had grown ten pounds heavier. Apparently he was still "getting his growth." But he was confident that the severe training would pare him down as it had done in previous years.

He was pulling a smoother and stronger oar than ever; this was the verdict of the coaches during the early months of this season of '93. They were kind enough to tell him so. His horizon was unclouded. With a glow of honest pride he read this opinion of a Harvard observer, in the "Boston Globe":

Paine rowed Number Four for two years and will be remembered as the rosy-cheeked freshman who, together with the giant Heffelfinger, made the backbone of the ill-fated '91 crew which was so badly defeated by Harvard. He has really made wonderful improvement since then and with his experience will be one of the mainstays of the boat this year. Thrown entirely on his own resources, he has been obliged to work very hard while in college. Not only has he maintained a good standing in his studies, but he has found time, by means of newspaper correspondence, to make an income sufficient for all his wants.

He is chairman of the board of editors of the "Yale Literary Magazine," the highest distinction in the Junior class, and is one of the men sure to be tapped for Skull and Bones. He has been an editor of the "Yale Courant" and has written a large part of the play which is to be produced in the Hyperion Theater to-morrow night by undergraduates. He has the satisfaction of being one of the most popular men in his class and is certain of election as captain of next year's crew.

All went well with this fortunate young man until the season was advanced into the month of May, when the crew began to look forward, with restless eagerness, to the sojourn at New London. The time trials over the harbor course had been satisfactory. It was not as fast as the '92 crew and lacked that finished artistry which had been so conspicuous, but it possessed a consistent speed and power and seemed good enough to win.

There came an unexpected loss of form, a slight break in the harmony among those eight men. The crew was out of tune. We felt it in the boat. The coaches did not have to tell us. Paine was conscious that his hard-won mastery of the oar was almost imperceptibly slipping away from him. The fine edge of his essential quickness was dulled. Seated at Number Six, a rhythm and coördination even more perfect was required than when he had been in the waist of the boat. But he had been able to meet these exactions until this perplexing difficulty occurred.

Number Six was a trifle slower. To feel for the water and grip it solidly, to find a firm anchorage for the blade, with the shell moving at the rate of twenty feet in a second, demands the instantaneous effort of a sprinter leaving the mark.

This was what had been lost. For some time the coaches failed to take it seriously, but I knew that my strength and weight were not effectively applied. The boat was running away from me. What was the cause of it? The most plausible answer was told by the scales in the boat-house. A hundred and ninety-two pounds, in the month of May! And there was no getting rid of another pound of it. Extra work in a pair-oared boat, besides the daily routine of the eight in warm weather, and perhaps five pounds would be melted off in an afternoon, but it was all there again the next day.

Sad were the reflections and dark the forebodings. For a man who was naturally slow, who had overcome this handicap by two years of the most strenuous schooling and exertion these few added pounds of weight were in the nature of a tragedy. Aside from rowing they meant nothing more than rugged health and the filling out of a tall, big-boned frame. Number Six was even guilty of stealing away in secret to spend hours in a Turkish bath, but those merciless scales in the boat-house granted him no solace.

It happened as he had feared. The crew went to the Gales Ferry quarters and "Bob" Cook arrived to apply the master touches. He was not at all satisfied. Men were shifted about in the boat and tirelessly studied. He found the crew to be slow and ragged, afflicted by that athletic malady known as a slump. It was cruelly decreed that Paine should bundle himself in woolly sweaters until he resembled a polar bear and run miles and miles over the country roads in the summer heat. This punishment reduced him by two or three pounds, but he could not stay reduced.

No radical changes were made in the organization of the crew until a week before the Harvard race, and the five veterans still held their places undisturbed. It was taken for granted, at this late hour, that no more experiments would be tried. On the whole, the work showed a slight improvement. Then there dawned the saddest day in the young life of Paine at Number Six, a day more distressing than when, as a freshman, he had sat in the floundering shell ten lengths astern of Harvard.

Ten years later one of his early attempts at fiction was published in "Scribner's Magazine." The short story was called "A Victory Unforeseen," and part of it was so thinly disguised that it was not fiction at all. It had happened to Ralph Paine and this is how he described it:

The next morning sparkled with a cool breeze from the Sound, and its salty tang was a tonic after the sultry days which had tugged at the weights of all the men, excepting Hastings, until they were almost gaunt. When the crew was boated for the forenoon practice, the exhortations of the head coach were almost hopeful. But after he had sent them away on the first stretch at full speed, even the blasé old engineer of the launch could see that things were going wrong in the same old way. The emotions of the head coach were too large for words and with sinister patience he made them row another spurt. Before he could begin to speak, Hastings knew that there was still a break in the swing at Number Six, and the confirmation came in tones almost of entreaty from the bow of the launch.

"You are still behind, Six, while the rest of the crew is swinging better. Try, for God's sake, to get your shoulders on it and swing them up. Do you want seven other men to pull your hundred and ninety pounds of beef like so much freight in the boat? I have told you these things a hundred times, and you must hang on to them or I can't risk bothering with you any longer. All ready, coxswain, steer for that red barn across the river."

Within thirty strokes Hastings felt that he was rowing in no better form than before, although he had never been so grimly determined to row better. Stung to the soul by the taunt of the coach, he strove always to be a little ahead of Number Seven whose instant of catch was signaled by the telltale tightening of the crease in the back of his neck.

"Slo-w down on y-o-u-r slides!" yelled the bobbing coxswain. "*You are b-e-h-i-n-d, Number Six.*"

Hastings could have throttled the coxswain. He had heard this plaint so often that it cut him like a whip. The head coach picked up the cursed refrain:

"*You are behind, Number Six.*"

The futility of his flurried effort became maddening. Soon the crew ceased rowing. The launch steamed alongside and the head coach called out, with sincere regret:

"I'm afraid I'll have to make a change at Number Six. Better get out and take a rest, Hastings."

A substitute crawled into the vacant seat and Hastings went aft to the cockpit of the launch where he could be alone. He watched the substitute grip the oar still warm from his calloused hands. Nor did he yet realize what had befallen him and felt vague relief that the struggle was done.

When he went ashore at Gales Ferry, the impulse was to flee the place, away from the sights and sounds that hurt him so. It seemed a thing greatly to be desired even to row on a beaten crew. While he lingered, he saw one of the substitutes standing idly in the boat-house door. To Hastings's questions he replied:

"They put my partner in the 'varsity boat and there is nobody to man the pair-oar with me. And I ought to be over at the start right now, for the tip is out that Harvard intends to try the four miles on time. How am I going to hold a stop-watch on 'em?"

Hastings helped him shove the pair-oar into the water and said:

"If I can be any use as a substitute, why, that's what I'm here for. I came near playing the baby act and running away, but if I can help the crew to row faster by getting out of it, I am honestly glad of it."

In one way this was an ignominious finish of a rowing career, to serve as a substitute during the last few days before the race and watch your own crew sweep past while you trailed after the Harvard eight with field-glasses and stop-watch. But it was illumined by that simple and stead-fast gospel of duty which a grieving youngster had learned to accept without question during his three years of associa-tion with the men and the traditions of that generation in Yale rowing history. No inherent virtue of his own had in-spired him to feel with unaffected sincerity that he was glad to help the crew win the race by getting out of the boat.

A few days later he saw the race from the deck of a yacht, and the other guests were kind and tactful and seemed very sorry for the derelict Number Six. With him was "Josh" Hartwell who had been the captain of that famous '92 crew in which they had sped down this shining river together, eighteen lengths in front of Harvard, with no break in the swing from stroke to bow, and the oars flashing in faultless unison.

Now they were nervously waiting to catch the first glimpse of the contestants as they came into the last two miles of the course downstream. Oh, but it was a long, hard race for men to row, with a heavy wind against them all the way and white-caps flecking the roughened water. It was like rowing five miles instead of four.

They passed at a slow, dogged stroke, a grim test of endurance, the spray flying over the outriggers, and Yale had a lead of three lengths. In the last mile this was increased by another boat-length and a safe margin of victory. Thankfully I went ashore to seek the telegraph office and write the story of the race. It was also my epitaph as an oarsman, for I was careful to state that in taking Ralph Paine out of the boat at the last minute, "Bob" Cook had displayed his usual shrewdness and wisdom.

The jubilant Yale oarsmen hastened to New Haven for the celebration, tally-ho coach, fireworks, parade, and the rest of it. I was in no mood to join them and tarried in New London until midnight. Troubles never come singly. While in a crowd at the railroad station, some scoundrel picked my pocket of twenty-seven dollars which happened to be my entire fortune just then. It seemed to be one thing too many. From a belated Yale straggler the price of a ticket was borrowed and so I returned to the campus.

At breakfast next morning in Mory's snug tavern I encountered "Bob" Cook and said to him:

"There is one thing I want to talk to you about, Mr. Cook, but you were too busy at Gales Ferry."

"Spill it, my son," smiled the bronzed, robust coach. "We missed you at the crew banquet last night. Some nice things were said about the way you took your medicine."

"Oh, I deserve no credit for that," was the hasty exclamation. "You know I have been planning to go into newspaper work when I finish college next year, and — and you offered me a bully job on your paper, the 'Philadelphia Press,' and I expected to take it — "

"What's the matter now?" demanded Robert J. Cook the publisher. "Trying to hold me up? Is some New York paper offering you more money?"

"Great Scott, it's not that, Mr. Cook. But, of course, you don't want a poor fat-head that was kicked off a crew in disgrace. It probably means that he will make a failure of it when he tackles a real job. You need n't feel under any obligation to hold that position for me, after what happened at New London."

"I expect you to report to my city editor in September of next year," severely returned Robert J. Cook. "Now forget that nonsense, and we'll have a few more poached eggs and some sardines on toast and another pot of coffee. If you weigh as much as two hundred pounds you don't have to worry any more."

VII

A YOUNG MAN IN SEARCH OF TROUBLE

IT was a minor episode of history, but gorgeously romantic against the quiet background of twenty-five years ago, when American life was unvexed by wars or foreign relations or the loud cries of the Young Intellectuals as they cease from praising one another long enough to toss overboard the morals, manners, and ideals of all the generations of mankind that have preceded them.

This placid current of things became disturbed by the struggle of the Cuban people to wrest their unhappy island from the cruel and corrupt misrule of Spain whose red and yellow banner floated over a few fragments of that vast empire which had once extended from California to Peru. Other Cuban rebellions had blazed or smouldered in cane-field and jungle, one of them lasting ten years, but none had so deeply stirred sentiment in the United States as this final upheaval which was begun in 1895.

The barbarous severity of the Spanish armies, the policy of laying waste the country and using starvation as a weapon where the sword had failed, aroused greater indignation than did the invasion of Belgium by the gray-backed German columns. This was because Cuba was so much nearer home. Our orators eulogized the cause and its leaders. Antonio Maceo and Maximo Gomez and their barefooted black battalions were hailed as patriots whose spirit was akin to that of Washington and his ragged Continentals. They deserved American recognition and support in their courageous fight for freedom, but, as in a more recent instance, the Government of the United States for a long time maintained an attitude of punctilious neutrality.

In pitiful need of arms, supplies, funds, the scattered bands of Cuban insurgents carried on a guerrilla warfare for three years against Spanish forces which finally numbered two hundred thousand men. The revolution would have been stamped out but for the unofficial aid of its friends in this country. Their activities were directed by a Cuban *Junta*, or revolutionary committee, whose chief headquarters were in New York and Washington. Large sums of money were raised by popular subscription.

The American Government offered no objection to this, but, as soon as these funds were converted into rifles and machetes and cartridges and sent to Cuba, international law was defied, offense given the friendly power of Spain, and violent liberties were taken with the solemn edicts of the State Department. In short, it was an utterly lawless business, and those engaged in it were likely to cool their heels in a Federal prison. Some of them did, and were considerably older when they emerged. The American Navy patrolled the coast from Sandy Hook to Key West to discourage this forbidden industry of filibustering, with orders to capture all vessels so suspected.

Spain had, of course, established a close blockade of the island of Cuba with its own naval forces, and the policy was simple but effective. Any vessel caught in the attempt to run the blockade with cargo for the rebels was to be blown out of water. It was waste motion for a filibustering skipper to wave the Stars and Stripes when overtaken by a Spanish cruiser. He was a man without a country.

Such was the situation in 1896 when the Cuban cause was undeniably righteous and immensely popular, and yet, incongruously enough, those who saved it from disaster were lawless sea-rovers pursued from their own coasts to the blue waters of the Caribbean, dodging every smudge of smoke that showed on the horizon, tricking their own navy and a swarm of shore officials to shove the cargo aboard, and fleeing to take chances with the Spanish blockading fleet in some lonely, palm-fringed bay.

In that day and generation, when the opportunities were few for those in quest of high adventure, it was the finest game one could play. Beyond argument, it gave him a run for his money from start to finish.

Two years out of college, and therefore not old enough to know better, this business of filibustering in Cuban waters appealed to Ralph Paine as eminently desirous. As a newspaper reporter, life had not lacked flavor or variety, but now it seemed flat and unprofitable. The thing was to get afloat in one of those notorious steamers whose voyages had an air of mystery, whose departures and escapades were clouded in a baffling secrecy, and whose sailormen had the temper of the buccaneers who had cruised in those same seas long, long ago.

"The trouble with you," said the managing editor, in a friendly mood, "is that you are suffering from an attack of *damfoolitis*. It is a very common malady at your age. You have a good job here. Better stick to it. There is not another young reporter in Philadelphia who pulls down a salary of sixty a week, or anything like it. And sometimes you actually earn it. The Cubans won't let you join one of those crazy expeditions, and if they did you would n't be allowed to send any news back. I don't propose to stake you."

The swarthy gentlemen of the Cuban *Junta* were found to be as unreceptive as the managing editor. American volunteers were in disfavor just then and there was no eagerness to send more of them to Cuba. Misfortune had happened to one or two ships. It was suspected that there had been spies on board, or somebody had talked too much. It was necessary to take the strictest precautions. Courteous but vague was the assurance that possibly something might be done at some future time. Scores of private detectives in the employ of the Spanish Legation were seeking evidence against the filibustering vessels. . . .

There followed several weeks of endeavor to convince these suspicious patriots that one's devotion to the cause of *Cuba Libre* did not mask some sinister motive. They had good reason to be careful, no doubt, when one mischance might mean a precious cargo lost to those tattered regiments which had neither ordnance plants nor munition factories of their own. At last the coveted permission was granted, but all information concerning the time, place, and means of departure was to be withheld until the very time of sailing.

Mr. William Randolph Hearst was then a novel sensation in New York journalism, a young millionaire with a hobby who flung his money right and left. He had undertaken to lead the United States into war with Spain in behalf of bleeding Cuba and was making a tremendous noise about it. This was a cause more laudable than some of those which he championed later. His correspondents, famous writers and illustrators among them, were depicting the horrors of Spanish military administration under Captain-General Weyler, "The Butcher," and the savage extermination of a whole population in *reconcentrado* camps.

The late Richard Harding Davis, probably the most brilliant war correspondent of his generation, was sent to Cuba by Mr. Hearst, but all his efforts to evade the elaborate espionage of the Spanish officials were thwarted. He saw what they permitted him to see. This was the usual fortune of the American observers who went openly to Havana. To the few men who had succeeded in sending news from the camps and flying columns of the insurgents, Richard Harding Davis offered this ungrudging tribute:

They are taking chances that no war correspondent ever took in any war in any part of the world. For this is not a war — it is a state of lawless butchery, and the rights of correspondents, of soldiers, and of non-combatants are not recognized. Archibald Forbes and "Bull Run" Russell and Frederick Villiers had great continental armies to protect them; these men work alone with a continental army against them. They risk capture at sea and death by the guns of a Spanish cruiser, and, escaping that, they face when they reach the island the greater danger of being cut down by a guerrilla force and left to die in a road, as Govin was cut down, or of being put in a prison and left to die of fever, as Delgado died, and as Melton is lying now. . . .

The fate of these three American correspondents has not deterred others from crossing the lines, and they are in the field now, lying in swamps by day and creeping between the forts at night, standing under fire by the side of Gomez as they stood beside Maceo, going without food, without shelter, without the right to answer the attacks of the Spanish troops, climbing the mountains and crawling across the *trochas*, creeping to some friendly hut for a cup of coffee and to place their dispatches in safe hands, and then going back again to run the gantlet of Spanish spies and roving cavalry and of the unspeakable guerrillas.

In case you do not read a New York newspaper, it is well that you should know that the names of these correspondents are Grover Flint of the "Journal," Sylvester Scovel of the "World," and George Bronson Rea of the "Herald." I repeat that, as I could not reach the field, I can write thus freely of those who have been more successful.

It occurred to the restless young reporter who had received permission to sail with a filibustering expedition that Mr. Hearst might be interested in the adventure. He proceeded to obtain an interview with the prodigal publisher in his office in New York, and a bargain was promptly struck. From the editorial point of view, it was merely another gamble which might result in a good story. You never could tell.

The energetic Mr. Hearst, sitting upon his desk and swinging his long legs, said quite casually in closing the interview:

"You may get nowhere and if you do the Spaniards will probably scupper you. By the way, you remember the big fair held in Madison Square Garden to raise money for the Cuban cause. They voted on a sword, at so much a vote, to be given to the greatest living soldier. Of course General Maximo Gomez won in a walk. Then I gave them two thousand dollars for the sword, to help the cause along, and of course I intend to present it to Maximo Gomez. Do you want to see it?"

With dazzled eyes I beheld the costly weapon as it rested in a mahogany case. The scabbard was ornately adorned, the hilt plated with gold and sparkling with small diamonds. It had been made by a famous firm of Fifth Avenue jewelers. Here was a sword which looked like two thousand dollars. Displaying the blade, Mr. Hearst called attention to the engraved inscriptions, such as "*To Maximo Gomez, Commander-in-Chief of the Army of the Cuban Republic,*" and "*Viva Cuba Libre.*"

"Very handsome," said I. "Old Gomez will be tickled to death, when he gets it."

"That is the idea, *when he gets it,*" observed the bland, debonair Mr. Hearst. "I have been trying to find somebody foolish enough to carry this elegant sword to Gomez. I am perfectly frank with you. These inscriptions would be devilish hard to explain to the Spanish army, if you happened to be caught, would n't they?"

"And you want me to try to present this eighteen-karat sword to Gomez, with your compliments?" I suggested.

"If you don't mind," was the hopeful reply. "I swear I don't know what else to do with the confounded thing. Of course if you are nabbed at sea, you can probably chuck it overboard in time —"

"And if I get surrounded on land, perhaps I can swallow it, Mr. Hearst. Never mind that. I am the damn fool you have been looking for. Tuck the glittering weapon in the mahogany case and I will lug it along right now."

He shook hands with me and I passed out into the night, the long, polished box under one arm. As I regarded it, the incident dwelt in the realm of the true romance. There had to be no waiting until the low, rakish filibustering steamer should flit to sea. To be young and foot-loose and robust, to be carrying a sword to Gomez with your own death-warrant artistically engraved on the shining blade, to expect that Spanish spies would soon find your trail — all this was entrancing beyond words.

As soon as possible the sword was put into a snug leather case instead of the unwieldy mahogany box. It became one item of a private arsenal which included two revolvers and a sheath-knife. Just what was the purpose of this ridiculous burden of hardware, I am at a loss to explain. There must have been some notion that sailing the Spanish Main implied being armed to the teeth, or that with the sword of Gomez as fatal evidence one was in honor bound to sell his life dearly. Had Ralph Paine fallen overboard, with the added weight of a stuffed cartridge belt, there would have been a splash like a ship's anchor and an instantaneous plunge to the bottom.

The final word, whispered by a stealthy messenger of the Cuban *Junta*, was:

"Go to Jacksonville and report to Señor José Huau" (pronounced *Wow*).

"Wow! That is easy," I said to myself. "I was raised in Jacksonville and Señor Huau runs the cigar-store at the corner of Bay and Main Streets. No doubt I went to school with some of the other conspirators."

Florida had become the active base of the filibustering industry, after several unlucky experiences out of the ports farther to the northward. Captain Hart, who had run the Laurada out of Philadelphia, forfeited his ship to the Government and was sentenced to a prison term, and the same hard fate befell Captain Wiborg in Baltimore. But the famous Three Friends, the Dauntless, and the Commodore were stealing out of the Florida harbors and inlets with their lawless freightage and picaresque crews, so cleverly handled that they defied capture and left not enough evidence to trip them.

In a sleeping-car south-bound, the glittering sword of

Gomez was watchfully guarded night and day. There was
the thrilling surmise that an attempt might be made to lift
it as a trophy for the Spanish Legation. Such are the gratifying illusions of youth! The uneventful journey was disappointing.

Portly Señor José Huau was found behind his cigar counters, and in a corner was the well-remembered soda fountain
where he had aforetime served me many a fizzing drink as a
thirsty urchin with a nickel in my fist. It seemed odd to contemplate him as a leader in affairs so delicate and dangerous
and important.

An affectionate greeting and he led the way into a dingy
little back room where men drifted in to talk in hushed voices
around a card table or vanished on secretive errands, shrewd,
daring Cubans, like General Emilio Nuñez and Alphonso
Fritot, or sun-reddened, close-mouthed shipmasters like
"Dynamite Johnny" O'Brien, "Bill" Lewis, or Napoleon
Broward and his brother Montcalm. They knew their trade
and unemotionally diced with the devil and the deep sea.

"When will a ship sail? *Quien sabe?*" murmured Señor
Huau, with a shrug and an habitual glance over his shoulder.
"I will send you word at the hotel. We have had some trouble. But our soldiers need the guns and the ammunition terribly and we must send them soon. A few days? A week?
A month? Ah, I wish I could say. But you will know in
time."

Señor Huau lighted a fresh cigar and there was a twinkle
in his black eye as he remarked:

"It is lucky, perhaps, that your esteemed father is no
longer the pastor of a church in Jacksonville, Ralph, my boy.
If something slips, and you are arrested, it might be a little
awkward for the Reverend Samuel Delahaye Paine — his
only son in jail."

"He would feel proud of me, Mr. Huau. At least, that is
my guess. A man who fought in the trenches before Sevasto-

pol and at Inkerman and Alma when he was a kid of seventeen in the British army, and led a battery of light artillery in our Civil War, is n't going to be upset by a little thing like filibustering. If he were young enough, he would be apt to take a whirl at it himself."

"Ah, but he is now the father of a son," was the wise comment of Señor Huau. "I will let him know where you are, after you go to sea, and send him any news that comes back. He is still living at Sanford? We must not make more worry for him than can be helped."

Sooner than expected the summons came to the hotel from this little room in the rear of the cigar-store. A Cuban sauntered along the piazza early in an evening of this same week and halted to whisper:

"Come to the freight yard at midnight and you will find friends. Good luck, if I never see you again."

This was in the month of December when the winter visitors were flocking to Florida like birds of passage. The hotel orchestra was playing after dinner. Plump matrons gossiped in groups and tired business men loafed in wicker chairs. The young people danced and flirted and were bored for lack of more exciting diversion. It was all so safe and conventional and usual that it seemed extraordinary to be getting a kit together of saddle-bags, blankets, weapons, and so on, not forgetting the sword of Gomez, in readiness to go surging off God knew where.

Shortly before midnight I faded out through a side door as unostentatiously as possible, although a man weighed down with such peculiar luggage was bound to clank and jingle as he walked. The noise suggested a portable blacksmith's shop. Skulking in the shadows of back streets and fetching a wide circuit, it was found possible to approach the freight yard down among the wharves without raising an alarm. The place was in darkness, purposely so. Stumbling around at random, I began to encounter men singly and in bunches.

They swore in Spanish, at me and at each other. That I asked questions in English appeared to disturb them. Their accents became challenging.

To be mistaken for a Pinkerton hireling in Spanish employ was not auspicious, but presently these leaderless Cuban patriots were taken in charge by two or three competent agents who herded them over to a train consisting of several freight cars and one darkened passenger coach with the shades pulled down. Into this they piled, groping to find seats, encumbered with bags and bundles, falling over the seats like blind men in a cavern. If one chattered in his excitement, all the others hissed for silence like a den of snakes. It was impossible to count them, but there must have been forty or more in the party, Cuban cigarmakers and other exiles who were returning to fight for their native land.

Presently the cigarettes glowed like fireflies and there were intermittent glimpses of dark faces, flashing teeth, hands weaving in nervous gesticulation. Not a word of English was heard in this rustling mutter of voices cautiously subdued until I fell over a leg in the aisle and the owner exclaimed:

"Ouch! Right on the shin! Why in blazes don't you sit down and keep calm?"

"Beg pardon, brother. Please move over," said I. "Any more *Americanos* in this madhouse?"

"You can search me, son. My name is McCready, and would n't this give you the yips? It was wished on me by my sheet, the 'New York Herald,' which has an inside drag with this Cuban outfit. The news editor wrenched me from Broadway, despite my loud shrieks, and told me to go to it. He had it all fixed up with the ace cards of the *Junta*."

"What's the idea now?" I asked. "Where do we proceed from hence? Sealed orders?"

"Rolling down to Cuba in a freight train, apparently. Misery loves company. I am glad you came," answered the sardonic Ernest W. McCready. As an adventurer, he appeared to lack enthusiasm. His demeanor was undismayed, but it was all in the day's work and he wished it understood that he did not make a practice of hunting trouble. He was a sensible young man. It seemed wiser to defer confiding the story of the sword of Gomez. McCready would have been ready to agree with Mr. Hearst, that it was a fool and his errand.

In that little back room behind the cigar counters and the soda fountain, Señor Huau and his friends had planned this midnight excursion to the last detail, with keen and subtle intelligence. A few minutes after the Cubans had crowded into the gloomy passenger coach, the train moved quietly out of the yard. Soon it gathered speed and was, indeed, a fast freight as it rumbled across the flat landscape of pine and palmetto and saw-grass. Inside the curtained car it was impossible to guess in what direction the train was moving or where the destination might be.

Several miles beyond Jacksonville there was a brief halt. A number of men clambered aboard with their bundles, emerging from behind a shanty of a way station. Two or three of them used the English language vigorously, like true soldiers of fortune. They had been hiding in the woods, it was learned, waiting for the expedition. The train delayed a little longer. Two limber Cubans strapped climbing irons to their legs and ascended the telegraph poles beside the track. Methodically they cut all the wires for reasons quite obvious. No Government official could now send word ahead to intercept this fugitive freight train and its contraband cargo.

Again the expedition rattled along and nobody tried to sleep. So far, so good, but there would be no certainty that the various hostile agencies were outwitted until the party should be stowed aboard ship, with the coast astern and the merchandise crammed under the hatches. Two hours passed, and then the train slowed its pace and proceeded with more caution. The engineer in the cab must have enjoyed this escapade. It was not on his routine schedule. Ahead of him was the gleam of water beneath a sky spangled with stars. He let the train roll out upon a long, creaking trestlework and it came to rest at a wharf in the harbor of Fernandina.

Moored alongside was a large, sea-going towboat with a bold sheer and the suggestion of speed and power. Painted white, she loomed tall and spectral against the dusky curtain of night. Lanterns were hung at the gangway and thirty negro roustabouts stood ready to hustle the freight into the hold.

This vessel was the Three Friends. To the Spanish Navy she was the perfidious and accursed *Tres Amigos* which had been as elusive as the Flying Dutchman, which had been harried and chased from Cape Maysi to the Yucatan Channel, and for whose capture or destruction the Captain-General of Cuba had offered many thousand pesos.

Low in the water, she was much less conspicuous at sea than the high-sided tramp steamers which had been employed earlier in the game. And as a towboat she required no clearance papers for a specified destination. A wrecking license was sufficient and this could be made to cover a multitude of sins. On this particular occasion she had steamed out of Jacksonville, innocently enough, a week or so earlier to look for a wreck reported on the Florida Reef.

It was quite by chance, of course, that the industrious Three Friends should be tied up to the wharf in Fernandina at the very moment when the wandering freight train stopped abreast of the gangway. The doors of the box-cars flew open. The roustabouts jumped like sprinters. A torrent of merchandise flowed into the vessel, which was manifestly in a hurry. Boxes and barrels, bales and crates, they erupted from those freight cars, and the forty-odd Cuban patriots spilled out of the passenger coach to help load the ship.

The cargo was harmless enough. The stenciled markings proved it, "condensed milk," "salted codfish," "breakfast bacon," "prime lard"; but when a case of hams was dropped and smashed, out clattered a dozen Mauser rifles.

A serene little man with a mop of gray hair and a pugnacious Irish face stood and looked on, his hands in his pockets. When a brawny nigger let a big box slide down the planks to fetch up on deck with a terrific thump, the calm little man spoke gently:

"Easy, boy, if I was you. That there case of canned tomatoes is nitroglycerin. If she goes off, it's liable to muss us all up."

"My Gawd, Cap'n Johnny, yessuh," was the agitated response. "This cargo sure is mighty ticklish an' deceivin'. Nex' box o' termaters come so easy she ain't gwine crack a egg."

Captain Johnny O'Brien, epic hero of many such wild voyages as this, a man with a price on his head, strolled to the engine-room door to chat with the fat, perspiring chief concerning certain technical matters, the amount of coal in the bunkers, the steam pressure, the condition of the boiler tubes. Upon such practical details hung success or a most unpleasant finish. It was worth noting that the Three Friends had been a week away from port, and yet there was all the coal in her that could be stowed below. Somewhere off the coast floated a small schooner with an empty hold and a grimy crew. Taking on coal at sea is a difficult trick, but it can be done.

There was never a trace of tropical languor in the celerity with which those freight cars were emptied of their incriminating and explosive contents. All hands toiled to get the ship away by daybreak. The risk of discovery, the urgent need of haste, whipped them into amazing energy. The Collector of the Port of Fernandina, whose duty it was to thwart the enterprise, had been decoyed elsewhere by an ingenious telegram for which that suave cigar merchant, Señor Huau, may have been responsible.

But there were other hazards, such as the meddlesome Navy or an incursion of deputy marshals. There could be no resisting Uncle Sam and his legal documents. They were always persuasive.

The cargo vanished into the open hatches and was hastily stowed by a gang below — thousands of rifles and machetes, millions of cartridges, pieces of field artillery and brass shells for them, saddlery and shoes, medical supplies and what not — the essentials of equipment for troops whose situation was forlorn beyond description. Dawn began to flush the sky when the last heavy case of cartridges was dumped on deck.

Then the roustabouts and the crew of the vessel flew at a great heap of coal which was tied up in sacks. It was flung aboard from the wharf and piled wherever space could be found, aft beyond the towing bitts, between the boats, on the cabin roof. For the forty-odd patriots, likewise for McCready and Paine, there was no other place to live than this open deck amid the sacks of coal. The Cuban colonel in charge of the party and a wounded major were given the spare stateroom. The Three Friends had not been fitted out for the passenger trade. It was vastly more important to find deck-room for this extra coal.

"Rather poor stuff to sleep on," said the critical Mc-Cready, "but it might be worse. Soft coal, please observe, not anthracite! Ah, yonder is my cabin de luxe, with a hawser for a pillow. Bully ventilation! Plenty of fresh air! I always did hate a stuffy room."

VIII

'HELL-BENT WITH "DYNAMITE JOHNNY"'

CAPTAIN O'BRIEN climbed into the wheel-house, poked his head out of a window, and waved a hand. There was no farewell toot of the whistle. The niggers on the wharf cast off the lines. Alphonso Fritot, the efficient agent of the *Junta* who had managed the railroad excursion, flourished his hat and shouted farewell in musical Spanish phrases. The patriots huddled amidst the coal sacks raised a quavering cheer for *Cuba Libre*.

The Three Friends throbbed to the beat of her powerful engines and moved out of the shining harbor which was aglow with the flush of sunrise.

It was now possible to make the acquaintance of this ship's crew, to discover what manner of sailormen had been tossed together to persist in undertaking such voyages as this. The exploits of Captain "Dynamite Johnny" O'Brien were, of course, familiar. In the Three Friends he had been often to Cuba, but there were other hot and turbulent countries washed by the Caribbean which had known him in earlier years. This was the trade he followed for a livelihood, to deliver arms and munitions where revolution brewed. In the cause of Cuba, however, he was risking his neck for something more than gold. The sentiment of it had taken hold of him. He believed in this fight for liberty.

Very quiet and intrepid and sparing of speech, he had lived a life as fantastic as fiction, and regarded it as commonplace.

The nickname of "Dynamite Johnny" was a souvenir of a landing in Haiti during one of its chronic upheavals of government. He had agreed to deliver forty tons of dynamite to the insurgent forces which held a certain port. The federal

CAPTAIN "DYNAMITE JOHNNY" O'BRIEN AND AN EXPEDITION OF HIS FILIBUSTERING
OUTLAWS BOUND FOR CUBA

(The arrow indicates Captain O'Brien)

troops happened to be shelling the town at the time, but Captain O'Brien dropped anchor in the bay and sent his boats ashore. It was not his habit to evade a bargain. He and his sailormen had lugged twenty tons of the dynamite up on the beach in front of the town and were pulling back to the ship for more when the federal artillerymen neatly planted a shell in this particular spot of the shore.

When the smoke cleared, the Haitian rebels had lost the twenty tons of costly explosive, but what was more disconcerting, the town had been violently erased from the map. Captain O'Brien viewed this incident as no concern of his. He had agreed to deliver the cargo. Thereupon he cussed his startled sailormen into action and they loaded the remaining twenty tons of dynamite into the boats and rowed ashore with it.

Having stacked the boxes neatly on the beach near the large hole where the Haitian town had been, they shoved off and returned to their low-browed, dissolute packet. The artillery hurled a few peevish shells after them, but the episode was closed. Captain "Dynamite Johnny" O'Brien departed at twelve knots to seek other traffic elsewhere.[1]

He was employed by the Cuban *Junta* as a sort of fleet commander, to be consulted in the secret conferences with respect to the general plan of operations afloat, or to be shifted from one vessel to another if the occasion should require. With him in the Three Friends sailed Captain "Bill" Lewis, skipper of the towboat and hired by her owners, whose charter terms were for so many thousand dollars a voyage and a bonus for every cargo safely landed. A stout-hearted, jovial seafarer was "Bill" Lewis, who honestly enjoyed the game. He was paid double wages, but this was the minor inducement.

---

[1] This was the version current aboard the Three Friends. In a biography of Captain O'Brien called *A Captain Unafraid*, by Horace Smith (Harper & Bros., 1912), it is stated that he was carrying the cargo of dynamite to Colombia in the yacht Rambler.

The same thing could be said of fat John Dunn, the chief engineer, who swore to stay ashore at the end of every voyage and quit this durn-fool performance which was no place for a family man and growin' old at that. But he could no more let go than could the noisy braggart of a black cook, Jim Bell, or the stocky, hard-fisted first mate and his toughly seasoned deck-hands, or the firemen who stoked her in the inferno of a boiler-room as she fled under the blazing skies of the tropics. Kipling knew the breed and told it for them in the lines:

> "For to admire an' for to see,
> For to be'old this world so wide —
> It never done no good to me,
> But I can't drop it if I tried!"

This was the crew of the Three Friends, bold men and competent, who had been carefully recruited. Some of them might get drunk ashore, and they were always ready for a fight or a frolic, but they never blabbed and no money could buy them.

What of the forty-odd passengers who bestrewed the decks as the vessel raced to the southward of Fernandina on that fine winter morning with a lively breeze and a swinging sea? Alas, their aspect was excessively unromantic. Seasickness speedily afflicted these Cuban patriots. They sprawled among the sacks of coal and a litter of valises, pasteboard suitcases, bundles wrapped in newspapers. They wore all kinds of clothes, even to hard-boiled shirts and derby hats. Heroes they actually were, moved by exalted motives to enlist in a forlorn hope, but you would never have guessed it as they lay inanimate with the spray pelting them.

They were not all cigarmakers. Here was a handsome lad, trimly equipped for service, who had been a student at Harvard. A middle-aged man with an air of distinction had been a consulting engineer, with offices in New York. The love of country, the appeal of a flag with a single star, was dearer than life. Among them were a few adventurers, soldiers of fortune from Porto Rico or Venezuela or Colombia whose hatred of Spain was hereditary.

The Three Friends held a course within sight of the Florida coast until early in the forenoon, when a steamer's smoke was seen close inshore. We veered out to give it a wide berth. Soon the stranger was made out to be the revenue cutter Boutwell, making her best speed out across the St. John's bar. It was her evident intention to intercept and capture the Three Friends, but something faster was needed than this venerable tub of a cutter whose gait was known to a fraction of a knot.

Chief Engineer John Dunn made no effort to crowd on more steam. Folding his huge, tattooed arms, he leaned against the rail as a mildly interested spectator. Talking to himself he prattled along:

"She won't ketch us, but supposin' she did! There's enough evidence in this durned hooker to send me up for twenty years. No alibi this time, eh? I really ought to have more sense — skyhootin' around with this scandalous bunch. Durn my fool hide, it's the last time."

Soon the plodding revenue cutter was left astern. She could not come close enough to make it worth while to fire a shot as a summons to heave to. Disgustedly she jogged back into the St. John's River to cable a warning to the cruisers at Key West to watch for the Three Friends and head her off in the Florida Strait. Several weeks later we learned more about this pursuit by the cutter Boutwell. And it was again in order to admire the nimble wit of Señor Huau and his partners. Another well-known filibustering vessel, the Dauntless, had been tied up at a wharf in Jacksonville, unable to escape official vigilance. She was under the guns of the Boutwell which lay in the stream abreast of her. At dusk of the day of our own departure, Cubans had begun to trickle aboard the Dauntless, one or two at a time, with every sign of stealth. They were most anxious to avoid scrutiny.

Later in the evening it had been also observed that the fires of the Dauntless were no longer banked. Smoke curled from her funnel. A subdued and suspicious activity had led to the conclusion that this audacious craft intended to make a run for it, to catch the revenue cutter napping, and once under way to show a clean pair of heels down the river. The bluejackets of the Boutwell cleared ship for action. The cable was hove short, ready to slip. The tricky Dauntless was checkmated this time.

Such had been the circumstances when the freight train carrying the genuine expedition had stolen away at midnight from the freight yard. Official attention had been artfully diverted to the Dauntless. Having served the purpose, the dummy patriots had trickled ashore again, and the fires were banked.

Naturally elated by the success of the stratagem, the actors had been too loquacious, and in this manner it was learned that the real quarry was the Three Friends. Thereupon the revenue cutter had hastened down the river, but had reached the sea a bit too late to make it anything more than a wild-goose chase. It was a gleam of comedy in a drama grimly serious to those whose fortunes were involved.

In this jumble of humanity sloshing about the spray-swept decks of the Three Friends, a few personalities began to detach themselves and to arrest attention. There was the squarely built, powerful young man, for instance, with the stubbled beard and the blistered nose and the cheery grin. No Cuban blood in him! He had an air of taut, masterful self-reliance, and the candid blue eye regarded life with an engaging sparkle. He was the kind that took the cards as they were dealt and played a poor hand well; this you perceived at a glance. I had mistaken him to be one of the ship's crew.

"Mike Walsh is me name," said he, by way of introduction, "and the *Cubanos* promised me a commission in the field artillery. I was a chief gunner's mate in th' hoodooed old battle-wagon of a Maine, servin' me third enlistment. I jumped her at Key West, having a mind to insert meself into this entertainin' disturbance."

The amiable deserter beckoned a lanky man of at least twoscore years and a mournful countenance and presented him as follows:

"Sergeant Jack Gorman, gentlemen — a veteran of the regular army, havin' done hitches as a bugler, a doughboy, and a trooper. He was in the last Indian battle, at Wounded Knee, unless he's as big a liar as most soldiers. Explain yourself, Jack. Buck up an' look pleasant."

With a manner profoundly serious, the sergeant elucidated himself in this wise:

"I showed the Cuban bosses my sharpshooter's medals and they said they'd give me a thousand dollars for every Spanish officer I picked off. It looked like easy money. No Mauser or Krag for me! I packed along the old Springfield and two hundred rounds. Allow for some poor shootin', and I ought to clean up a hundred thousand dollars."

"You want to look at his old cannon, Mr. Paine," said Mike Walsh. "She slings a slug as big as your thumb, and this comical Gorman sets an' counts his cartridges to pass the time an' rolls up a dazzlin' fortune. However, he's no more a lunatic than the rest of us or he would n't be here."

"You are bright, Mike," observed McCready, breaking a long silence. "But please don't include me. I am the victim of an editorial press gang."

In rambling, mellow accents the chief gunner's mate told us how he had departed from the Maine which, two years later, was to be shattered by an explosion that was the immediate cause of the war with Spain and forced the United States into new paths of destiny. Key West being a speck of an island in an emerald ocean, Mike Walsh, deserter, had been hard put to it to elude the naval patrol sent in search of him. By night he had swum out to a small schooner while the crew was ashore and had tucked himself in the hold. The schooner made sail the next day and stood up the Gulf with a cargo of green bananas.

This diet became distasteful to the bold deserter and he also craved water to drink.

"How long did you stand it, Mike?" I asked.

"Two days, sir, and then I boiled out of the hatch and captured the schooner."

"Of course you did. How many men were there?"

"A lantern-jawed skipper with whiskers on his chin, an' two fo'mast hands an' a cook. That was all. They were surprised to see me an' I picked up a handy bit o' firewood beside the galley an' we mixed it up. The skipper fell down the companionway an' one sailor bumped his head or something, an' the other one tumbled into the hatch among the bananas. I disremember what happened to the cook. Anyhow, we come to terms an' they agreed to give me rations an' set me ashore up the Gulf."

"And then what?" demanded McCready, who displayed symptoms of interest.

"Oh, I hitched up with the *Cubanos* in Tampa an' they shoved me through to Jacksonville, an' me an' this bloodthirsty Jack Gorman lived in the woods till the train picked us up, as ye know. 'T is th' fact that the Navy is all spit and drill an' polish in time o' peace, an' nothin' ever happens. This Cuban ruction looks like it might keep a man busy an' cheerful-like."

So much by way of introducing Mike Walsh, a rare jewel of a man and shipmate, who was to save the skins of all this company before the end of the voyage. And it may be that you will feel inclined to forgive and overlook his sin of desertion. How could you have expected him to remain tied to his peaceful battle-wagon with a lovely ruction raging almost next door?

IX

"GOOD–NIGHT, LADIES!"

THE sky clouded in the afternoon of this first day at sea. Dirty weather was brooding and it soon came in gusty squalls and driving rain that drenched the sodden, seasick Cubans. The gray seas climbed over the low bulwarks and broke on deck. It was a wet ship, rolling deep-laden, and there was no respite through the night.

Wedged between sacks of coal, with the heavy coils of hawser as an anchorage to save us from going adrift, McCready and I slept by fits and starts, mostly fits, and were perplexed to find the romance in it. The ship was wrapped in darkness, every ray of light from the deck-houses carefully screened. Lighting matches or cigarettes on deck was a punishable offense. If you tried to move about, you were almost certain to step upon the face of a comatose patriot.

It was different next morning with a dimpling sea and skies of blue. Our sad-eyed comrades began to revive. A few of them scrambled to the galley door with tin plates and cups and were served with hash and bacon, hard biscuit, and coffee with a noble kick to it. The chaotic decks took on a slight semblance of order. The patriots were beginning to unscramble themselves. Odds and ends of cargo overlooked until now were passed below. Colonel Perez Calvo showed a wan countenance in the stateroom doorway and issued certain commands to which nobody paid much heed. He was a courageous leader on dry land, but this uneasy, disturbing ocean — *caramba!!*

Meanwhile the crew of the Three Friends went about its own accustomed business, one watch relieving the other, viewing the unhappy patriots as so much dunnage to be dumped ashore at a designated place along with the rest of the cargo. Upon the small bridge above the wheel-house, Captain Johnny O'Brien chewed a dead cigar and swept the horizon with an excellent pair of glasses, a battered straw hat shading his eyes.

In the afternoon we passed the tall lighthouse at Jupiter Inlet and ran close to the beach. There was a curious sense of contrast in gazing at the huge Palm Beach hotels and the long pier. For my own part I felt no desire to be idling there nor envy of those who could afford it. McCready was of the same mind.

"I begin to like the rotten life we lead," said he, with his slow, quizzical smile. "I wonder why it is. It sort of gets you and you want to see it through. Palm Beach? Nothing doing."

He was a young man particular about his clothes, habitually well groomed when in civilization. Now he was unshaven, smeared with coal dust, stripped to a torn undershirt and grimy breeches rolled to the knees, and he was beginning to like it. Yes, it was sort of getting you, just as it had gotten hold of the sea vagabonds who manned the Three Friends.

At night the sea was again rough and I find this brief mention in my diary:

More rain and heavy squalls. Ship making bad weather of it. Slept on coal, but got washed out several times and tried all sorts of places, finally fetching up against three boxes of nitroglycerin which were lashed against the side of the cabin. They had worked a little loose and slid some, but not enough to hurt. McCready said they made him nervous. He slept poorly. Ditto me.

A stiff norther was blowing next morning and the Three Friends shipped it green over the bow, easing her speed to ten knots. The air was wonderfully bright and clear, and finely etched on the sky-line were the stumpy masts and fighting-tops of two cruisers. A little while and they were identified as the Newark and the Raleigh which based on

Key West. They were so much larger and higher out of water than the Three Friends that we were able to see them first. It was imperative to avoid these interfering cruisers whose errand it was to spoil this voyage.

Off to starboard were the Florida Keys, a lonely labyrinth of low, mangrove-covered islands and coral reefs and shallow channels. Engineering genius and the millions of John H. Flagler had not yet flung across them a marvelous seagoing railroad to Key West. They were familiar only to a few fishermen and spongers. Adroitly the Three Friends swung to seek refuge in this watery wilderness before she could be spied by the lookouts of the Newark and the Raleigh. A twisting fairway was followed, with Captain "Bill" Lewis as pilot, and in a snug retreat beyond the leafy curtain of Bahia Honda Key the anchor was let go. There we lurked all day in a quiet lee while the norther whistled outside and the surf foamed across the reefs.

When the slippery Three Friends ventured seaward in the kindly dusk, the cruisers had vanished. We saw them again, quite unexpectedly, during the night. They had anchored in the outer roadstead of Key West, perhaps a mile apart. Slightly vexed that he had been compelled to waste his good time behind Bahia Honda Key, Captain Johnny O'Brien was in no humor to shift his course again. He held straight on, between those two sleeping cruisers with their rows of twinkling lights. Like a dim shadow the hunted vessel stole between them. There was no alarm of bugle or boatswain's pipe along the quiet decks where the bluejackets swung in their hammocks. The astute Captain O'Brien had reasoned that if he were detected, so much time would be required to get the cruisers under way that he could lose them in the night.

It was a farewell, in a way, to home waters where capture meant no more than serious inconvenience and perhaps indictment by a Federal Grand Jury. This was a disagreeable risk to run, but by no means fatal. Later in this same night the Three Friends left the Dry Tortugas light over her stern and steered for the Yucatan Channel to pass around the western end of Cuba. She was making for the Caribbean and for a coast where Spain maintained the right to deal with law-defying interlopers as His Most Christian Majesty's admirals and captains might see fit.

It impressed one, this bold invasion by an unarmed, sea-going towboat whose destruction with all hands had been decreed in resounding phrases from the palace of administration in Havana. It had the flavor of bygone centuries, of an era when the little ships of England had sailed to the West Indies and the South Sea to singe the beards of the viceroys of Spain and to laugh at the tall galleons with their tiers of carronades and culverins. Nor was it far-fetched to think of "Dynamite Johnny" O'Brien as a comrade in spirit to Hawkins and Dampier and Edward Davis.

Such romantic musings as these were broken into by the sensible McCready who remarked:

"We did n't hear some of this stuff until it was too late to swim back — how sincere these Spaniards are in yearning for O'Brien's scalp and so on. A life insurance agent would certainly call *him* a bad risk anywhere within sight of Cuba."

"It would have made me hesitate, Mac," I admitted. "Have you learned any more Spanish to-day?"

"You bet! *Americano! El Corresponsal New York Heraldo! Pacifico! No piratico! No insurrecto! Help! Help!* And a precious lot of good it will do. When we get shot up in this sinful packet, who will stop to listen to my impassioned cries of neutrality? However, sink or swim, this is the life."

This last opinion was violently altered and shortly thereafter. Out in this empty stretch of sea, between the southernmost Florida keys and the western cape of Cuba, a large steamer was sighted in a moonlit evening hour. The day had been tranquil, better weather, the Cubans almost blithe, some of them cleaning the rust from rifles and machetes, singing the battle hymns of their beloved republic, pinning colored rosettes on their upturned hat-brims as a militant decoration.

This strange steamer attracted the prompt attention of the Three Friends, which edged away from force of habit. There was no alarm until it was perceived that the stranger had also shifted her course. Presently it became a pursuit. There was no doubt of it, and the pursuer, as vaguely discerned, was a thumping big vessel. The smoke gushed thick and black from the funnel of the Three Friends. The chief engineer was not among the spectators. He had tumbled below to exhort his stokers with strong words and the flat of a shovel. It was absurd to try to run away from this big steamer. She was coming up at a great pace.

That veteran regular, Jack Gorman, ambled aft to clear the old Springfield for action. In that mournful voice of his he informed us:

"I always did aim to finish with my boots on, boys. I was standin' under the bridge just now, and I heard Johnny O'Brien say to the mate that this vessel yonder looked like it might be the Viscaya or the Oquendo, them wallopers of armored cruisers that come out from Spain not long ago. Twenty knots, and big guns — say, one shell 'ud blow us plumb to blazes."

"Livin' in a battleship did have its drawbacks," observed Mike Walsh, chief gunner's mate, "and I never thought I'd regret sayin' good-bye to the old Maine, *but* —"

Ralph Paine gulped and had little to say. It was most infernally disquieting to watch that big steamer steering to overhaul the Three Friends. The diary sums it up with that brevity which is said to be the soul of wit:

Chased. Emotions. Lots of them.

Some of us moved forward and gazed up at the shadowy bridge of the Three Friends, for lack of anything better to do. There was a place where nobody spilled his emotions. The strange steamer was now so clearly visible, looming so portentously, that at any moment we expected to hear the report of a heavy gun. McCready was relating the story of the filibuster Virginius in the last Cuban revolution — caught by a Spanish cruiser, just like this, and the crew shot against a stone wall in Santiago, most of them Americans, just like us.

I was ready to throw to the fishes that resplendent sword of Gomez, with the diamonds in the hilt and the inscriptions on the blade, which would have been so wretchedly awkward to explain to a group of Spanish naval officers.

Just when all seemed lost save honor, we overheard Johnny O'Brien say in his quiet, even way:

"She scared me some, honest she did, putting after us that way. It's a Mallory liner, and all that ails her is fool curiosity to find out who we are — running hell-bent without any lights."

The sigh of relief that swept the crowded decks of the Three Friends sounded like a safety-valve blowing off. The Mallory liner, which had so seriously impaired my own heart action, came steadily closer until a biscuit could have been tossed aboard. Passengers lined her rail. The electric lights of the promenade deck revealed a few women, two or three of them young and seemingly fair. They waved handkerchiefs and shouted to us. Gold-braided officers called down from the lofty bridge:

"Three Friends ahoy! Bully for you! Good luck and God bless you!"

"Here's to Johnny O'Brien! You're the stuff! Take care of yourself!"

"*Viva Cuba Libre! Adios, Tres Amigos!*"

In this manner we parted company and the ladies had something to talk about. The episode was unimportant, and yet it lingers vividly in memory. To us amateurs who had taken it all so carelessly for granted, there was vouchsafed another aspect, a realization of what might have been. We felt a deeper respect for the courage of the men who made voyage after voyage, when any strange steamer might have turned out to be a twenty-knot armored cruiser flying the Spanish ensign. And there was a touch of sentiment which appealed to the heart of youth in the glimpse of those girls on the deck of the liner, waving us a bonny fare-ye-well.

The Three Friends went her solitary and furtive way until she passed around Cape San Antonio into the Caribbean, a thousand miles from a home port and still hurrying toward a destination known only to those in command.

X

THE SHADOW IN THE RIO SAN JUAN

It was not in accord with the temperament of Mike Walsh, chief gunner's mate, to twiddle his thumbs in idleness during this voyage of the Three Friends. In the cargo was a Hotchkiss field gun, a very efficient piece of ordnance which was expected to annoy the Spanish troops with twelve-pound shell and shrapnel. Inasmuch as the bold Mike had been promised a commission in the Cuban artillery, it occurred to him to hoist this gun out of the hold and assemble it on deck. From among the forty patriots he would recruit a gun crew and proceed to drill them while at sea. This would enable him to be ready for business as soon as the expedition was landed, or, as he put it, to hop into the trouble *pronto*.

So crowded were the decks of this nefarious vessel that Mike was perplexed when he sought a clear space in which to set up his twelve-pounder. In fact, the only spot he could find was far forward, right up in the bow, which was so narrow that the wooden bulwarks interfered with the activities of the gun crew. The ingenious Mike Walsh solved this difficulty by making a platform or foundation high enough to raise the gun clear of obstructions. The only available material consisted of heavy boxes of Mauser rifle cartridges which were hoisted out of the hold to serve the purpose.

These made a substantial, stable platform, and yet it seemed a trifle odd to mount a gun upon such an explosive base as this. However, it was a most unconventional voyage and no one objected. Those who preferred the quiet life had no business to be sailing with "Dynamite Johnny" O'Brien.

Having set his field piece upon its wheels and lashed it fast with a hawser, Mike Walsh turned to the task of schooling his gunners and putting the fear of God into them. One was a long, pock-marked lad who confessed to eighteen years and service in three revolutions in his native republic of Colombia. Another was a bearded Cuban who had been graduated from an American technical school. Of course that veteran regular of many experiences, Jack Gorman, laid the old Springfield aside to show them that he could qualify for the artillery as an assistant instructor. As Mike Walsh sagaciously suggested:

"If you could find some way of mountin' that private blunderbuss of yours, Jack, it would give us a battery instead of one gun."

"Quit your joshin', Mike," replied the serious-minded Gorman. "When I start to poppin' off Spanish officers at a thousand dollars per head, and that's the agreement, you'll treat my old Springfield with more respect, lemme tell you."

The Three Friends was rolling to the southward, almost a week away from her port of departure. The sacks of coal heaped on deck had been fed to the hungry furnaces and the company which lived under the open sky was not quite so grimy and uncomfortable. The vessel steered well out into the Caribbean to avoid the Spanish blockading craft, but in the bright weather it was possible to discern the mountains of Santa Clara Province, blue and misty, from a distance of thirty or forty miles to seaward. The sight of them inspired the Cuban patriots with valorous emotions, with clamorous eagerness to join their comrades in the audacious warfare against the ponderous, dull-witted battalions of Spanish infantry. The curse of seasickness was forgotten.

The leaders served out blankets and haversacks, rifles, machetes, ammunition to equip every man. From the voluble chatter, the fiery gestures, it was to be inferred that these heroes were about to exterminate numerous Spanish regiments on their own account and to storm fortified cities.

One small episode disturbed these happy warriors. They were presumed to subsist on their own rations, but in the haste of getting the expedition to sea, some of the stores had been left behind. Now that they had regained the appetites of which the heaving billows had robbed them, to be put on short allowance was a serious grievance. The ship's crew displayed no sympathy. These hardy seafarers had their own stock of provisions and they did not propose to share the grub with any blankety bunch of Cuban lubbers. The negro cooks were ready to prepare any stuff which the Cuban colonel might deal out, but this was as far as it went.

This situation so annoyed a herculean patriot called Black Sam that he was for starting a mutiny. He was a loud-mouthed, bullying African with the scars of old wounds slashed across his naked chest, as ugly a customer for a scrimmage as the fancy could conjecture. Having won over a few truculent spirits, he chose the breakfast hour for declaring himself.

The Cubans were crowding to the open door of the galley with their tin plates and cups while the ship's cook, Jim Bell, and his mulatto assistant dished out the meal as allotted. It was slim fare for hungry men, and Black Sam, towering in the foreground, demanded a menu more generous. In his fist was a heavy machete with which he threatened to slice the cook, who stood his ground and reached for a kettle of hot water. Several other mutineers pulled pistols as they shoved toward the galley door, while Black Sam roared his curses in broken English and crackling Spanish.

Now the sailormen of the Three Friends were fond of this cheerful cook of theirs and they had no idea of letting him be carved or perforated just because the Cubans found fault with their breakfast. The watch on deck speedily surged in the direction of the galley while the men in the bunks turned out with magical celerity. It was to be observed that they came not empty-handed. The scene was distinctly animated.

The uproar indicated that Black Sam proposed to raid the galley and stand the ship upon its head.

Bloodshed was averted by a voice from above. It proceeded from the roof of the wheel-house which overlooked the lower deck where the hostile forces were mustered. The speaker was little Captain Johnny O'Brien who gazed down with an air of mild curiosity. At his elbow was the stalwart figure of Skipper "Bill" Lewis who was fingering what appeared to be a Colt's forty-five. Black Sam rolled his eyes upward and seemed to have forgotten his intention of slaying the cook. The noise suddenly subsided.

"Go on away and behave yourselves, boys," said gray-headed Johnny O'Brien, waving a hand at his own sailormen. "Let 'em alone. I'll take care of this rumpus."

The crew of the Three Friends grinned in a sheepish manner and began to drift away from the galley. At the same time the Cuban mutineers were edging away from the terrible Black Sam.

"Hi there, you Jim Bell, what's it all about?" called down Johnny O'Brien.

The cook emerged from the galley, still clutching his kettle of hot water, and answered in quavering accents:

"Please, suh, this yere triflin' big nigger say he gwine slice mah gizzard if I don't feed him same as you-all."

"Give me that gun, Bill," said Johnny O'Brien to Captain Lewis. "Now you listen to me, Black Sam. Another word of your lip and I'll shoot your brains right out through your heels. The rest of you Cubans go chase yourselves. *Vamoose!*"

The efficient Captain O'Brien beckoned the stocky mate and told him: "Go get that pesterin' Sam nigger and tie him to the winch and play the fire hose on him. And see that he gets no dinner. Seems like I can't get any peace or quiet at sea."

The mutiny was in the past tense. Thereafter if a Cuban

felt dissatisfied with the bill of fare, he kept the matter to himself. It had been demonstrated that Captain O'Brien was master of his own ship and that when it came to peace and quiet he was almost fussy about it.

All the dangers and discomforts of the voyage seemed of no consequence when the word was passed that the vessel would soon attempt to land her cargo. She had made this long voyage, around the western end of Cuba and far into the Caribbean, in order to deliver the precious arms and supplies to the forces of General Maximo Gomez himself, who was operating in the eastern provinces. Thus far luck had favored the adventure, which was even more hazardous than usual because of this prolonged cruise in the enemy's waters. The total steaming distance would be at least three thousand miles before the Three Friends could hope to regain her home port.

"It's queer," said the mate, during a trick at the wheel, "but this is sure an educated old hooker. You can *feel* her begin to sheer off the minute we sight a smoke on the horizon. On the level, she beats you to it, even before you start to give her the helm. I reckon she has dodged till she is just naturally shy."

The only vessels sighted in the Caribbean were merchant craft and these had been given a wide berth. It was in the middle of a clear afternoon, with a gentle wind, when the Three Friends slackened speed for the first time and came to rest, twenty miles off the coast of Cuba. The hard-driven engines were given a little respite while the wary ship reconnoitered and waited for darkness.

The portly chief, John Dunn, ambled on deck to announce in aggrieved accents that she was afflicted with leaky tubes and a bum condenser and how could you expect her to make any speed if she got ketched inshore and had to run for it! Anyhow, he would fish out the clamp for the safety-valve and be ready to stick it on, same as usual, and all hands could shovel the coal to her and hope her boilers would n't bust and blow her to hell.

The Santa Clara Mountains lifted dimly from the sea, and through the powerful glasses on the bridge it was possible to descry a break in the bold outline. This was a pass through which the Rio San Juan flowed down into a small bay on the shore of which the expedition was to be landed. It was the secret rendezvous of which General Gomez had been informed and to which he was expected to send troops enough to safeguard the cargo against capture after it had been put on the beach.

Until eight o'clock in the evening the Three Friends idled far offshore while her officers attentively scanned the tranquil sea. It was known to them that a Spanish coastwise merchant steamer was due to leave Cienfuegos in the afternoon, on a regular sailing schedule, and it was advisable to be certain that she had passed on to the northward. The canny Johnny O'Brien had also a certain acquaintance with the habits, speed, and patrol areas of the Spanish naval vessels blockading this part of the coast.

The merchant steamer plodding on her course from Cienfuegos failed to discover the large, white towboat which drifted twenty miles out from the bay of the Rio San Juan. A rusty, wall-sided British tramp wallowed by in the dusk, bound to some port of the West Indies, but the errand of the Three Friends was no concern of hers.

Aboard this lonely and fugitive filibustering vessel, rocking so gently in the cradling swell of the Caribbean, there had begun to stir an amazing amount of activity. There was no leisure to admire the effulgence of the rising moon and the beauty of a silvered ocean. No longer were the forty-odd patriots permitted to slosh about the decks like so much bothersome freight.

Colonel Perez Calvo, the Cuban leader, had conquered the infernal sea which had laid him low. It was a kind of resurrection from the dead. He was in uniform, even to the boots and spurs, and he spoke commands that were obeyed. There was a certain method and order in the ticklish enterprise of putting one of these expeditions ashore, and now that the hour was at hand affairs moved with an admirable precision and celerity. Some of the Cubans swarmed into the hold where the husky deck-hands joined them. Others were stationed at the open hatches where they handled the weighty cases, bales, and barrels as they were laboriously passed up from below.

Among these sweating toilers of the sea were McCready and Paine, who were alleged to be neither sailors nor warriors, but a species of newspaper correspondent and as such bound to maintain the attitude of non-combatants. As things had turned out, this was all nonsense. It would have been a waste of breath to try to explain the distinction to an exasperated enemy which had been hunting this diabolical Three Friends for a year on end.

This hard job of helping to get the cargo hoisted on deck was found to be congenial. It was much more satisfactory than to sit and look on. And so we heaved and grunted and emptied the stifling hold of as much stuff as could be tiered the length of the lower deck, on both sides of the ship. Securely lashed on the overhang, or after part, were six wide-bottomed surf-boats, nested like fishermen's dories. The procedure was to shove these boats overboard as soon as the vessel was inside the little bay, string them along to port and starboard, and dump the cargo into them.

In this matter the landing could be swiftly managed. Haste was an essential factor. Nothing was apt to prove more unhealthy than a deliberate style of action, for to be trapped inside the bay by a prowling cruiser or gunboat would mean abandoning ship for all hands and taking to the bushes. As soon as McCready had it figured out, he murmured a couplet from Kipling which nicely fitted the circumstances:

"But I would n't trust 'em at Wokin';
  We're safer at sea again."

In the eruption of cargo from below, Captain Johnny O'Brien was not conspicuous. He remained upon the roof of the wheel-house where the chief engineer joined him now and then for amiable confabulation. They would set the Cubans and their freight on the beach as the bargain called for. What happened to the patriots after that was no affair of the Three Friends. If the Spaniards jumped them, they were out of luck.

It was nine o'clock at night when the vessel headed straight for the coast, moving as fast as the screw could kick her along. You could feel it in the quivering hull and see it in the foaming waves as the bow ripped through the sparkling sea. Power had been held in reserve for this final sprint. Thrilled by the excitement of the moment, the Cubans flourished their bright machetes in the moonlight and sang that battle hymn, or national anthem, which had the fire and lilt of a trumpet call.

The handsome lad, Edgar Carbonne, who had forsaken a college campus, was for leading his comrades straight against the town in which his Cuban sweetheart dwelt. It was held by two thousand Spanish troops, but what mattered the odds when a man had not kissed his girl in an eternity?

The Three Friends ran ten miles and then stopped her engines to wait and watch. There was nothing to cause alarm. Everywhere the glimmering sea was lonely and un-tenanted. A long pause, and the dash for the coast was resumed. The ship halted again when no more than three or four miles from the shadowy mountain range. Captain O'Brien began to search the dark, rugged slopes for the red wink of a friendly signal light to assure him that the coast was clear.

Young Lieutenant Edgar Carbonne and ten men were ordered to drop one of the surf-boats overside and let it tow astern. They were to form a scouting party which was to be sent ashore as soon as the vessel should enter the bay. If they were not wiped out by an ambushed force of Spanish troops, it could be safely assumed that the general disembarkation might be ventured.

Again the Three Friends stole onward, this time at a gait more cautious. The mountains seemed to cast a black curtain of shadow far out to sea. This made it difficult to obtain a clear vision of the small bay and the headlands which guarded it. The entrance was obscured by this deep adumbration, so different from the brilliance of the tropic moonlight some distance out to seaward. It was like passing into the night from a lighted room.

The bay slumbered, however, in a profound silence. There was no reason for hesitating to enter it. A little way to the southward, the expected signals were observed, quick flashes, red and white, according to some prearranged code. The landing of the expedition was as good as accomplished.

This was my own elated opinion. Tucked under my arm in its leather case was the effulgent sword, valued at two thousand dollars, which I had been commissioned to carry to General Maximo Gomez, with his name and various eulogies engraved on the blade. The donor, Mr. William Randolph Hearst, had candidly mentioned his failure to find a cheerful idiot to undertake the errand until I had wandered into his office. Well, I was about to show him that this uncomplimentary dictum had been too harsh. Perhaps to-morrow the grizzled commander-in-chief of the Cuban Army of Liberation would receive this splendid weapon as a token of the sympathy and admiration of the American people!

The scene was readily pictured, fierce old Gomez surrounded by his staff — a background of tents and palms — myself advancing with a graceful bow of homage, the sword dazzling all beholders — a brief speech of presentation translated by the headquarters interpreter — cheers by the cavalry escort and the bugles blown — the gratified response of General Maximo Gomez, preferably in writing so that Mr. Hearst might publish it and have something to show for his two thousand dollars.

For a rival journalist, McCready displayed a most unselfish spirit. This performance would shove him into the background, as he said, and the "New York *Heraldo*" had the short end of it, but if the soldiery of Gomez should be shy of enthusiasm he would distribute enough pesos to buy rum for the outfit and also lead the claque.

To the best of my recollection, and the diary confirms it, I was rehearsing the simple but elegant oration that was to accompany the diamond-studded sword, when things began suddenly to happen to the well-laid plans of Captain "Dynamite Johnny" O'Brien and the notorious Three Friends. She was quietly moving into the black shadows of the bay and Lieutenant Edgar Carbonne and his ten Cuban scouts were about to tumble into the surf-boat and pull for the shore.

Keen eyes and good night-glasses just then detected something like a moving shadow against the somber wall of the jungle, inside the bay. It was in motion close to the water, or so these seasoned observers fancied. They would not have sworn that they saw anything at all, but the vague impression was enough to make them wary. Promptly the vessel was swung about to head out to sea, and she proceeded to leave the bay astern.

These experienced buccaneers were not to be frightened by phantoms, however, and presently the Three Friends reversed her engines and began to back into the mouth of the bay. The strategy of this was obviously correct. In the event of trouble, she was now all set to depart without lost motion. Very slowly she worked her way in, crab fashion, while John Dunn stood by his engines and swore to himself and at his firemen. Now he was dead sure that this was no place for a fat man with a family and growin' old at that.

XI

A COMPETENT CHIEF GUNNER'S MATE

THERE was no occasion for alarm until the vigilant vessel had backed well inside the bay, almost into the position where it would be convenient to drop anchor and send the boats away. Then against that dark screen of woodland, perhaps four hundred yards distant, where the shadow had appeared to move, there flew up a shower of sparks. Nothing vague about that! These sparks gushed from a steamer's funnel and she had opened up to drive ahead for all she was worth. It was extraordinarily fortunate for the Three Friends that she had concluded to back into the bay. In this awkward moment she was on the mark, as you might say, to make a straight-away run for it.

Captain O'Brien did not have to give her the jingle-bell for full speed ahead. The chief had seen that shower of sparks fly upward, and with an agility amazing for his bulk he popped into the engine-room and caught up the clamp which he deftly applied to the safety-valve. His forebodings had come true. The old hooker had been ketched inshore, durn her soul, but he'd make her lay her ears back and run like a scared rabbit if he had to bust her wide open.

The fireroom was no place for a nervous stoker while the chief bellowed at them to wallop in the coal and keep their eyes off the steam-gauge. He proposed to raise a blankety sight more steam than the boilers were expected to stand. A zealous old filibuster was this fat man in the greasy overalls.

Meanwhile the mysterious craft which had been lurking in the darkness of the bay was driving ahead, her sinister intentions no longer masked. She flew the flag of the Spanish

Navy. This was comprehended when her bow gun flashed flame and the echoes of the report clamored between the headlands and in the mountain pass. Without doubt the gunners must have been able to see the target, the long tow-boat with the deck-houses painted white and the moonlit sea beyond her.

But Spanish gunnery was notoriously wild, and the first shell, fired at point-blank range, splashed well over the Three Friends. At a guess, the two racing vessels were no more than five hundred yards apart when the attack opened.

The Cuban patriots were painfully surprised, more so than the sailormen who had learned that this trade of theirs consisted largely of the unexpected. They had their own duties to engage their attention, and that masterful skipper, "Bill" Lewis, saw to it that they earned their wages during this bad hour. The deck-hands whipped off their shirts and leaped into the fire-room to wield slice-bar and shovel. They went at it as though trained by previous experiences of a critical nature.

The hostile vessel astern was still obscured in the shadows cast by the mountains as she came tearing out in pursuit, but it was reasonable to assume her to be a small gunboat of the class employed in the coastwise patrol. Her crew may have been poor marksmen, but they were serving that bow gun with the perfervid energy of a hornets' nest. The shells were dropping around the Three Friends and one of them tossed spray on the after-deck, but no splinters flew from the wooden hull which one projectile would have raked fore and aft.

Watching the flashes and listening to the sharp, reverberating reports, we were of the opinion that the angry gunboat was not quite as fast as the fugitive filibustering steamer. At any rate, in this first few minutes the distance between them had widened a little. It was still no more than a few hundred yards and the Spanish gunnery was positively disgraceful.

In this present era, with the Great War in Europe a tragic yesterday, the episode which I am describing may seem to be the merest trifle, but one must take into account the historical perspective. Twenty-five years ago it was when the Three Friends fled out to sea from the Rio San Juan, an American vessel fired at with the intent to destroy her by a naval craft of a European power. It was sensational, particularly to those who wondered where the next shell might alight.

The Cubans were raw recruits, for the most part, and some of them had never fired a rifle. They lacked the cohesion of drilled men and it was natural enough that the scenes on deck should have been somewhat confused. Many of them were blazing away with their Mausers in a manner so excessively careless that you were likely to have your head blown off if you showed it on the upper deck. They shot at the wide, wide world and incessantly yelled "*Cuba Libre.*" A few of these agitated patriots sought shelter. Foolish panic had laid hold of them. As though one could hide from an explosive shell in this big, wooden towboat! The stentorian accents of the chief engineer were heard to complain:

"Hi there, somebody! Send a couple o' hands to haul these yere condemned Cubians out of my stoke-hole. They are divin' down here head-first and we ain't got elbow-room. How the devil can I make steam with a mob of bug-eyed patriots under foot, hey?"

The Three Friends and the Spanish gunboat hurried out into the moonlit expanse of the Caribbean, clear of those curtaining shadows, and the interval between them slowly increased until they were perhaps a half-mile apart. Now it was to marvel that a gunner could miss the mark, with a smooth sea and this brilliant illumination of an unclouded moon.

One incident was more like fiction than fact. The old regular, Sergeant Jack Gorman, had unlimbered that treasured Springfield of his to fire a few rounds with the deliberation of a man who valued each leaden slug at one thousand dollars cash. Then he paused and fished out of his knapsack the mouthpiece of a cavalry bugle. It was a souvenir of some frontier Indian fight at which he had sounded the charge. Into the capacious muzzle of the old Springfield he rammed the mouthpiece of the bugle and threw open the breech.

Holding the rifle at arm's length, he rested the butt upon the rail of the upper deck and blew one call after another, "Boots and Saddles," "Reveille," "Assembly." Shrill and clear the notes floated over this quiescent sea. The gunboat astern actually appeared to swerve and slacken speed and then to come on again. We could imagine the Spanish officers as puzzled and astonished. What sort of a ship had they tackled, with a bugle sounding the call to quarters? *Valgame Dios*, was this an armed cruiser of the Cuban Republic? Filibustering steamers were not supposed to behave in this peculiar fashion, blowing bugles and firing fusillades at a Spanish man-of-war!

It may have occurred to you that the competent chief gunner's mate, Mike Walsh, was not a man to find contentment merely as a spectator. Quite right! That Hotchkiss field piece of his was still mounted upon its platform of cartridge cases in the bow. He had been about to take it down for stowage in a surf-boat when the impetuous gunboat had disrupted the whole programme. No sooner had the two vessels sped clear of the darkened bay than he was beseeching Captain O'Brien to let him cut loose with shrapnel.

"Dynamite Johnny" had not the slightest objection to shooting up the navy of His Most Christian Majesty, and international complications were the least of his worries, but he delayed action for another reason. When the Three Friends had backed into the bay, the twelve-pound gun was, of course, mounted at the wrong end of her. And to bring it to bear from the bow, during a stern chase, meant swinging the ship almost broadside to. This maneuver would have presented a huge target at such close range that even those erratic Spanish gunners could not have missed it. Therefore the intelligent Captain O'Brien had preferred to run for the open sea, get clear of the coast, and open up a more agreeable distance before advising Mike Walsh to go to it.

The hawser which lashed the wheels of the field piece had been cast loose in readiness. The Lord only knew what would prevent the gun from jumping overboard when discharged, as it was certain to rear and kick back upon its platform of rifle cartridges, but this disturbed Michael Walsh not at all. He had mustered his crew, the long lad from Colombia, the bearded Cuban, and Jack Gorman, who was willing to suspend operations with the old Springfield. They slewed the gun around to train it as much astern as possible without blowing the forward end of the deck-house to smithereens, and impatiently waited for Johnny O'Brien to swing the ship.

At length he waved his hat from the bridge and shouted in cheerful tones:

"All ready, Mike? Then let her go. I don't like the way those Spaniards have been heavin' shells at us. I hope you blow the daylights out of 'em."

A jubilant yell from the gun platform was carried along the decks. Nobody had liked the discourteous reception in the little bay of the Rio San Juan. The Three Friends veered from her headlong course in order to coöperate with the baleful intention of Mike Walsh, who had deserted the American Navy because, forsooth, there was nothing but drill and polish in time of peace. He was crouching behind his twelve-pounder while his mates handed up a shell or shoved at the wheels in obedience to his commands. Mike knew his business.

The gunboat was something like nine hundred yards distant, as Mike calculated it, when he laid his sights and timed the shrapnel fuse. With a jerk of the lanyard he jumped aside and the gun spat a crimson streak. By the width of a mosquito's whisker the agile Mike Walsh escaped being smashed against the heavy bulwark as the field piece bounded in the recoil and drove back across that platform of cartridge cases. These were solid timbers that formed the bulwarks of the bow, but the gun kicked a hole through which a man could have crawled.

Through the glasses it was noted that the bursting shell had flung the water into gleaming spray a few yards in front of the amazed Spanish gunboat.

"Hold her as she is, Cap'n Johnny," roared Mike, in happy anticipation, as he leaped to haul the gun into position. "That one was a sighting shot. I'll be messin' them Spaniards up in a minute if this drunken old —— of a gun don't waltz overboard."

Speedily he fired another shrapnel shell while Captain Johnny held the ship steady to give him a clear range. The explosion indicated that a clean hit was scored. It was Mike's assertion, and he had been rated an excellent chief gunner's mate aboard the Maine, that the shrapnel bullets had scattered to sweep the gunboat's deck. This opinion was confirmed when we saw the little war vessel check her pursuit and come to a sudden halt. Up soared one rocket after another, streaking the sky with crimson, to signal for assistance. It was the appeal of a craft disabled and helpless. The gunboat rested like a log upon this mirrored ocean.

Providence and Michael Walsh having interposed in behalf of the Three Friends, it seemed reasonable to surmise that Captain O'Brien would let well enough alone. His temper had been seriously tried, however, and he felt resentful. He had agreed to deliver a certain cargo in the bay of the Rio San Juan and the meddlesome enemy had thwarted him. In fact, the gunboat, although crippled, was still in the way.

The word was passed from the bridge that Johnny proposed to turn and ram that cussed gunboat, and if he failed to sink her the intention was to *board* her!

A few days earlier in the voyage I had been maundering about the romance of the Spanish Main. Well, here it was, and served piping hot, the real thing as they had lived it in bygone centuries — *boarding* the Spaniard, with a brace of pistols, and your cutlass between your teeth, and all that sort of thing. The actual prospect, however, was not pleasing at all. It failed to appeal. Such is the difference between fact and fancy.

"*Board her?* Did you hear that?" said McCready, with his cynical grin. "This little O'Brien man gets on my nerves. He ought to be locked in his cabin before somebody is hurt. You and I did n't *have* to get into this, you know. To think I was swapping lies over a mug of ale in Brown's Chop House three weeks ago, and trying to fake up a new way to pad my expense accounts, and sensible things like that. It seems years and years. How do you feel, anyhow?"

"Like a silly ass, Mac. This impossible O'Brien person has begun to swing the ship clean around to head straight for that disabled gunboat. We had better collect the necessary weapons."

"Come on down to the lower deck," advised McCready. "We may as well make ourselves useful in these last moments of two frivolous and misspent careers. They seem to be yelling for more rifle and revolver ammunition. It sounds mostly like Mike. He knows. We will help to break open a few boxes. Leave it to me and I should open with prayer."

We scrambled down the ladder and over the heaps of cargo between the deck-house and the rail. The sight which met our gaze was very trying for two young men already nervous. One of the patriots, a large, impassioned man with jetty black whiskers, was also endeavoring to obtain small-arms ammunition for the boarding party. He happened to be plying an axe in a frenzied manner. It smote a tier of the flat, heavy boxes with rope handles which we knew to be filled with Mauser rifle cartridges.

These boxes rested upon three much larger cases which we instantly identified as containing nitroglycerin. Of this there was no doubt whatever. Through more than one night we had slept in the lee of them and on other occasions had watched them go adrift with the most intense interest.

The black-whiskered patriot raised his axe for another mighty blow. All he had to do was to hit one of those rifle cartridges upon the cap and send the bullet down, bang, through a case of nitroglycerin, and the good ship Three Friends would be strewn in small bits over a considerable area of the Caribbean. Fascinated with horror, McCready breathed aloud:

"My God, it's one thing after another. Could you beat it?"

With this, he uttered a hoarse shout and fell upon that misguided patriot who crashed to the deck, the fingers of McCready locked in his whiskers. My own mouth had hung open so that my chin scraped the second button of my shirt, but no sounds issued forth. It was momentary paralysis, the case of a man scared out of what few wits he normally packed under his hat.

Together we dragged that wretched patriot away from the scene and hammered him with the handle of the axe by way of dissuading him from doing it again. Later it was learned that he had been a brass-bound *comandante* of the Volunteer Fire Department of Havana. This explained it perfectly. It is never safe to trust a volunteer fireman with an axe. His ruling impulse is to chop the house down with his eyes shut.

Recovering from this shock, McCready and Paine noted, with marked disapproval, that the sailors of the Three Friends were actually gleeful over this boarding party. They were methodically arming themselves, and even the pot-bellied chief engineer, released from his absorbing duties for the moment, reckoned he'd go get him a Spaniard if the rest of the boys aimed to prance into the ruckus.

The preparations were hasty, of course, because the affair was singularly impromptu, but at least fifty very earnest men could be relied upon to take a hand in it, including the best of the Cubans. The two alleged correspondents were in the picture by sheer force of circumstances. Of a truth, this thing had been wished on them. It was not mentioned in their editorial contracts.

Johnny O'Brien was a fine little man who deserved to have what he wanted. And his idea of ramming and sinking and boarding and so on was consistent enough. Any obstacles which interfered with his job were to be eliminated. He was a man of his word, with a professional pride in his calling. Almost had he hauled the ship around to dash straight at the inert gunboat when, boom, a much heavier gun was fired from close in to the coast and somewhat to the southward. Intent on its own affairs, the Three Friends had failed to observe this larger war vessel hastening to respond to the distressful message of the rockets.

This interruption spoiled the pleasure of Johnny O'Brien. The second or third shell, fired at a range of a mile or more, splashed far to starboard of the Three Friends, and Mike Walsh announced that he could do a blame sight better than that with his jumpin' little old twelve-pounder. However, this second gunboat, or whatever it might be, was heaving heavy metal, by the sound of it. She was also moving rapidly in the direction of the Three Friends. Reluctantly Captain O'Brien called off the boarding party.

They were coming too fast for him. Farther to the southward, down Cienfuegos way, a searchlight was talking in shafts of white light that swept the sky. This indicated a formidable ship, and the Spanish Navy was mobilizing in force. Even Mike Walsh agreed that he could not stand them all off with his twelve-pounder. The man at the wheel climbed the spokes and threw her hard over. The chief engineer trundled himself below to his clamped safety-valve and his gasping stokers. The Three Friends bade farewell to the Rio San Juan.

Now she was no destroyer for speed, and when sufficiently scared had been known to turn up fourteen knots. In this crowded hour, however, with two Spanish war vessels pelting in chase, she was going an easy fifteen knots because she had to. When a fireman collapsed he was hauled on deck by the heels and another volunteer took his place. The tall funnel glowed red-hot and the needle of the steam-gauge flickered at forty and fifty pounds more than the law allowed.

It was out of the question, while the pursuit continued, to run for a home port in American waters. This meant the long flight around the one end of Cuba or the other, almost to Haiti on an easterly course, or close to Yucatan if the Three Friends should drive to the westward. The nearest neutral refuge was the British island of Jamaica, across the Caribbean, where, once in harbor, there would be no danger of attack. Even a crew of filibustering outlaws might find safe waters inside the three-mile limit.

And so Johnny O'Brien pointed her nose for Jamaica and chewed a frayed cigar and reflectively rubbed his stubbled chin while he gazed astern. He had been almost trapped in the Rio San Juan, and only the efficiency of Mike Walsh had saved the expedition from sudden and fatal disaster. But with the first gunboat disposed of, there were still two hostile vessels crowding in chase of the Three Friends, and it was, indeed, time to go.

However, it was known that most of the Spanish warships, even the fast cruisers, of this blockading fleet were unable to make their rated speeds because of fouled bottoms and slovenly engine-rooms. The fifteen-knot gait of the Three Friends enabled her to draw slowly away from the second gunboat which had appeared from in close to the coast. The dangerous cruiser far to the southward, whose searchlight had raked the sky, was otherwise invisible, but, at a distance of several miles, she fired two or three shells and the dull detonation of the guns was like the growl of thunder.

Half an hour later it was probable that if the boilers held together, the Three Friends would escape from her awkward predicament. The pursuing vessels had ceased firing. The gunboat astern was no more than a tiny, black dot.

XII

A SHIP WITH NOWHERE TO GO

AFTER midnight Captain O'Brien shifted his course, steering away from Jamaica, which was no longer an imperative haven of refuge. The peril was past, but it had left a confused situation. The Cuban leaders had arranged no other rendezvous on this southern coast, so confident had been their expectation of success. This was the first expedition which "Dynamite Johnny" had failed to put on the beach. Colonel Perez Calvo swore that the plans must have been betrayed, else how could you account for the friendly signals which had winked on the mountain-side, and then that thrice accursed Spanish gunboat so artfully ambushed in the bay of the Rio San Juan?

To dodge about the Caribbean in the hope of finding a landing-place unmolested by Spanish troops, or without getting into communication with the Cuban insurgent forces, was out of the question. It meant burning much coal and there was no more than enough to carry the vessel clear of hostile waters. Besides this, the news that she had fired at and disabled a gunboat of the coast patrol would be telegraphed to every port from Santiago to Pinar del Rio. The audacious *Tres Amigos* was certain to be hunted, as by a swarm of angry hornets.

On the other hand, to attempt the long voyage back to an American port with this cargo of munitions and patriots would be out of the frying-pan into the fire. It meant arrest and confiscation and the disagreeable indictments of a Federal Grand Jury. The Three Friends was a ship with nowhere to go.

These were complications which hastily presented themselves while those in command were debating whether to attempt an exit from the Caribbean by way of Cape Maysi or by the western course around Cape San Antonio. Both passages were likely to be menaced by all the Spanish blockading craft which could be hurried thither on the chance of intercepting a filibustering vessel which had turned pirate.

So far as most of us cared, such problems could await decision until the morrow. It had been a busy night and all hands felt fatigued. There was all that confounded cargo to be passed below and restowed in the hold, but the weather was so calm that this back-breaking labor could be deferred a few hours. The patriots curled up to sleep wherever nooks and corners could be found among the cases and bales and barrels on deck. Johnny O'Brien turned the ship over to Captain "Bill" Lewis and guessed he would turn in for a little snooze. The Spaniards had certainly pestered him, said he, but the chief engineer had put the boots to her in great shape, and taking it by and large you could call it a pretty close shave.

McCready and I sought sleeping quarters in one of the nested surf-boats upon the overhang and agreed that we had a corking fine story to write. And the Cubans would be in no mood to suppress it. Those on board were bursting with pride and elation. They had fought the only naval engagement of the Revolution! *Viva el Tres Amigos! Viva el Capitan Johnny O'Brien!* He had dared to defy a Spanish man-of-war, to sweep its decks with shrapnel shell, to riddle the wicked gunboat so that it appealed for help! Who had ever heard of such courage, such boldness? *Viva Miguel Walsh! Viva Cuba Libre!*

"We did n't fire the shot that was heard around the world," said McCready, "but it is a safe bet that it stirs up a few echoes in Washington and Madrid. That was piracy, old man. We shot up a friendly power, the same being the kingdom of Spain. This is an American ship, built, owned, and registered as such, and manned by an American crew, from bridge to galley. That sort of thing is not done in polite maritime circles. Pirates, according to Hoyle — not a doubt of it!"

"Bully, is n't it, Mac," said I, with worthy pride. "Probably the only living pirates! Now if it were larceny or forgery, or some disreputable crime like that, you might feel ashamed of yourself, but think of taking your grandchildren on your knee and letting 'em play with your long white whiskers while you tell how you sailed the blue Caribbean as a red-handed pirate in your wild youth, just like Captain Kidd!"

"We are a long way yet from Broadway, my boy," drowsily observed McCready before slumber overtook him. He was an optimist only in spots.

One could hear many a voluble yarn next day, of incidents which had escaped attention during the famous battle of the Rio San Juan. Notable had been the experience of the black cook, Jim Bell. During the voyage he had been a noisy blow-hard, a man of blood-curdling ferocity, to hear him tell it, who fairly yearned to hit the beach with the Cubans and make them doggoned Spanish sojers hard to find. Yessuh, boss, if he had n't done signed articles to stay with the ship, he suttinly would hone a machete and be the fightines' man on old Gomez' pay-roll. Trouble just did come natural to him, but of cou'se he could n't do the Three Friends no dirty trick by desertin' that-away.

When the ship had slowly backed into the bay of the Rio San Juan, with engines reversed, this blatant Jim Bell had been standing far aft on deck, breathing fire and slaughter. He had been tremendously startled when the hidden gunboat came bolting out from the shadows, shooting vicious shells. With a sagacity that did him credit, the sea-cook instantly perceived that he was at the wrong end of the ship. The stern, closest to the enemy, was no place for him to be.

Whirling about to flee forward, he happened to spy an open cargo hatch right at his feet.

"Why ain't I broke mah fool neck when I flew into that enticin' hatch?" he orated to an interested audience. "Man, I jes' took a header *an' lit on three o' them Cuban patriots that had beat me to it.*"

Far down in the gloom of the after-hold, Jim Bell organized his scrambled mentality sufficiently to comprehend that his position was still unsound. He was at the wrong end of the ship. One of those Spanish shells was bound to hit the Three Friends in the stern, and then where would he be? Right smack in the way of it!

Thereupon he scrambled up a ladder to the deck and began to crawl forward upon his hands and knees, "scroochin'" as low as possible. The goal was the galley, his own familiar realm, which occupied the extreme forward part of the deck-house, well up toward the bow and farthest removed from the Spanish gunboat.

Now at this moment, Mike Walsh was slewing the twelve-pounder around to train it on the target astern and presently the blast of the first shot blew all the glass out of the galley windows and played havoc with the dishware. It had not occurred to the cook's disordered wits that this field piece in the bow might be brought into action. He failed to connect Mike Walsh and the gun with the terrifying crash of glass and crockery in the galley, and his belief was that another Spanish war vessel had appeared in front of the Three Friends and was blowing her all to pieces.

Stunned by the concussion, bewildered by the débris that showered him, as he popped into the darkness of the galley, the mind of Jim Bell was more disconnected than ever. The Spaniards would be climbing aboard the ship in a minute, at the rate they were shooting up the deck-house and everything, and, once inside the galley, he flattened himself upon his stomach to wriggle in behind the range.

Now it so befell that the limber mulatto, the assistant cook, had already sought this same hiding-place, and he, too, was suffering acute delusions concerning the blast of that twelve-pounder and the resultant wreckage. Naturally enough, when Jim Bell came piling in on top of him, behind the range, the mulatto refugee mistook this invader for a Spanish assailant whose motto was no quarter. In the same manner Jim Bell felt absolutely certain, when his throat was clutched and a pair of hysterical feet kicked the wind out of him, that he was engaged with the enemy.

It was a spirited combat waged in the darkness by two strong men sincerely endeavoring to kill each other bare-handed. They fought their way out from behind the range, and then it was possible to lay hold of stove-lids, frying-pans, and other useful weapons. Pantry shelves which had been loosened by the concussion of the gun came tumbling down when these interlocked warriors banged against them, and they were bombarded by such bric-à-brac as canned tomatoes, iron kettles, and earthen crocks.

They flopped about in the broken glass which was not good for their hides, and continued to thump each other until weakened by exhaustion. Just when the enemy was trying to bite his ear off, Jim Bell surmised that they might be victims of mistaken identity. He rolled out on deck, wiped the blood and soot from his eyes, and discovered that the Three Friends, unscathed, still rode the seas. These twain were the only casualties of the unique naval engagement of the Rio San Juan.

On the lower deck McCready picked up three Mauser cartridges, the brass shells of which were dented. As souvenirs they interested him. The axe of the whiskered volunteer firemen had dealt a top layer of these rifle cartridges a slanting blow, as the dents signified. Slipping one of them into his shirt pocket, McCready commented, in a pensive voice:

"I have been blown up by managing editors for failing to get a good story, but I never did come so near to losing one entirely. By the way, I wonder whose feet I saw sticking out of a ventilator at the climax of the excitement last night? They were tan shoes — no, your feet are too big, Ralph, and you could n't crawl down a ventilator anyhow. They don't carry 'em your size on this packet. Perhaps it is better not to know. Too many brave men suffered a loss of reputation last night."

During this same day it was learned that the Three Friends would attempt to steal back through the Yucatan Channel under cover of night, running the gantlet of whatever Spanish craft might be sent to the westward to intercept her. Once clear of Cuban waters, she would make for one of the lonely keys off the southern coast of Florida. There the cargo was to be dumped and the patriots marooned while the vessel ventured into port to obtain coal.

Captain O'Brien hoped to be able to convince the American authorities that the Three Friends, returning with empty holds, had been engaged in the innocent task of helping some ship in distress, as covered by her wrecking license. If his lies were plausible enough, he would come back to pick up the cargo and the people and make another voyage to Cuba with them.

"Marooned is a good word," was McCready's comment. "Apparently we are in for the whole show, from soup to nuts. Are n't you getting filled to the neck with this romance-of-the-Spanish-Main stuff?"

"You like it, you know you do, you old grouch," said I. "But what about carrying this two-thousand-dollar sword to Gomez? I still have that eloquent presentation speech in my system."

"Don't let it mildew in this damp sea air," scoffed McCready. "You will have lots of time to compose and rehearse a new one on our desert island. This flinty-hearted O'Brien person proposes to leave us there to cast lots for the victim that goes into the pot as a stew for the rest of us. I suppose it will come to that. This piece seems to be played in character, I will say that much for it."

XIII

MAROONED ON NO NAME KEY

THE day after the naval action of the Rio San Juan passed very quietly. The Three Friends headed west for Cape San Antonio and did better than thirteen knots with a strong wind behind her and a following sea. At night we kept an anxious lookout for hostile cruisers, as we are sure that both ends of the island will swarm with them. If they catch us, we are gone ducks. Two lights were sighted during the evening, but they did n't see us, as we are running dark. Boiler tubes leaking and mighty little coal left. *Am stuck on the life!*[1]

This I find scribbled on a page of the smudged, sea-stained diary. That last remark was intended to be confidential, the exclamation of a young man thinking aloud. It makes entertaining reading for the Ralph Paine of to-day, a sedate, bald-headed citizen of such conventional propriety that his fellow townsmen elected him to the New Hampshire Legislature to help make laws instead of smashing them, and His Excellency, the Governor, appointed him a member of the dignified State Board of Education. Seldom has a pirate of the Caribbean been so thoroughly reformed, outwardly, if not at heart.

The gods of wind and weather favored the endeavors of the Three Friends to elude the interference of the irritated Spanish naval forces. The brilliant moon was covered with watery clouds and the sea took on an aspect gray and misty and melancholy. The signs foretold a rough blow and a wet ship.

Another day and she was wallowing in rain and spray while the strident gale twanged the funnel-stays, and the

[1] To the younger generation this crude slang may be obsolete. It means that the author was enjoying himself.

combers leaped over Mike Walsh's twelve-pounder lashed at its station in the bow. That pot-valiant cook, Jim Bell, was flooded out of his galley, loudly protesting that he wa'n't hired to drown hisself in no swimmin' races, no, suh. He properly refused to try to kindle another fire, and so we rummaged in the hold for hardtack and sardines, and huddled on deck wherever a lee could be found.

Nobody cursed the weather although it wickedly racked and pounded the Three Friends. It was not beyond conjecture that her abused engines might quit or her seams open and let her founder like a blooming basket, but in this whirling smother of clouds and rain and foam the ship was effectually concealed against discovery. Slowly, with infinite labor, she crept far over to the coast of Yucatan and then changed her course to continue the détour well into the Gulf of Mexico. It was the part of discretion to avoid those cramped and populous waters between Cuba and Florida.

As soon as this heavy weather had subsided, there arose much excitable discussion concerning the scheme of leaving the party of patriots and the cargo on some God-forsaken key or other while the vessel went off to find coal and supplies. It was not a popular idea. There was much grumbling and some talk of mutiny, but it simmered down when Captain O'Brien offered a few brief, well-chosen remarks. These were to the effect that he was running the show and they could stow all that fool nonsense. He would give them the surplus grub that belonged to the crew and come back to take 'em off somehow.

It may be remarked in passing that this wiry, gray-haired terrier of a little man was drawing near to sixty years of age. He had led a battering life on many seas and had suffered innumerable anxieties and hardships, but he was still vigorous, not to say forceful, as I have tried to indicate. This may interest the landsman who, in sheltered comfort, feels that he must begin to ease up on the shady side of fifty. And the

example of this indomitable sea-rover ought to stimulate the
tired business man who wears himself out in a few hours a
day at a desk and has to play golf to fit him for the ordeal.

Somewhere off Key West, early in the night, the Three
Friends dropped a surf-boat and manned it with four Cubans
who rowed into port with secret messages for their friends
and confederates. They carried also for transmission to New
York by cable the stories written by McCready and Paine
of that unexpected encounter with the Spanish gunboats.
These narratives had been submitted to Colonel Perez Calvo
and Captain Johnny O'Brien for censorship, but they could
not bear to mutilate them. Pride forbade, and the devil take
the consequences! They had no intention of hushing the
exploit.

With his customary intelligence McCready appraised the
situation as follows:

"These newspaper stories of ours will not be accepted as
legal evidence of piracy. For one thing, they can't find us to
make us swear to the truth of them. And if they did, we
could not be compelled to incriminate ourselves. The crew
of the ship will not squeal, you can gamble on that. And the
Spanish Navy can't depose, under oath, that the vessel
which shot 'em up was the Three Friends. The story will be
played up on the front page and it is liable to raise a fuss,
but in the eyes of the law all newspaper men are liars until
proven to the contrary."

This sounded so logical that worry was dismissed. The
sea-worn Three Friends moved northward in the Florida
Strait and skirted the far-flung tangle of shoals and keys
among which she had sought a hiding-place from the two
American cruisers during the voyage outward bound. Finding deep water in the Hawk Channel, inside the barrier reef,
she ran forty miles and then slowed down to turn in among
the scattered and innumerable keys which were, at that time,
so remote and unpeopled.

In the light of the moon they disclosed themselves as dark dots or mere threads spread over an immense area of quiet, shallow water. As the vessel cautiously picked her way, we were once more hoisting by main strength all that heavy cargo out of the hold, passing up the cases of cartridges with rope handles, grunting over the boxes of rifles and machetes, shoving at that uneasy consignment of nitroglycerin. And it all had to be heaped on deck to dump into the surf-boats strung alongside.

The ship dropped anchor at midnight and we looked in vain for the landing-place. It was four miles away, explained Captain O'Brien, and the water was so shoal that he could steam no nearer. To this distant and invisible destination it was necessary to transfer the cargo, the patriots, the supplies, by means of small boats and to tug at the oars eight miles for every round trip to the beach.

Fond memory declines to weave any romance into that weary performance. It was disgusting. After twelve days at sea in the Three Friends, the party was not in the pink of condition for such a task. You might have called us a bit overtrained.

However, we could not reasonably expect to enjoy such sport as potting Spanish gunboats all the time. In a surf-boat laden to the gunwales I plied the stroke-oar and reflected that a Yale-Harvard race was never like this. The Cubans who manned the other thwarts may have been excellent cigarmakers but they were infernal duffers in a boat. The wide-girthed, flat-bottomed craft progressed in a drunken manner, occasionally sidewise or wrong end to, amid the most prodigious splashing and banging and cursing.

A Cuban military officer pretended to steer. It was diverting to hear him invoke an endless category of saints whose intercession seemed highly advisable if we were ever to fetch up anywhere.

Earlier in his career, one of these unhappy oarsmen professed to have sailed in a sponging schooner frequenting these waters. He it was who found the objective, called No Name Key, after two hours of spasmodic toil. By night the place looked unpleasant, a tiny strip of sand and a dense growth of mangrove bushes barely lifted above the tide. It was worse to discover that reefs of coral and limestone surrounded the key and that the boats could be hauled no closer to the beach than several hundred yards. This meant that every bit of cargo had to be lugged that distance by tired men who floundered and stumbled or fell down under their burdens and found it very rough going indeed.

My boat set some stuff ashore with which to make a camp, and it was soon learned that the centipedes and various other ill-natured bugs were holding a district convention or something of the sort on No Name Key. It was a swampy islet with an evil smell of rotten vegetation and tidal mud. As a hiding-place for a band of outlaws it had been chosen because no one would think of looking for them there. Fragments of driftwood were lodged in the mangrove branches several feet higher than the level of the beach. This served to show that the key had been swept by more than one hurricane. It was evident that the weather signs would be scrutinized with a peculiar interest.

Having rigged a rude tent and stowed the personal dunnage in it, my boat-load of heroes embarked for the return trip to the Three Friends. A strong breeze came up with the dawn and the tide raced wickedly through the channels and lagoons. That four-mile pull was almost hopeless at times, for the current drove us far astern of the anchored steamer, and then it was to claw ahead against the wind, gaining an inch or two at a stroke. When my Cuban comrades of the oar lost their breath and their expectation of ever regaining the Three Friends, I addressed them with violent words.

Here was my chance to coach a crew and to hurl at it the well-remembered insults and epithets which had bruised the

THE *THREE FRIENDS* AND THE *DAUNTLESS* AT A WHARF IN JACKSONVILLE

The *Three Friends* is the white steamer at the left of the picture

soul of that clumsy Yale oarsman, Ralph Paine, at Number Four. Earnestly I bellowed at those exhausted patriots:

"For the love of Heaven, wake up, you poor dummies."

"Holy suffering cats, can't you ever learn to swing an oar?"

"Close to the water now. Blast your eyes, swing in time."

"*One — two — three — four — lift it all together!*"

"Look here, you Jesus Maria Betancourt up in the bow there, if you catch another crab I'll throw you overboard."

In a worse plight than this was the valiant Mike Walsh who had set out for No Name Key with a boat-load of munitions. Tide and wind drove him straight out to seaward. In the rough water his Cubans were a tangle of sprawling oars, of feet waving against the sky. It was different from landing an expedition, close to the shore, in some sheltered bay of the Cuban coast. Mike was seen to knock a man off his seat and take an oar himself. He rowed as strongly as he swore. His voice just then would have drowned the whistle of the Three Friends. Remorselessly his boat drifted out across the wide reach toward the Hawk Channel and an empty horizon until it seemed unlikely that he could steer to make one of the intervening keys.

As the distance from the Three Friends increased, his expostulations could no longer be heard. He and his crew resembled some fantastic mechanical toy in furious but futile motion. Captain O'Brien was intent on getting the cargo out of the ship before any meddlesome cruisers or revenue cutters from Key West might come poking about. There was no time to dally with a rescue party and all that the vanishing Mike Walsh got was sympathy.

He passed from view behind a fragment of an outer key, still driving for the great beyond. It was consoling to feel an implicit faith in his ability to master any emergency, and one could fancy him as organizing an impromptu filibustering expedition of his own, with his derelict boat-load of patriots and rifles and ammunition. At any rate, he was bound for the coast of Cuba when last seen.

It was eight o'clock in the morning when McCready and I shoved off for another trip to No Name Key. The sailormen of the Three Friends were now helping to navigate the surf-boats, having perceived that the job was in a bad way without them. In the afternoon the last of the stuff was put ashore, and the marooned company dropped in its tracks, on the little strip of beach or among the muddy mangrove bushes, to rest its aching bones and to sleep profoundly.

It was more than physical weariness. The results of all this exertion seemed so wretchedly disheartening! After the long voyage into the Caribbean, the enterprise was in a situation much less hopeful than when it had sailed out of Fernandina. It seemed foredoomed to disappointment and failure.

Toward nightfall the party awoke from the dead and began to bestir itself. The Cubans employed their machetes to cut boughs and rig shelters with bits of canvas, rubber blankets, and so on, slinging their hammocks to the stouter bushes. McCready, Jack Gorman, and I made our own camp and saved a place for Mike Walsh, even though he was missing with all hands. Cuban sentries were posted along the shores of the key and there was a semblance of military routine with shrill challenges of "*Quien va*" and a whistle blown to command silence after dark. My diary includes this comment:

Jack Gorman is a bully forager and we got our share of grub and water and decided to take turns guarding it, watch and watch. In the twilight I waded out and took a bath and put on a clean shirt and white duck breeches. The moral effect was excellent. Felt better than at any time since the voyage began. Laid around a fire in the evening and wondered what was going to happen to us. Some of the Cubans are very peevish and hollering for more to eat. Major Morales expects a schooner from Key West with more stores. This is a darned funny way to spend Christmas.

The wind veered into the northward next morning, blowing strong, with a clouded sky. The sea beat against the key and two of the surf-boats had been so carelessly secured that they went adrift and were lost. Two others remained, but in such boisterous weather it was impossible to go exploring in search of a refuge more habitable, nor, for the present, was there any way of obtaining more food and water. The isolation was complete.

It was a cheerful Christmas Day, nevertheless, with a gift welcome beyond compare, for at a yell from the beach the Cubans scampered out of their shelters. A speck of a boat was lunging in from the Hawk Channel, a low, inert lump of a craft that wallowed over the crested seas like a cow jumping hurdles. After a while a rag of blue fluttered from an oar raised in the bow, while in the stern the figure of what appeared to be the solitary occupant gleamed white from the waist up.

"It's nobody else but Mike," shouted Jack Gorman, "but what's become of his bunch of waterlogged patriots?"

The astonishing surf-boat grounded far out among the reefs. The commander was seen to flourish an oar in the manner of a harpoon, or as though he were stirring a kettle of soup in the bottom of the boat. Feeble wails arose.

"Mike is wakin' up his crew," said Gorman. "I begun to think he had eaten 'em raw."

One by one the Cuban castaways bobbed up from inside the boat and went overboard in close contact with an energetic oar, followed by a roar from Mike Walsh:

"The beach ahoy! Send off some hands to help me get the stuff out, an' report me to the *comandante* as arrivin' in good order."

We stumbled through the surf and fell upon the neck of this competent chief gunner's mate. Stripped to the waist, his hairy chest was tattooed with a spread-eagle and the American ensign. No fear of his striking his colors! His greeting was affectionate, but he hastened to protest:

"God bless ye, boys, an' there's no place like home, but first let me get rid of the cargo. Then I'll spin the yarn. 'T is clear to the coast of Africa and back I have been, with a bum crew. And me only shirt that I set for a sail is blown out of the bolt-ropes, for I could n't stop to reef after I once got her h'isted."

Mike carried more ammunition from his boat to the beach than any other three men, reported to the Cuban *comandante* in person, apologized for his delayed arrival, and was then joyously hauled into our camp where he ate enough for three men, rebuilt the makeshift tent in handy sailor fashion, and insisted upon washing the tin plates before he sat himself down to rest.

"It was kind of cir-circuitous," explained Michael Walsh, with his boyish grin and humorous twinkle. "When I went driftin' off to hell-an'-gone, I exhorted th' brave but helpless *Cubanos* until me tongue hung out, but 't was no use. Whenever they will be comin' to, they'll say I made 'em work their passage. The boat shipped a lot of water, being loaded deep, but I would not permit them to jettison cargo, the same havin' great value to old Maximo Gomez over yonder. So I ordered 'em to bail ship an' they did so until they fell off their perches an' washed about in the bilges. And then I prodded 'em again.

"When day broke, me good ship was in the Florida Straits and I begun to worry a bit. If I was to bump the coast of Cuba, there might be difficulty in explainin' this infant expedition of arms an' rebels, an' me the same Mike Walsh that had been tossin' shrapnel into the Spanish Navy. But the wind shifted, please God, an' so I come drivin' back. What with bailin' an' wrastlin' them long oars, the enlisted men of me force is wore to a frazzle."

For several days longer the stormy weather held the party as prisoners on No Name Key. The rations were running short and there was no sign of the promised schooner from

Key West. The cleaning rods of rifles were lashed to bits of stick and served to spear the giant crayfish out on the reefs. These had the size and flavor of lobsters and were boiled in a kettle of salt water. When the gale subsided, Mike Walsh and a boat's crew explored other small islands two or three miles distant and found brackish water for drinking and a few bunches of green bananas.

Quarrels over food and water touched off several lively scrimmages and the Cuban surgeon patched and plastered the wounded. The water was doled out on short allowance, and it was prudent to keep an eye on your own share if you wished to husband it against a greater need. The morale of the expedition was beginning to break. The privations endured were not enough to account for this. It was the sense of failure, the feeling that rescue had been somehow thwarted, that the party had been abandoned to its fate.

As was bound to happen in such dismal circumstances, some men displayed unquenchable courage and fortitude while others whimpered and would have stolen the boats and fled by night if the sentries had not been on the alert. The Cuban leader, Colonel Perez Calvo, had preferred to stay in the Three Friends and seek *terra firma* at Key West. The scourge of seasickness had made him of little account and there was no mourning when he vanished from this melodrama.

The command had been assumed by the one-eyed Major Morales, a brave soldier of Cuban campaigns, but not the man to coax and cheer and compel these forlorn and emotional castaways. He threatened, cursed, beat them with the flat of his machete, and they sulked the more.

What held them together and saved the situation, as much as anything else, was the personality of a blithe soldier of fortune, Frank Pagiluichi by name, an Italian by birth, a Cuban by adoption, and for some time an engineer officer in the Argentine Navy. He was a linguist, a gentleman, a rover who found himself at home in the ports of every sea, and he had the gift of shining in adversity. While frying a mess of green bananas in a tin plate you might have heard him caroling an Italian love song, breaking off to tell in Spanish some broad anecdote that made the Cubans yell with laughter, or strolling over to chat in French with a disconsolate lad from Haiti. As a diplomat he displayed his talent in such episodes as this, which my diary briefly mentions:

Another gun play this afternoon. Major Morales ordered the fiery little chap nicknamed Porto Ric' to go in a boat and hunt for water. Porto Ric' properly refused, having worked like a dog while the loafers took siestas in the shade. Morales pulled his artillery and Porto Ric' was there with a machete which he had been sharpening with a file. Before they could mix it up, Pagiluichi waltzed in and pried them apart. Then he delivered orations and gestures and smoothed it out in a jiffy. Lively disappointment among the Cubanos who were hoping that Major Morales was about to be given a military funeral on No Name Key.

XIV

PIRACY ON THE HIGH SEAS

AFTER a week and more of this unpleasant but vivacious existence among the mangrove bushes, a small schooner appeared in the offing and brought provisions, also news from the swarthy conspirators of Key West who operated a *Junta* and secret service of their own. It was made known that the Three Friends would be unable to return and embark the expedition for another voyage to Cuba. For one thing, her engines and boilers were unfit to risk the adventure without a thorough overhauling in port. Even John Dunn, that fat and garrulous chief, had been compelled to admit that she could n't stand being chased by no more Spanish gunboats, durn her old soul, and it was a miracle she had n't laid down and quit on him anyhow. All he could do was to patch her hastily in Key West and limp home to the shipyard in Jacksonville.

Report and rumor indicated that the Three Friends would be tied up hard and fast in Jacksonville, by official decree, with United States deputy marshals on board to prevent her from playing truant. That armed ruction off the Rio San Juan had involved her in difficulties which her plausible, deep-sea liars were unable to brush aside. Already in Key West they had found it awkward explaining that ragged gap in the bulwark where Mike Walsh's acrobatic twelve-pounder had tried to kick itself over the side while in action.

Vainly had Captain Johnny O'Brien and Skipper "Bill" Lewis argued the matter with candid, clear-eyed sincerity. They had been looking for a wreck reported adrift. The quest had kept them in the Caribbean until the coal bunkers were empty. It was easy enough for the officials to search the vessel. There was nothing suspicious on board, no militant Cubans, no explosive cargo. As for that hole stove in the bow — a collision on a thick night with an unknown steamer — that ought to satisfy the most skeptical inquiry.

Those newspaper stories cabled to New York? Reporters' guff! Fakes hatched in Key West! The place was notorious for its newspaper liars. What would the poor old Three Friends be doing but trying to earn an honest living as an offshore towboat? Shooting at a Spanish man-of-war? Nonsense! What did she have to shoot with?

All this gossip was entertaining to the derelicts on No Name Key, but it lacked the essential fact. What ship would be sent to rescue us and when? The reply was that nobody knew. Every effort had been made, but *quien sabe?* Then it was that McCready and Paine decided to go to Key West in the little schooner and try to find information less vague than these disquieting rumors.

To Mike Walsh was entrusted the custody of the sword of Gomez, that noble weapon which had been carried over many a league of salt water and was as remote from its destination as ever. Proud and gratified was Michael Walsh to take charge of the sword, and it went without saying that the surest way to court sudden death would be to try to steal it from him.

He had mounted his twelve-pound field piece to sweep the beach and from a pole beside it flew the lone star flag of Cuba. It was his habit to organize himself as efficiently as possible and even No Name Key could not daunt him.

Dirty, ragged, unshaven, the two correspondents drowsed upon the schooner's deck while she ran for Key West with a fair wind, reaching there late at night. Down among the wharves a Cuban was luckily encountered and he was a cordial pilot to a restaurant of one Palacho who was deep in the plots of the *Junta*. In those days it was a Key West without a railroad, a lazy tropical town, much more Cuban than American, a little exotic island set far out in a sun-bathed ocean. For us two refugees it was easy enough to find cover in the Cuban quarter and to remain there safe against discovery.

Ah, it was superb to comprehend that we were heroes, brave men from the *Tres Amigos* which had defied the powerful navy of Spain. And we were impatiently awaiting the chance to go and do it again! That midnight supper in the restaurant of the excitable, admiring Palacho — the idea of payment insulted him — it was little enough to do for two veterans of the battle of the Rio San Juan — a sirloin steak, broiled pompano, turtle stew, guava jelly, cheese, coffee, big cigars, and red wine!

And while we ate, the Cubans surrounded the table and we refought for them the glorious naval action — tracing a map on the tablecloth, a salt-cellar as the Three Friends, a bread crust as the disabled gunboat, a bottle as the cruiser firing her big guns down Cienfuegos way.

One of the company flourished a copy of the "Times-Union" of Jacksonville and sonorously read aloud:

La Lucha, a Havana newspaper, in the issue of Saturday, printed a story to the effect that a Spanish patrol boat had entered the harbor of Havana with part of its pilot-house gone, the captain reporting that it had been carried away by a shot from the Three Friends while the patrol boat was chasing the filibuster near the San Juan River. If this report has been received in Havana, the American Government officials say there is little doubt that the matter will be reported to Washington and may lead to serious complications between Spain and the United States.

The restaurant of the kindly Palacho rang with cheers. What was intended to be a square meal and nothing more had become an ovation and a celebration. It was a very

late hour when the two well-fed correspondents rolled into
bed at Sweeney's lodging-house. They were disturbed by
several drunken sailors who seemed to make a pastime of
falling downstairs. One of them loudly announced, over
and over again, that his name was "John J. McCarthy,
E-S-Q with a period," and he could lick any six men in Key
West. After a while somebody hit him with a chair and threw
him out. His challenge came more faintly from the sidewalk, the last stand of "John J. McCarthy, E-S-Q with a
period."

Sleepily McCready murmured, during his last waking
moments:

"We'll have to pack up all the fancy grub we can lay our
hands on to-morrow and take it back to Mike Walsh and
Jack Gorman — also a case of beer, and a box of those bully
cigars. It's coming to them."

"Sure thing," said I; "and if you want to make Mike perfectly happy, take him John J. McCarthy, E-S-Q with a
period, who can lick any six men in Key West. Mike deserves
to have a little mild amusement."

It was learned the next morning that, although warrants
had not been issued for the arrest of the pirates of the Three
Friends, such proceedings might occur at any moment and
it was advisable to remain shy and inconspicuous. However,
we ventured as far as a Cuban barber shop, and there we met,
by chance, Richard Harding Davis and Frederic Remington
who were returning from a trip to Havana and other ports
and towns held by the Spanish forces. Both men have died
since then, "Dick" Davis, the facile journalist and gifted
story-teller who won distinguished success in the flush of his
youth; burly, big-hearted Fred Remington whose genius with
brush and pencil preserved for future generations the vanishing life of the Western frontier.

They seemed to find entertainment in the pair of vagabonds from No Name Key, and Davis declared that it was too good to be true — the delightful flavor of piracy — marooned on a lonely tropical key — and our thoroughly disreputable make-up.

"First-class stories you chaps wrote, both of them, of the Three Friends and the gunboat," said Davis. "The 'Herald' and the 'Journal' displayed them as big stuff."

The compliment pleased us tremendously. A word of praise from Richard Harding Davis was valued by a young reporter.

"I thought you were a brace of tough niggers who had just broken out of the county jail," chuckled Remington.

"It's the coal dust," explained McCready. "You sleep in it for twelve days and it rubs into your skin. Washing in salt water does n't start it. We scrubbed off a few layers this morning. As for our clothes, please take it from me that an honest heart beats beneath these ragged breeches."

"And will you kindly avoid the mention of jail?" I suggested. "It is n't really tactful."

"Better dine with us to-night, at Palacho's," urged Davis. "We can post trusty scouts and see that you are n't pinched. I want to hear all about it. Pirates are a rare treat."

"Thanks, but we must be heading back to our desert island," replied McCready. "Our pals will worry if we don't turn up. Mike Walsh is liable to capture a sponging schooner and bombard Key West if he thinks anything has happened to us."

They wished us good luck and laughed some more. From the barber shop we drifted unobtrusively into the office of a Cuban official through whose hands passed all confidential information of importance. Key West was a whispering gallery of revolutionary plots and counterplots, the base of secret communication with Cuba. First we looked through a pile of newspapers and found them intensely interesting. Mr. William Randolph Hearst had emblazoned a dispatch from a special correspondent in Jacksonville with these startling headlines:

"*PIRACY*" STRIKES TERROR

THREE FRIENDS FILIBUSTERS IN FEAR OF THEIR LIVES

IF CONVICTED OF THE CRIME THEY WILL BE SENTENCED TO DEATH

THE HOTCHKISS GUN PLAYS AN IMPORTANT PART IN THE CHARGES

ADMINISTRATION WILL PROSECUTE

Other newspapers regarded the affair as worthy of serious editorial discussion. The "Nashville American," for example, took this gloomy view of it:

It is reported that the steamer Three Friends, engaged in the filibustering business, while on a recent trip to Cuba had a regular battle royal with Spanish warships and gunboats and by means of a Hotchkiss gun ably handled drove off the Spanish vessels. If this story is correct, it details a thrilling encounter and will inspire the Cubans to attempt to operate a naval force. If true, does it not make the Three Friends a pirate? If she hoisted the Cuban flag she will have to be seized by the United States authorities, for our Government has not recognized the Cubans as belligerents, and if the Three Friends fought the Spanish men-of-war, claiming to be a Cuban vessel, she cannot be other than a pirate and will have to be treated as such.

The Spanish Legation in Washington affected to pooh-pooh the incident. If there had been the slightest shred of truth in the sensational yarn, the Spanish Minister would have been promptly informed of the facts by Acting Captain-

General Ahumada in Havana and it would have been an imperative duty to have demanded the surrender of the boat and its crew to the Spanish Government, to be dealt with according to the universally recognized law of nations. Absolutely no report of any such alleged and absurdly improbable occurrence had been received.

This was obviously for publication. The United States was rapidly drifting into war with Spain at this time and the American people were in no temper to listen to a demand that the crew of the Three Friends should be surrendered and shot against a wall as had happened to the sailors of the Virginius.

The "Jacksonville Citizen" ruffled the sensitive feelings of Ernest McCready and Ralph Paine by calling them liars in this blunt fashion:

Of all the exaggeration and misstatement that have been published by both sides regarding the Cuban war, this last story of a naval battle in which the Three Friends proved a victor is about the most nonsensical. In the first place, there is no armament on the boat, as claimed in the published accounts, and in the second place, she is only a fast tugboat and consequently unfit to engage one of even the least important class of naval vessels. If there was any encounter between the two vessels, it is safe to say that the Three Friends owes her preservation to prompt and speedy flight and not to her prowess at arms.

Nothing is more natural than that when the enterprising correspondents boarded the vessel, eager for news, upon her arrival at Key West, the inquiries should have been evaded. And there are jokers even on a filibuster who like to have fun with the marines. The entire matter can probably be attributed to the zeal of correspondents who hold sensationalism above truth in news-gathering and who first publish their fiction and then let the public make investigation as to its veracity.

Another entertaining report had filtered through the Cuban sources of information. In the formidable legal document which was said to be in preparation, Ralph Paine was to be named as among "the certain persons then engaged in armed resistance to the Government of the King of Spain, in the island of Cuba, to cruise or commit hostilities against the subjects, citizens, and property of the King of Spain, with whom the United States is at peace."

This distinction was presumably accorded me because I happened to be well known in Jacksonville where the years of my youth had been spent.

"You have put one over on me," remarked McCready, without envy. "They fail to mention me as included among those present. The Jacksonville papers print your photograph, I notice, and seem proud of you as a native product. The rising young pirate — son of the former pastor of the Ocean Street Presbyterian Church. It listens well."

After reading a few more excerpts from newspapers in New York and elsewhere, it occurred to me to say:

"We may never be famous, Mac, like Richard Harding Davis, but for a couple of common or garden reporters we have come pretty near making ourselves notorious."

At noon our Cuban friend and advisor received a cable message in code which startled us into impetuous action. The steamer Dauntless had been able to get to sea from Jacksonville and was southward bound to attempt to rescue the cargo and the exiles from No Name Key and to convey them to Cuba. She was already on her way and might be expected to arrive in the Hawk Channel within the next twelve hours. Here was a slant of good fortune when hope had been almost abandoned. Somehow the clever Dauntless had euchred the officials and the American naval patrol. In the latter case it was to be suspected that the officers of the cruisers and revenue cutters might have winked the other eye.

Their private sympathies were with the bold seafarers who played the filibustering game, and they must have applauded the stories of the fight and escape of the Three Friends off the Rio San Juan. Also they must have forgiven a certain chief gunner's mate named Mike Walsh his sin of deserting the battleship Maine.

It was for McCready and Paine to make hasty departure from Key West and rejoin their long-suffering comrades on No Name Key. Flitting to a wharf, they managed to hire a decrepit sloop. The skipper was a sun-dried, elderly negro who seemed dubious about getting to the key at all, with the wind blowing dead ahead. He hoisted a patched mainsail and a frayed jib and stood out through the fairway to the inside channel which wandered through the maze of islets to the northward.

The tide was also against him and the sloop had to make short tacks to clear the reefs and muddy shoals. The afternoon wore on, and by dead reckoning it was conjectured that a rheumatic terrapin could have given the sloop a ten-mile start to No Name Key and have won in a walk.

Twilight came and the laggard craft was stirring the soft mud with her keel while the black mariner grumbled to himself:

"She's a-grubbin'. Ain't no water in this channel a-tall. How you reckon a vessel gwine sail if she got to keep on a-grubbin'?"

McCready and I rustled a supper on the rusty stove in the dirty box of a cabin and then stretched out for a nap upon the pig-iron ballast which served as a floor. An hour later the sloop had quit grubbin' and was hard and fast aground. The lights of Key West twinkled no more than five miles astern. It was an utterly impossible voyage. The situation impressed our youthful emotions as immensely critical.

A question of honor was involved. If the Dauntless should take off the expedition and leave us behind, the stain would be ineffaceable. Sink or swim, we were bound to see the thing through. Perish the thought that we should be regarded as quitters, renegades! And there was the sword of Gomez, left in the faithful custodianship of Mike Walsh, which it was my

own sacred duty to deliver in *Cuba Libre*. It went against
the grain to confess to defeat, but we were in the deuce of a
fix.

Just when all seemed lost, there came to one of us a flash of
inspiration, a possible solution of the problem. In Key West
harbor we had seen the steam yacht Vamoose, built to break
records and famous for speed. This vessel had been chartered
by Mr. Hearst to expedite his news service between Key West
and Havana and also to circumvent the Spanish military
censorship. The trick for us was to shove the wretched sloop
out of the mud, run back to Key West with a fair wind, and
beseech the Vamoose to whisk us to No Name Key.

It was humiliating to contemplate, in a way, because we
much preferred to seek our own fortunes and to trust to our
own resources as filibusters and pirates. The expedition on
No Name Key was a strictly private project which resented
intrusion. However, we were compelled to swallow our pride
and to go humbly begging a favor of the Vamoose. It was
this, or the shame and disgrace of failure.

Plunging overboard from the sloop, we tugged and hauled
and pushed while the ancient skipper handled a pole, and
after a bitter struggle the miserable craft floated clear of the
mud. No longer grubbin' or obliged to tack every few minutes, she followed the channel and soon ran clear of the keys,
with the breeze mostly astern. The instant the bowsprit
scraped a wharf in Key West harbor, two young men scrambled ashore and began to ransack the town. This was no time
for stealth or the fear of the law. It was a search incredibly
fevered and anxious.

In charge of Mr. Hearst's news service, which included the
operations of the Vamoose, was Charlie Michelson, a first-
class journalist, whom we had known in New York. He was
sauntering out of a billiard-room, on his way to bed, when we
fell upon his neck, jabbering both at once. We were a pair
of hard cases, he said with a grin, and deserved no sympathy

whatever, nor did he wish to be seen with us, but the Vamoose was ours for the asking, of course. He would send off word to her captain at once, telling him to get up steam. And the swift yacht would be bowling up the Hawk Channel by midnight.

When we tried to thank Michelson, words failed us. He had saved our honor and lifted us from the depths of misery. Back to the sloop we went on the run to collect our stuff, mostly supplies for Mike Walsh and Jack Gorman, and to persuade the black mariner to paddle us off to the yacht in his dinghy.

If this narrative has conveyed a true impression of the life aboard the Three Friends and on No Name Key, it will be realized that to be escorted into the staterooms of a luxuriously appointed yacht by a respectful steward in a white jacket was in the nature of a shock. The steward was even more shocked, no doubt, when he beheld the guests, but he had been well trained and so dissembled his feelings. Supper was served a little later. This brief experience was a respite and an interlude which seemed positively unreal. We crawled into clean, soft beds instead of nestling between sacks of bituminous coal or being dented by pig-iron ballast. Ah, but it was a grand night!

XV

THE WRATH OF GENERAL EMILIO NUÑEZ

As in a blissful trance we heard the anchor lifted and felt the Vamoose vibrate to the thrust of her twin screws as she passed out into the wide Hawk Channel. This forty-mile run would be no more than a mere two-hour jog at twenty knots. Because it was ticklish business finding No Name Key in the night, the yacht proceeded as near as she dared to go, and then dropped her hook in the bight of Loggerhead Key to wait for daylight.

At five o'clock she was again under way, moving with caution to keep in deep water, while her disreputable guests enjoyed an early breakfast. Enjoyed it? They almost wept into the finger-bowls. The touches of elegance, the refining influences of civilization, were too much! It seemed ages since this brace of ruffians had passed as young gentlemen.

Not long after this memorable breakfast, the Vamoose veered around the end of a wooded islet and sighted No Name Key. There it was, a distant, swampy patch of mangrove almost submerged in a sea of shifting green and blue. But it had ceased to be lonely and unfrequented. An amazing activity was manifest.

Four miles out from the key lay a black-hulled, powerful towboat with red deck-houses. It was the Dauntless! Alongside were two or three native sloops and schooners while other small sailing vessels were moving to and from No Name Key. This flotilla was engaged in bringing off the cargo. The white sails dotted the bright water which was swept by a lively breeze. Spongers and fishermen from Key West and Nassau, they were making brisk work of it, and the scene was uncommonly picturesque.

"By Jove, Mac, we did n't have very much time to spare," said I. "This looks like a mighty well-managed affair. The Dauntless will be loaded and on her way in short order. And we'll be there, with the sword of Gomez. *Viva Cuba Libre!*"

"Wait a minute," cried McCready who had borrowed a pair of glasses. "You are one of those chronic, darn-fool optimists. The expedition has gone bug-house again, as sure as you live!"

This was a strange assertion, but presently the lamentable fact became visible to the naked eye. Dementia had suddenly, mysteriously afflicted the orderly procession of sailing craft that moved between the Dauntless and No Name Key. They were scattering hither and yon, scudding before the wind or beating frantically against it to seek refuge in the crooked passages among the more distant keys. Those which had snuggled close to the filibustering steamer were casting off and making sail in the most violent haste.

Never had a well-contrived expedition been so curiously disrupted. And in this helter-skelter flight the hysterical little sloops and schooners were carrying away with them the hundreds of cases of Mauser rifles, the millions of rounds of cartridges, the many boxes of machetes and all the rest of that precious cargo. In all directions they were fleeing with it and there was no intention of coming back. A spectacle more bewildering and disconcerting could not have been imagined.

"It beats me," said the master of the yacht Vamoose which was slowly steaming in the direction of the Dauntless. "Old Gomez has a fine chance of getting that stuff, I don't think. If ever there was a busted party, this is easily it. There is no use in my trying to chase those crazy little vessels and rounding 'em up, for they are all in shoal water and still going it. And the Dauntless is worse off than we are. She draws twelve or fourteen feet."

Two or three of the sloops were already vanishing beyond

the keys to the westward. McCready rubbed his eyes and was heard to mutter that this filibustering game gave him the yips, likewise the fantods. It was as bad as that. The yacht stopped her engines within hailing distance of the Dauntless. Upon the roof of the wheel-house stood Captain "Dynamite Johnny" O'Brien, and for once his demeanor indicated a distraught state of mind. He rumpled that mop of gray hair with both hands and desisted to adorn his remarks with gestures. One of these conveyed an emotion unmistakable. He was shaking his fist at the Vamoose. For some reason he deeply, passionately disliked the beautiful yacht.

How he had managed to dodge out of the Three Friends and into the Dauntless, with the Federal officials yearning to lay hands on him as a pirate, was an extraordinary puzzle in itself, but just now it seemed commonplace. There were other things more baffling to engage the attention. The language of Captain O'Brien was unheard. The wind blew his words away. For us he was an artist in pantomime.

The real orator of the day was a dark, active person with an air of authority who showed the whites of his eyes while he spouted curses like molten lava. His voice was resonant, and where his best phrases rebounded from the side of the Vamoose, the white paint curled in blisters. He used both Spanish and English, mixing them fluently. I recognized him as a man of distinction, General Emilio Nuñez, one of the foremost Cuban leaders, with a record of valor in the field. Evidently he had taken it upon himself to see that this expedition was handled with no more mishaps.

"Do you get that?" exclaimed McCready, who had aucked and thrown up an arm to ward off a double-shotted expletive. "What he is trying to say is that we have spilled the beans, or words to that effect. And I infer that if we go aboard the Dauntless he will take great pleasure in shooting us deader than Judas Iscariot."

"He means it, Mac. Now do you realize what we have done? Those idiotic sloops and schooners mistook the Vamoose for a revenue cutter from Key West as soon as she showed herself around the point. This yacht is built like a small cruiser and she is a stranger in these waters. Now do you see what ailed them? They were seized with acute panic and started elsewhere. And they are still going. Vamoose is their motto, likewise *muy pronto*."

This was the answer as pieced together from the incoherent denunciations of General Emilio Nuñez, who was fairly bounding from one deck of the Dauntless to the other. The yacht was long and low and painted white, like the naval vessels of that era, and her lines were unfamiliar to these spongers and fishermen. To escape being caught in the act, this was the motive which had sent them scurrying over the face of the waters. It was every man for himself and the devil take the hindmost. Unavoidably they carried the cargo with them. It was dispersed in a manner heartrending to behold.

The whistle of the Dauntless blew long, imploring blasts to recall the fugitives, but they took it as a warning and continued to steer for far horizons, in a dozen different directions. Without discussing it, McCready and I determined to delay presenting ourselves on board of the Dauntless and shaking hands with Johnny O'Brien and General Emilio Nuñez. It seemed too much like suicide, and we were not quite ready for that, even though our young lives were blighted.

As a forlorn hope we jumped into one of the yacht's boats and, with two sailors to row it, set out in chase of the nearest munition-laden sloop which appeared to be "grubbin'." If one of the flotilla could be overtaken and reassured, probably the others would turn back at seeing her make for the Dauntless or for No Name Key. Alas, the approach of the yacht's boat, with its sailors in blue uniforms, spurred the crew of the sloop to such superhuman exertions that they avoided stranding and shot ahead, with the wind abeam, into a wide lagoon.

Wearily, with not the slightest prospect of success, we turned to attempt to head off a schooner which had been compelled to tack clear of obstructing shoals. Our friendly, beseeching signals were ignored. McCready and I babbled at each other. Cowards, we envied those runaway spongers and fishermen. To us was denied any way of escape. We were bound to the wheel of fate.

The yacht blew a signal to recall her boat. The captain was in a hurry to return to Key West. He had other business in hand. No doubt he would be willing to take us along, two disconsolate young pirates whom circumstances had vanquished, but the temptation was thrust aside. We had to go aboard the Dauntless and endeavor to rejoin our comrades. There was no alternative although we turned pale at the thought of engaging General Emilio Nuñez at close quarters.

At this most doleful moment there came chugging into view, from the direction of Key West, a small steam launch which proved to be filled with Cuban partisans who had come to bid the patriots *adios* and to lend a hand in towing the surf-boats out from No Name Key. Instead of obeying the yacht's signal of recall, we rowed like mad to intercept the launch. In broken accents we told those Cubans what had happened to the expedition.

Viva Cuba Libre, the day was saved! Presto, the tragedy was no more than a comedy of errors. The launch sped away to pursue and corner those daffy little sailing vessels. Now they could no longer find security in shallow water. The skipper of one sloop, still suffering delusions, imagined that the launch had been sent to capture him. He let his vessel drive for the beach of the nearest key and the instant she took the bottom he hopped overboard followed by his four men. Into the mangrove thicket they crashed, heels over head, and were moving with extraordinary rapidity when last seen.

The launch had better luck with the next attempt. A schooner was fairly trapped in a pocket of reefs between two islands and after much shouting and scolding it was possible to calm her fears. Soon this vessel was sailing back toward the Dauntless. Another of the fleet, and then another, was prompt to descry the maneuver. The stampede was checked. It was a pretty sight to see the white-winged craft returning like a flock of birds which had been driven to flight by a hawk.

The orderly programme of transferring the cargo was resumed. The episode had turned out to be an interruption, not a disaster. It was conceivable that General Emilio Nuñez might waive the death-sentence, but I still quaked at the thought of meeting him face to face while McCready was easily startled.

Taking our lives in our hands, we scrambled up the side of the Dauntless in a very furtive manner, suggesting the arrival of two burglars engaged in a second-story operation. By using great care we were able to avoid the immediate notice of General Emilio Nuñez, who was absorbed in more urgent affairs. All that concerned him now was getting the steamer safely to sea, with the cargo in her. Most of the patriots had been brought off from No Name Key, but Mike Walsh and Jack Gorman were not among them. To a question our boyish friend, Lieutenant Edgar Carbonne, replied:

"Mike is waiting for you on the key, Señor Ralph Paine. And Sergeant Jack Gorman wished to keep him company, I think. Unless you go ashore and report yourself, Mike will stay right there. It is an obligation, he told me, to guard the sword of Gomez and your stuff until you came back from Key West. He had given his word."

Yes, this was it — the simple, unquestioning fidelity of a man who would never go back on a pal. A rough man by your standards, gentle reader, was Mike Walsh, but in the sight of God I venture to say he was rated a gentleman. Failure to join the Dauntless would have been a mighty serious business for him, the end of his high ambition to gain a commission in the Cuban artillery, the risk of arrest and punishment as a deserter from the American Navy, but he was ready to face it sooner than break his word.

And Sergeant Jack Gorman, hardened old regular trooper, had preferred to stay with Mike Walsh because they were bunkies and pals during this filibustering adventure — Jack Gorman with that obsolete old Springfield rifle of his and the two hundred rounds which were to bang out a fortune for him in popping off Spanish officers at a thousand dollars per head. Chivalry is not dead. The world may laugh at Don Quixote, but his soul goes marching on to rebuke ignoble motives and sordid interpretations of life, and to illumine the spirit of the Golden Rule.

I went ashore in the Cubans' launch and found these two musketeers in a camp almost deserted. My personal luggage had been neatly bundled together and Mike Walsh stood waiting, the sword of Gomez under his arm. Jack Gorman was counting his cartridges to pass the time.

"Sure, I knew you'd turn up," said Mike as we thumped each other. "I had some words with Major Morales, who jumped me for refusin' to budge, but Gorman waved the old blunderbuss at him."

"Come on, you bully old fools," I shouted, "and hop into that launch."

"The elegant sword is intact, diamonds and all," said Mike as he formally surrendered it. "I slept with it."

It seemed strangely out of place to offer them praise and gratitude. I tried to express something of the sort, but Mike brusquely interrupted:

"Stow it! For the love o' God, man, what else would ye expect me to do? Now let's shove off for another promenade in the Caribbean Sea and maybe it'll get us somewheres this time."

By four o'clock in the afternoon the Dauntless had the cargo mostly under hatches and the party strewn about her decks. Out clear of the sheltering keys she ran and plunged into a lively sea. Again the course was set to steal around Cape San Antonio, at the western end of Cuba. It was the old story — decks awash with rain and spray, seasick Cubans, the open sky for a roof, and a diverting gamble with destiny.

McCready and Paine were not easy to find during the late afternoon of this first day of the voyage. They were hidden behind a lifeboat where General Emilio Nuñez would be unlikely to discover them. It was their pious hope that his emotions might cool to a normal temperature overnight.

"He displayed all the symptoms of a bad *hombre*," murmured McCready in the windy twilight. "If we can stall him off until the morrow, there is a fighting chance that he may not throw us overboard. If ever a man had provocation to do murder, he was it."

"The Vamoose seemed a happy idea, Mac. I thought we were bright."

"We were, buddy, but bright men stir up most of the trouble in this world. Whew, I have aged ten years since morning."

Upon the small bridge surmounting the wheel-house, Captain Johnny O'Brien loitered with a dead cigar between his teeth and a tattered straw hat pulled over his eyes. He was placidly sweeping the horizon with a good pair of glasses. A distant smudge of smoke was visible and he called down to the helmsman to let her go wide of it.

XVI

THE VOYAGE OF THE DAUNTLESS

FOR two or three days the weather was like the temper of General Emilio Nuñez, stormy and overcast. The Dauntless was a staunch sea-boat and rode out the worst of it hove to while the deck-load of half-drowned humanity hung on by its eyelids. For McCready and Paine it was not such an ill wind, because the attention of General Nuñez was thereby diverted from these two miserable objects of his wrath. And when the sky cleared, he, too, had ceased to be tempestuous. It was no longer necessary to contemplate walking the plank or being strung up to a derrick-boom in lieu of a yardarm.

Rumor hinted that the expedition was to be landed on the coast of Pinar del Rio Province, in the western part of the island, instead of another long cruise in the Caribbean to deliver the cargo to Maximo Gomez. The reasons for this change of plan were not divulged. The leaders had been influenced, no doubt, by the latest advices from the field.

It seemed as though the escapade of the Three Friends and the failure of her voyage had hardened the resolution of little Captain Johnny O'Brien. There was to be no more waiting offshore to make a final dash in the darkness. He was driving the ship straight for a destination.

It was early in a bright afternoon when the Dauntless turned into the wide entrance of Corientes Bay which is a little way below Cape San Antonio on the southern side of the island. To us amateurs in maritime deviltry, this procedure seemed hazardous in the extreme. The bay was large enough to contain a fleet without crowding, an expanse of tranquil water supremely beautiful, with gleaming white beaches and feathery groves of palms. There was no sheltered anchorage for the Dauntless. From seaward she was boldly conspicuous, a steamer loitering where no steamer ought to be. A Spanish gunboat or cruiser passing outside would have trapped her beyond hope of escape.

The Cubans were packing their kits to go ashore, and once again all hands buckled to and lifted that everlasting cargo out of the hold. The heat was cruel, a blistering sun and no breeze, and down below the ship was an infernal sweat-box, with all that weighty stuff to be moved. Several Cubans collapsed and were hauled on deck. Hardships had sapped their endurance. They showed pluck, these forlorn adventurers who had been so unmercifully hammered about by sea and land. They were tremendously admirable.

One of them was an old man, or so he seemed to us youngsters, with his patient, wrinkled face, white mustache, and bent frame. In his worn, shabby aspect there was nothing heroic. He wore the remnants of a black alpaca coat, and his hat was a grotesque ruin of a derby which looked as if it had been played football with. One of his sons had been wounded while serving with Garcia, and Spanish guerrillas had tied him to a tree and chopped him to death with machetes. Another boy had fought with Antonio Maceo until that magnificent black warrior was killed in Pinar del Rio.

This gentle old man had kept a little shop in Tampa until the love of country and the call of duty had compelled him. He had been ailing while on No Name Key and now he was shaking with malarial chills or flushed with fever. He stood upon his thin, shaky legs while the Cuban major served out the rifles and ammunition before landing, but the surgeon whispered something and the old man moved aside. He was pronounced unfit to land. He would surely die or be a burden for the others. They would have to send him back to Florida in the Dauntless.

He leaned over the rail, staring at the green shores of Cuba, tears running down his cheeks. His hand fumbled with the tiny flag with a single star which he had pinned to his soiled shirt. The first man to console him was Sergeant Jack Gorman, the veteran regular who had seemed to be as tough as rawhide. But the tropical fever had gripped him also, and he was in bad shape, trying to pull himself together, making a pitiful pretense of fitness for duty. The Springfield rifle was red with rust and he bragged no more of his marksmanship or told us how he had sounded the charge for the troopers at Wounded Knee.

Jack Gorman would pick off no Spanish officers, at a thousand dollars a head, with slugs from that deadly old blunderbuss. Amassing a fortune had ceased to interest him. He was too sick to care, and the doctor told him to stay aboard the ship. He took it with the philosophy of a man who had found life a hard road to travel.

"I'll hit the beach with the next outfit that comes over, boys," said he. "You can't lose Jack Gorman. I'll be there with bells on to help you lick them Spaniards to a frazzle."

"We'll wait for you before capturin' Havana," replied Mike Walsh. "What will we be doin' for siege artillery unless you pack that old cannon on your shoulder, Jack?"

McCready and Paine had assembled their personal luggage, blanket rolls, saddle-bags, canteens, and weapons, including the sword of Gomez, and were preparing to disembark with the forty-odd patriots. If it had been left to them, they would have preferred to land elsewhere than in the western end of Pinar del Rio Province, but they had to take things as they came. As has been said before, Captain Johnny O'Brien was not in the habit of consulting the convenience of his passengers.

The Dauntless had steamed well inside Corientes Bay when General Emilio Nuñez beckoned the two correspondents to the wheel-house. He had forgotten the harrowing episode of the yacht Vamoose which had so nearly wrecked a perfectly good filibustering expedition. His manner was friendly, even solicitous, as he began to explain:

"Pinar del Rio is not a good place for you. Here you will be four hundred miles from Gomez. You will not get to him by land — impossible! Antonio Maceo, who commanded in the West, is dead. General Ruiz has been captured. It is quiet in Pinar del Rio — our soldiers are scattered — they will need time to reorganize. This cargo is to equip them while they wait for a new campaign — it is to show them they are not forgotten."

"Then you advise us to try it again, General Nuñez, with another expedition from Florida?" I asked.

"That is my advice. We can send you soon in a ship that will carry arms and men to Gomez, to the coast where the Three Friends was driven away. The Commodore, I expect, will be ready when you get back to Florida."

The argument was persuasive, but there was a factor of the equation which General Nuñez had overlooked. It was wholly personal. In sharing the perils and privations of these shipmates, especially Mike Walsh, we had learned to feel that we belonged with them. To be separated from them would seem akin to desertion. Blurred was the fact that we were in the employ of New York newspapers, paid to get the news and send it, under obligation to render the fullest possible measure of service, not as pirates, but as correspondents.

General Nuñez answered an unspoken question when he went on to say:

"There will be little news to send from Pinar del Rio, and much trouble in sending it. And that beautiful sword with the diamonds — the sword of two thousand dollars — to cross the *trocha* with it, the Spanish barricade across the island, of forts and block-houses and trenches and wire — no, it can never be done."

It did appear to be a difficult mission — several hundred miles of hostile wilderness and perhaps a hundred thousand

Spanish troops betwixt me and that eloquent presentation speech to the commander-in-chief of *Cuba Libre*. McCready and I thanked General Nuñez and retired for consultation. My diary mentions it as follows:

A painful hour. Acute distress, mental and spiritual. Mac and I wavered and could n't decide what was best to do. We were bound to be unhappy either way we played it. To prance into this jungle meant that we would be of mighty little use to the "Herald" and the "Journal." It was n't at all where we wanted to go. Our plans had been flubbed by that rumpus off the Rio San Juan, in the Three Friends. On the other hand, we hated to quit our pals. They could n't understand it. You could n't expect them to. Of course they would think we had cold feet. Parting from Mike Walsh is what worries us most.

In this crisis we turned to Captain O'Brien for counsel and he also urged trying our luck in another voyage. Of course these piracy charges might put a crimp in filibustering out of Florida, said he, but there was more than one way to skin a cat, and as long as the *insurrectos* needed the stuff he would try to get it to 'em. This verdict should have clinched the decision, but how could you feel reconciled to quitting a comrade like Mike Walsh? There was a wistful look in those bold, blue eyes of his as he sidled up to ask:

"You an' Mac will be goin' ashore with us? I'll be feelin' fine if there's the three of us to be company for one another. Now that Jack Gorman has been took with chills an' fever, I'd be lonesome-like with nothin' but these *Cubanos*."

Again we wobbled in our minds and could not read our duty clear. Mike was ready to invade Cuba even though this was a luckless jumping-off place. We were endeavoring to make our own situation plain to him, with respect to the bonds of journalism, when, as was usual, the unexpected happened. Never was a ship less anxious to attract attention to herself than was the Dauntless as she moved two miles inside the wide harbor of Corientes Bay on this bright afternoon. Something went wrong with the valve of her whistle which suddenly bellowed a hoarse, tremendous blast, and it was a whistle with a voice for an ocean liner.

Caramba! It kept on bellowing while the engine-room force erupted madly from below with spanners and wrenches in their fists. The infernal whistle could have been heard for miles in this quiet air. It summoned, fairly implored, the Spanish coast patrol to come and get this nefarious vessel, its cargo, its patriots, and Captain Johnny O'Brien with a fancy price on his head. And while the whistle persisted in its clamorous raving, it was blowing off steam from the boilers and so diminishing the speed of the Dauntless if she should have to cut and run for it. Here was an incident which got on one's nerves. It was a complication that seemed entirely superfluous.

They choked that temperamental whistle after a while, and the Dauntless sheered shoreward to find an anchorage and hustle out the surf-boats. The Spanish naval forces had failed to respond to the stentorian invitation, perhaps because it was the hour of the siesta. However, certain precautions were taken. A lookout climbed to the head of each stumpy mast and clung there with a pair of glasses. A hempen hawser was used as an anchor cable, and in the bow stood a deck-hand with an axe, ready to chop at the word. Chunks of resinous fat pine were fed into the furnaces or piled ready for an emergency. Alas, there was no John Dunn to put the clamp on the safety-valve and shove it to her, durn her old soul. The portly chief had been detained in the Three Friends to wrestle with the processes of the law. They had ketched him at last.

It was rather ticklish work when the first boat shoved off for the beach, a few hundred yards distant. The dense jungle ran down to the high-water mark, and a regiment of Spanish troops might have been screened in this ambuscade. All was quiet. The landing was unmolested. There was nothing to indicate that any other human beings had set foot in this lush, tropical wilderness, not a hut or a clearing or a fisher-man's wharf. It was as primeval as when Columbus had skirted the coast of Cuba.

The boats were rapidly filled and sent away with much shouting and splashing. As fast as the cargo was heaped on the beach, a gang of toilers moved it into the undergrowth where it would be hidden from any passing vessel. A Cuban cavalry force was expected to arrive shortly and escort the precious store of munitions and arms inland, to the nearest fortified town held by the insurgents.

The one-eyed Major Morales stood with folded arms in the shade of a palm and issued orders. The pose suggested Na-poleon, but the army consisted of these twoscore sea-weary patriots, undrilled, in motley garments, looking like refugees from a flood or a fire. They managed to raise a cheer for *Cuba Libre* when they saw the landing accomplished without misfortune, and the flag was unrolled to flaunt a bright patch of color above the tiers of boxes and bales and casks.

The crew of the Dauntless labored mightily to clear the decks with the least possible delay. There had been another steamer caught in daylight, on the northern coast, with half a dozen boats plying to the beach. She had escaped, but the Spanish man-of-war had raked the boats with shrapnel and some of them had vanished in splinters and bloody whirl-pools. It was not easy to realize, in this lovely blue harbor of Corientes Bay, that the Dauntless was taking a grimly sporting chance and winning it by sheer audacity.

During one of the trips to the beach, I was wading through the gentle surf with a box of Mauser cartridges when Mike Walsh came along with a boat-load of shells for his field piece and those bothersome cases of nitroglycerin for making dynamite. It was uncertain footing in the surf, with a rough coral bottom, and in spite of Mike's exhortations, two patri-ots fell down with a case of nitroglycerin. He helped them ashore with it and remarked, with that bland, untroubled grin:

"Looks like that stuff was no good, don't it? That bump ought to ha' touched her off. And it was bangin' all around in the deck in heavy weather, more 'n once. I figured on blowin' up some Spanish railroad trains full o' troops."

"Thank the Lord she did n't go off that time, Mike," said I, with feeling. "Please don't let them drop another box. Well, it seems as if McCready and I ought to go back in the Dauntless and try to land closer to old Gomez next time. I won't say good-bye yet, Mike, for we want to talk it over once more with General Nuñez when I go aboard."

" 'T is a hard choice to make," reflected the experienced chief gunner's mate. "Only a fool will tell ye that the signal of duty is always easy to read. Look at meself, for instance. Here I went and jumped ship in the Navy to take on with these *Cubanos* an' help 'em fight for liberty. Does it make me a blackguard or a hero? I wonder. See you later. We've got to rustle this stuff."

There was to be no farewell word with Mike Walsh. He was on the beach and we were on the Dauntless, as it so happened, when the last surf-boat left the ship. No sooner had it cast off than Johnny O'Brien shouted to the mate:

"All clear! Your men aboard? Then let those boats go. We won't bother to pick 'em up empty. Cut that cable. I'm sort of anxious to get out of here."

The ship was churning ahead as the axe bit through the hempen strands. The Cubans in the last surf-boat ceased rowing to wave their hats and yell *adios* and good luck. On the white beach the rest of the company stood silently watching the departure. Conspicuous among them was the strong, indomitable figure of Mike Walsh, a leader of men and a master of circumstances. McCready and I flourished handkerchiefs and shouted something. Then we walked to the other side of the deck. We were very unhappy.

This last glimpse of Mike was like a poignant reproach. Newspaper work inspires a spirit of tenacious and ungrudging loyalty in the hearts of the young men whose vocation it is, and this constrained us to seek another filibustering voyage, but the sense of loyalty to Mike Walsh was no less imperative, and there you were — one of those riddles for which there is no satisfactory answer. General Nuñez broke into the gloom of the conversation. He was in excellent spirits. The enterprise had been highly successful. Again he assured us that we had done the right thing. He was buoyantly sanguine of getting us away in another expedition, possibly in a week or two.

"It sounds convincing enough," sighed McCready, "but I feel like a whipped pup."

"So do I, Mac, confound it. The trouble is that we forgot we were newspaper men, and the big stunt seemed to be to play it to a finish with our friends of the *Tres Amigos*. Nobody ever did find it agreeable to lead a double life."

We fretted and worried and attacked this problem of conduct again and again while the Dauntless ran out of Corientes Bay in the dusk and sought that familiar passage around Cape San Antonio. A kindly fortune had been vouchsafed this adventure, and the vessel sped homeward in smooth weather and without pursuit. General Nuñez and his aide left her off Key West and the course was laid for Jacksonville. There were no alarms until the cruiser Newark was sighted at anchor inside the jetty of the St. John's bar. Reluctant to answer awkward questions, Captain O'Brien hauled out to the northward and entered the river after dark.

Then he slipped in past the cruiser and encountered the Dolphin a little later. Both war vessels let their searchlights play on the Dauntless, but made no effort to detain her. They knew from experience that overhauling a suspected filibuster inbound would yield no evidence of crime. It was lucky that the two cruisers took this for granted, because the

Dauntless had certain passengers who would have been difficult to explain, the militant Jack Gorman and the Springfield rifle, the pathetic old Cuban with the derby hat, and two alleged correspondents, heavily armed, who looked like dissolute buccaneers.

That the steamer would be closely scrutinized and thoroughly searched by the Government officials in Jacksonville was anticipated as a matter of course, and therefore it was arranged that the incriminating passengers should be set ashore a few miles below the city. Sergeant Gorman and the sorrowful Cuban were told where to find friends who would take care of them.

XVII

A CASTAWAY OF THE COMMODORE

CAPTAIN O'BRIEN had strongly advised Ernest McCready and Ralph Paine to insert themselves into a convenient hole or other hiding place, and pull it in after them. They were sure to be entangled in the legal proceedings against the Three Friends, and the deputy marshals were already on the watch for them. Detention might mean missing the next expedition to Cuba and the fat would be in the fire. Paine had one of his happy ideas. Four miles below Jacksonville, on the river, was a comfortable hotel which catered to winter tourists. Here was the place to lie snug, and as it was enthusiastically explained to McCready:

"I spent a winter there with my folks when I was a boy. The landlord and my father are old friends, and we can dig in there as long as we like. Nobody can find us. And a few luxuries will recuperate us a whole lot."

It listened well, agreed McCready, who confessed that all this chatter about deputy marshals annoyed him. Roseland ought to be an excellent retreat for two fatigued pirates who were suffering from too much excitement. At eight o'clock in the evening the Dauntless dropped us off in a boat. Jack Gorman and the old Cuban wished to find a street-car into Jacksonville where they had been instructed to report to Señor Huau in the back room of the cigar-store. They were still a bit wan and shaky, but ever so much stronger than when the Cuban surgeon had refused to let them go ashore in Corientes Bay. Both men swore to meet us on the next expedition to the shores of bleeding Cuba.

Having convoyed these comrades to the highway, the two correspondents walked across the lawn of the Roseland hotel, lugging their impedimenta of saddle-bags, blankets, rifles, and what not. For lack of a mirror they had no conception of their forbidding appearance. Their big straw hats were cocked up in front, Cuban army fashion. Their clothing was torn and incredibly grimy, like their faces. Sun-painted noses, stubbled beards, and a furtive, guilty manner were details of the picture. One of them had forgotten to slip a holster from his belt. The other carried under his arm the sword of Gomez to which a machete was tied with bits of cord. From head to foot they were villainous.

Clattering along the piazza, they entered the large office or lounging room, and strode up to the desk, letting their baggage fall with a crash. Addressing a gentlemanly clerk, they asked to see the manager. The clerk mumbled something and shied violently. He was suddenly pop-eyed. The manager was out for the evening. He was in luck, thought the clerk. You could read it in his countenance.

"Oh, well, I can see him in the morning," was my easy reply. "Will you put us in a couple of rooms? We are not at all fussy."

"Not a room left, nothing whatever," gulped the clerk. "We can't possibly take you in. No use waiting."

McCready nudged me. There was a scraping of chairs in this large room, the sounds of hurrying feet, of agitated exclamations. The guests were moving out rapidly. Two or three elderly persons advanced to implore the clerk to telephone for the police, to do something, quick.

"Are we as bad as that?" I implored. "Look here, Mac, we have touched off another panic, just like the Vamoose."

McCready was scanning a printed placard posted beside the desk. It informed the public that the Roseland hotel was no longer a hotel, but a sanitarium for nervous invalids in need of rest and skilled treatment!

"*For nervous invalids — a quiet sanitarium,*" chuckled McCready. "A few of the patients are suffering a relapse.

Could you beat it? Come on, you old blunder-head, before we get locked up for disturbing the peace."

It was an error, no doubt, this breaking in on these invalids who had been afflicted with jumpy nerves even before they caught sight of us. Snatching up our strange baggage, we fled to the piazza and vanished in the darkness. There was a note of regret in the voice of McCready as he murmured:

"I am rather sorry they were so anxious to throw us out. I can't blame them harshly, but I, for one, can qualify as a nervous invalid in need of rest and skilled treatment. How about you?"

"On the verge of the yips, Mac. We are stranded on a lee shore. I can't show myself in one of the Jacksonville hotels. I know too many people in the town. Shall we camp in the woods until we can figure out the game?"

"Not me," declared McCready, halting in his tracks. " I am going to sleep in a bed to-night if I have to commit murder. Let's trail along into the city and trust to luck. She has been a good friend of ours in spite of your bright ideas."

"Ah, yes, that Roseland hotel was another of my bright ones," I sighed.

Timidly we boarded a street-car and were regarded with disquieting interest. If the other passengers did not point with pride, they at least viewed with alarm. Naturally I expected to encounter some old boyhood playmate, or one of my father's friends. As the car left the open country and passed into the eastern end of the city, more people got on. A few blocks and we should be among the stores and hotels of busy Bay Street.

The strain was breaking us. It was any port in a storm. McCready glanced out with a hunted air and spied a signboard on a corner. We laid hold of our unusual personal property and leaped from the car. Into the saloon we scuttled and the swinging doors closed behind us. Now those whose trade it is to write fiction are often accused of overworking the machinery of coincidence. Why, bless you, the coincidences of fact are stranger and more frequent than imagination ever invented. Here we were, with our feet on the brass rail and a kind bartender reaching for a bottle of private stock when a voice droned aloud from behind a newspaper at a table in a corner:

Havana via Key West. — It is known here that the steamer Three Friends has landed at Juaraco the expedition carried from Fernandina, and it is reported that Ralph D. Paine, the correspondent who was on the filibuster, has been captured and with three Cubans has been placed in the Cabañas fortress.

Somebody else at the table disputed this, saying:
"That's not so. I'll bet you the drinks on it. Henry Fritot saw Ralph Paine in Key West, at Palacho's café, after the Three Friends came back from Cuba. Henry's brother, Alfonso, told me so yesterday. They hid on a key somewheres."

"Maybe they did. I'd like to see Ralph Paine. We used to go duck-hunting together out Trout Creek way when we were in high school. And we were in swimming one day when a big alligator pretty near got him, and —"

Two feet slid off the brass rail. The kind bartender was left with the bottle in his hand and two untouched glasses upon the mahogany. Having rehearsed an exit from the Roseland sanitarium, we were experts at moving the aforesaid feet in the direction of a door. Before you could have winked twice we were out of that saloon. McCready breathed hard. He said he felt far from rugged. Whither? We had intended asking the bartender. At this moment there glimmered across the street, down by the river-front, a rudely lettered square of canvas with a candle behind it. The welcome words were:

LODGINGS. 25 CENTS

At full speed we steered for this humble haven and found a frowsy woman who led us up a rickety flight of stairs into two chicken-coops under the roof. There were cots in them.

McCready peered out of a dingy little window. The lights gleamed in the saloon across the way, symbols of sympathy and good cheer. Marooned again! We sighed and kicked off our boots. The romance of the Spanish Main was beginning to show signs of wear and tear. Compared with this unlovely place of confinement, Sweeney's Key West lodging-house had been palatial. Even John J. McCarthy, E-S-Q with a period, would have been greeted with open arms as a diversion. At least, he could have been sent across the street on an errand. We passed a melancholy night.

A nigger boy was sent with a note to Señor Huau next morning, informing him where two hunted correspondents could be found when the expedition was ready to sail. The messenger returned with a brief reply, instructing us to keep hidden and sit tight. Señor Huau was also thoughtful enough to send a bundle of newspapers. The "Times-Union" had published the document framed by the United States Government in the case against the Three Friends and her crew. The headlines and opening paragraphs were as follows:

THREE FRIENDS AS A PIRATE IS TAKEN — THE CUBAN STEAMER SEIZED AS SOON AS SHE ENTERED THIS PORT — SHE WENT TO SEA ARMED TO FIGHT SPANISH SHIPS — AT LEAST THAT IS THE CHARGE BROUGHT AGAINST THE VESSEL BY THE UNITED STATES GOVERNMENT

RALPH PAINE, MIKE WALSH, CAPTAIN LEWIS, AND OTHERS ARE ACCUSED — THE STEAMER IS RELEASED ON BOND UNDER THE COURT'S RULING AND DEPUTY MARSHALS PLACED ON BOARD

A steamer charged by the United States Government with being a pirate entered port yesterday, but instead of being an object of suspicion and hatred, was welcomed by the river craft and hundreds of citizens. The alleged pirate is the steamer Three Friends which tied up at the foot of Ocean Street. Before the vessel had been at the wharf half an hour, she was seized by the Collector of Customs of the port of St. John's on instructions from the Secretary of the

Treasury, and during the afternoon was taken in custody by United States Marshal McKay on a charge of piracy, the charge being made in a libel filed by Cromwell Gibbons, Assistant United States District Attorney, by direction of Attorney-General Harmon.

The libel is a peculiar one and is the only one of its kind ever filed by the United States Government against a regularly licensed American vessel, and while the charge is most serious the owners of the boat are not worried about the final outcome. . . .

This prefaced the document itself which was long and foolishly verbose, after the manner of lawyers. It was not stupid reading, however, for the pair of refugees in the twenty-five-cent lodging-house, and they perused it with scrupulous attention, particularly these concluding paragraphs which were the nubbin of the argument:

That the said steam vessel, Three Friends, to wit, on the 14th day of December, in the year of our Lord 1896, did within the Southern District of Florida and within the jurisdiction of this court, was then and there by certain persons, to wit, John O'Brien, William T. Lewis, John Dunn, Henry P. Fritot, August Arnau, Michael Walsh, Ralph D. Paine and divers other persons to the said attorneys unknown, heavily laden with supplies, rifles, cartridges, machetes, dynamite and other munitions of war, including one large twelve-pound Hotchkiss gun or cannon and a great quantity of shot, shell, and powder therefor, and said vessel was then and there manned by fifty men in addition to the crew, the names being to the said attorneys unknown, with intent that said vessel should be furnished, fitted out and armed for the purpose of being employed in the commission of piratical aggression, search, restraint and depressions upon the high seas, on the subjects, citizens, and property of the king of Spain in the island of Cuba, and wilfully and with intent to injure, and without legal authority or lawful excuse, to commit depredations upon the subjects, citizens and property of the king of Spain in the island of Cuba. . . .

That the said steam vessel, Three Friends, on or about the 21st day of December, while upon the high seas, in or about the neighborhood of the waters at the entrance of the San Juan River, in the island of Cuba, was then and there by certain persons, to wit, John O'Brien, William T. Lewis, John Dunn, Henry P. Fritot, August Arnau, Michael Walsh, Ralph D. Paine and divers other persons to the said attorneys unknown, furnished, fitted out and armed with wilful intent to commit piratical aggressions and depredations, and that said persons did then and there discharge the Hotchkiss gun or cannon mounted in the bow of the said vessel, on a certain Spanish gunboat, and that the persons being on the said vessel also discharged their rifles on the said Spanish gunboat, all of which was done wilfully and with intent to injure, and without legal authority or lawful excuse, the subjects, citizens and property of the king of Spain in the island of Cuba.

McCready read this aloud, in an impressive voice, and commented:

"A good copy-reader with a blue pencil could improve that stuff, but I must admit that it carries a punch. Again I regret that I was n't raised in this Jacksonville, as a playmate of some of these divers outlaws. I might have had my name in the cast. Ah, ha, listen to this shriek on the editorial page of the 'New York Journal.' Mr. Hearst seems to be getting all stirred up about you."

The United States Government has announced its purpose to proceed against the Americans who took part in the naval skirmish between the filibustering steamer Three Friends and two Spanish craft in the Caribbean Sea last month, as pirates!

THE PENALTY FOR PIRACY, IT WILL BE REMEMBERED, IS DEATH!

President Cleveland has obliged Spain in many ways, has done all in his power to save a corrupt and venal monarchy from paying the penalty for the barbarous oppression of the Cubans. He has put the United States Navy at the service of the Spaniards, and has trodden down the Constitution in order to balk the will of the American people.

But when he undertakes to have American citizens hanged by the neck until they are dead, because they beat off Spanish armed vessels which sought to board their craft, he exceeds even his limit of power.

THE JOURNAL does not question the zeal with which the Cleveland administration will strive to send these men to the gallows for the comfort of Spain, but it thinks the United States District Attorney of Jacksonville will have to send to Alaska for a jury not absolutely certain to acquit the accused.

"Um-m, I suppose you will plead not guilty," observed the cynical young McCready while he searched for a cigarette. "A fine chance you have to get off as a correspondent and a non-combatant and all that rubbish. You worked harder and cussed louder than any four Cubans, lugging cargo and rowing boats and shooting at the subjects, citizens and property of the King of Spain."

"It seems to me you were blazing away with a rifle and yelling your head off, Mac. Am I mistaken?"

"Absolutely. My only act of violence consisted in trying to beat the brains out of the volunteer fireman with the black whiskers. And then I was quite mad with fright. I refuse to be named in the indictment, and the coarse phrase used by Mr. Hearst, '*hanged by the neck*,' bores me beyond measure."

We found other newspaper comment, in a more temperate vein, including interviews with members of the Senate Committee on Foreign Relations. The predicament was not as black as it had been painted in the opinion of the "New York World" which discussed it in these consolatory words:

According to the views of Senator Cushman K. Davis and other students of international law, the courts must first prove the offense of which the Three Friends has been guilty. Will the officers of the Spanish gunboat come to the United States to confess their own defeat and discomfiture? The newspaper correspondents will not testify because they are now with the insurgent troops in Cuba. Captain O'Brien and Captain Lewis have sense enough to keep their mouths shut. The crew are silent. They are not testifying against themselves. Although the Spanish Minister, Dupuy De Lome, may call the attention of Secretary Olney officially to the depredations of the Three Friends, his action will be merely a formal discharge of his ministerial duties.

The whole episode is humiliating to Spanish prowess and naval skill and courage. If the Three Friends had been captured or sunk by the Spanish war vessels, Spain would have had all the glory and no American citizen could make lawful complaint. As it is, the

Cubans are delighted, the Americans are rather proud of the dexterity shown by the gunners of the Three Friends, and the Spanish are too disgusted to talk.

An item of news was discovered which more immediately concerned the fortunes of the two stowaways in the twenty-five-cent lodging-house than all this furor over the alleged act of piracy. The filibustering steamer Commodore had sailed for Cuba with a cargo of munitions a few days sooner than had been expected, having found an opportunity to load and get away. Off the Florida coast, near Mosquito Inlet, she had foundered in a heavy gale of wind. It was the Commodore in which we had planned to make the next voyage to Cuba, as advised by General Emilio Nuñez.

Among the survivors of this disaster was Stephen Crane who had sailed as a correspondent. He was a young man of only twenty-five years, but already a novel of his had been published which displayed the rare flame of genius. It was called "The Red Badge of Courage," a singularly vivid and profoundly intimate study of the experiences and emotions of a boyish private soldier in the American Civil War. Poor Crane never lived to hear the innumerable novelists of to-day prattle about realism as though they had invented it. Precious few of them can write like Stephen Crane who blazed his own trail a quarter of a century ago.

The news that Crane had been wrecked in the Commodore held a personal interest for me because we had known each other in Asbury Park during summer vacations from college. We had been engaged in the same sort of work, reporting for daily newspapers the frivolous activities of that swarming seashore resort. It was one way to earn money. A curious training, this, for Stephen Crane, the youth with the soul of a poet and a psychologist, whose *tour de force* was to be "The Red Badge of Courage" written when he had never seen a battlefield or heard a shot fired in action.

But even in that futile, inconsequential environment of

Asbury Park in midsummer, he had been learning his trade, the intuitive selection of detail, the ironic humor, the sensitive eye for color. I had taken writing seriously, as most young newspaper men do, hoping to do better things and striving to acquire the magic of the necessary word. It had made an impression, that Stephen Crane, loafing on the beach at Asbury Park, could write so entertainingly about a trifle so absurd as a misfit bathing suit.

A bath-clerk was looking at the world with superior eyes through a hole in a board. To him the freckled man made application, waving his hands over his person in illustration of a snug fit. The bath-clerk thought profoundly. Eventually, he handed out a blue bundle with an air of having phenomenally solved the freckled man's dimensions.

The latter resumed his resolute stride.

"See here," said the tall man, following him, "I bet you've got a regular toga, you know. That fellow could n't tell — "

"Yes, he could," interrupted the freckled man. "I saw correct mathematics in his eyes."

"Well, supposin' he has missed your size. Supposin' — "

"Tom," again interrupted the other, "produce your proud clothes and we'll go in."

The tall man swore bitterly. He went to one of a row of little wooden boxes and shut himself in. His companion repaired to a similar box.

At first he felt like an opulent monk in a too-small cell, and he turned round two or three times to see if he could. He arrived finally into his bathing-dress. Immediately he dropped gasping upon a three-cornered bench. The suit fell in folds about his reclining form. There was silence, save for the caressing calls of the waves without.

Then he heard two shoes drop on the floor in one of the little coops. He began to clamor at the boards like a penitent at an unforgiving door.

"Tom," called he, "Tom — "

A wail of wrath, muffled by cloth came through the walls. "You go t' blazes."

The freckled man began to groan, taking the occupants of the entire row of coops into his confidence.

"Stop your noise," angrily called the tall man from his hidden den. "You rented the bathing-suit, did n't you? Then —"

"It ain't a bathing-suit," shouted the freckled man at the boards. "It 's an auditorium, a ballroom, or something. It ain't a bathing-suit."

The tall man came out of his box. His suit looked like blue skin. He walked with grandeur down the alley between the rows of coops. Stopping in front of his friend's door, he rapped on it with passionate knuckles.

"Come out of there, y' ol' fool," said he, in an enraged whisper. "It 's only your accursed vanity. Wear it anyhow. What difference does it make? I never saw such a vain ol' idiot."

As he was storming, the door opened, and his friend confronted him. The tall man's legs gave way, and he fell against the opposite door.

The freckled man regarded him sternly.

"You 're an ass," he said.

His back curved in scorn. He walked majestically down the alley. There was pride in the way his chubby feet patted the boards. The tall man followed, weakly, his eyes riveted upon the figure ahead.

As a disguise the freckled man had adopted the stomach of importance. He moved with some sort of procession, across a board walk, down some steps, and out upon the sand.

There was a pug dog and three old women on a bench, a man and a maid with a book and a parasol, a seagull drifting high in the wind, and a distant, tremendous meeting of sea and sky. Down on the wet sand stood a girl being wooed by the breakers.

The freckled man moved with stately tread along the beach. The tall man, numb with amazement, came in the rear. They neared the girl.

Suddenly the tall man was seized with convulsions. He laughed and the girl turned her head.

She perceived the freckled man in the bathing-suit. An expression of wonderment overspread her charming face. . . .[1]

The two lugubrious prisoners in the lodging-house found something to talk about — Stephen Crane and the lost

[1] From the short story, "The Reluctant Voyagers." This is included in the latest collection of Stephen Crane's stories, *Men, Women, and Boats.* (Boni & Liveright, 1921.)

Commodore, "The Red Badge of Courage" which we were sufficiently intelligent to admire as a significant work of art, and the technique of writing in general. It was a merciful dispensation that for a little while we could forget ourselves and our own peculiar tribulations.

Then there climbed the rickety stairs a visitor who was like a tonic breeze. This was Napoleon Broward, managing owner of the Three Friends, who had commanded her in several expeditions to Cuba. He was a big, stout-hearted man, very able, who had been a sea-cook, fisherman, towboat skipper, wrecker, and sheriff.

"It does look as if you boys needed to be cheered up," said Napoleon Broward, after listening to our tale of woe. "All this piracy holler will blow itself out. They can't hang anybody. And no Grand Jury in Jacksonville will return indictments carrying any penalty like that. Shucks, folks would ride 'em out of town on a rail, and they know it."

"What will happen to the Three Friends and the divers persons, like Paine here?" anxiously inquired McCready.

"Oh, I reckon they may be tried for breaking the neutrality laws, same as usual. I'm sick and tired of giving bonds for the vessel and bail for Johnny O'Brien and the rest of the bunch. But I won't be able to get the ship to sea, not for some time. The United States Court is acting mighty mean and stubborn about it. They seem dead set on confiscatin' the Three Friends and sending all hands up the road for two or three years. Those busy-bodies at Washington talk powerful brash about piracy convictions and so on, but the sovereign State of Florida won't stand for any foolishness like that."

The very appearance of this tall, broad, courageous managing owner of the Three Friends was as comforting as his words. As the sheriff of Duval County, it had been taken for granted that whenever a bad nigger ran amuck, Napoleon Broward would go out and tote him in, dead or alive. As for this filibustering industry, he cheerfully regarded trouble with the United States Government as habitual. He went on to mention that they had plastered another libel on the Dauntless, for taking our expedition off No Name Key, and she was tied up with deputies aboard and Pinkertons watching her, like hound dogs with a 'possum up a tree. However, the owners hoped to habeas corpus or replevin her or something like that.

"The Government thinks you two boys are in Cuba," said he, "so there has been no active search for you. They have got you named in the legal papers, Ralph, and of course they'd like to grab McCready as a witness. All you have to do is hole in right like you are, and hope for things to break right. They can't prove a case unless somebody turns state's evidence. And that's where we've got 'em by the short hairs."

With this Napoleon Broward departed to attend to his own complicated affairs which seemed to disturb his massive composure not in the least. For several days longer we endured confinement in that wretched lodging-house which was no better than a jail. For exercise we ventured to walk out after dark, avoiding the busy end of Bay Street and taking the direction of suburban, unlighted East Jacksonville. Once we halted at the wooden bridge over Hogan's Creek, beside which stood a humble grocery store. And there McCready had to listen to a chapter of my earlier life.

"It was there I toiled, Mac, at the tender age of fifteen, and some day a tablet will mark the spot. The high school was rather primitive and I had received my diploma at fourteen, delivering a superb commencement oration called 'The Claims of the Age We Live In'! My father hoped to send me North for more schooling, but he could n't afford it just then, so while marking time I applied for a job in the Bridge Grocery Store and got it, at six per week.

"Besides selling grits, salt meat, molasses, and canned

goods to a clientèle largely colored, a high-school course in bookkeeping enabled me to keep a double-entry set. The groceryman was declared a bankrupt soon after I left him, but I am sure it was not the fault of the bookkeeping. There was another clerk, a red-headed boy named Pasco, and we used to climb aboard a rotten old derelict of a schooner beached in Hogan's Creek and imagine refitting her for a cruise in the Caribbean, and then the boss would catch us and read the riot act, and — "

"He should have taken a club to you," interrupted Mc-Cready, in a tired voice. "Look what that childish nonsense led you into."

"That Pasco kid would have made a bully pirate, Mac. But that was n't what I started to tell you. We did a big trade with the nigger hands in those sawmills over yonder by the river, especially on Saturday nights. And I invented the brilliant scheme of selling them molasses in paper bags. If a man was careful not to bump it, he could carry home a couple of quarts in a paper bag without leaking a drop.

"The store was crowded one Saturday night when two strapping niggers got into an argument. Instead of reaching for a razor, one of them swung a two-quart bag of molasses and smote the other on the head. You never saw such a gorgeous explosion. That store *rained* molasses. Every nigger's wool was full of it. And of course it touched off a general ruction, and every other mill-hand that had *his* molasses in a paper bag hit the nearest nigger behind the ear with it. Then the deadly weapons got mixed up with it, and the boss had to send a hurry call for the police, and the Bridge Grocery Store was a wreck. I offered my resignation and it was instantly accepted. But it was a bright idea, Mac, selling molasses in paper bags."

"I have been in contact with your bright ideas," ungraciously spoke McCready. "They usually explode."

At length, the drab life of the lodging-house aroused in us

a desperate mood. After nightfall we sallied forth and chartered a cruising hack, imploring the negro navigator on the box to find a quiet place where a decent dinner could be ordered.

"Yessuh, I knows jes' th' restaurant wid teenty little rooms fenced off same as box-stalls where nobody don't meddle in other folkses business."

We dived into the musty hack, buttoned the curtains down, and he flogged the bony steeds. The café was excellent, as it turned out, and we lingered in a comfortable seclusion. Two men were dining in another curtained alcove adjoining, and the voice of one sounded vaguely familiar. It was not identified, however, until he began to read aloud to his companion something which was evidently in manuscript. He stopped reading to say:

"Listen, Ed, I want to have this *right*, from your point of view. How does it sound so far?"

"You've got it, Steve," said the other man. "That is just how it happened, and how we felt. Read me some more of it."

Now I knew who these two men were, Stephen Crane and Captain Edward Murphy, commander of the lost filibustering steamer Commodore. Last to leave the sinking vessel, they had flung themselves into a skiff with the cook and an oiler. After struggling all night to keep the little skiff afloat, they had been washed ashore in a heavy surf which had drowned the oiler. Stephen Crane's story, as he wrote a first draft of it shortly after the event, and as we overheard bits of it in the restaurant, was called "The Open Boat." It was then, and still is, one of the finest short stories in the English language.

It was deeply interesting, to be long remembered, this listening to these two men discuss their mournful and terrible experience made the more realistic by the passages from Stephen Crane's story as he read them aloud to the fine young Irish shipmaster.

The injured captain, lying in the bow, was at this time buried in that profound dejection and indifference which comes, temporarily at least, to even the bravest and most enduring, when, willy-nilly, the firm fails, the army loses, the ship goes down. The mind of the master of a vessel is rooted deep in the timbers of her, though he commands for a day or a decade; and this captain had on him the stern impression of a scene in the grays of dawn, of seven turned faces and later a stump of a topmast with a white ball on it that slashed to and fro at the waves, went lower and lower, and down. Thereafter there was something strange in his voice. Although steady, it was deep with mourning and of a quality beyond oration or tears.

"Keep her a little more south, Billie," said he.

"A little more south, sir," said the oiler in the stern. . . .

A silence in the alcove and Captain Edward Murphy commented:

"The Commodore was a rotten old basket of junk, Steve, but I guess I did feel something like that when she went under. How do you wind it up, when poor old Billie was floating face down and all those people came running down to pull us out of the breakers?"

Then he saw the man who had been running and undressing, and undressing and running, come bounding into the water. He dragged ashore the cook, and then waded toward the captain; but the captain waved him away and sent him to the correspondent. He was naked — naked as a tree in winter, but a halo was about his head, and he shone like a saint. He gave a strong pull, and a long drag, and a bully heave at the correspondent's hand. The correspondent, schooled in the minor formulæ, said, "Thanks, old man." But suddenly the man cried, "What's that?" He pointed a swift finger. The correspondent said, "Go."

In the shallows, face downward, lay the oiler. His forehead touched sand that was periodically, between each wave, clear of the sea.

The correspondent did not know all that transpired afterward. When he achieved safe ground he fell, striking the sand with each particular part of his body. It was as if he had dropped from a roof, but the thud was grateful to him.

It seemed that instantly the beach was populated with men with blankets, clothes, and flasks, and women with coffee-pots and all the remedies sacred to their minds. The welcome of the land to the men from the sea was warm and generous; but a still and dripping shape was carried slowly up the beach, and the land's welcome for it could only be the different and sinister hospitality of the grave.

When it came night, the white waves paced to and fro in the moonlight, and the wind brought the sound of the great sea's voice to the men on shore, and they felt that they could then be interpreters.

"Do you like it or not, Ed?" asked Stephen Crane.

"It's good, Steve. Poor old Billie! Too bad he had to drown. He was a damn good oiler."

When there came a lull in their talk, Paine and McCready pushed the curtain aside and made a party of it. Here were four of us, all in the same boat, as one might say, foregathered by a singular chance, and our combined experiences embraced all the vicissitudes of filibustering. And so we sat and wove together those recent voyages of the Three Friends and the Dauntless and the Commodore. Young Captain Murphy was a man without a ship, but he hoped to get another one and play the game again.

Stephen Crane had never been robust and there was not much flesh on his bones, at best. Sallow and haggard, he looked too fragile to have endured his battle for survival with the furious sea, but his zest for adventure was unshaken. His thin face, mobile and very expressive, brightened when he talked of attempting another voyage. His indifference to danger was that of a fatalist. In appearance, in the careless indifference to conventions, in a manner of speech extraordinarily brilliant when his interest was aroused, there were many suggestions of Robert Louis Stevenson.

Incessantly smoking cigarettes, the long fingers straying to the straggling brown mustache, Crane sat slumped in his chair and discussed the fine art of filibustering in a drawling, unemotional voice, now using the slang of the street and the bar-room, again flashing in some bit of finished prose like this:

"The captain went to the stoke-room and what he saw as he swung down the companion suddenly turned him hesitant and dumb. He had served the sea for many years, but this fire-room said something to him which he had not heard in his other voyages. Water was swirling to and fro with the roll of the ship, fumbling greasily around half-strangled machinery that still attempted to perform its duty. Steam arose from the water, and through its clouds shone the red glare of the dying fires. As for the stokers, death might have been with silence in this room. One lay in his berth, his hands under his head, staring moodily at the wall. One leaned against the side, and gazed at the snarling water as it rose, and its mad eddies among the machinery. In the unholy red light and gray mist of this stifling, dim inferno they were strange figures with their silence and immobility. The wretched ship groaned deeply as she lifted, and groaned deeply as she sank into the trough, while hurried waves then thundered over her with the noise of landslides."

XVIII

FAREWELL TO THE SWORD OF GOMEZ

A DAY or so after the night with Stephen Crane, McCready received a telegram from the "New York Herald," sent in care of Señor Huau. It commanded him to return to Broadway and there await the plans of the next filibustering expedition instead of hiding somewhere in Florida. How could a nervous editor, dealing out assignments in Herald Square, be expected to comprehend the intricacies of life in the Caribbean? He had sent McCready to join the Cuban insurgents weeks and weeks ago, and he was n't there.

"No use of my wiring any more explanations," sighed McCready. "Imagine trying to make them understand. Here is where the combination breaks up, old man. And I did want to be among those present when you handed the sword to Gomez."

"I am still some distance from the big scene, Mac. What *am* I going to do without you?"

"*Viva Cuba Libre! A la machete! Caramba! Piratos!*" answered he, which sentiments seemed to do as well as any others. That same night witnessed the sad separation. I went to the railroad station in a hack with McCready, or as near as I dared approach that populous terminus, and bade him *adios*. He was a prey to consuming anxiety at the thought of trying to unwind the tangled skein of circumstances to the satisfaction of a hard-driven managing editor. How absurd to say that youth is care-free and happy! Youth takes itself too seriously for that. It discovers every little while that life is blighted, and suffers accordingly.

I was left to worry alone, which was much more distressing than worrying in partnership. No message of recall came from Mr. William Randolph Hearst. He had so many correspondents wandering about in strange places that one more or less made no difference, and Ralph Paine was lost in the shuffle. Existence alone in that unspeakable lodging-house was intolerable. Twenty-five cents a day was too much to pay for solitary confinement. Any more of it and there would be no lucid intervals at all.

A despairing wail for succor brought the interposition of the benevolent Señor Huau. He had notified my father of the whereabouts of his disreputable son, and that robust clergyman, the Reverend Samuel Delahaye Paine, who had been a bold soldier in his youth, hastened to Jacksonville from his home in Sanford, bringing my only sister with him. They were invited to the house of Señor Huau and I was smuggled in to meet them by night. It was a most enjoyable surprise party for all concerned. The career of piracy was warmly endorsed by that admirable parent of mine, who possessed a sense of humor. He had this agreeable suggestion to offer:

"You know J. V. Fairhead, who was one of the elders of the Ocean Street Church during my pastorate. I saw him to-day and he will be very glad to have you stay with him — in hiding, of course. He has a tower room where you can look up and down the street, and there is a convenient side door if you wish to leave suddenly. He is a discreet man, and he understands — er — why you are in Jacksonville."

It was novel but most attractive — for a pirate to take shelter with a Presbyterian elder, and I moved into the Fairhead residence that very night. The tower room was blissfully comfortable and strategically advantageous. But the days dragged very slowly past, and although the ceremony of being hanged by the neck had ceased to be painfully imminent, no summons came from Señor Huau.

The Three Friends and the Dauntless were still tied up hard and fast, and no pretext was plausible enough to release them. No sooner were bonds furnished by the owners to cover one dereliction than other proceedings were instituted. There was every reason to conclude that the United States Government intended to put a stop to this reckless business of shooting up the Spanish Navy. First thing you knew, Captain Johnny O'Brien might damage an expensive Spanish battleship or cruiser.

Finally Ralph Paine betook himself to a quiet little hotel in Green Cove Springs, twenty-five miles up the St. John's River, where a fugitive from justice would be unlikely to find acquaintances. He changed his name and had difficulty in remembering his *alias* when visiting the post-office in quest of letters from the Cuban conspirators in Jacksonville. Meanwhile the piracy case was hanging fire for lack of witnesses. Those honest sailormen could not be expected to take the stand and confess to the grave crime of which they were accused. Stephen Crane had them in mind when he wrote:

"I have got twenty men at me back who will fight to the death," said the warrior to the old filibuster.

"And they can be blowed, for all me," replied the old filibuster. "Common as sparrows — cheap as cigarettes. Show me twenty men with steel clamps on the mouths, with holes in their heads where memory ought to be, and I want 'em. But twenty brave men merely? I'd rather have twenty brave onions."

At the end of a month of irksome inaction in Green Cove Springs, the prospect was no brighter. Filibustering was in a bad way. It was time to admit to one's self that he had tried and failed. And failure hurts like a wound when one is too young to realize that every life is strewn with thwarted ambitions, with vanished dreams of achievement. Yes, we had tried, McCready and I, but it made it no less ignominious in our sight that we had been compelled to quit.

If this were fiction in the romantic vein, instead of truth sober and unadorned, the glittering sword would have been delivered to General Maximo Gomez as the neat climax of the tale. The melancholy fact was that I had carried the costly bauble some 5000 miles and had been almost frightened to death times beyond counting, and now all that could be done was to turn Mr. Hearst's two-thousand-dollar gift over to Señor Huau as an official custodian, request a receipt for it, and wish him luck in forwarding it to Maximo Gomez.

The sequel was even more of an anticlimax. Señor Huau, it seems, sent the sword to the wife of General Gomez in San Domingo and she treasured it until she was able to rejoin her warrior husband, after Spain had been driven out of Cuba by American ships and soldiers. It is credibly related that when fiery old Gomez examined the sword, so splendid, so costly, so ornate, he exploded in one of his turbulent denunciations, this white-bearded, gimlet-eyed, shriveled little man who was feared by friend as well as foe.

"Ah-h-h, it cost so much money? A trinket good for nothing? Would I be so shameful as to wear it instead of my San Domingo machete? Nonsense! Those imbeciles in New York, with two thousand dollars to waste! It would have bought shoes for my barefooted men, shirts for their naked backs, cartridges for their useless rifles. Take it away. It exasperates me. If the *majace*, the idiot who was sent on the stupid errand, had found me in camp, I should have been tempted to stick him in the belly with his wretched gold sword!"

This, I assert, was realism to please the taste of the modern school of dyspeptic novelists, the severe avoidance of a happy ending and everything gone to pot for the hero. The only bright phase of the finish concerned Michael Walsh, chief gunner's mate. He had reason to feel as happy as Pollyanna, for the report was received through Cuban sources that he had blown up a railroad bridge in Pinar del Rio, and a Spanish troop train with it, and had thereby earned swift promotion. That nitroglycerin must have been converted into potent dynamite, after all.

For years I sought to find some trace of the admirable Mike Walsh. The most reliable information was that when peace came to distracted Cuba, he settled in a fishing village on the coast and found prosperity and contentment, organizing the community, of course, and lording it as a sagacious and benevolent dictator. He was a rare jewel of a man, and here's to his health!

Republics are not always ungrateful. Until old age overtook him, Captain "Dynamite Johnny" O'Brien was in the employ of the Cuban Government. When the United States finally raised the wreck of the Maine from the mud of Havana harbor, it was towed out to sea for ceremonial burial and Captain O'Brien was chosen to act as pilot in honor of his heroic services in the cause of Cuban freedom. He was pensioned by the Cuban Government and died full of years and extraordinary experiences.

At a dinner in New York, in celebration of his eightieth birthday, President Menocal of Cuba was personally represented by Señor Victor Barranco who brought this message:

In Cuba's darkest days, Captain O'Brien's clear head, stout heart, and steady hand guided the ships which carried the arms and ammunition to the patriots in the field. The pay was low and often came in driblets. The risk of imprisonment for violating the neutrality laws was great, and greatest of all was the risk of capture and death at the hands of the Spanish patrol fleet.

Our brave and gallant *"Captain Unafraid"* chanced these dangers and sacrifices because of his innate love of liberty and his warm sympathy for a people struggling against tyranny. By direction of the President of the Republic of Cuba, your old companion in arms, Johnny, I tender you, for the Cuban people, our renewed testimonial of affection and gratitude, and our best wishes on this your birthday.

Even in this land of opportunity it would not be easy to find a career, for romance and inspiration, to match that of Napoleon Broward, the stalwart managing owner of the Three Friends. As orphan boys not yet in their teens, he and his brother Montcalm had been left to shift for themselves in a log cabin with a wattled chimney on a forlorn farm in a wilderness near the St. John's River. They decided to stand by the old homestead and fight it out alone, asking no help of their kinsfolk. As best they could, these ragged urchins made their crops and kept track of their drove of razor-back hogs and struggled with their primitive housekeeping.

The usual meal was a mess of hominy, sweet potatoes, and a piece of pork boiled together in a pot over a fire of fat pine knots. Panthers screamed in the near-by hammock land, and after supper the lads would bar the door, stand the shotgun against the wall close to the bed, and stick a bowie knife in a chink between the logs alongside the corn-husk pillows. Forlorn and lonesome and fearful these babes in the woods must have been, but they were not quitters, and they lived and toiled in this fashion for two years.

Then an uncle persuaded Napoleon to work in his logging camp, and, Montcalm refusing to be left behind, the stripling brothers were raftsmen for another two years. They were really getting on in the world, for they next became wage-earners on their grandfather's farm, Napoleon at seventy-five dollars a year, Montcalm at fifty. When Napoleon was seventeen he forsook the land and sought to improve his fortunes on the water, shipping as cook and assistant fireman on a small St. John's River steamboat. He succeeded in saving enough money to board with the lighthouse keeper at the fishing hamlet of New Berlin for two school terms, and this completed his education so far as the inside of books was concerned.

The spirit of adventure led him to ship in a lumber schooner bound to Boston. There he was discharged in the dead of winter. He had never before seen snow, but, shivering in his Kentucky jeans and gingham shirt, the boy from Florida sought employment in this frigid region with no thought of retreating to his balmy homeland. Whooping-cough laid him on his back until all his money was gone. As soon as he was able to get about again, he decided to try to ship aboard one of the fishing fleet bound to the Banks. Fearing lest his racking cough might cause rejection as an able-bodied sea-man, he waited until he hove in sight of Captain Newcomb of the Emma Linwood, and then scurried into a near-by store to gulp down a dipper of water. Having checked the cough-ing spell, he hurriedly asked the skipper if he needed a man and was able to pass muster.

In his flimsy clothing, Napoleon Broward sailed for the Newfoundland Banks with the ice-floes grinding off Boston harbor and the spray freezing where it flew on deck. Yearn-ingly he eyed the woolens and boots of his shipmates, but the boy had learned to take his medicine and work for what he got. During the voyage he whipped the bully of the fo'-castle and gained merit with the hard-bitted skipper by accepting the hardships and dangers with a cheerful, dogged fortitude. His speech was drawling and slow, but his hands were not soft and he stripped like an athlete in training.

From fisherman to seaman before the mast in a south-bound sailing vessel, Napoleon Broward worked his way home again and continued to follow salt water, as a roust-about and wheelsman. By the time he was thirty, this almost illiterate deck-hand had become so much of a man in river traffic that he was able to buy a part ownership in a steamer which carried passengers and mail between Mayport and Palatka. His courage and ambition were not to be denied, and Napoleon Broward was already known the length of the St. John's as a man who "toted fair," talked straight, and handled men and steamboats with masterful energy.

His business ventures prospered, and his reputation in Jacksonville was such that when he decided to stay ashore as a candidate for sheriff of Duval County, his election was in the nature of a landslide, and he held the office for nine years. Six feet by two hundred and ten pounds were his dimensions, and, kept in fighting trim by a battering life, he was a first-class sheriff for any emergency. If you asked the particulars of some stormy episode in a turpentine camp, he would reply in the lazy, placid accents of the native Floridian:

"Oh, I just located him and got him. I reckon that's all there was to it."

While Napoleon was engaged in his shore-going activities Montcalm, who had become a successful towboat man, looked after the river interests, and the brothers formed a partnership. In 1895 they came to the conclusion that a powerful seagoing tug built for offshore towing and wrecking along the Florida Reef would be a profitable investment. The estimated cost of building such a vessel was forty thousand dollars, and they could scrape together less than half the amount. A third partner, George Decottes, was enlisted, but like the Broward brothers he had more pluck than cash, and the stout craft weathered severe financial stress before she was launched from a Jacksonville shipyard.

They named her the Three Friends and expected to set her at her lawful business, but her paint was no more than dry when secretive, soft-footed men were exploring the Florida ports in behalf of the Cuban Republic, searching to find vessels fit to engage in filibustering. These agents offered the Broward brothers ten thousand dollars for every cargo the Three Friends might be able to land on the coast of Cuba. Napoleon Broward commanded the vessel during her first voyage, preferring to share with his men whatever hazards were to be faced in this untried enterprise. As he told it to me, the adventure turned out as follows:

"Early in the winter of 1896, General Colasso and sixty-five men were hiding on the Gulf coast, waiting for a chance to run a cargo of arms. This expedition was loaded aboard a schooner which slipped down among the Florida Keys, while at the same time the Three Friends started from Jacksonville to meet her and transfer the men and stuff. Once across the St. John's bar, I removed the name boards from the pilot-house, and ordered no lights to be shown.

"The schooner was found at Indian Key, the transfer made, and the Three Friends sailed for a landing place on the north coast of Cuba, near Cardenas. It was new business to most of the men aboard and they shivered at the sight of a steamer's smoke. The Cuban pilot, who was relied upon to find the landing place, lost his bearings and in thick weather anchored the vessel fair abreast of a Spanish fort. The surf-boats, which we quickly filled with Cubans and cargo, had no sooner hit the beach than they found themselves in a hornet's nest. The men were fighting the Spanish garrison at close quarters, unable to retreat through the heavy surf, and the noise of the engagement soon drew a gunboat from Cardenas. I did n't want to lose my vessel, and I was n't going to forsake the men of my own crew who had rowed the boats ashore, so I told the hands that were left on board:

"'Don't use your guns. The firing will bring more gun-boats down on top of us. Get your axes and lie down under the bulwarks. If this pesterin' gunboat tries to board us, take her men as they come over the rail. There's two boats of our crew to come off from the beach and I won't leave 'em adrift.'

"The boats were recovered in the nick of time and the Three Friends stood out to sea with the Spanish gunboat popping at us, and crowding in chase.... Before we got very far toward Key West, the morning star suddenly showed through a rift in a cloud. Old John Dunn, the chief engineer, poked his head on deck for a gulp of cool air, mistook the star for a vessel's light driving straight at us, and rushed forward, while he hurled a tin plate and spoon over the rail, and shouted:

"'Durn you, Broward, throw the cargo overboard and lighten the vessel. The Spaniards have got us sure. Can't you see that masthead light showin' dead ahead of us?'"

The dashing success of the Three Friends, in voyage after voyage, won great popularity for the steamer and her crew throughout Florida, whose people could see no crime in the thrilling escapades that recalled the days of buccaneering. Sympathy with the Cuban cause was rampant and filibustering was regarded as a game of wits in which the Governments of Spain and the United States held the losing cards. Not a solitary conviction was secured against the Three Friends or her men. The prosecutions, which included the famous charge of piracy, were delayed and hampered by lack of evidence to build up a winning case until quashed by the declaration of war against Spain in 1898.

When there were no more cargoes to be landed on the beaches of Cuba, Napoleon Broward and his brother Montcalm took the Three Friends to Key West to employ her in the profitable business of pulling stranded vessels off the deadly Florida Reef. It was a heroic life which these brothers led as wreckers, fit only for the hardiest and bravest men and the most consummate seamanship. In storms when it was an even guess whether the towboat would float or founder, she was driven out to sea to race for the salvage of imperiled tramp or square-rigger. They took big risks, but they were gambling for handsome stakes, and the staunch Three Friends stayed under them.

In 1903 this towboat man, Napoleon Bonaparte Broward, announced his intention of making a fight for the Democratic nomination for Governor of Florida. His cause looked like a picturesque forlorn hope. The railroad and corporation interests were against him and nowhere were they more powerful than in the State of Florida.

"I don't intend to go after the folks in the cities," declared Napoleon Broward. "Their newspapers are against me, and they don't take me seriously. But I'm going to stump every cross-roads village between Fernandina and Pensacola and talk to the farmers and crackers and show 'em that their top ends were meant to be used for something better than hat-racks. I'm going to make them sit up and think. They won't mind mistakes in grammar if they find I'm talking horse sense."

Under forced draft, this big, forceful native son charted his course up and down and across Florida, hammering away at his fellows of the pine lands, scrub palmettoes, wire grass, and prairie, wasting no time in attempted eloquence, but telling them exactly what he proposed to do if they made him Governor. They flocked to hear him from curiosity, as the owner and master of the Three Friends, and they liked this new display of grit.

But they found also that he had employed a rarely retentive memory to pack his head full of facts and figures to buttress his arguments, and that he carried ammunition for fighting at long or short range. He had handled men for many years, and he had a masterful presence and address. He told them that what he wanted most to do was to safeguard and develop the public lands of the Commonwealth. His speeches carried the conviction that he was a strong and honest man who would fight in the last ditch for the gospel of the square deal, wherefore the Floridians elected him their Governor for four years. From start to finish, he had fought and won his own aggressive campaign against tremendous political odds.

Napoleon Broward's crusade to develop the public lands meant nothing less than an imperial scheme for the reclamation of the Florida Everglades. He preached it as the greatest possible benefit that could come to the State. For more than half a century engineers and public men had thrashed over this problem, agreeing that its solution would give to Florida more wealth than all the rest of her arable acreage. But nothing had been accomplished, in a large way. Like most men of adventure, Napoleon Broward had vision and imagination. As he told the folks of his State:

JOHN DUNN, CHIEF ENGINEER OF THE *THREE FRIENDS*, ON THE DECK OF HIS DREDGE IN THE FLORIDA EVERGLADES

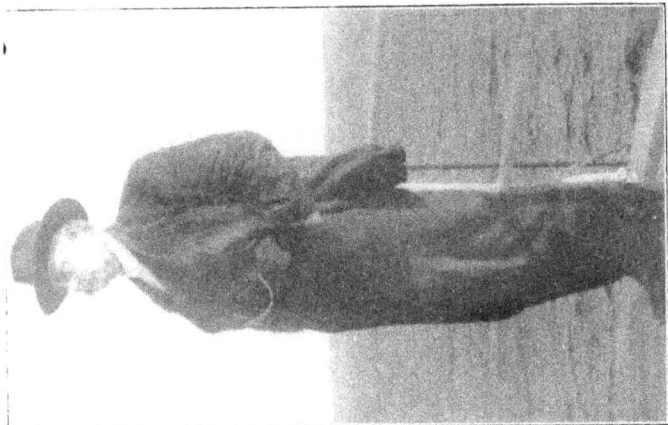

NAPOLEON BROWARD, FILIBUSTER, GOVERNOR OF FLORIDA, UNITED STATES SENATOR ON THE BRIDGE OF THE *THREE FRIENDS*

"Shall the sovereign people of Florida supinely surrender to a few land pirates and purchased newspapers and confess that they cannot knock a hole in a wall of coral and let a body of water obey a natural law and seek the level of the sea? To answer yes to such a question is to prove ourselves unworthy of freedom, happiness, or prosperity."

As Governor Broward he mobilized the energy and resources of the State to launch this reclamation project which would make available for cultivation three million acres of fat, black bottom land. He designed the first dredges which opened the main drainage canals from the Everglades to the tidal water of the east coast. When twenty governors and many senators and congressmen met at Memphis to discuss inland-waterways projects, Florida discovered that she had reason to be proud of her own governor. This self-taught towboat skipper talked with such convincing force and breadth of knowledge that he was cheered beyond all his fellow orators.

Later, at Baltimore, during a National Drainage Congress, Napoleon Broward was the most prominent figure of a distinguished company of delegates who elected him president of the organization. President Roosevelt found no more valuable and better-informed ally in his far-reaching plans for the conservation and development of the natural resources of the nation than Governor Broward, who was conspicuous among the governors called in convention at the White House to discuss these vital problems.

Because of this record, his people elected him to the United States Senate where he served with genuine distinction. His colleagues admired his personality and respected his ability. It was as Senator Napoleon Broward that he died, cut off in the prime of his vigor and usefulness, a man who had made his own career, who had received no favors from fortune.

While he was Governor of Florida, I made a trip into the

Everglades with him. An uncouth monster of a dredge was eating its way through the wilderness of submerged swamp where roamed a few Seminole Indians. In command of the dredge was a portly man in greasy overalls, grayer and stouter than of yore, but the same old John Dunn, once chief engineer of the Three Friends. Napoleon Broward had loyally provided his old shipmate and filibustering comrade with a comfortable berth.

"Durn my eyes, but I'm glad to see you, Ralph," shouted the veteran of the Caribbean. "This ain't nothin' like the good old days, is it? I was tellin' Broward that I get a restless fit now and then, even if I am growin' old and a family man at that. I had it on my mind to write you a letter. There's a lot of them old churches and cathedrals along the Central American coast with all kinds of gold and jewels in 'em. I have a notion that a fast boat and a few good men could pull off some raids if they planned it right, and get away with it. If we could get hold of Mike Walsh, say, and some more like him, we might clean up a nice piece of loot."

Regretfully I declined to consider it. Of necessity the point of view had changed, for I had become a family man. A buccaneer born in the wrong century was John Dunn, as genial a law-breaker as ever clapped a clamp on a safety-valve and put the boots to her. He, too, has slipped his cable and made the last, dark voyage, and may he sip his grog and spin his yarns in the haven of Fiddler's Green where the souls of all good mariners go.

Twenty years after the famous naval engagement of the Rio San Juan, I was making a voyage in a five-masted schooner out of Portland, Maine. While she loaded coal in Norfolk, I happened to be idling on the balcony of a shipping office which overhung the river. Outward-bound there steamed past a long, powerful seagoing towboat painted white. Her appearance was familiar, even before I read the name on her stern, *Three Friends, Jacksonville.*

Of the figures at the wheel-house windows, one was much like jovial Captain "Bill" Lewis. The Three Friends was like a phantom ship, conjuring memories of youth and high adventure and bitter disappointment. Staunch and faithful, she was still towing off the St. John's bar, or wrecking on the Florida Reef, or trailing the strings of barges coastwise, as far as Baltimore and Norfolk. A gallant ship with a peculiar distinction! She had fought the only sea-fight of the Cuban Revolution and earned for her company the honorable stigma of piracy.

Ernest W. McCready is now a substantial newspaper publisher in Canada, and occasionally he visits my New Hampshire farm for a serious-minded week of golf. Not long ago he had unlimbered an excellent brassie shot, but after watching the flight of the ball he stood wrapped in meditation. Without any preface whatever, he turned to say:

"What do you suppose Mike Walsh really thought of us, when we let him hop ashore without us in Corientes Bay?"

"You can search me, Mac, but I know I have waked up in the middle of the night, more than once, to fret about it."

XIX

"REMEMBER THE MAINE!"

In January of 1898, a dozen or more staff correspondents of as many newspapers were sent to Wilkes-Barre to report by wire the trial of Sheriff Martin and his deputies for shooting down seventy miners as a bloody episode of a strike in the anthracite region during the preceding autumn. The sheriff and the coal operators called it a battle, but it was popularly known as "the Lattimer massacre."

As a sequel, a brigade of the Pennsylvania National Guard, three thousand strong, had been hurried to that bleak and somber region of culm-banks, unkempt hamlets, and polyglot toilers. For several weeks the rebellious resentment was repressed by infantry regiments, cavalry troops, and field batteries scattered over a wide area. It was the next thing to war.

Most of these newspaper correspondents had been in the field during this campaign and when they met again in Wilkes-Barre to "cover" the spectacular court proceedings, it was like a congenial reunion of old friends. Among them was Ralph Paine whom a tolerant managing editor had forgiven and welcomed back to Philadelphia after his wanderings with the sword of Gomez. The young man could lay claim to none of the wisdom of Ulysses, but he could piously echo the declaration that "many griefs also in his mind did he suffer on the sea, although seeking to preserve his own life."

This prolonged tour of duty in Wilkes-Barre was unusually pleasant, an interesting story to handle and leisure enough to enjoy the hospitality of the clubs and the homes which had opened their doors to the visiting correspondents.

The community had determined to regard them as a social event. No matter how diverting the evening's entertainment might be, however, it was their habit to saunter into the telegraph office before bedtime in order to make certain that their stuff had been forwarded without delay. One of them was chatting with the operators a little before midnight, on February 15th, when this brief bulletin was picked off the wire:

Battleship Maine blown up in Havana harbor. Most of her crew killed. Probably a Spanish plot.

The startled correspondent loped up the street and burst into the Press Club, where he wrecked a poker game. It was like tossing a cannon cracker into the room. The tragic news meant war with Spain. The opinion was unanimous. War was a novelty almost incredible to an American generation which had grown up in happy ignorance of it. In the clamorous discussion the correspondents forgot the sheriff and his panicky deputies who had riddled the marching miners with sawed-off shotguns. Every man was hoping for the summons to proceed post-haste to Havana. The big story was there.

The round of work next day was perfunctory and absent-minded. Then the first lucky correspondent flourished his telegram and the rest of them trooped to the station to see him off and made an undignified amount of noise about it. My own orders were not long deferred and it was *au revoir* but not farewell to those left behind, for this was one of the happy phases of the trade we followed, that you met your newspaper comrades again in Havana or San Francisco, in London or Shanghai, and were not in the least surprised.

The route to Cuba this time was respectable, by rail to Tampa and thence by passenger steamer, and not in a low-browed filibustering packet with a crew of piratical shipmates. There was one disturbing regret. In the haste of departure the young man had failed to stage a parting scene with some particularly nice girl or other. It was missing a dramatic opportunity, this dashing off to war at a moment's notice. Destiny was kind, however, for while waiting a day in Tampa for the steamer Olivette, he met a most delightful girl who happened to be an old friend.

Promptly he invited her, with her mother, for a drive in one of those leisurely two-horse vehicles which hovered in the offing to cajole the winter tourist. All went well until the drowsy old negro took a sandy road out among the pines and palmettoes and the live-oak hammock land. There he attempted to drive across a railroad track at a blind crossing. The infatuated young man turned and beheld a freight train not twenty feet away and coming rapidly. The paralyzed colored person endeavored to yank his horses to one side, but they were deliberate animals, faithful rather than sudden or impulsive.

The agitated Ralph Paine was clutching at the ladies and yelling to them to jump. An instant later they experienced the sensation of being in collision with a freight train. It side-wiped the unfortunate vehicle and tossed it clear of the track, horses and all. The elderly African described a splendid parabolic flight and landed upon his head, which was, of course, impervious to injury. He could have done it no better with numerous rehearsals.

The ladies were flung into the deep sand while the freight cars thundered past no more than a few inches from their heads. The young man responsible for this little pleasure excursion crawled out of the wreckage of the carriage and discovered that he was not a total loss. The poor ladies were alive, but somewhat incoherent, and he made them as comfortable as possible with cushions and robes. Strange to say, they had suffered nothing more than slight bruises.

Meanwhile the freight train was halted and the crew came running back. The engineer was amazed at finding nobody killed, and he relieved his emotions by swearing heartily at the old fool of a nigger, who had troubles of his own, with his horses crippled and the carriage so much splintered junk.

In a passing wagon the ladies and the correspondent were conveyed to the Tampa Bay Hotel. That same night he sailed for Havana with a strip of plaster on his brow and various aches in his bones. The incident is here recalled merely to indicate what risks and hazards a correspondent may encounter in the line of duty. In this instance it cannot be denied that it was an obvious duty to devote one's self to a girl so uncommonly charming as she was, and it would have been a pity to have missed the cue for a farewell remark, that it was a freight train which really threw us together.

There was nothing to make light of in the scene disclosed when the steamer entered Havana harbor on that February morning — the ghastly tangle of twisted steel protruded above the surface of the water, all that was left of a powerful, immaculate American battleship — boats clustered about it and the grotesque helmets of divers searching for the shattered bodies and fragments of two hundred and sixty-six brave men who had worn the Navy blue — and a barge piled with waiting coffins. It bit into one's memory as though etched with acid.

The tragedy had stirred the Spanish people of Havana, soldiers and civilians, not so much with sympathy as with a hostile spirit which smouldered like tinder ready for the spark. They had bitterly resented the act of sending the Maine to Havana when diplomatic relations were strained almost to breaking, and they were the more incensed when Spanish agencies were openly suspected of causing the disaster. They foresaw war as the result and felt no fondness for Americans. It was a very interesting city to be in, with the lid likely to pop off at any time. And yet the Spanish army officers displayed their traditional courtesy of race when you met them in the cafés. One of them took pains to explain to me, tracing a map on the tablecloth:

"If there is war, Spain will conquer your boastful United States. How? Permit me to show you in a word, Señor. The thing is absurdly simple. In the opinion of foreign experts, our navy is stronger than the American fleet which recruits the riff-raff of all nations, British deserters, Scandinavians, and so on. As for the army? What is yours? A regular force of twenty-five thousand men, a bagatelle! Spain has two hundred thousand men in Cuba. These are seasoned troops. She will pick one hundred thousand of these, leaving the others to garrison the island against the insurgents. This army of invasion will divide itself, one column landing at a Gulf port, the other on the Atlantic coast, perhaps at Charleston. Marching north and sweeping your handful of regulars before them, they will sustain themselves off the country, exacting fabulous ransom from your rich cities, and unite to capture New York, Baltimore, Washington. Ah, you Yankee dollar-hunters. So wealthy a nation and yet so helpless! May I offer you another glass of cognac, Señor?"

The populace was not so courteous. The talk of stringing the Yankee pigs to lamp-posts was prevalent, and the special target for threats was the American Consul-General, Fitz-hugh Lee. A fighting Lee of Virginia of the old strain was this ruddy, jocund gentleman with the white mustache and the tuft on his chin. In his youth he had commanded the cavalry forces of Robert E. Lee, and he had led the last charge of the Lost Cause. Would you have expected such a man to quit Havana merely because sundry wild-eyed Spanish partisans expressed an intention of killing him?

Punctually at the dinner hour he took his accustomed seat at a table in the Hotel Inglaterra, close to a long window which opened on the pavement. There the passing crowds beheld him and he could overhear their remarks, which were often superheated. Suave, leisurely, he lingered to smoke a cigar and sip his wine, and perhaps reading aloud, with a chuckle, to the correspondents who dropped in to join him, a few more of the anonymous letters that breathed death and destruction. He was urging Americans to leave Havana and most of them obeyed, barring naval officers, correspondents, and a few business men.

It was done with kindly forethought, this choice of a conspicuous place in the café every night. Not that Fitzhugh Lee had to parade any proof of his own courage, but he knew it would hearten the rest of us who might feel nervous symptoms. And after a chat with him over the coffee, one felt ashamed of dodging dark streets or the slums down by the water-front.

"Well, boys, you can stick around town until you see me grab my hat," he would say. "I don't plan on getting left when the last boat pulls out, and I can move mighty spry, let me tell you. I learned how to retreat in good order a good many years before you-all were born."

Meanwhile the American Naval Board of Inquiry was investigating the pitiful wreckage of the Maine and taking the testimony of the survivors. Upon the verdict hung the declaration of war. One bit of evidence seemed conclusive. We could behold it for ourselves while we watched the divers at work day after day. The keel-plates of the battleship had been blown to the surface. They were identified as such by the naval constructors familiar with the ship's building plans. No internal explosion, of magazines or boilers, could have driven these bottom plates upward, to the surface of the harbor. And this, in a word, was the final verdict, that the Maine could not have destroyed herself by accident, but the cause is still an unsolved riddle of history.

And now the center of tension and expectancy shifted to Key West where the American fleet soon mobilized in command of Rear Admiral William T. Sampson. Long since obsolete, sent to the scrap-heap or used as targets for flocks of bombing planes, those battleships, Iowa, Indiana, Massachusetts, were the pride of the nation and superbly efficient for their day. The Navy was ready, as usual, in respect of personnel and discipline, and the keen-edged fighting spirit. Ships have vastly increased in size and speed and hitting power since then, but the dominant factor is still the men behind the guns.

Key West swarmed with them in the spring of '98, the types eternal in the naval service, from the grizzled, steadfast captains who had been afloat on every sea, to the taut, downy-cheeked young ensigns fairly rampant for war, and the two-fisted bluejackets who were ready for a fight or a frolic whenever they hit the beach. On the day when the order came to put the gray war paint on the ships, over the dazzling white which was their normal garb, the yell that went up from the fleet must have carried across to Havana. It was the first tangible portent that the trouble was about due to break loose.

Correspondents poured in by every steamer from the mainland. Just how they were going to report this war was a matter of hazy conjecture. Later there would be an army to accompany to Cuba, but for a while it was the Navy's affair, and things might happen anywhere over an area of a thousand miles of salt water. Seagoing tugs and yachts were chartered at enormous expense to follow the fleet and serve as dispatch boats. Only a few newspapers could afford such outlay, but the correspondents kept coming to Key West with orders to get the news somehow. Most of them were first-class reporters, assigned to cover this story as they would have been sent to a big fire or a railroad wreck.

We did not aspire to be called war correspondents. This dignity belonged to Richard Harding Davis and to the Englishmen who joined the throng, entertaining veterans who had seen hard fighting in numerous campaigns on the Indian frontier, who had marched with the Turks, with the Chinese and Japanese armies, who had gone to Greece as Stephen Crane had done in '97. To us novices they were the real thing, like Archibald Forbes, or with the flavor of Kipling's fiction. We never tired of listening to their yarns.

The Key West Hotel was a bedlam of a place while we waited for the war to begin. And when other diversion failed, you could stroll around the corner to the resort known as the "Eagle Bird" where a gentlemanly gambler, as well-groomed and decorous as Jack Oakhurst, spun the roulette wheel. And there you would be most apt to find Stephen Crane, sometimes bucking the goddess of chance in contented solitude, a genius who burned the candle at both ends and whose spark of life was to be tragically quenched before he was thirty years old. With his tired smile he would drawl these cryptic lines, when about to take another fling at the "Eagle Bird":

> "Oh, five white mice of chance,
>   Shirts of wool and corduroy pants,
> Gold and wine, women and sin,
>   All for you if you let me come in —
>   Into the house of chance."

There was a month of this waiting day by day for the fleet to sail cleared for action. My own newspaper had not hired a dispatch boat, but had made an arrangement with the "New York World" to share the cost of the service. This would enable me to cruise in whatever boats the "World" might send with the fleet. Other plans quite unforeseen, however, were suddenly devised on the very night the message came that war had been declared against Spain.

XX

A GUEST OF SAMPSON'S FLAGSHIP

AMID the surging excitement of Key West, no figure moved with calmer assurance than the great Sylvester Scovel. Yes, you could rightly call him that. He had won his laurels in the field with Maximo Gomez and the Cuban insurgent forces as a correspondent of the most remarkable bravery, dash, and resourcefulness, taking his life in his hands and succeeding where others had failed. He had been imprisoned by order of the Spanish Captain-General and sentenced to be shot. The protests of the American Government saved him and he had rejoined the insurgents. His nerve and audacity were proof against dismay.

He was a public character and deserved all the praise that had been given him. The title of correspondent was inadequate. The "World" called him its "Special Commissioner." His exploits were trumpeted on the front page. To be ignorant of Sylvester Scovel was to argue yourself unknown. He was as ready to interview a Pope as to advise a potentate. Through the daily journalism of his time this energetic young man whizzed like a detonating meteor.

It was Scovel who drew me aside, during the confusion of that memorable night in Key West, and confidentially imparted:

"You are not to go in the 'World' dispatch boat with me. I have made different arrangements. You will sail in Admiral Sampson's flagship New York, and you had better hustle yourself aboard."

"What's that? You must be dreaming, Scovel, old man. No special correspondents will be allowed on the flagship.

That was all settled days ago. Nobody but the two men from the Press Associations —"

"Oh, yes, I know, but I fixed this up with the Admiral to-day. He expects you. Of course the 'World' will get the use of your stuff. Your own paper will attend to that."

"The Admiral expects me?" said I. "The deuce he does. I can see him waiting at the gangway. He has a war on, but of course he won't let a little thing like that interfere —"

"I am not joking, Paine," was the severe rejoinder. "If you are not out there by midnight, you'll get left."

"All right, I'll be there, Scovel I know you are a great little fixer, but —"

Sylvester Scovel turned on his heel and dismissed the topic. When he arranged things, they were as good as done. On the hotel piazza I discovered a young naval lieutenant who was in charge of the last boat that would go off to the flagship. He was a friend of mine and I frankly stated the case. It was risky business for him, putting a civilian aboard without orders, but he was willing to take a chance if the Admiral had really invited me. If it turned out to be a false alarm, it would be up to me to swim ashore.

Presently the launch moved out of the harbor to roll in the open sea and find the outer anchorage, several miles distant. The fleet showed no lights. They were straining at the leash, ponderous battleships, slim cruisers, skittish little torpedo boats, the first American squadrons under orders to seek and engage the enemy since the Civil War.

Up the tall gangway of the armored cruiser New York clambered the uneasy young Paine with a suitcase into which he had hastily scrambled a change of clothes at the last moment. The officer of the deck eyed the suitcase. It seemed to annoy him. Then his coldly critical gaze took in the stranger in civilian garb. Glibly, but with an inward trepidation, was this officer informed:

"The Admiral expects me. I am to sail with the fleet."

"First I have heard of it," snapped the other. "No orders given to let you come aboard. The Admiral is asleep."

"Oh, don't bother to wake him up," was my idiotic reply. "I can see him first thing in the morning."

The officer of the deck removed a brass-bound cap and rubbed his head. Then he bawled to the boatswain to hoist the launch inboard. This was according to schedule. The last boat was to be swung away and secured on arrival. It looked as though the unwelcomed visitor might have to swim for it. But the confident mention of the Admiral had granted him a respite and he was finally permitted to make his way down to the steerage mess where dwelt the youngest officers, ensigns and naval cadets, and they hailed him right cordially. Nobody had the smallest desire for sleep, and so we cocked our heels upon the long table and noisily fought the war in advance until shortly before daybreak when the signal ran from ship to ship and the anchors were weighed and the jubilant fleet steamed out to begin the blockade of Havana.

There was a flurry of excitement when the light cruiser Nashville dashed off to capture the Spanish merchant steamer Buena Ventura as the first prize of the war. Some time after this, when the warships were spread in orderly array over a sapphire sea, Admiral Sampson paced the quarter-deck of the New York, a spare, erect figure in white uniform. The short gray beard carefully trimmed, the precise and studious manner, suggested more the scholar than the sailor. From the list of captains he had been selected for this most important command because of the superior intelligence and efficiency with which he had performed the duties of a career begun during the Civil War.

On this particular morning his mind was preoccupied with problems of momentous gravity. This war was to be won or lost by sea. Its dominant concern was with the powerful squadron of fast armored cruisers under the Spanish Admiral Cervera whose whereabouts were unknown. Until this force could be made harmless or destroyed, it would be impossible to send an American army to Cuba.

To Admiral Sampson, then, wrapped in his anxious reflections, commanding a fleet untried in battle, came this inconsequential correspondent, Ralph Paine, and attempted to explain his presence aboard the flagship. The young man was distinctly ill at ease. He felt conscious that his midnight arrival had been informal. The Admiral halted in his measured stride, his hands clasped behind him, and his severe features failed to warm in a smile of greeting. He listened for a moment and spoke curtly:

"Scovel told you to come aboard? Are you sure of that? And I consented to the arrangement?"

"There must be some misunderstanding, sir," was the flustered exclamation, with a hunted glance over the side. It was, indeed, a long swim to Key West. The Commander-in-Chief briefly agreed to this statement and resumed pacing the quarter-deck. The unhappy correspondent was left rooted to the spot from which he presently removed himself to a refuge more secluded. His young friends of the steerage mess offered condolence as did also the debonair "Chappie" Goode,[1] representing the Associated Press, who enjoyed a privileged status.

The situation was befogged, but one could not hold the buoyant and irrepressible Sylvester Scovel guilty of deception. He had mentioned it to the Admiral, no doubt of that, as a stroke of enterprise which should benefit the "New York World." And whatever Scovel suggested was thereby arranged. For him life was one superb and compelling gesture after another. The only difficulty was that the interview concerning Ralph Paine had failed to impress itself upon the burdened mind of Admiral Sampson. This was the unavoidable conclusion.

[1] Now Sir William Goode and until recently Chairman of the Austrian Section of the Reparations Commission.

The day passed and the fleet took station off the Cuban coast, from Havana to Matanzas, grim and vigilant and wary of torpedo-boat attack. The correspondent who had failed to obtain official sanction and recognition was still on board, and his ribald messmates called him a burglar who had crawled through a hawse-hole. He was an item overlooked in the conduct of the war and apparently it had been decided to make the best of him. Thus it happened that he remained a guest of the flagship through the first fortnight of the war with Spain.

It was a gorgeous opportunity for a zealous young journalist, permitting him to skim the cream of episodes, impressions, color and movement which were all unfamiliar to American newspaper readers. He wrote columns and columns of it, to be cabled from Key West, and the stuff was prominently displayed and double-leaded. It carried the line, "*From a Staff Correspondent Aboard the Flagship New York*," but it failed to state how he got there.

In the midst of this singularly fortunate experience there was one unhappy episode. The enemy was observed to be constructing a series of earthworks to defend the harbor of Matanzas, and mounting coast batteries behind them. Admiral Sampson resolved to discourage this pernicious activity and ordered a bombardment. It was undertaken by the New York, the light cruiser Cincinnati, and the monitor Puritan. Now this was the first action of the war, a fact which made it more than a minor episode. The thunder of American broadsides was a spectacular event.

By this time Richard Harding Davis had been granted a special dispensation to visit the flagship and we stood together upon the superstructure, tremendously interested in the show and especially in the Spanish shells which passed overhead. The bluejackets of the New York served their guns with an enthusiasm which Davis described in this vivid style:

At first I tried to keep track of the shots fired, but soon it was like counting falling bricks. The guns seemed to be ripping out the steel sides of the ships and to be racing to see which could get rid of the most ammunition first. The thick deck of the superstructure jumped with the concussions and vibrated like a suspension bridge when an express train thunders across it. They came crashing from every point, and when you had steadied yourself against one salvo you were shaken and swayed by the backward rush of the wind from another. The reports seemed to crack the air as though it were a dense body. It opened and shut and rocked you about with invisible waves. Your eardrums tingled and strained and seemed to crack. The noise was physical, like a blow from a baseball bat; the noise itself stung and shook you. The concussions were things apart; they shook you after a fashion of their own, jumping your field glasses between the bridge of your nose and the brim of your hat and hammering your eyebrows. With this there were great clouds of hot smoke that swept across the decks and hung for a moment, hiding everything in a curtain of choking fog which rasped your throat and nostrils and burned your eyes.

The ship seemed to work and fight by herself; you heard no human voice of command, only the grieved tones of Lieutenant Mulligan, rising from his smoke-choked deck below, where he could not see to aim his six-inch gun, and from where he begged Lieutenant Marble again and again to "Take your damned smoke out of my way." Lieutenant Marble was vaulting in and out of his forward turret like a squirrel in a cage. One instant you would see him far out on the deck, where shattered pieces of glass and woodwork eddied like leaves in a hurricane, and the next pushing the turret with his shoulder as though he meant to shove it overboard; and he would wave his hand to the crew inside and there would be a racking roar, a parting of air and sea and sky, a flash of flame vomiting black smoke, and he would be swallowed up in it like a fairy in a pantomime. And instantly from the depths below, like the voice of a lost soul, would rise the protesting shriek of Lieutenant Dick Mulligan, "Oh, *will* you take your damned smoke out of my way!"

I quote at this length to indicate that in the brisk bombardment of Matanzas there was excellent material for a newspaper dispatch. The American people were clamoring for action and powder smoke, and here was the first taste of it, three ships banging away with every gun that could be brought to bear, and the yellow streaks of earthworks spouting like geysers as the shells tore into them. The Spanish batteries were soon silenced, without damage to the American naval force.

When our bugles blew to cease firing and the smoke had cleared, a tug came churning alongside the New York, having witnessed the spectacle from a discreet distance. It was the "New York Herald's" dispatch boat, waiting for Richard Harding Davis to finish writing his story and eager to dash for Key West with it. Now the "World" boat was supposed to be trailing the fleet, and to be on the *qui vive* for such an episode as this bombardment. Vainly I searched the horizon to find it. Because of his intimate acquaintance with Cuban waters, Sylvester Scovel had betaken the boat and himself elsewhere along the coast, "to take soundings for the Admiral," as transpired later.

I could not write like Richard Harding Davis, but I had the news and there was no way of sending it. Politely but firmly the "Herald" man megaphoned from the bow of the tug that he liked me personally, but he'd be hanged if he would carry my stuff to Key West to be printed in a rival sheet, to wit, the "World." And he grinned when he said it, for he was assured of the first real scoop of the war. Much as I admired Sylvester Scovel the magnificent, it was to wish that he might have attended more strictly to the newspaper game and left the management of the war to Admiral Sampson.

Sorrowfully I beheld Davis toss his copy to the deck of the tug in a weighted envelope. The boat's whistle blew two or three derisive snorts and she tore off at top speed for the hundred-and-twenty-mile run to Key West. This was how the "Herald" scored a notable beat on the bombardment of Matanzas, leaving a profoundly disappointed and unreconciled correspondent with his adjectives and paragraphs bottled up and no way to uncork them. Destiny had properly scuppered him.

A few nights later there was another story, but it could not even be told, much less written. Secrecy sealed it until the end of the war. The flagship had returned to the blockade of Havana and was moving slowly within easy range of Morro Castle. In black darkness, with the weather thick and muggy, she drifted some distance from her station. The heat had driven me from below and I was asleep upon the super-structure. The awakening was tumultuous.

A gun barked from some vessel obscured in the darkness. The call to general quarters sounded through the quiet decks of the New York. Five hundred men leaped from their hammocks and raced to their stations. A minute or two of this prodigious commotion and the ship was silent and ready. From her signal mast the Ardois lamps were flashing red and white, and presently a reply winked in the night, a little distance off to starboard. It was repeated and the flagship also reiterated her own private code signal. Then the crew streamed back to the hammocks and cursed the false alarm.

The rest of the story was confidentially imparted by Ernest McCready of the "New York Herald," my old ship-mate of the Caribbean. He had been permitted to make a cruise in the torpedo-boat Porter, by way of an experience, and was down in the stoke-hole, in dungarees, to see what that was like. The commander, Lieutenant "Jack" Fremont, was of the dashing, intrepid type best suited to this job, and while rolling about in his little tin-pot of a craft he had sighted the looming shadow of a large ship where he thought no friendly man-of-war ought to be.

Promptly he flashed his own code signal for the night, but through some blunder the signal quartermaster of the New York displayed the wrong combination of numbers. The Porter signaled again, and again the twinkling answer was unsatisfactory. This was enough for the bold "Jack" Fremont. It looked as though he had encountered one of Cervera's armored cruisers trying to steal into Havana. Instantly he cleared a torpedo tube and trained it on the great, spectral shape that floated so near. The torpedo crew was set and ready to launch the terrible missile at the target.

Fremont told them to wait a minute, and with his own hand he let drive with a three-pounder gun as his final word. The shell flew over the flagship, which was much amazed and in the very nick of time displayed the correct night signal. It was by this narrowest of margins that the Admiral and five hundred men and a correspondent who felt a certain fondness for existence, although he did n't amount to much in the general scheme of things, escaped being blown to glory by the little torpedo-boat Porter, which was everlastingly on the job.

"And 'Jack' Fremont certainly would have done it," said McCready when next we met. "I popped out of the fire-room hatch when he called 'em to quarters, and you never saw such a sincere little crew in your life. They stood on their toes and fairly yelped for the word to let go. And the skipper came so near saying it that I really dislike to discuss the affair."

An edict from the Navy Department finally banished the fortunate Paine from the flagship. He had fared ever so much better than he deserved. The editors of certain other newspapers were righteously protesting that their staff correspondents were discriminated against. Why should n't they be allowed to cruise in the flagship? What was the excuse for this man Paine, anyhow? As a matter of fact, there was n't any. He had just happened. And so, in the best of spirits, with a sense of gratitude for benefits received, he went ashore at Key West to seek other means of seeing the war.

XXI

ONCE ABOARD THE GUSSIE!

AMONG the opportunities offered was the voyage of the good ship Gussie. It was mostly comedy. What else would you have, with a vessel of that name? Yes, she had sailed the high seas as the Gussie for more than thirty years, a lumbering, red, paddle-wheeled ark which had been a transport in the Civil War, so the legend ran. In raking the coast for troop-ships, the Government had discovered this venerable relic plying down New Orleans way, and she was added to the collection of maritime curiosities in which the American Army risked drowning during the war with Spain.

The strategists of the War Department were anxious to ascertain how much coöperation could be expected from the Cuban insurgent forces in the event of a siege of Havana by land or sea, or an attack at Santiago. It was known that they were in urgent need of munitions and supplies, and the Gussie was therefore loaded with a valuable cargo and sent from Tampa. She carried also two companies of the First Infantry, a seasoned regular outfit which had been stationed in the Far West for many years and whose older officers had seen hard fighting in campaigns against the red Indians.

These troops were intended to protect the landing of the cargo, and three Cuban officers went with them to act as scouts and to get in touch with the insurgent detachments nearest the point of destination. It was to be a secret expedition, of course, in order that the enemy might not concentrate to spoil the plans and blow the Gussie and her people out of water. The Gussie waddled into Key West harbor on her way across to Cuban waters, and her pilgrimage was enshrouded in as much secrecy as a well-advertised excursion to Coney Island.

When she departed, two newspaper dispatch boats followed in her wake, just to make the voyage unostentatious. All that was lacking to make it absolutely stealthy was a brass band and a plentiful supply of fireworks. As an escort, the Navy offered the little revenue cutter Manning. On board the Gussie were six or eight correspondents who prayed for fair weather. One moved gingerly lest he stub his toe and kick a hole through the side of this hoary old tub. Her merchant skipper was a kind-hearted, elderly man with moth-eaten whiskers who preferred an uneventful life. A correspondent reported him as complaining:

"Why those Spaniards have no idea what one shot will do to my vessel if they happen to hit her. Honest to God, young man, one of them fat regular soldiers stumbled down the companionway this morning, and before we could stop him he had busted through the planking of three decks and landed in the lower hold. What I can't figger out is what kept him from going through the bottom."

Incidentally, this seafaring expedition, including two companies of infantry, was in command of a colonel of cavalry. The proper senior officer would have been Captain Jinks of the Horse Marines. During the first night the Gussie wandered close to Havana, inside the cordon of the blockade. She blazed grandly with lights from every port, like a hotel afloat. The American warships had not been informed of the coming of the Gussie, and therefore when they beheld this singular phenomenon they shot at it and afterward hauled alongside to ask questions. The excursion lacked a naval signal boy who could have told the blockading force what it was all about. This made the situation excessively embarrassing for the Gussie. It was an entertaining night, with the report of a gun every now and then as a peremptory mandate to heave to, then the disgusted accents of an officer on the bridge of a cruiser or battleship, demanding to know what in hades kind of a lunatic asylum had gone adrift.

The Gussie was like a flustered old lady caught in a jam of street traffic. The merchant skipper lamented in his whiskers and plaintively informed the Navy that he did n't know where he was going, and wished he was n't. It was no place for a respectable vessel that had seen better days. And would they kindly leave him alone because he had never meant any harm to nobody. Then the Navy turned its searchlights on the Gussie and laughed at her in a ribald manner, with a shocking lack of reverence for her sex and her age.

When morning broke, the secretive Gussie had drifted so close to Morro Castle, off Havana, that you could count the guns in the embrasures. One fanciful excursionist swore that he could smell breakfast cooking in the houses along the Alameda. The Gussie gasped and scuttled seaward with a startled air. All hands wondered why she was not fired at and sunk. The most plausible theory was that the Spanish gunners could n't believe she was true. If they were subject to delusions like that, it was time to swear off drinking Cuban rum.

The Manning came along to chaperon the Gussie, and the trim converted yacht Wasp joined the party. On deck the two companies of regulars sprawled upon their gay Navajo blankets, and down below the mules of an army pack-train brayed for more water. The Gussie sauntered off to the westward, within plain sight of the coast, while Spanish heliographs talked about her from the red-roofed stations on the hilltops and the round Martello towers on the headlands. The excursion was already common gossip.

At noon the Gussie stood in toward the coast in order to send the Cuban scouts ashore near Mariel. She ran close enough to see that the landscape fairly buzzed with Spanish troops who were eager to welcome her. It was vexatious enough to be peppered at by clusters of infantry who scampered out of the block-houses, but the thing was carried entirely too far when the Gussie was attacked by cavalry!

A hundred of these Spanish horsemen broke out of the verdure and raced along the beach for a mile or more, firing from the saddle until the Wasp tossed a few shells among them and they wheeled into the jungle. The American colonel of cavalry in command of the Gussie expedition was much impressed. He was a veteran campaigner, but this was something new. It was all he could do to restrain himself from telling the bugler to sound "Boots and Saddles" for a counter-charge. In many respects, this was an unconventional sea voyage.

Having survived a cavalry attack, the Gussie went on to the westward. The Cuban scouts had declined to go ashore at Mariel. The vote was unanimous. Near the inlet of Cabañas a small fort crackled with rifle volleys and the bullets came singing over the Gussie. A four-pounder on the Manning discouraged this sport. We began to surmise that the Pinar del Rio Railroad was running special trains out of Havana and advertising the Gussie as a holiday attraction.

She hovered in the vicinity of Cabañas for some time, slowly diifting to the westward of the inlet, until the coast was veiled in a tropical downpour of rain. Then it was decided to put the scouts ashore and start them inland. If they should return with favorable information, the munition and the mules could be transported to the beach. What this expedition needed most was the professional skill of Captain "Dynamite Johnny" O'Brien.

The Gussie dropped anchor a quarter of a mile from shore where a heavy surf broke white across the coral reef. The three Cuban scouts, wearing boots and spurs, reluctantly got into a small skiff to find a passage through the reef. They were supposed to know. Very promptly they were capsized in the breakers and salvaged themselves by swimming, wading, and turning involuntary somersaults during which it seemed odd to catch the gleam of their spurs.

Then the ship's boats were ordered away and into them jumped the husky regulars of E Company, under Captain O'Connell and Lieutenant Crofton, sixty men in all, while G Company was held in reserve on the Gussie. There was nothing farcical about these American infantrymen and the way they went about their business. They were samples of the magnificent little regular army which was to fight and win the war at Santiago, regardless of a commanding general who was too fat-bodied to climb a horse and too fat-witted to plan a campaign. In time of peace this army had been scattered at small posts, and it was therefore at its best in such a minor operation as this landing at Cabañas, the unit a company led by its own officers.

Captain O'Connell's big lifeboat was upset in the surf, which caused delay, while Lieutenant Crofton gained the beach with his detachment and deployed them as skirmishers. The blue shirts and brown hats instantly vanished in the luxuriant jungle. The men went at it as though they were trailing Apache Indians. Presently the captain and his force scrambled out of the breakers and also disappeared inland, but at some distance up the beach.

Meanwhile the Manning and the Wasp had taken positions to shell the woods should the enemy be flushed by the skirmishers. Aboard the Gussie it was discovered that three horses would have to be sent ashore for the use of the Cuban scouts. Here was an occasion when a certain Ralph Paine displayed a misguided initiative which again proved that he required a keeper. These horses were nothing in his young life, but nobody else seemed anxious to conduct them to the beach and he therefore offered to take one of them along with him.

Two sailors manned a small boat and waited near the ship. Half a dozen infantrymen laid hold of a large black horse and dragged him to an open cargo port. He objected violently, but they shoved all together and he dropped twenty feet with a mighty splash. When his head emerged from the ocean, the small boat paddled close, and the aforesaid Paine, who was seated in the stern, grabbed the poor beast by the halter rope. It was very much of a disgusted, hysterical horse. This quarter of a mile to the beach was a long swim, but by holding the beast's head up he was enabled to strike out bravely.

Progress was slow and arduous, and the struggling horse absorbed one's attention. The journey was a little more than halfway accomplished when those busy skirmishers ashore made contact with the enemy. An infernal racket suddenly filled the jungle, the Spanish firing volleys, the cool-headed Yankee doughboys snap-shooting at will and picking them off from cover. Smaller noises, like angry hornets, were in the air as the bullets flew toward the Gussie. There was also an impression that they were aimed, by unanimous consent, at a little boat and two profane sailors and a perplexed correspondent who towed a large black horse by the nose.

This journey to the beach was like a one-way street. You had to go ahead. To turn and haul that floundering horse back to the Gussie was out of the question, for there was no method of hoisting him on board again. At least, this was my belief at the moment. The two sailors were obsessed by this same notion, that they could not abandon the horse as a derelict. Therefore they pulled steadily at the oars, glancing over their shoulders, and communing with each other in phrases that required expurgation.

The beach seemed to be miles and miles away because the horse was like a sea anchor astern, although he swam nobly, snorting like a grampus. It was hard work holding his head above water when he began to tire. After a certain number of minutes or hours or days, or whatever they were, the boat reached the surf which broke over the edge of the reef.

By this time an impetuous American infantryman had come running out of the jungle to strip off his shirt and brandish it in the wig-wag code. What he had to say was evidently comprehended by the Wasp and the Manning, for they began to shell the woods. The projectiles flew high, to pass over the invisible skirmishers, but the noise of them overhead increased the discomfiture of two sweating sailors, a large black horse, and a two-hundred-pound correspondent who felt himself to be the most conspicuous object in or about the island of Cuba.

The fact that rifle bullets were spattering just outside the surf and that a short-sighted shell from the Manning almost got the horse, added to the impression that here was too much publicity.

No sooner was the boat fairly in the surf than it capsized. The breakers were boisterous, rearing white-crested. Their blows knocked you down as with a club. The two sailors clung to the gunwales of the boat, and one of them was heard to remark that this was a bum place to be wastin' time on a blankety-blanked livery stable. They gained a foothold on the coral bottom and managed to swing the boat around bow on to the surf. Then they scrambled in and shoved the oars into the thole-pins. The boat reared like a bronco, but air tanks made it buoyant and they drove it seaward, pulling like madmen. Without another upset they fought clear of the breakers and made for the Gussie.

They had done their duty by the horse. He had touched solid bottom, although in the surf. The equation had resolved itself into a short halter rope with the horse at one end and a fool of a correspondent at the other. It could not be said, with accuracy, that they were on *terra firma*. First a ponderous breaker knocked the horse down and he stepped on the correspondent, and then it was *vice versa*, with several encores. However, they were gradually approaching the beach and finding shoaler water. Short of wind and with various abrasions, due to scraping on the coral and stepping on each other, they finally stayed right side up, to their mutual relief.

On board the Gussie was one of the most famous illustrators of his time, Rufus F. Zogbaum, best known for his pictures of the naval service. For "Harper's Weekly" he made a double-page drawing called "*Landing Horses Through the Surf Under Fire from the Shore.*" Although done with spirit and fidelity, it failed, of course, to portray the inner emotions of the young man with the large black horse. Art has its limitations.

Once clear of the breakers, the beach seemed to be no more hospitable. Bullets came singing across it from the Spanish force engaged with the American skirmish line. However, the idea persisted that the horse had to be delivered to somebody and the transaction completed. He was a leg-weary animal and moved with reluctant feet. Also it seemed a long journey to find a tree to tie him to, for nobody was waiting to receive him. Moored in this manner, the young man concluded that it would be unreasonable for the horse to demand any more of his time.

The outstanding fact was that one was permitted to join the first American troops to land on Cuban soil in the war with Spain. The altercation with the horse had been incidental, another episode in the career of a young man who could never seem to learn to mind his own business.

He found a trail from the beach into the jungle and soon came to a row of old rifle pits from which the Spanish soldiers had been driven out. Here a squad of E Company had tucked themselves in and were firing to discourage the enemy from crossing the trail and so flanking the outfit.

It was learned that the skirmishers had encountered a body of Spanish irregulars, a hundred or so of them, some mounted, who had been hastily sent from Cabañas to annoy the landing party from the Gussie. In a running fight they had been scattered, and the shells from the Manning and the

Wasp had, no doubt, hastened the retirement and held back reënforcements from the coastwise garrisons near by. They had carried their wounded with them. In the dense undergrowth the American infantrymen stumbled over four dead bodies. One of them was the officer commanding the Spanish party, a handsome man of middle age, wearing a spick-and-span uniform, with medals and ribbons on his breast.

This was the end of him, of his long years of honorable service, of his ambitions and affections, to be killed and left to rot in a shallow grave of the Cuban jungle as a tragedy entirely negligible. He had been blotted out as an incident of this absurd Gussie expedition which would leave not the slightest impression on the war. It was something to remember as typical of the enormous futility of most bloody quarrels between nations. He symbolized the primitive stupidity of it all.

The American soldiers suffered no casualties. Schooled in the traditions of frontier warfare, they had taken every advantage of the thick cover and had handled their rifles with methodical accuracy. The only casualty was a correspondent, James F. J. Archibald, who had gone ashore with E Company. He was pinked in the arm by a Mauser bullet, a slight flesh wound which was very precious in his sight. He was the first American wounded in Cuba. It was a distinction. And those who knew "Jimmie" Archibald were aware that he would make the most of it.

Two more horses came safely ashore and the three Cuban scouts were firmly told to straddle them and ride for the camp of the insurgent leader, Perrico Diaz, at the foot of the Caraca-Jicara mountains which loomed darkly a few miles distant. They remonstrated until irate doughboys whacked their steeds. Then with theatrical gestures of farewell they clapped home the spurs and crashed into the jungle trail as if shot out of guns.

The skirmishers trooped back to the beach in the late

afternoon and piled into the boats. They wrestled with the surf and escaped drowning and so rejoined the Gussie, dripping wet and in excellent humor. They had chased the Spaniards through the brush and taught them to leave the old First Infantry alone. It had been a nifty little scrap while it lasted.

The Gussie lifted anchor and churned her paddle-wheels to get away from a lee shore before night. It had been decided to attempt another landing somewhere else. Again she obtruded herself into the blockade of Havana where the Navy called her a chronic nuisance. She was scolded and insulted in a manner more scandalous than ever, particularly when the gunboat Vicksburg chased her no less than three times before morning.

Then the patient Manning and the courteous Wasp resumed their chaperonage, and the Gussie steamed into a broad bay near Baraçoa. Here was another rendezvous with the Cuban forces. Ah, they were waiting! A white flag waved from the top of a royal palm in the chaparral. It was the friendly signal. The Gussie forgot all the trepidations and previous shocks to her nerves and boldly advanced within three hundred yards of the beach. Who had dared to call this voyage a nautical jest?

Two masked Spanish field batteries opened on her at this close range. They had decoyed the poor old hussy of a steamboat inshore for this very purpose. The marksmanship was perfect for direction, but a trifle high. The first flight of shells passed a few feet above the spar deck. The Gussie reversed her engines so suddenly that she almost broke herself in two. Like other invalids confronted by unexpected peril, she moved more rapidly than the doctors had believed possible.

This disarranged the aim of the Spanish batteries and they failed to pot her. The Wasp was enjoying herself by knocking to pieces a Martello tower near the beach while the Mann-

ing practiced on the batteries hidden in the grass. The
merchant skipper of the Gussie thought it high time to protest to the colonel of cavalry. This foolishness had gone far
enough. The Gussie was liable to get hurt if they proposed
to let the Spaniards use her to shoot at all up and down the
coast. It was n't unreasonable to ask the Army to be more
careful of her.

But the Army had resolved to try it once more, and so the
Gussie proceeded toward Matanzas. A Cuban pilot was put
ashore, the jolly, fleshy old Ambrosito, with instructions to
find the camp of Betancourt. The Gussie drifted offshore all
night, awaiting his return. A boat from the Manning found
him hiding on the beach and fetched him off. Miles and miles
had he crawled on his belly through the grass, vociferated
Ambrosito, and the country was full of Spanish patrols.
They swarmed like *cucujos*, fireflies, and there could be no
landing the mules and the guns and things between Cardenas and Matanzas.

"So I have come back to you," concluded Ambrosito,
"and, ah, my brothers, my little brothers, it is good to live
on the Gussie, much better than being killed with bullets and
machetes on the beach. Here we are all doing well — divinely
— *como papas* — like potatoes."

Three times was out, as far as the Gussie was concerned.
Thrice had she tried and failed, but no one could accuse her
of lacking the best intentions in the world. Back she sailed to
Key West and the voyage belonged in the archives of history.

In a restaurant I found McCready, ordering ham and eggs
every few minutes, after a rough week at sea in a dispatch
boat.

"What kind of a time did you have in the silly old Gussie?"
he asked, in greeting.

"Don't ask me, Mac. You go find a big black horse and
ask *him*."

XXII

IT HAPPENED IN HAITI

ROVING the high seas in a newspaper dispatch boat during the Spanish War was a hard life, but seldom monotonous. Among the steamers chartered for this purpose was the Three Friends in which sailed, for a time, correspondents both of the "World" and the "Herald" as the result of an amicable working agreement. It was a congenial coincidence, to find myself again afloat in this vessel which, as a filibuster and pirate, had so boldly aided the Cuban cause two years earlier. Captain Montcalm Broward was in command and with him were perhaps a dozen of the old crew, including the mate and several of the deck-hands. They enjoyed this knocking about to follow a war. Even in this new rôle, habit was strong in the wary Three Friends. It required a vigilant man at the wheel to prevent her from shying at every smudge of smoke on the horizon.

The blockade of the American fleet extended two hundred miles along the northern coast of Cuba while Admiral Sampson awaited trustworthy tidings of the enemy's dangerous squadron, flying Cervera's pennant, which had sailed from Spain to vanish like ghost ships. The newspaper boats kept closely in touch with the blockading force, remaining at sea for several days or perhaps a week, until something happened to write about. Then they ran for Key West, blow high, blow low, to reach the cable office.

The Navy was astonishingly patient with this meddlesome flotilla of tugs and yachts. It stipulated that they should stay ten miles offshore at night, beyond the blockading lines, but otherwise they did as they pleased and were sometimes a nuisance to the fleet. The powers in Washington were acutely sensitive to public opinion. This war was not unique in that the politicians were unwilling to leave the management to the professionals. You may remember that when the Army went to Santiago and a whole shipload of correspondents disembarked, the Cuban insurgents mistook them for an advance regiment of the expeditionary force, but that is another story.

Among my comrades in the Three Friends were McCready, Stephen Crane, and Harry Brown, dean of the "Herald" war staff, who chanted a strange salt-water dirge of his own composing when things went wrong or the weather was too rough for comfort. It went like this, rolled out in deep and mournful accents:

> I would rather sing a song
> To a harp of one string,
> Than to hear the water gurgle
> Or the nightingale sing.

> *(Chorus)*
> A bottle o' rum, the ship's a-sinking,
> *Two* bottles o' rum, we'll all be drowned,
> *Three* bottles o' rum, she'll go to the bottom,
> *Four* bottles o' rum, we'll
> > never
> > > be
> > > > found.

Now and then these cruises had the flavor of other and wilder days in the Three Friends. There was a stormy twilight off Cardenas when a suspiciously minded and hasty gunboat, the Machias, concluded that she had sighted an enemy ship. Her gunners aimed a shell which nicked the top of the funnel of the Three Friends and showered all hands with soot, besides spoiling their tempers. Ranging closer, the Machias discovered the error and the officer in charge of the bridge offered a handsome apology.

He was rather grumpily forgiven while we wiped the soot from our eyes, but it was more than sinful human nature could endure when he cheerily bellowed:

"By the way, can you spare us a couple of sacks of potatoes? The supply ship overlooked us, and we've been off here ten days."

"Look what you did to my funnel!" roared Captain Montcalm Broward. "I like your blasted nerve! Tried to blow my vessel into the middle of next week and then ask me for two sacks of potatoes! Not a damn spud! You've got a fine way of introducing yourself when you want to ask a favor. Goodnight!"

The day on which we were lucky enough to see a fine little naval action in the bay of Matanzas was also in character with the former career of the Three Friends. The torpedo-boat Dupont and the converted yacht Hornet had observed that Spanish troops and laborers were concentrating to rebuild the works damaged by the bombardment of the American cruisers, and also mounting big guns in the forts across the harbor. Now these plucky midgets, a flimsy torpedo-boat and a small gimcrack of a yacht, had no business whatever to be poking about in Matanzas harbor in such circumstances as these, but their doctrine was to keep busy and ignore the odds.

While they reconnoitered the industrious activities of the foe, the Punta Gorda battery opened on them with an eight-inch gun. Instead of taking the hint and beating for the open sea, the two midgets darted inshore and swept those Spanish works with rapid-fire from their nasty little one- and six-pounder guns. They took them in flank, moving so rapidly that they were as hard to hit as a couple of agitated fleas. They peppered the Spanish soldiers in the open and drove them scampering into a block-house which was presently shot full of holes. The squads of laborers abandoned the carts and mules. The enemy was anxious to knock off work and call it a day.

The vivacious Dupont and Hornet waltzed up and down the bay, at a thousand yards range, and there was no manning the land batteries to retaliate while the contented blue-jackets were pouring shells, like a hailstorm, across every embrasure and gun mount. Having perforated the landscape in this laudable manner, the two midgets came out to tell the Three Friends about it, not boastfully, but by way of a sociable chat. It was not in the rules of the game for small vessels to go bombarding, they explained, but if you did n't stir up something once in a while this blockade duty would bore you to death.

It was a lively little story, and worth writing, and the Three Friends therefore departed for Key West. The hour was early in the forenoon and it was hoped to file the dispatches in time for the next morning's editions. There were perhaps fifty miles left to run when another boat was sighted, the old filibuster Dauntless, in the employ of the Associated Press. She, too, was hurrying toward Key West, from the Havana sector of the blockade.

Now the cable service was jammed and overloaded with the dispatches of half a hundred correspondents and the procedure was first come, first served. It often happened that belated copy was delayed a whole day in reaching New York, and unreasonable managing editors shot back undeserved rebukes, threatening some unhappy correspondent with dismissal.

For this reason the Three Friends thought it inexpedient to let the Dauntless arrive in port ahead of her, and now began as thrilling an ocean race as you could have found in a month of Sundays. These were two stubborn and reckless vessels, veterans of escapes and pursuits when Captain Johnny O'Brien and John Dunn had sailed in them. And there were enough old hands aboard to infuse this race with the spirit of "let her go and here's hoping she don't bust herself wide open."

There were volunteers to shovel coal and the two shapely towboats tore along, side by side, over a sea that slept in a breathless calm. The afternoon was waning and they still raced on even terms when the sun went down and Sand Key light shone like a star. The funnel of the Three Friends glowed hotter and hotter until its color was a dull red. It stood just abaft the wheel-house, between this wooden structure and a box of a bunk-room on the upper deck which had been built as quarters for the correspondents.

Key West was still an hour away when it was observed that this upper cabin had begun to char and smoulder from the heat of the incandescent funnel. And presently there was a gush of flame, while the curling smoke almost enveloped the ship. The mate yelled to the men to fetch the fire hose and start the steam pump, but Captain Montcalm Broward interfered to say:

"You let that pump alone, understand? I'm not going to waste good steam on a pump. Look at the Dauntless! We have n't put her astern yet. Douse the fire when you hit the wharf in Key West."

The Three Friends was the victim of a conflagration, no doubt of that, but Montcalm Broward added that he guessed he could steer her by the emergency hand-wheel aft if he got chased out of the pilot-house with his shirt-tail blazing.

And so, trailing sparks and smoke and apparently doomed to be burned to the water's edge, the Three Friends continued on her way to Key West. The mate organized a bucket brigade, and those of us not otherwise engaged handed along pails of salt water. This checked the blaze, but the upper works still smoked and sizzled and the danger was by no means past. The burning vessel swept close to the gunboat Annapolis, standing by a Spanish prize, and the Navy lads cheered and waved their hats. They knew a sporting finish when they saw one.

The Three Friends foamed into Key West harbor with the Dauntless no more than two lengths away. In the last resort, it was now a problem of getting a man ashore first. The master of the Dauntless executed a neat bit of strategy. He was making for his own wharf, when at the foot of a street, near another pier-head, he spied a loafing one-horse hack made visible by an arc light at the corner. Toot, toot, toot, and the sonorous whistle drew the attention of the darkey driver.

The Dauntless sheered in and slackened way. As she bumped the piling and rebounded, a long-legged Associated Press correspondent took a flying leap, rolled like a shot rabbit, gathered himself up, and sprinted for the hack. Almost at the same moment, the Three Friends had been adroitly swung in to scrape the end of a wharf close by. The spare and nimble McCready hurtled through space and was running when he lit. He knew a short cut through an alley and he went skimming into the street where the cable office stood, just in time to see the hack kicking up the dust ahead of him.

The race was lost, but hold! — the winner fell and turned heels over head at the very threshold of the building. A fist had caught him behind the ear. The man behind the fist, who was a trifle near-sighted, peered at the prostrate journalist and became aware that he had blundered. As though explaining it to himself, he was heard to mutter:

"My God, I thought it was a 'New York Journal' man!"

McCready was the victor because of this case of mistaken identity, but he was too good a sportsman to take the decision on a foul, and my recollection is that they tossed a coin to decide who should have precedence with the cable operators.

Late in the month of May the scene of action shifted eastward to the St. Nicholas Channel, between Cuba and the Bahama Bank, where Admiral Sampson kept watch and ward with the best of his fighting ships to prevent Cervera's squadron from slipping through to Havana by way of the northern passage. Day after day the fleet idled and drifted in the tropic heat, days painfully anxious for the silent, brooding American admiral seeking contact with an elusive enemy. The Three Friends hovered within sight of the flagship, vainly hoping for something to happen.

Then occurred an incident so splendidly dramatic that it was like a splash of bright color against a dull background. The battleship Oregon joined the fleet after her spectacular voyage from the Pacific, fourteen thousand miles around the Horn in sixty-eight days, risking attack by Cervera's armored cruisers or by the torpedo craft which were lurking off South American ports, driven harder and faster than had been thought possible for a coast defense battleship of her type, enduring the ordeal so magnificently that she was ready for battle on that very day she joined the fleet in the St. Nicholas Channel. It is literally the fact that the nation had awaited news of her safe arrival with breathless interest and suspense.

At full speed she came steaming past the flagship, her flaghoists gay with fluttering bunting, the bluejackets massed on deck and some of them wearing cap ribbons of their own devising, "*Remember the Maine.*" And as with one great lusty voice the fleet cheered the Oregon, which, a few weeks later, was to win laurels even more notable as the fighting ship in the forefront of the naval battle outside Santiago that obliterated the finest squadron of the Spanish Navy.

Admiral Sampson was by this time convinced that Cervera's ships had taken refuge at Santiago where the dilatory and stupid tactics of Commodore Schley had failed to establish an effective blockade with the vessels of the Flying Squadron under his command. The admiral hastened to Santiago with the New York, Oregon, and Mayflower, and found that the enemy was indeed inside the narrow harbor while Schley was keeping his ships from ten to twenty miles offshore instead of closing in to bar the exit.

Promptly Sampson established a masterly blockade. The harbor was sealed by a line of ships which held their stations day and night, and there was no possibility of escape for the doomed Spanish squadron. To make assurance doubly sure, Lieutenant Richmond P. Hobson undertook to sink the collier Merrimac across the harbor entrance, and so drive a cork in the bottle. For this perilous and daring adventure, a forlorn hope if ever there was one, a crew of only seven men was required, but, as the Admiral said, "enough officers and men volunteered to man a fleet of Merrimacs, there being hundreds of offers from a single ship."

The dispatch boat Three Friends rolled in the seas off Santiago harbor, beyond range of the shore batteries, while the Merrimac was stripped and equipped with explosive mines to sink her rapidly. It was after three o'clock in the morning when Lieutenant Hobson took her in, a shadowy hulk of a ship stealing slowly shoreward in the moonlight. Soon the heavy guns of the Morro and Estrella batteries began to thunder and flash, and it was unbelievable that the Merrimac and her devoted crew could have escaped instant destruction.

Soon after sunrise, a Spanish steam launch cautiously approached the wreck of the sunken collier and discovered Lieutenant Hobson and his seven men clinging to the débris. As prisoners of war they were taken aboard the cruiser Reina Mercedes and hospitably entertained by the Spanish officers, including Admiral Cervera himself. Lieutenant Hobson was permitted to write a letter to his own admiral:

I have the honor to report that the Merrimac is sunk in the channel. No losses, only bruises. We are prisoners of war, being well cared for.

The message was carried out to the flagship New York, under a flag of truce, by Commander Joaquin de Bustamente. This and all other information available was obtained by the correspondents of the Three Friends who perceived that this was one of the superb stories of the war at sea, and they were anxious to send it home as soon as possible. The nearest cable bases were Port Antonio, Jamaica, and Mole St. Nicholas, at the western end of Haiti. As to distance, there was little to choose between them. It was more than a hundred miles if you ran southward to Jamaica or crossed the Windward Passage to the Haitian port.

Wind and weather were apt to influence the decision. It so happened that our previous trips had been made to Port Antonio, but this time it was decided to try the French cable service at Mole St. Nicholas. The sea was rough all the way. The correspondents endeavored to write, braced in the bunks with pads of papers on their knees, and found that they were performing acrobatic feats. The scene lacked that composure essential to literary production. As a rule, not much good prose is turned out by a man who persists in standing upon his head.

However, these correspondents solved it by lying flat on their stomachs, having discovered that they could not fall off the floor, and although they slid about more or less they managed to write many hundred words describing the glorious feat of Lieutenant Hobson and the Merrimac.

In the midst of his exhausting labors, Harry Brown, dean of the "Herald" staff, paused now and then to inform all hands, in a melancholy baritone, that he would rather sing a song to a harp of one string than to hear the water gurgle or the nightingale sing. Stephen Crane occasionally expressed the opinion that the sun was over the yardarm and that there were times when the corkscrew was mightier than the pen! He abominated this drudgery of grinding out news dispatches, with an eye on the cost of cable tolls. And seldom could he be coaxed to turn his hand to it. His was the soul of the artist, slowly, carefully fashioning his phrases, sensitive to the time, the place, and the mood.

All day long the Three Friends bucked into it, unable to maintain decent speed, and it was late in the evening when the mountains of Haiti loomed as a dusky landfall. The vessel made her way into a placid and very beautiful bay almost rimmed by these dark heights, and dropped anchor a few hundred yards from the beach of Mole St. Nicholas.

The lustrous sheen of the moon revealed a village of huts, whitewashed and thatched, spread among tall clusters of palms. Crowning the headlands were the ruins of stone forts built very long ago, when the Spanish, the French, and the English had fought over the romantic island of Hispaniola. From the jungle across the bay came the cadenced thump, thump of a drum. It suggested the Congo, and naked black dancers, and the incantations of witch doctors.

A boat was lowered from the Three Friends and two sailors rowed the correspondents to the beach. The curious populace trooped down to the strand, jabbering the corrupt French patois which is the language of Haiti. There was not a white man among them. In color they shaded off from ebony to gingerbread. A ragged, noisy mob it was, and strangely excited. They crowded about us as we stepped ashore. Their behavior seemed almost hostile. One of the sailors of the Three Friends decided to trail along. The symptoms interested him. He was an enterprising young man whom we christened "the astute deckhand" before the night was over.

It was conjectured that the arrival of this big white towboat, so clearly discernible in the moonlight, might have been misinterpreted. Possibly some one had recognized her as a ship of an unholy reputation, her career linked with that of Captain Johnny O'Brien who had once meddled, in a violent manner, with the political affairs of Haiti. This was the first visit of the Three Friends as a dispatch boat, and she had come stealing in by night.

Not much was required to agitate the people of this black republic in which revolutions were casually touched off between meals. At any rate, Mole St. Nicholas appeared to regard us as sensational. Strangers in a land most decidedly strange, we had one fixed idea, to find the French cable office. The crowd on the beach mysteriously expostulated, and several tattered soldiers came scuffling their bare feet and lugging guns with long, rusty bayonets attached.

The impatient correspondents hurled volleys of bad French to right and left and shoved ahead. They knew not where they were going, but they were on their way. They saw crooked streets and vistas of those low, whitewashed huts among the trees, and beyond them the overshadowing mountains.

The crowd on the beach followed after, but soon dwindled, too sleepy for sustained interest in anything. The visitors rambled on, and presently came to a sudden halt. Where two streets crossed, a small camp-fire glowed and around it squatted several Haitian soldiers. Others loafed to and fro on sentry duty, and they were unexpectedly alert.

One of them advanced and opened his face to emit a shrill yell of "*Qui vive.*" The cry was taken up and repeated by one invisible sentry post after another, throughout the town, until it caromed in faint echoes from the nearest mountains. The effect was startling. The soldier whose "*Qui vive*" had sent this vocal explosion going was barring the path with a musket of some antique pattern. The bayonet was particularly distressing. It looked like a boarding-pike, and he handled it so carelessly that McCready was seen to clap both hands to his stomach. The gesture was eloquent. We all felt that way.

There was no such thing as argument with this stubborn black warrior. The street was closed to traffic, as far as we were concerned. There was a hasty retreat and a consultation during which it was noted that a two-story frame building projected from the center of the town, the only one of its kind. At home it would have been about as pretentious as a village grocery store, but in Mole St. Nicholas it was indubitably the palace of the Governor-General, or the City Hall, or something of the sort.

This was the logical destination. It offered the hope of

coherent information. Otherwise the quest of the cable office was hunting a needle in an insane haystack.

Accordingly the correspondents tacked into another street, but again they saw the flames of a little fire and soldiers warming the soles of their feet, or watching the coffee-pot. There was another interview with sentries and excessively lengthy bayonets, and that infernal "*Qui vive*" went racketing from one group to the next beyond, like setting off a new kind of watchman's rattle.

There was no breaking through to reach the two-story frame palace. But these four newspaper men had been trained to find some manner of beating the devil around the bush, wherefore they executed another détour.

It would be tiresome to explain the next encounter, and the one after that, the camp-fire in an open space where the streets met, the bizarre group of black infantry, the infernal clatter of "*Qui vive*," the tableau with the voluble but implacable sentries, and the retreat in good order. For us the thing was becoming monotonous, and, with a little more of it, one of those rusty bayonets might damage an expensive correspondent.

We drifted in the direction of the beach to talk it over. Of the quartet, only Stephen Crane was enjoying the experience. As usual, he refused to take the responsibilities of daily journalism seriously. He had been known to shorten the life of a managing editor. A night in Mole St. Nicholas had its appeal for the artistic temperament.

"It is your move, Crane," said McCready. "Fiction is your long suit. Here it is. Things like this don't happen in real life. Let us have a few remarks from the well-known young author of 'The Red Badge of Courage.'"

"Me?" grinned Crane. "If I caught myself hatching a plot like this, I would n't write another line until I had sobered up. Steady, boys, the night is still young, and I have a hunch that there'll be lots more of it. This opening is good."

Harry Brown, in charge of "The Herald" war service, was an older man and less frivolous, who kept an eye on the ball. He began to issue commands.

"There must be some way of breaking through this silly blockade of armed ragamuffins. You come along with me, Steve Crane, and we'll work along the beach and try to get by at the western end of the town. Paine and McCready can scout in the other direction. If we are still out of luck, we can meet down at the boat landing so as not to lose each other."

The youthful deck-hand from the Three Friends listened to this counsel and wandered off alone. He was having the time of his life. Half an hour later, the four correspondents were reunited down at the boat landing. Their strategy had been futile. They merely had more tales to tell of sentries and little fires and "*Qui vives.*" It was their opinion that Mole St. Nicholas was enjoying another revolution. Certainly it was well guarded against surprise. Martial law was rampant.

"I tried to bribe the last nigger soldier that stopped me," sadly said Harry Brown, "but when he saw me stick 'my hand in my pocket he jabbed at me and, say, I had no idea I was so fast on my feet. I don't know but what we shall have to go aboard ship and wait for morning. This seeing Haiti by moonlight is getting too dotty for me."

"Stick around, Harry," advised Stephen Crane. "Age has dulled your feeling for romance. We can beat this game yet."

After some more useless conversation, the solitary deck-hand came sauntering to the beach, wearing the air of a young man immensely well pleased with himself. His serenity was inexplicable. To the disgruntled group he announced:

"Sure, I busted the jam. It was dead easy. I went sailin' through them nigger soldiers, one bunch after another of 'em, with a fair wind and tide. They saluted me like I was a brigadier-general with a feather in his hat. After a while I come to the big, two-decked shack with a piazza on it, and I got a couple more salutes outside, and they woke up a hefty smoked ham of a man that was the first mate or something, and he came rollin' out in sky-blue pajamas, and —"

"Stop it, Bill," broke in Stephen Crane. "You make us dizzy. Unravel yourself, for God's sake! Go back to the salutes and start again."

"Oh, did n't I tell you? It was comical. One of them nigger obstructions in the channel had fetched me up all standing — you know, a little fire in the road and those wall-eyed boys *qui-vivin'* like hell — and I went around the corner and leaned against it to study what next — when along come a shiny big buck of an officer, and the soldiers hopped to attention, and he gave 'em the password. I could hear it plain as anything, and so I slid along to the next outfit of sentries —"

"And tried the password on them?" exclaimed McCready. "Look here, Bill, how could you wrap your tongue around this Haitian French lingo? It stumps us, and we went to college one time."

"French, nothin'," replied the astute deck-hand. "It was good United States. All I had to do was to parade up to these chocolate drops, and say to 'em, 'I-am-the-Boss!' Just like that!"

"I-am-the-Boss" slowly echoed the bewildered correspondents. It was beyond them to guess what phrase of this bastard French dialect could have sounded like the deck-hand's magic sesame.

"And he said it just like that, Bill?" demanded Harry Brown.

"Did n't I tell you? 'I-am-the-Boss.' Mebbe he thought he was talkin' French, but I knew better."

"Bill, you are a wonder," solemnly declared Stephen

Crane. "But, darn you, you are too impossible for fiction. I shall have to get good and drunk to do you justice. And you told them you were the boss and got away with it?"

"Come along and see," readily answered the deck-hand. "I'll show you. And, listen, I met an awful pretty girl, and there was mighty little tar baby about her, I could see that, an octoroon, mebbe, and I made a date with her —"

"That will do for you, Bill," chided Harry Brown, as the official chaperon. "Forget your immoral love affairs and lead us to the palace."

Young Bill moved on ahead with a touch of swagger in his gait. He had this town eating out of his hand. Boldly he approached the nearest flickering fire and the loafing soldiery. Throwing out his chest, he sharply proclaimed:

"I-am-the-Boss! Salute, you black sons-of-guns."

At his heels marched the four correspondents, chanting in unison: "I-am-the-Boss! Salute, you black sons-of-guns."

The effect was as magical as the astute deck-hand had foretold. The slouching sentinels rolled their eyes and bobbed their heads in recognition of the pass-word. One or two even attempted to present arms, but the result was sketchy. Their hands strayed to their straw hats. A salute was evidently intended. Past them strode the conquering deck-hand and the admiring correspondents. Crane was murmuring aloud:

"I wonder if we could blast the secret out of a French dictionary. Probably not. We shall never know. It is just one of those things."

XXIII

THE SUBLIME BUTLER OF NEW ROCHELLE

THE cordon was broken. We were inside the lines. Unimpeded, the advance was continued to the pretentious frame building, in front of which a sentry bawled a challenging "*Qui vive*" but Bill told him even more loudly who was the boss and there was no argument. In the light of a lantern hung on the piazza stood a large, round man of a saddle-colored complexion, clad in blue pajamas and straw slippers. He beamed cordial good nature and welcomed the strangers as his guests. To their profound relief, he spoke English, racily, as though perfectly familiar with it.

"Ah, ha, it is a pleasure, gentlemen, you bet your sweet life," he cried, shaking hands effusively. "I am the Chief-of-Staff to the Governor of the Arrondissement of Mole St. Nicholas who is the General of the Army also. He is fatigued and have hit the hay. In the morning he will be dee-lighted, *n'est pas?* You found some trouble with the brave soldiers of *mon général?* There is a war, a little one, in Haiti. Pouf, we will win in a walk. The soldiers were on the job? You found them awake? Two of them had to be shooted yesterday for sleeping too much on guard. It made the army buck up, you bet."

The urgent errand was explained, concerning the French cable office, and the rotund Chief-of-Staff was all sympathy and action. The two cable operators would be in bed at this hour, but he himself would summon them *vitement*, in a jiffy. He slipped on a blue coat adorned with tarnished gold lace and fringed epaulets, and yelled at a colonel or something, the officer of the guard, who paraded five soldiers as an escort. Thus honored, the correspondents ambled along with the Chief-of-Staff who imparted the following information:

"You admire how I speak English, eh? Pretty smooth! I twist her by the tail. Why not? Four years I was a butler in New Rochelle, New York!"

Stephen Crane made gestures with both hands, then propped himself against a tree while he gurgled:

"Hooray for the Chief-of-Staff! *He buttled in New Rochelle!!* My hunch was a winner. This is a purple night with spangled trimmings."

Thereafter Crane insisted upon addressing our host as Alice-in-Wonderland. We yearned to know what fantastic nudge of destiny had thrust the butler into this martial niche. It could have happened only in Haiti. But he prattled of other things until the procession halted in front of a low-roofed house which, nevertheless, could boast of an upper story and windows therein. The colonel of the guard was tripped by his sword which was too long for his stature, but he yanked it from between his legs and sternly commanded the five soldiers to stand at attention, all in a row.

They were drawn up across the street from the dwelling of the two French cable operators. The Chief-of-Staff advanced to shout at the upper windows. He spoke in French, and the noise he made was tremendous. It was like pounding a bass drum. He paused to refill those capacious lungs. The house was dark and silent.

Again the Chief-of-Staff shattered the night with his stentorian alarum. There was never a sign of a cable operator's head at an upper window. It was explained to the correspondents:

"Their ladies have arrive by the mail-boat from Cape Haitien, only yesterday. I am, what you call a damn intrusion, *n'est pas?* I will show them — these two cabbages of the cable company."

He raised another clamor, and by now the genial Chief-of-Staff was quite angry. They were called imbeciles, pigs, and he swore by the name of a cow. During this outburst, a tousled head appeared in an upper window and the voice of a cable operator advised the Chief-of-Staff to close his mouth and go to bed. Any business of the cable company could wait until morning. This disturbance was idiotic.

Was this how these wretched insects of the cable company defied the Chief-of-Staff of the Governor, of the General, of the Arrondissement of Mole St. Nicholas? *Sacré baptême ! Nom d'une pipe ! Mille tonneres !* He would let them know. He spoke to the colonel, who barked at the five bare-footed soldiers.

Morbleu! They raised their guns and aimed them at the upper windows. The hammers clicked. Five black forefingers made contact with the triggers. They awaited the word to fire. Of a sacred truth, this Chief-of-Staff was no man to trifle with! He addressed the darkened house, briefly, conveying the sinister fact to the reluctant cabbages that in two minutes their rooms would be full of bullets.

Voilà! Here was an argument marvelously persuasive. Its results were instantaneous. In those upper rooms there was the sound of rapid movement, the swift patter of feet. Not even was there delay to say *au revoir.* The first cable operator fell down the stairs, emerging into the street with his trousers in one hand.

The other followed him by a margin so close that it was almost neck and neck. This one seemed to have inserted one leg into his white linen trousers while in midair.

The five soldiers still held their guns ready. They grinned from ear to ear, but there was that in the nervous demeanor of the cable operators which convinced one of their belief that the Chief-of-Staff had meant what he said.

The march was resumed, the colonel now and then becoming entangled with his sword. A path had been cut through the jungle, almost half a mile to the building near the shore of the bay where the cable had been landed. There was a sense of gloomy isolation in this jungle trail which caused McCready and Paine some uneasiness. They were not wholly trustful of the Haitian soldiery, but Stephen Crane expressed all the confidence in the world in the saddle-colored ex-butler of New Rochelle. We were perfectly safe with Alice-in-Wonderland.

And so it turned out. The cable operators were in a ruffled mood, but they consented to start sending the dispatches without delay. While we lingered to make sure of this, McCready wandered to the beach to explore the ruins of an ancient stone fort. One of the soldiers followed him, it seems, and clutched him by the arm. As McCready told it later, he was scared and confessed it without shame. The black ruffian had led him some distance away, beyond the ruined fort, until they were remote from succor.

"He had a bayonet and a machete," said Mac, "and it looked like dirty work, me with a money belt on, and this ferocious nigger had seen me take it off to slip the cable operators a gold piece as a tip. But he did n't unlimber the deadly weapons, and I guess I was curious or paralyzed, for I let him tow me way down yonder, where my screams could not have been heard. Then he spoke for the first time, in English, mind you:

" '*Gib me one dollah, white man.*' "

"Did he get it? I shucked him out two silver ones and clawed my pockets for small change. It was cheap ransom, a regular bargain. Don't mind that rattling noise. It's only my knees knocking together. I can't make 'em stop."

With happier minds the correspondents returned to the town of Mole St. Nicholas, having done their duty by their several newspapers. It occurred to them to try, in some small degree, to display their appreciation of the courtesy of the Chief-of-Staff and the soldiery. The courteous impulse was to buy the Haitian Army a drink. This desire was conveyed to the Chief-of-Staff, who replied that all the rum-shops were

closed, for the hour was past midnight, but he would be glad
to open one of them.

The invitation was comprehended by the colonel and the
five soldiers. Presently, by some kind of telepathy, the news
seemed to spread throughout the army. Instead of five men,
more than twenty trooped along as a guard of honor, and the
mobilization was increasing rapidly. It looked as though the
reserves had been turned out as a compliment to the four
correspondents. The column turned into one street after
another, and the impression was that it grew longer in passing
the groups of sentries at the little fires.

A halt was ordered at the door of a stone-walled hut, and
the Chief-of-Staff shouted one of those mandates of his. The
response was too laggard to please him. *Nom de Dieu!* He
spoke to the colonel, and the foremost file of soldiers shuffled
up, reversing their muskets. With the steel-shod butts they
battered that door in and made kindling wood of its stout
planks. It was one way to open a door.

The landlady of the grog-shop was in the act of descending from a sort of loft in which she slept. When the door
crashed from its hinges, she was so startled that she missed
the ladder and hit the floor with a mighty thud, being a
negress of ample proportions and chastely clad in a brief
chemise. It was an unusual welcome to an inn, so we thought,
and she appeared to agree with us.

The Chief-of-Staff, however, made no comment. It was all
in the night's work. Stephen Crane admired him more than
ever. It was an affinity. They were becoming like brothers.

The dazed and ponderous landlady was requested to produce rum. Harry Brown laid three dollars upon the rude
counter. There was a row of bottles on a shelf. It was expected that the money would buy one or two of these. But
the landlady passed them by and turned elsewhere. In a
corner stood one of those huge glass carboys in which acids
are stored. It was empty. She began to fill it with rum.

Gallon after gallon gurgled into it. We were learning how to sluice the dusty throats of an army.

"Rum is forty cents a gallon, it seems," said Crane, who had conferred with the Chief-of-Staff. "A unique experience, this — entertaining an army at a cost of three dollars. By golly, boys, she intends to fill that carboy. And the night is still young. Was it a winning hunch? I ask you."

Two muscular soldiers slung the carboy from a pole, in a rope netting, and the army moved in the direction of the beach. You could not have separated it from that carboy short of a drumhead court-martial. There had been no pay-days in several months. It had been a long time between drinks. Soon after this, the white beach of Mole St. Nicholas was a scene of life and animation, all of that.

The correspondents began to wonder whether three dollars' worth of rum was not too much. They felt this way after the army began firing salutes as a token of its esteem. The guns wobbled too much at random. The Chief-of-Staff had tarried until the merriment was more like a riot. Then he excused himself, mindful of his dignified station and exalted rank, and promising to meet us in the morning. At that time His Excellency, the Governor, would expect us for an audience at the palace, you bet.

In the morning? It was morning already, with a flush of dawn in the sky, while the enthusiastic soldiery danced on the beach and the astute deck-hand taught them to sing, "There'll be a Hot Time in the Old Town To-night." And, between choruses, this useful young man danced with the pretty girl who "had mighty little of the tar baby about her, let me tell you."

There were hoarse cheers for the grand Republic of the United States, and eloquent eulogies of the peerless Republic of Haiti, jewel of the Antilles, as voiced with deep emotion by the younger correspondents. Never was an *entente cordiale* in better form. Harry Brown, having attained years of discretion, and realizing his responsibilities as manager of a newspaper war staff, forsook the party before sunrise and went off to the Three Friends to snatch a few hours of sleep.

The other correspondents remained as hosts to the army. Courtesy demanded it. They were hailed as eternal friends of Haiti, as long as a drop of rum was left in the carboy. When there was no more rum, the guests began to disperse, leaving wavering tracks in the sand as they moved away, still singing.

The three correspondents, rather weary, returned to the Three Friends for breakfast. The social whirl had not yet released them. They remembered the engagement with the Governor at the palace. They sat on deck in a row, holding their heads in their hands. The obligations of hospitality had been exhausting. The astute deck-hand, as blithe as a daisy, was scrubbing down decks.

They were aroused by a noise in the town, the blare of bugles, the squeak of fifes, the roll of drums. They asked the skipper for a boat. Mole St. Nicholas was calling them. They were good for a farewell appearance.

To the palace they trudged, collecting many a friendly but blear-eyed salute *en route*, and found the vivacious Chief-of-Staff awaiting them. He was very much in uniform, crimson breeches and cavalry boots, gold cords on the blue coat, a plumed cocked hat. In Crane's opinion, the ex-butler would have knocked New Rochelle cold. While we chatted with him, a tall and dignified black man came out on the piazza. He wore a frock coat, with a sword belt buckled on. His face was serious and intelligent. In French the Governor greeted the visitors with a courtly ease of manner.

He took himself and his position with deep seriousness. He wished it to be understood that a review of the troops was to be held. It was a tribute to the distinguished journalists who had so cordially fraternized with his own people, as citizens of sister republics. It was open to remark that His Excellency was either deaf or had slept like a dead man. Otherwise he would have mistaken the cordial fraternizing for an attack by the enemy in force. Revolutions have been started with much less racket than that moonlit party on the beach.

The military band straggled past, an odd assortment of musical talent oddly arrayed, and banged and tootled its way to the parade ground. The Governor, the Chief-of-Staff, and the correspondents walked in that direction, but when you tried to step in time with the martial music of Haiti, your feet pranced in a cake-walk. It could n't be helped. Back of the town was a cleared field in which the army awaited its commanding general. A shrill fanfare of bugles, and the troops began to march in review.

There were perhaps two hundred of these black infantry-men, with brigadiers, colonels, and majors sprinkled as thick as huckleberries in a pudding. For uniform most of the privates were lucky to have a shirt and breeches and a big straw hat. The officers strutted in extraordinary remnants of military trappings, but it would have been unkind to laugh at them. It was like children playing a game in ab-sorbed imitation of grown-ups. Solemnly the army straggled past in review, guns of all vintages carried at all angles while the officers waved their swords and yelled strange orders. In justice it should be said that the army was conscious of feel-ing a difference in the morning. It was not quite up to par.

Then the zealous brigadiers attempted to maneuver the infantry, and got in trouble with it. Across the field, beyond the parade ground, the ragged files loped at the double to charge the imaginary enemy, but the pace soon slackened and there occurred a perplexing phenomenon. Every few steps the army halted and many men stooped over to pick up one foot in their hands, and then the other.

Stephen Crane was appealed to, as an expert in the tactics

of war. The literary critics had given him credit for a rare insight into the psychology and impulses of battle-fields.

"You can search me, boys," said he. "I never knew an army to stop and take its feet in its hands that way."

"You poor stupids," exclaimed McCready, who had solved it. "If you steer a barefooted army into a field covered with cactus bushes, can you blame it for stopping to pull the thorns out?"

"Quite so," agreed Crane. "I have no doubt you will find it included in the Haitian drill regulations."

From the harbor echoed three long, impatient blasts of the Three Friends' whistle. It was time to return to the blockade of Santiago. We bade His Excellency, the Governor, a warm farewell, but he urged us to wait a little. A dozen soldiers had laid hold of a rope and were dragging an antique cannon which may have been left in Haiti by the artillery forces of Napoleon. They were about to fire a salute with this interesting curio. It was, indeed, time to put for the open sea.

Ralph Paine hurriedly addressed his comrades:

"When that thing busts, it's going to scatter far and wide. Without hurting anybody's feelings, I suggest that we waive this final ceremony."

The Governor understood. He had heard the steamer blow her whistle again. It was the call of duty which must be obeyed. The Chief-of-Staff came down to the beach with us. Stephen Crane, reluctant to part from him, was asking him for the story of his life, and what about that four years as a butler in New Rochelle, when again Captain Montcalm Broward jerked the whistle cord. We shook hands with our genial host and friend, who said:

"It was a hot time in Mole St. Nicholas, you bet your sweet life. *Au revoir*, but not good-bye, and stay longer next time. Those cable operators, they will be on the *qui vive*, *n'est pas?* I think so, by jingo."

Before the ship sailed we sent off to him, in a skiff pulled

by the astute deck-hand, a case of sardines, a ham, and a tin
of cigarettes, as slight tokens of our gratitude and affection.
The Three Friends steamed out of the bay set between the
lofty green mountains. Three correspondents kicked off their
shoes and crept into their bunks to fall asleep. McCready
murmured his favorite bit of Kipling:

> But I would n't trust 'em at Wokin',
> We 're safer at sea again.

Harry Brown was humming to himself that mournful
ditty of his own invention:

> . . . Than to hear the water gurgle,
> Or the nightingale sing,
> A bottle o' rum, the ship 's a-sinking,
> *Two* bottles o' rum, we 'll all be drowned,
> *Three* bottles o' —

Stephen Crane raised his voice in tired protestation:
"Please don't sing that, Harry, old man. The words offend
me. Rum is poison. Think what you did to an army with
your vile three dollars. You ought to have known better."

XXIV

THE MARINES HELD THE HILL

Looking backward from the tranquil environment of a New Hampshire farm and the perspective of a middle-age not without its dignity, I am honestly surprised at the singular capacity displayed by this Ralph Paine in his youth for surging into matters which were wholly foreign to the pursuit of journalism. It would be charitable to call it a surplus of energy that flew off at blazing tangents. The fact may be apparent, by this time, that he was unhappy unless life consisted of one — er — of one thing after another.

In the course of this patchwork of memories, he has now come to an episode for which he had the grace actually to blush. In so far as he was able to discover, after the event, there had been no extenuating circumstances. This was the verdict of numerous beholders.

Soon after the American fleet had established its grim and unwearied blockade of Santiago, Admiral Sampson became convinced that he required a harbor not too far away in which his ships could be coaled and minor repairs effected, and where refuge might be sought in violent weather or after a punishing sea battle.

An ideal base was found in Guantanamo Bay, thirty-eight miles to the eastward. It was wide and deep, with an outer roadstead in which the largest fleet could anchor without jostling. There was not a finer harbor in the West Indies, but Spanish commerce had made almost no use of it. Near the entrance was a cable station and a small fishing village. Otherwise the shores and richly verdant hills were untenanted.

The light cruiser Marblehead, Captain Bowman McCalla,

reconnoitered the bay on June 7th, in company with the armed liner Yankee, and drove the Spanish gunboat Sandoval into the shoal water of the inner harbor. They also shelled the cable station, destroying it, and putting to flight the guard of Spanish troops.

Three days later, the transport Panther arrived from Key West with six hundred and fifty marines on board, in command of Lieutenant-Colonel Robert W. Huntington. Their job was to occupy and hold a shore base, and make the enemy hard to find. It goes without saying that the United States Marine Corps viewed this errand with enthusiasm.

For more than a hundred years this illustrious force of sea-soldiers had slung its hammocks between the decks of the ships of our Navy. Its traditions of valor and service were a priceless inheritance. These "leather-necks," as the blue-jackets called them, had been deadly with musket and boarding-pike when, from the shattered poop of the Bon Homme Richard, Captain John Paul Jones was trumpeting that he had not begun to fight. They had manned the tops when ruddy Isaac Hull was sinking the Guerrière with immortal broadsides which thundered from the wooden walls of the Constitution frigate. They had lined the bulwarks of the Hartford when the great-hearted Farragut damned the torpedoes; and they had swung the breech-blocks and slammed home the brass shell-cases with Dewey at Manila.

Soldier and sailor, too! From seaports exotic and remote had come the frequent and familiar message:

The marines have landed and have the situation well in hand.

This fight at Guantanamo Bay was an incident in the ordinary and accustomed routine, but it possessed a larger significance because it welded a little more enduringly the spirit and traditions of the Corps. It played its part in passing along to the next generation that temper and habit which is, after all, a spiritual equation and which causes men of all

sorts and conditions to believe that honor is to be preferred
to life.

This is what the regiments of American marines were
to show to all the world in Belleau Wood and at Château-
Thierry, with the slogan of —

Come on, you ——, *do you want to live forever?*

These six hundred and fifty marines aboard the Panther
desired to be put ashore, the sooner the quicker. Impatience
was a mild word for it. For days and days they had been
cooped in a ship which, as a floating barracks, was wretchedly
equipped. Nobody had seemed to know what to do with
them. Shafter's army was supposed to be ready to sail
from Tampa for the decisive invasion of Cuba, but never was
an army more unready. It could not be said that the high
command changed its mind, for the reason that it had no
mind to change. Confusion was its middle name. Fortu-
nately this was an army of brave soldiers who were determined
to win in spite of the War Department.

By way of contrast, it was worth noting that this battalion
of marines was intelligently equipped for a campaign in the
tropics. They were in uniforms of khaki. Suffering American infantrymen later strewed the Santiago trails with those
red-lined blue woolen overcoats with heavy capes, familiar in pictures of the Civil War. They had been thought-
fully prepared for marching into the Hudson Bay country.
Through some official oversight, the snowshoes and fur caps
had been omitted from the kits.

The dispatch boat Three Friends followed the Panther
into Guantanamo Bay, and the correspondents looked on
while the Marblehead and the Dolphin raked the wooded
hills and valleys with shrapnel to drive back any lurking
Spanish forces. Swiftly the marines filled the whaleboats and
cutters from the naval vessels and were towed to the beach
by steam launches. It was done with order and precision.

Within an hour the battalion was disembarked with its tents and supplies.

The marines climbed the hill selected for a camp, rifles on their shoulders, belts stuffed with cartridge clips, canteens filled, rations in their haversacks. They had discarded their coats and rolled up their sleeves, sinewy, active men hardened by incessant drill. To their eager questions, the obliging bluejackets of the Marblehead had made answer:

"Will you big stiffs get action? Listen! These woods are full of Spanish gorillas, the *Escuadra de Guantanamo*, the finest sharp-shootin' outfit in Cuba — three thousand of 'em — and they let out a hearty laugh when they saw you guys shove off. What they figure on handin' you will be plenty. Huh, don't you worry about *action*. You'll be combin' bullets out of *your* hair, all right."

The hill rose rather sharply from the beach. On top was an area more or less level, and perhaps two acres in extent. It was a rolling country, and, where the hills dipped, the intervales were dense with trees and creepers and tall grass. The camp-site was well chosen, at an elevation which overlooked the other hills near by, and with a line of communication and retreat open to the bay and the guns of the warships.

Through the afternoon the marines pitched camp and the tents blossomed in rows. Possibly there was too much confidence in the ability of the battalion to chase the enemy to a safe distance. At any rate, little was done in the way of digging trenches. When nightfall came, the marines were still in the open. They had not dug themselves in with their shovels and broad bayonets. The camp was on the alert, of course, outposts vigilant, and the officers a dashing and competent lot.

It was near midnight when the Spanish guerrillas began to creep nearer under cover of darkness. You could not call it a concerted attack. It was desultory sniping, snap-shooting at the embers of the camp-fires, at the vague outline of the assemblage of tents, a procedure cunningly calculated to rasp the nerves of these detestable *Marinos Americanos* and rob them of sleep.

There was no hitting back excepting as the exasperated "leather-necks" of Camp McCalla fired at the flash of the rifles in the undergrowth. The sibilant little voices of the Mauser bullets, as they drove across the hill, persuaded the battalion to make the dirt fly with whatever tools were handiest. They were in a mood to give the humble mole credit for a superior intelligence.

Daybreak disclosed the thin lines of marines lying flat behind small brown ridges of earth, shooting intermittently, very sore at an enemy that squibbed at them from the thickets. There had been no sleep in camp and this was only the overture. The Navy signaled to know whether reënforcements were needed, but the marines growled, "No, thank you"; and guessed they could hold the hill and maybe make things interesting for the Spaniards.

Meanwhile the Three Friends had left in a hurry for Port Antonio, Jamaica, to cable the news of the landing and the opening skirmish. This was the first attempt of an American armed force to seize and hold enemy territory in Cuba, a curtain-raiser in advance of the grand entrance of the Army. Stephen Crane stayed ashore with the marines because he foresaw much personal enjoyment. A hawser could not have dragged him away from the show. As I have said, the haste to file cable dispatches never troubled him. It was his business, as he viewed it, to gather impressions and write them as the spirit moved.

The Three Friends wasted no time during that run of a hundred and ten miles to Jamaica. It was the intention to return to Guantanamo Bay as soon as the Lord would let her. The weather was unusually favorable, but after reaching Port Antonio she was delayed several hours for engine-room repairs. As a result, it was in the middle of the night when the

Three Friends approached the Cuban coast and then went more cautiously lest she become entangled with the blockading fleet or with scouting cruisers. Also, she had been told by crisp and emphatic naval commanders not to go blundering into Guantanamo Bay until after sunrise.

In the early morning, therefore, she passed in from the sea and dropped anchor not far from the Marblehead and within a short distance of the marines of Camp McCalla upon the hill. They were still there, and Old Glory stirred in the faint breeze that breathed with the dawn. The petulant pop of rifles indicated that the fight was unfinished. For more than thirty hours there had been no cessation. The marines had taken their punishment. Between the tents they had laid their dead in a row on the grass and decently covered them with blankets. There had not yet been leisure for digging graves.

Stephen Crane came down to the beach and waved his hat in token of his desire to be taken aboard the Three Friends. He was dirty and heavy-eyed and enormously hungry and thirsty. It was all he could do to drag himself into the ship's galley where he gulped down food and black coffee. Then he sprawled on deck, rolling cigarettes and talking in a slow, unemotional manner as was his wont, but the thin, pallid face kindled and the somber, weary young eyes brightened when he told us how it had fared with the battalion of marines. And as he went on, he used words as though they were colors to be laid on a canvas with a vigorous and daring brush.

What had particularly impressed him was the behavior of the four signalmen, who, through the night, had kept the Marblehead informed of events upon the hill. These marines had a cracker-box, placed on top of a trench. When not signaling, they hid the lanterns in this box, but as soon as an order to send a message was received, it became necessary for one of the men to stand up and expose the lights.

"And then — oh, my eye!" drawled Crane, "how the

guerrillas hidden in the gulf of night would turn loose at those yellow gleams. How in the name of wonders those four men were not riddled from head to foot and sent home more as repositories of Spanish ammunition than as marines is beyond my comprehension. To make a confession, I, lying in the trench, invariably rolled a little to the right or left in order that, when he was shot, he would not fall on me. . . . Whenever the adjutant, Lieutenant Draper, came plunging into the darkness with an order, such as 'Please ask the Marblehead to shell the woods to the left,' my heart would come into my mouth, for I knew that one of my pals was going to stand up behind the lanterns and have all Spain shoot at him.

"The answer was always upon the instant, '*Yes, sir.*' Then the bullets began to snap, snap, snap at his head while all the woods began to crackle like burning straw. I could lie near and watch the face of the signalman, illumined as it was by the yellow shine of lantern light, and the absence of excitement, fright, or any emotion at all, on his countenance was something to astonish all theories out of one's mind. The face was in every instance merely that of a man intent upon his own business, the business of wig-wagging into the gulf of night where a light on the Marblehead was seen to move slowly."

Crane had joined the daylight sortie of a hundred and sixty marines under Captain Elliott who had burned the headquarters of the guerrilla forces at Cusco. Small incidents had impressed him, for it was of such that he had builded "The Red Badge of Courage," and this bit from his novel, written before he had seen a man killed in war, was precisely what he had found on the trail to Cusco:

Once the line encountered the body of a dead soldier. He lay upon his back, staring at the sky. He was dressed in an awkward suit of yellowish brown. The youth could see that the soles of his shoes had been worn to the thinness of writing-paper, and from a great rent in one the dead foot projected piteously. And it was as if fate had betrayed the soldier. In death it exposed to his enemies that poverty which in life he had perhaps concealed from his friends.

The ranks opened covertly to avoid the corpse. The invulnerable dead man forced a way for himself. The youth looked keenly at the ashen face. The wind raised the tawny beard. It moved as if a hand were stroking it. He vaguely desired to walk around and around the body and stare; the impulse of the living to try to read in dead eyes the answer to the question.

Rested and refreshed, Stephen Crane was eager to go ashore from the Three Friends and rejoin his pals, the marines, but McCready made vigorous objection.

"For heaven's sake, Steve, sit down and write some of this stuff. We left you here to cover the fight, and you've got it all. As soon as we catch up with the story, I must run this vessel back to Port Antonio and keep the cable busy. Duck into the cabin and write."

Crane paid no attention, but continued to talk about the marines. These practical, uninspired newspaper men were a confounded nuisance. They and their absurd demands were to be brushed aside. McCready tried bribery — beer and cigarettes — and Crane consented to dictate a dispatch, although very much bored. It was a ridiculous scene — McCready, the conscientious reporter, waiting with pencil and paper — Crane, the artist, deliberating over this phrase or that, finicky about a word, insisting upon frequent changes and erasures, and growing more and more suspicious. Finally he exclaimed:

"Read it aloud, Mac, as far as it goes. I believe you are murdering my stuff."

"I dropped out a few adjectives here and there, Steve. This has to be *news*, sent at cable rates. You can save your flub-dub and shoot it to New York by mail. What I want is the straight story of the fight."

Ralph Paine left them wrangling bitterly, with small hope of a satisfactory adjustment. He had been so absorbed in

Crane's recital of events that he had forgotten his haste to get ashore and investigate this small battle at first hand. He noticed that the scattering fire from the camp and from the chaparral had ceased. It was a morning lull. The Spanish sharpshooters had bethought themselves of breakfast, or such was the deduction, and the marines were in a mood to second the motion.

His attention diverted by this interval of strange silence on land, Paine thought it an excellent time to visit the battalion upon the hill. He had overlooked breakfast while Crane was talking, and now it seemed inconsequential, not worth the delay. This was a serious error, as it turned out. By way of speedy nourishment, he poured out one drink of Scotch whiskey — one drink, mind you, and it was *not* a large one. This is important to remember.

A noble idea occurred to him. He drove the cork in the bottle and carried it along with him. It seemed a sin to leave it in the locker when those heroic marines were so sorely in need of comfort and sympathy. This was nothing at all like that moonlit picnic on the white beach of Haiti when the rum had gurgled so hospitably. The motive was entirely different. The most censorious critic could have found no fault with it. The bottle of Scotch was to be a friend in need and a tribute to valor.

It happened that another Colt machine gun had just then been landed from a ship. It was a heavy affair, mounted upon a pair of wheels, and, for some reason, more men were needed to drag it up the steep slope of the hill. Being a young man of some beef and brawn, I put my shoulder to the wheel and shoved. The foothold was crumbling and insecure, as the men on the drag-rope also discovered. The gun slewed and slid back.

I went with it, but even more rapidly, rolling into a tall clump of cactus after bumping over a rock or two. The first impulse, and a praiseworthy one, was to save the bottle of

Scotch. It had lodged unbroken. In the light of this good fortune, the altercation with the cactus clump amounted to nothing.

Two correspondents who had come ashore from another dispatch boat had also volunteered to help the marines haul the gun up the hill. One of these was H. J. Whigham, an Englishman who won the amateur golf championship in the early days of the game in America, and who was later the publisher of the "Metropolitan Magazine." Poor Whigham, too, fell down the hill, but was unlucky enough to finish the descent on his face which was scratched and cut and bruised in such wholesale fashion that, after a naval surgeon had criss-crossed it with strips of plaster, there was no recognizing him as Whigham at all. He was, beyond doubt, a casualty of war.

Another struggle with the Colt gun and it was pulled over the brow of the hill. The marines were found in their shallow trenches, haggard men fighting off sleep, but uttering no complaints. There was never a notion among them of withdrawing to the ships. To the nearest squads of them appeared a correspondent with a bottle of Scotch in his fist. They eyed him with a wistful fondness. He was more popular than a paymaster.

It was touching to see how sparingly each man drank, a swallow, and then he passed the bottle to the comrade at his elbow. A few of them were asleep during this lull, cheeks against the rifle-stocks, fingers ready to jerk the bolt and slide in another clip. A boyish second lieutenant refused to drink and handed the bottle to a hard-featured sergeant with a bloody bandage around his head. It was done with the grace of a Sir Philip Sidney.

"After you, sir," said the sergeant.

"Take a slug, you old fool!" snapped the lieutenant. "You men need it worse than I do."

The correspondent strolled along the line until a marine

tossed aside the empty bottle. One of the men had lost his cap during the night and his head was bare as he lay stretched in his furrow of earth. Already the sun had begun to beat down upon this bare hill and the little breeze had died. It was going to be a wickedly hot day, with an unclouded sky, and the prostrate marines were red and sweating like ship's stokers.

I gave this bareheaded marine my gray soft hat, expecting to rummage the Three Friends for other head-gear. He seemed very grateful. However, it was unnecessary to go out to the ship on this errand. In another part of the camp a big straw hat with a flapping brim was discovered. It had been picked up by a marine during the return march from Cusco. The guerrilla who had worn the hat had no further use for it.

Clapping this discarded souvenir upon my own head I was protected from the blazing sun. A detail so trifling as this big straw hat is mentioned because it was soon to become an affair of sinister significance to a certain correspondent named Ralph Paine.

XXV

MY FRIEND, THE SUGAR BOILER

THE lull in the fighting was loudly, abruptly broken by the hammering staccato of a machine gun. The drowsy marines in the trenches rolled over to their rifles as a man is startled in bed when an alarm-clock rings. An officer with field-glasses at his eyes had discovered a movement against the grassy hillside across a valley. Where the trees and bushes were less profuse, an opening in the jungle, a considerable number of Spanish guerrillas were in the act of crossing to another ridge of ground. All that made them visible were the big straw hats.

The machine gun sprayed that hillside with bullets. It flushed the enemy like shooting into a covey of quail. You could see the straw hats bob up and disappear in all directions. Having made themselves scarce, with amazing rapidity, the straw hats returned the compliment by resuming the action with rifle-fire. Once more the bullets buzzed across the camp, and the marines set their sights and pulled trigger at whatever they fancied to be a living target.

The young man named Paine decided to betake himself elsewhere. There seemed to be no trench to hold him comfortably. He was fastidious about a proper fit. He would return to the bottom of the hill, beside the bay, and see what was going on there.

Having reached this destination, he poked along the beach, perhaps two hundred yards, and found a detachment of marines. They were posted to keep the line of communication open, and also to guard a large heap of ammunition boxes and supplies from which the camp occasionally replenished its stock.

These marines were so placed that they commanded a little valley between the hills, a valley which ran down to the bay. On one side of it was the camp, on the other the ambushed enemy. The camp could not be rushed from this direction so long as the detail of marines was there to thwart it. When the machine gun had set things going again, these men had swarmed into line behind fortifications hastily improvised from boxes of ammunition and provisions. Out of the water scampered naked men who had been bathing. As they ran they arrayed themselves with cartridge belts and rifles.

Ralph Paine tarried to get acquainted with them and found the conversation agreeable. They were very fine men. He was glad to sit down upon a box of shells. The heat of the sun, that falling down the hill with the Colt automatic gun, and the omission of breakfast had combined to make him feel a trifle queer. He is ready to swear that the one drink of Scotch — not a large one, mind you — had nothing whatever to do with it. If he had tackled breakfast with his customary zeal, nothing sensational would have occurred.

A habit of these Spanish guerrillas was to wrap themselves in palm leaves and climb a tree where they baffled detection and could practice fancy sharpshooting in a leisurely fashion. It is the plain truth that Ralph Paine felt sure he saw one of these crafty marksmen in a distant tree. Immediately he wished greatly to shoot this Spanish assassin, which was an impulse perfectly proper.

The marines had done more than their share. To lend them a hand was nothing else than courtesy. In fact, the young man's admiration for the battalion was so great that he was ready to charge the entire force of guerrillas, by way of showing his appreciation. And this he proceeded to do.

Some time after this, the perfidious Stephen Crane wrote for "McClure's Magazine" a story cast in the fictional form which he labeled "The Lone Charge of William B. Perkins;

A True Story." I read it with embarrassment. As a disciple of realism, Crane had been conscientious. In order that you may visualize the incident as he saw it, and to save the chief actor from talking about himself for a few minutes, I quote, in part:

And now it befell Perkins to discover a Spaniard in the bush. In a loud voice he announced his perception. He also declared hoarsely that if he only had a rifle he would go and possess himself of this particular enemy. Immediately an amiable young corporal who had been shot in the arm said, "Well, take mine." Perkins thus acquired a rifle and a clip of five cartridges.

"Come on!" he shouted. This part of the battalion was lying very tight, not yet being engaged, but not knowing when the business would swirl around to them.

To Perkins they replied with a roar, "Come back here, you —— fool! Do you want to get shot by your own crowd? Come back, —— ——."

As a detail it might be mentioned that the fire from a part of the camp swept the journey upon which Perkins had started.

Now behold the solitary Perkins adrift in the storm of fighting, even as a champagne jacket of straw is lost in a great surf. He found it out quickly. Four seconds elapsed before he discovered that he was an almshouse idiot plunging through hot, crackling thickets on a June morning in Cuba. Sss-s-s-swing-sing-ing-pop went the lightning-swift metal grasshoppers over him and beside him. . . . Sshsh-swing-pop.

Perkins decided that if he cared to extract himself from a tangle of imbecility he must shoot. It was necessary that he should shoot. The entire situation was that he must shoot. Nothing would save him but shooting. It is a law that men thus decide when the waters of battle close over their minds. So with a prayer that the Americans would not hit him in the back nor the left side, and that the Spaniards would not hit him in the front, he knelt like a suppliant alone in the desert of chaparral, and emptied his magazine at his Spaniard before he discovered that his Spaniard was a bit of dried palm branch.

Then Perkins flurried like a fish. His reason for being was a Spaniard in the bush. When the Spaniard turned into a dried palm branch, he could no longer furnish himself with one adequate reason. Then did he dream frantically of some anthracite hiding-place, some profound dungeon of peace where blind mules live placidly chewing the far-gathered hay.

Sss-swing-win-pop! Prut-prut-prrut! Then a field gun spoke. *Boom*-ra-swow-ow-ow-ow-*pum!* Then a Colt automatic began to bark. Crack-crk-crk-crk-crk-crk, endlessly. Raked, enfiladed, flanked, surrounded, and overwhelmed, what hope was there for William B. Perkins?

But war is a spirit. War provides for those that it loves. It provides sometimes death and sometimes a singular and incredible safety. There were few ways by which it was possible to preserve Perkins. One way was by means of a steam-boiler.

Perkins espied near him an old, rusty steam-boiler lying in the bushes. War only knew how it was there, but there it was, a temple shining with safety. With a moan of haste, Perkins flung himself through that hole which expressed the absence of a steam-pipe.

Then ensconced in his boiler, Perkins comfortably listened to the ring of a fight which seemed to be in the air above him. Sometimes bullets struck their strong, swift blows against the boiler's sides, but none entered to interfere with Perkins's rest.

Time passed. The fight dwindled to prut . . . prut . . . prut . . . prut. And when the silence came, Perkins might have been seen cautiously protruding from the boiler. Presently he strolled back toward the marine lines with his hat not able to fit his head for the new bumps of wisdom that were on it.

The marines, with an annoyed air, were settling down again, when an apparitional figure came from the bushes. There was great excitement.

"It's the crazy man!" they shouted, and as he drew near they gathered tumultuously about him and demanded to know how he had accomplished it.

Perkins made a gesture, the gesture of a man escaping from an unintentional mud-bath, the gesture of a man coming out of battle, and then he told them.

The incredulity was immediate and general. "Yes, you did! What? In an old boiler? An old boiler! Out in that brush? Well, we guess not." They did not believe him until two days later when a patrol happened to find the rusty boiler, relic of some curious transaction in the ruin of the sugar industry. The marines of the patrol marveled at the truthfulness of war correspondents until they were almost blind.

Soon after his adventure, Perkins boarded the tug, wearing a countenance of poignant thoughtfulness.

This is how Stephen Crane interpreted it. To the reader it will be obvious that he pinned a leather medal, as a booby prize, on William B. Perkins. And the verdict will not be disputed. And yet it seemed a perfectly logical thing at the time, to shoot up the Spanish army as a token of hearty coöperation with the battling marines. Had it occurred a generation later, the students of psycho-analysis would be demanding to know what was the matter with the young man's complexes. But he would have had Dr. Freud and his disciples guessing, because the explanation was so simple. This was merely another attack of *damfoolitis!*

It was not an incident for Ralph D. Paine, *alias* William B. Perkins, to write about in news dispatches. The transaction might have been called personal, and extraneous to the war. When he returned home, and the thing followed him, he laughed it aside as utter nonsense, but the first informant, who was the hostess of a dinner party, made this retort:

"My brother is a major in the Marine Corps and he was with the battalion at Guantanamo. He saw you do it."

To set the matter right in this chronicle of fact, there were essential details which Stephen Crane overlooked. The most important of these concerned that big, flopping straw hat, for which a guerrilla had no more use because of his sudden death. I had worn it gratefully until that unsupported advance with the rifle of the wounded corporal. When those friendly marines were yelling at me to come back, one of them said something about throwing away that hat, for God's sake, but this had made no impression at the moment.

The fact that the marines on the hill shot at these big straw hats on sight, as almost the only targets visible, was well worth noting, but there was room for no more than one idea under this particular straw hat. It went bobbing up the valley, and the marines in camp attempted to drill holes through it. They failed to do so because the wearer of the

MARINES ON GUARD AT THE SUPPLY BASE NEAR THE BAY. THEY
CHEERED THE AUTHOR'S HASTY RETURN FROM THE SUGAR BOILER

THE AUTHOR AT GUANTANAMO BEFORE HE ACQUIRED THE BIG
STRAW HAT

hat was moving too fast to be hit by any one but an expert wing shot.

At Yale this man Paine had been called a clumsy oarsman and a sluggish football player. At Guantanamo the coaches would have offered him apologies. He would have been invited to join the track team and show the other hundred-yard sprinters how slow they were. His heels flew up behind and swished the brim of the straw hat. This is how he ran.

As Stephen Crane said of him, he did not burn the wind in this manner until after he had shot the borrowed rifle empty. At first, the purpose of potting that Spanish sharpshooter in the tree had fascinated him, and he had been more or less oblivious of the efforts of those who were trying to pot him. But with no more cartridges there was, indeed, a lack of occupation, that frame of mind which is sometimes called *ennui*.

To retreat may have been the part of wisdom, but it did not look so. It was my belief that the *Escuadra de Guantanamo*, three thousand strong, was shooting at the rapidly moving figure in the valley, having rightly assumed that no Spanish soldier would be in that particular position.

The sugar boiler stood among the trees, the ruins of a brick chimney close by. If the chimney had been intact, it is not boastful to affirm that I could have reached the top in one bound and dived down inside. In the end of the boiler was an opening. It was not where the steam-pipe had been. No two-hundred-pound man could have inserted himself through such a small aperture as that, although I might have tried. The furnace door was my appointed haven. I took it head-foremost, as clean as a whistle, without rubbing the rust from the door frame.

Nor could the art of Stephen Crane convey the sense of ineffable contentment with which I snuggled in that providential old boiler. A brave man would not have sacrificed his precious dignity in this manner. You could imagine such a one calmly strolling back to the detachment of marines behind their breastwork of cartridges and hard-tack, and easily exclaiming while he flicked the dust from his riding-boots with a silk handkerchief:

"Rather warm work out there, my lads. Devilish poor shooting, though. The marines on the hill disappointed me. I shall have to speak to the colonel about it. They ought to have bagged me."

Have you ever slept in an attic room and listened to the patter of an autumn rain on the shingles? Snug and comfortable to be all tucked in, was n't it? To sit hunched in the blessed old boiler was like that, only more so. The steel-nosed bullets rang against the iron plates with a musical tintinnabulation. There was a slight uneasiness, of course, lest a spot eaten by rust might let a bullet in. But it was a bully old boiler, and I loved it.

It was an excellent place in which to sit and think hard. A man with no breakfast under his belt could not lodge in this boiler all day. It was a splendid tenement for a transient visitor caught in a storm, but this was all you could say for it. There was nothing to indicate that the marines were eager to send a relief expedition. They had shown their friendship by lending the missing correspondent a rifle. And he had absconded with government property.

There now percolated the conjecture that the big straw hat might have had something to do with all that shooting at Ralph Paine. He removed it from his head and used it as a fan. You could have raised steam in that boiler without building a fire under it. As a summer resort, it was out of the question.

"This hat made trouble for me," was the lucid conclusion. "Of course the marines and the Spaniards were shooting at each other across the valley, but at least a million of those bullets flew entirely too low. Both parties disliked this hat, it looks to me. I won't wear it when I go back. I'd rather get sunstruck."

Go back? This was something that had to be done, but shiveringly. It was like jumping into a tub of ice water. However, this getting to the beach had one advantage over the Gussie expedition. I did not have to tow a large black horse. The fighting had died down. Bullets no longer rang bull's-eyes on the boiler plates. It was a propitious time for emerging like a hermit crab forsaking its shell. There was an acute feeling of homesickness in leaving this dear old rusty boiler.

The straw hat *was* not carried along as a souvenir.

This return journey down the valley was made with long strides, but, by contrast, it was as peaceful as going to church. The marines offered a vociferous welcome, as Stephen Crane has informed you, and the wounded corporal seemed pleased and surprised to get his rifle back. There was considerable discussion, a sort of informal court of inquiry, concerning the adventure. It was agreed that the correspondent was cold sober. And not all the marines were ready to say that he was crazy. A grizzled gunnery sergeant declared, after gravely pondering it:

"These newspaper boys have a hard time of it, what with bucketin' around in nasty weather with the blockadin' fleet where nothing seldom happens. Why should n't this lad enjoy himself when he gets a chance? It was like takin' a day off. Why did n't we give him a belt full of cartridges, and he could ha' set all tight in his boiler and made a real holiday of it."

"It was that straw hat that gummed the deal for him," said a tall private. "If he'd had sense enough to lose that lid, *pronto*, he would n't have got pestered with so many bullets. For a man as big as he is, I sure did admire the way he slung his feet. He must have looked funny from up in the camp. I'll bet them guys was sayin' there goes one swift Spaniard that don't waste no time on siestas."

The correspondent expressed his gratitude for these kindly opinions, and as he walked away, the marines began to whistle "Johnny Get Your Gun."

This was the last day of the fighting at Guantanamo Bay. Convinced that they could not dislodge the battalion, and severely mauled, the guerrilla forces retired inland and the harbor was safe for Admiral Sampson's ships.

The Three Friends made another trip to Jamaica and then returned to her station off Santiago. I went aboard the flagship New York for a chat with my friends of the ward-room and steerage mess. Among the officers pleasantly encountered were Colonel Robert L. Meade, commanding the marines with the fleet, and Major Mancil C. Goodrell of the flagship's marine detachment. We three finally adjourned to the colonel's stateroom to talk over the good fight of Huntington's battalion at Guantanamo.

The suggestion was made that I should try to get a commission, as a second lieutenant, in the Marine Corps. I listened with enthusiasm. It seemed most desirable. Just then no other career seemed so congenial.

The colonel and the major would be pleased to write letters of endorsement and recommendation, said they, and this they proceeded to do at the desk in the stateroom. These letters they would forward to Washington at once, along with my application. At that time the editor-in-chief of my paper, the "Philadelphia Press," Charles Emory Smith, was a member of President McKinley's Cabinet, as Postmaster-General. Naturally enough, I wrote a letter to Mr. Smith, acquainting him with my ambition and requesting him to use his influence in my behalf.

It meant losing a promising young journalist, but in time of war I thought that Mr. Charles Emory Smith might be willing to make the sacrifice. He was a kindly man with a sense of humor, and I hoped he had forgotten or overlooked my last interview with him in the "Press" office. He had run up from Washington to keep in touch with his newspaper, and while strolling through the city room he was good enough to stop and say: "How are you, Mr. Paine? What are you doing now? Anything interesting?"

"Not very, thank you, Mr. Smith. I shall have to be in Easton to-morrow to cover the laying of a corner-stone, or the dedication of a new building or something, at Lafayette College. You know what those things are — some tiresome, pompous orator delivers an address, all wind and platitudes, and you have to sit and listen to it. Misfortunes like that blight a reporter's life."

"Ah, yes," said Charles Emory Smith, with a smile that was not wholly spontaneous. "I believe I am to be the principal speaker at Lafayette College to-morrow."

Need I add that the eloquent address of the Postmaster-General was reported by Ralph D. Paine with what would have been called twenty years later "meticulous" diligence? And he felt uneasy until he saw the closing paragraph ticked off by the Easton telegraph operator.

To return to that afternoon aboard the flagship New York, the documents were made ready for mailing and the colonel, the major, and I felt sanguine that the United States Marine Corps would shortly acquire a new second lieutenant. We went up to the quarter-deck where the air was much cooler. Admiral Sampson paced to and fro, his hands clasped behind him, with that detached, introspective demeanor. He paused to remark, very graciously:

"Good afternoon, Mr. Paine. How has your conduct been since the night war was declared, when you came aboard — er — call it unceremoniously?"

"My conduct, sir?" was the hasty reply. This was too soon after Guantanamo for questions like that. "My record is active but excellent. Why, you can ask Colonel Meade and Major Goodrell. They have given me written testimonials. Would you like to see them?"

"Never mind," said Admiral Sampson, with a rare twinkle. "You had better hang on to those testimonials. They may keep you out of jail."

The sequel of this epistolary industry came several months later. The campaign of Santiago and its aftermath had given the aspiring correspondent other things to think about than his candidacy for the Marine Corps. It had been an impulse born of the time and place. The momentum of journalism whirled him into different orbits, and that afternoon with the colonel and the major had become a dimming memory. It was recalled when he chanced to meet Mr. Charles Emory Smith in Washington.

"Why did n't you accept that commission in the Marine Corps?" inquired the Postmaster-General. "I spoke to the President about it and he was most agreeable. He made a note of the matter and said he would look after it personally."

"I never heard a word from Washington, Mr. Smith. I was hoping to be ordered north for the examinations, but there was nothing doing."

"Well, let's look into this," he exclaimed. "I am rather curious to know."

Mr. Smith promptly investigated and discovered that another young man named Paine, from Connecticut, had been trying to secure a commission in the Marine Corps, but without results until the Postmaster-General had interviewed the President. Then the patient and thoughtful William McKinley, amid the tremendous pressure of affairs, had said a word in favor of bestowing this second lieutenant's commission, but the Marine Corps had given it to the other Paine. He made far better use of it, I have no doubt, and Ralph Paine was left to continue his career as a reporter of events.

That lone charge of William B. Perkins at Guantanamo did, indeed, cause its hero to wear an expression of poignant thoughtfulness at times, as Stephen Crane has related. More than once he found himself meditating over an episode of the Santiago blockade which, when witnessed, he had regarded as pure comedy. Now he viewed it in a different light and his sympathy was with the enemy.

The Dolphin had been cruising to the eastward of the Morro when Commander Henry Lyon descried a train of open flatcars loaded with Spanish troops, coming from the direction of Juricao and bound to Santiago. At this point the railroad skirted the beach, running through a succession of short tunnels and deep cuts with open spaces between.

The train was moving from one tunnel to the next when the Dolphin dashed shoreward and shelled the flatcars with a four-inch battery at a range of only six hundred yards. The Spanish engineer yanked the throttle open and rattled the train along to gain the next tunnel beyond him, like a rabbit racing for a hole. The refuge proved to be a lamentable misfit, for it was a bit too short to shelter the locomotive and its string of flatcars.

The train pulled a little ahead, and the Dolphin banged away at the locomotive. It backed violently and two cars were exposed at the hinder end of the tunnel. Chased by flying fragments of shell, the soldiers upon these cars departed for the bushes without orders. Then the Dolphin bombarded the side of the tunnel and filled the air with earth and masonry.

The Spanish engine-driver thereupon fixed his gaze on the next tunnel and the train went scuttling to reach it. The American blue-jackets were hilarious. Never before in their experience had they beheld an hysterical locomotive. It had almost gained shelter in a long cut when a shell exploded squarely in the boiler and the game of hide-and-seek ended then and there.

The Spanish soldiers instantaneously vanished from all those flatcars and continued to Santiago on foot. One was puzzled to know whether to call this a naval engagement or a train wreck. At least a hundred conscript youths of Spain, in uniforms of blue and white bed-ticking, could find no mirth in this excursion, for they were killed or wounded by the target practice of the Dolphin.

As I say, it no longer seemed uproariously comical to me. The misfortune of those poor devils was too much like the adventure of the young man who had dived into the rusty sugar boiler. And if his girth had been a trifle larger or the furnace door a few inches smaller, his plight would have very much resembled that of the panicky locomotive so frantically trying to find a tunnel long enough.

XXVI
COLONEL ROOSEVELT CUTS RED TAPE

It has been said, and without much exaggeration, that the American Army captured Santiago with its bare hands. A democracy is always unready for war, and the men in the ranks pay with their lives the bitter price of the ineptitude of bureaucrats and the ignorance of politicians. After three months of preparation, the resources of a mighty nation were able to send to Cuba a force of fifteen thousand men, mostly regulars, who fought without proper food or clothing or arms, whose wounded died of neglect and whose regiments rotted with fever because they lacked the most obvious and elementary details of equipment and organization. It was a campaign in many respects tragic and grotesque, but illumined by the achievements of men who had the will to win at any cost.

Their dead and wounded strewed the jungle trails and littered the slopes of San Juan Hill and the defenses of El Caney, but they rushed on like a torrent and compelled the surrender of a Spanish army vastly superior in numbers.

And on that unforgettable Sunday morning of July 3d, Admiral Cervera's cruisers had steamed gallantly out to be smashed and sunk and driven ashore by the guns of Sampson's ships. Thus ended almost four centuries of Spanish dominion over the storied city of Santiago de Cuba in whose gray cathedral were entombed the bones of the conqueror of the island, Diego Velasquez, and from whose land-locked harbor had sailed the great galleons of Hernan Cortes and Pamfilio de Narvaes in quest of the fabulous gold of Mexico and Peru, a hundred years before the Pilgrims set foot upon Plymouth Rock.

Ah, but this old and famous city of Santiago was a place of wretched misery when the first American cavalrymen rode into its cobbled streets and stared with curious eyes. Thousands of people, the women and the little children, had streamed out into the country during the bombardment by the American fleet. They had found neither food nor shelter, for the region had been swept bare by the Cuban insurgents. These pitiable refugees died like flies, and when the survivors returned to the city, after the surrender, they were so much fuel for the yellow fever and smallpox to feed upon. Dead bodies lay thick in the city streets and vultures tore them. Gaunt men and women stretched skinny arms from the windows and feebly begged the American soldiers for bread.

It was then that Brigadier-General Leonard Wood, late colonel of the Rough Riders, first displayed his splendid talent as an administrator. He was the government of Santiago, physician, soldier, statesman. The man and the opportunity were fused in an extraordinary accomplishment. Famine vanished. The streets were cleaned of their unspeakable filth. The dead were heaped like cordwood and burned with barrels of kerosene. There was work and wages for the able-bodied. Out of a chaos gruesome and sorrowful and hopeless, order began to appear within forty-eight hours. Leonard Wood was the salvation of Santiago.

I recall meeting him in the Venus Café the day after he had undertaken this task. The luncheon menu consisted of horse meat stewed with onions, at five dollars a plate. Leonard Wood and General Henry W. Lawton sat at a table together, two tall, keen-eyed, square-jawed men of the blond Anglo-Saxon strain, born leaders who had proven themselves in the ordeal of battle. They were two of a kind. Of Lawton's division at El Caney, a Spanish staff officer had said:

"I have never seen anything to equal the courage and dash of those Americans who, stripped to the waist, offering their naked bodies to our murderous fire, literally threw themselves on our trenches — on the very muzzles of our guns. We had the advantage of position and mowed them down by hundreds; but they never retreated or fell back an inch. As one man fell, shot through the heart, another would take his place, with grim determination and unflinching devotion to duty in every line of his face."

There was a singular contrast between this glimpse of Wood and Lawton and a scene at the ancient stone palace of the Spanish Governor on the plaza, a contrast and a scene almost incredible. It was a ceremonial occasion, of striking significance, the formal occupation of Santiago by the American Army and the display of the Stars and Stripes above the palace as a symbol thereof. Staff officers and foreign military attachés surrounded General Shafter. An escort of troops paraded. A regimental band played. The civilian populace looked on.

For some inscrutable reason correspondents were told to remain severely in the background, but upon the roof of the palace, beside the flagpole, there appeared the active, compact figure of the incomparable Sylvester Scovel, Special Commissioner of the "New York World." His hand grasped the halliards of the flag. At this spectacular moment in the histories of Spain and the United States, what was more natural and to be expected than that Scovel should be in the center of the stage?

This was journalism, as his career had interpreted it. He had a flamboyant audacity which would have made him a dazzling motion-picture hero. There was only one Sylvester Scovel.

Behold him, then, defying martial edict, conspicuous upon the hoary palace roof, ready to assist in hoisting the American flag, while the commanding general and his staff glared in blank amazement. Scovel was told to come down. He paid no attention. The rude hands of soldiers pulled him down.

He was tremendously indignant. The affront was unpardonable. To General Shafter himself he rushed to argue the matter, this interference, this insult to the "New York World."

The corpulent General Shafter had suffered much in Cuba
and his temper was never amiable nor his language colorless.
He told Sylvester Scovel to shut up or be locked up, and
brushed him to one side. Sylvester Scovel swung his good
right arm and attempted to knock the head off the major-
general commanding the American Army in Cuba.

It was a flurried blow, without much science behind it, and
Scovel's fist glanced off the general's double chin, but it left
a mark there, a red scratch visible for some days. Then, indeed, was the militant young journalist hustled away and
locked up. It was an incident of war without precedent.

This was a strange climax of the luckless career of General
Shafter in the field, and yet perhaps this ridiculous assault
expressed a sentiment which had spread through the Army.
It was reflected in such an indictment as that of Richard
Harding Davis, a competent observer, who said:

A man who could not survive a ride of three miles on horseback
when his men were tramping many miles on foot with packs and
arms, and under a tropical sun; who was so occupied and concerned
with a gouty foot that he could not consider a plan of battle, and
who sent seven thousand men down a trail he had never seen,
should resist the temptation to accept responsibilities his political
friends thrust upon him, responsibilities he knows he cannot bear.
This is the offense I impute to Shafter, that while he was not even
able to rise and look at the city he had been sent to capture, he still
clung to his authority. His self-complacency was so great that in
spite of blunder after blunder, folly after folly, and mistake upon
mistake, he still believed himself infallible, still bullied his inferior
officers, and still cursed from his cot.

Well, the self-complacency of General Shafter had been
jarred, for once, and there was a red mark on his chin to
prove it. A day after the event, I met Louis Seibold, in

charge of the "World" service, in the entrance hall of the Governor's palace. Quiet, self-contained, never exploiting himself, it may be imagined that Seibold was not entirely in sympathy with the latest adventure of Sylvester Scovel. But it was his duty to see what could be done for the fellow member of the "World" staff who was a prisoner in the guard-room of the palace.

"I saw Scovel just now," said Seibold. "This is the first time he was ever really worried. He knows he would be shot in any country with a military system. Shafter insulted him, says he, and he could n't stand for it, so he hit him. Scovel is in no mood to apologize. I am going in to talk to the old man. Want to come along?"

"It will do no good to have me shove into the interview with Shafter," said I. "I'll stand by and wait for you, Louie."

It was a picture to linger in the mind, as perceived through the open door of the stately room in which Spanish Governors had held their stern and autocratic sway, the great bulk of Shafter overflowing a carven chair, his voice booming angrily, his pudgy finger straying to that red scratch on his chin; — Seibold engaged in courteous expostulation and holding his temper perfectly in hand. Now and then the general's remarks could be heard:

"Of course he ought to be shot, —— it! He ought to have been shot down in his tracks. But the people at home think this war is a pink-tea party. You know they do. . . . It would kick up an infernal rumpus . . . the war is about over . . . It is none of your damned business what I do with him. You have carried out your mission by appearing in behalf of the fool. You can do nothing more . . ."

Seibold came out, rather warm, and said in his dour way: "The old man thinks Scovel is crazy. I don't know about that. Deportation will be the sentence. Put him on a ship and send him home. And that is a whole lot better than I expected. Now if some bright young correspondent had punched the jaw of the commanding general of a French or German army in time of war — deported in a wooden box, eh?"

That torrid summer filthy Santiago was not always as diverting as this, Santiago with its stenches and miseries, with its smallpox and yellow fever, and among the hills outside the city an American army waiting to be taken home, an army with half its men disabled by fever and dysentery.

Frequently Colonel Theodore Roosevelt came riding into town, long stirrups like a cow-puncher's, polka-dot handkerchief flapping from the back of his campaign hat, eye-glasses gleaming, flannel shirt and khaki breeches, and only one idea in his head — to rustle supplies for "*my regiment*." He raided the wharves, the ships, the warehouses, and loaded the stuff upon pack-mules, into army wagons or native carts, and boasted of his ability as a wholesale forager.

When Colonel Roosevelt made his first raid in search of supplies, he snapped at young Lieutenant Wise who was the acting American Quartermaster:

"Well, I don't know and I don't care a whoop what the regulations are. My men need supplies and I've come after them, and I'm going to get them."

"You can have them, Colonel," replied Wise, "if you will find something to carry them away in. You ought to know that the Quartermaster does n't transport supplies to brigades."

"I 'll fix that," retorted Theodore Roosevelt, turning on his heel. In a jiffy he had commandeered five absurd little native mule carts. Having heaped them high with his plunder, the colonel of the Rough Riders shook hands with young Wise and said in farewell:

"Of course, you have to obey your fool orders because of red tape. But I don't have to. No harm done. You have done your duty and I 've got the stuff."

Red tape and regulations be hanged! *"My regiment"* needed other food than pork and beans. It needed medical stores. And its colonel would get them, by the Eternal, without waiting for a mare's-nest of requisitions and endorsements. And to the end of his life he snapped it out with that same proud, intense affection, *"my regiment,"* and no other honor, of those great distinctions bestowed upon him, was so close to his heart as the leadership of the First Volunteer Cavalry, better known as the Rough Riders.

There were only a few of us correspondents in Santiago. Most of them had gone home or to Porto Rico to join the troops of General Miles for the brief campaign in that island. We found quarters in the Anglo-American Club, an old Spanish house with its patio and galleries where, in the drowsy days of peace, foreign merchants and shipping agents and sugar planters had played whist and cooled themselves with whiskies-and-sodas. It offered lodgings to the newspaper waifs. The veteran steward, an elderly colored man, served meals of a sort. The world had tumbled about his ears, but he faithfully endeavored to put his little corner of it together again.

And into the club would breeze Colonel Roosevelt to find out what news we had and to tell us about his regiment with a delightful and infectious enthusiasm. You may have heard a father talk like that when the boy has scored the winning touchdown in a big football game.

Colonel Roosevelt came striding into the club one morning with a mien even more earnest and intense than usual. He called the correspondents together, I think there were five of us in the group, and pulled a sheet of paper from his pocket. It was the rough draft of a letter to the Secretary of War and was the genesis of the famous "Round Robin," signed by the commanders of the fighting divisions and brigades, which was tossed into Washington like a bombshell and resulted in getting the army out of Cuba before fever obliterated it.

The preliminary draft was shown to the group in the club, not to newspaper men as such, but in confidence to friends and gentlemen. It was not then ready for publication. Colonel Roosevelt wished to obtain other opinions than his own, explaining:

"What do you boys think of it? Have you any changes to suggest? It is a plain statement of fact. There is no more use for the army here, and it is dying on its feet, but the War Department refuses to listen. A little longer and the camps will be swept by yellow fever. We must budge those old fossils in the swivel-chairs somehow. How will the American people take it? Will it alarm them and set the mothers to worrying about their boys?"

"What about Shafter?" asked one of the group.

"He is anxious to have such a protest forwarded and will be glad to sign it. As a volunteer officer I am willing to be the scapegoat. If this stirs up a rumpus among the swivel-chairs, the regular officers ought not to risk censure, if it can be helped."

This was always Theodore Roosevelt's way with newspaper men. He trusted and respected them then, as he did later in the White House, and I am quite sure that his confidence was never betrayed. We read the letter and strongly approved of it. He thanked us and hastened off to consult with Leonard Wood. This letter, together with one much like it which was written by General Ames, also a volunteer officer, was then given to General Shafter who permitted the Associated Press correspondent to cable both documents to the United States.

They did, of a truth, raise a rumpus among the fossils in the swivel-chairs. Publication was what grieved these somnolent gentlemen most, a flagrant breach of Army regulations, but it was vitally necessary, as Theodore Roosevelt had foreseen, to arouse public opinion, even though the Secretary of War, General Russell Alger, wailed loudly that "it would be impossible to exaggerate the mischievous and wicked effects of the 'Round Robin.' It affected the country with a plague of anguish and apprehension."

However, the country learned that the Army, after a victorious campaign, was perishing of stupidity and neglect, and in no uncertain voice it demanded that the troops come out of Cuba. They began to move, as fast as the transports could be loaded in Santiago harbor. Most of the correspondents planned to leave with the Army. Louis Seibold and Ralph Paine decided to stay longer, for there were still stories to be gleaned in Santiago — more than twenty thousand Spanish prisoners of war to be transported to Spain, American regiments stationed on garrison duty in the city, and the pathetic efforts of the stricken population to recover from the stupor of disaster.

XXVII

TWO KNIGHTS OF SANTIAGO

THERE chanced to be another story, and it was worth waiting for in this torrid pest-hole of a Santiago. It came like a precious bit of flotsam washed up by the surf, wholly unexpected. I was walking across the plaza when two young men halted to ask where they could find the headquarters of the Red Cross. One was an American, the other a Frenchman. They wore the faded brown linen uniforms of Cuban insurgent officers, with roughly woven straw hats and clumsy, dilapidated leather leggins, also made out in the "bush."

They looked like men just out of a fever hospital. Their faces were drawn and pinched, and sunburn could not hide the pallor of hunger and exhaustion. Suffering seemed to have benumbed their faculties. They spoke in listless, apathetic voices.

As soon as it was discovered who they were and what errand had brought them to Santiago, I invited them to the Anglo-American Club for breakfast. In more than two years this was their first meal at a table with knives and forks, china, and napkins. It affected them profoundly and they wept a little.

The youthful American derelict was named Cox. The spirit of adventure had led him to enlist under the Cuban flag in '96, and all this time he had been with the roving bands of General Calixto Garcia. The hardships had been continually much worse than those endured by the American troops for two months outside of Santiago.

For more than a year he had not had a cent of money in his pocket. His food and clothing he had to find for himself. He had lived on mangoes, plantains, and parched corn, and often these were unobtainable. There had seldom been shoes to wear, and through the drenching summer rains he had lacked even a rubber blanket for shelter, sleeping in a hammock under a palm-leaf thatch. For seven months he had been ill with malarial fever, hidden away in a swamp, and always in danger of being discovered and slain by Spanish guerrillas. There were no medicines, not even quinine.

The Cubans did nothing for him and would not even assist him to leave the island and go home. Young Cox held a major's commission with the insurgents, but nobody cared very much whether he lived or died. This had been the experience of other American adventurers in Cuba. He was homesick, worn out, utterly despondent, and expected to die in the bush, in the *manigua*.

In May of '98 he had heard that the American soldiers were coming to Santiago. He began to dream of undertaking the long journey of three hundred and thirty miles from his camp near Puerto Principe, in the hope of finding his countrymen. The young Frenchman, Captain Cathard, was ready to join him. They had been bunkies for some time.

The pair of them had three little raw-backed Cuban ponies in wretched condition. The preparations for the march were not at all elaborate. A couple of woven grass blankets were thrown across one of the ponies. There was no other bedding to pack. The only cooking utensil was an iron pot. For rations they must forage or beg from friendly country people.

Thus equipped, with two hardy Cuban peasant soldiers as servants or "strikers," Cox and Cathard set out to reach distant Santiago through a country made incessantly perilous by Spanish troops and guerrillas who gave no quarter. A hundred miles of the route lay across the mountains of Puerto Principe, over rocky trails where riding was impossible. Then they descended into the plains and valleys where the ponies had to be pried out of sloughs which bogged them to the bellies.

Wet to the skin every day, shaking with fever, managing somehow to find enough to eat to hold body and soul together, the two young men struggled on through the steaming heat that smote them like a bludgeon. They made wide détours around the towns and the Spanish garrisons, and the fear of violent death was never absent. They were twenty-eight days on the march, a journey which would have sorely tried an expedition equipped with a pack-train and shelter tents and abundant supplies.

The experience, and what they had suffered previously, had scarred their minds. They told it in bits, in stumbling, halting fashion. Two years of it had frightfully aged young Cox. Sometimes his narrative wandered, like a man talking in his sleep.

A whole year had been spent in trying some way of ending the wretched exile, said he, but he was too weak and helpless to venture through the Spanish lines alone, without money, without anything, and the Cuban leaders did n't care . . . they were not very grateful to Americans. . . .

We told him to take it easy and be comfortable. There would be no trouble about outfitting him and Captain Cathard with clothes and shoes and money, and obtaining passage for them in a transport bound to God's country. But young Cox had not finished his story. His eyes filled at mention of a ship homeward bound, and he sat in a rapt, tense silence when a steamer's whistle bellowed hoarsely from the harbor-side, with its magical suggestion of the open sea and the long trail.

Then he resumed talking in his listless, broken manner which was as eloquent and moving as the words he said. He had no idea of going home from Santiago — we had misunderstood him — that was n't his reason for making the hard march from Puerto Principe — of course he was terribly homesick — but he had left a friend way back there in the bush, a fellow named DeVinne — he came from Kansas City

— and they had been through some pretty rotten campaigns together. DeVinne had been shot through the hip six months ago by a Mauser bullet — got caught in a Spanish ambuscade.

The bone was shattered and had refused to heal — and poor old DeVinne had been spraddled out all this time — hidden in a palm shack in the woods near Puerto Principe. What he needed was good food and dressings and medicine to give him some strength and sort of build him up — then there might be a chance of moving him to the coast.

"So I thought the Red Cross people might give me some stuff to pack on the ponies, and we'd hike back with it. If we don't, there is no chance for DeVinne."

Young Captain Cathard, a Frenchman with gentle manners and a wistful smile, a soldier of the type you would occasionally find in the Foreign Legion, was heard to murmur like an echo:

"What else would you, gentlemen? Forsake a wounded comrade? It is not done. You understand."

"Well, we could n't go back on a pal, could we?" awkwardly resumed Cox. "Anyhow, I guess I'll ramble down to the wharf after a while, just to see the ships. Gee, but it's good to hear Americans talk. All I heard in the bush was Spanish. I sort of forgot how to sling my own language."

A commonplace lad, to look at him, was this Major Cox, and in a crowd you would never have picked him for a hero, but he inspired an immense respect and admiration. He found himself shaking hands with American army officers when they strolled into the club, and they knew a good man when they met him. Soon it became an ovation to these two forlorn pilgrims from the bush, these two knights of Santiago.

It manifested itself in practical fashion. Dr. Egan, chief surgeon of the Red Cross, was delighted to supply all medicines, surgical dressings, malted milk, chocolate, and so on, that could be carried. New shoes, khaki clothing, flannel shirts, ponchos, were furnished from the Army quarter-master's stores. The three wretched ponies, nothing but skin and bone, were unfit to be used again. General Joseph Wheeler, commanding the cavalry division of the Fifth Corps, little "Fighting Joe" Wheeler, the gamecock of the Confederacy, who now wore the blue as proudly as he had worn the gray in his youth, contributed a sleek, stout army mule, big enough to carry a rich cargo of supplies.

In the shops of Santiago food was scanty and held at exor-bitant prices, but there was plenty of coffee, sugar, canned goods, bacon, and hard bread at the Army commissary store. And we saw to it that oatmeal, canned soups, and jellies were on the list for poor DeVinne, crippled and wasted in his shack and waiting for the pals who had refused to go back on him. Then the hat was passed and the gold pieces clinked into it right merrily. There would be no lack of money to tide them over the rough places.

The two young men could not be persuaded to tarry long enough in Santiago to recruit their strength, so eager were they to begin that long and arduous march to Puerto Prin-cipe. They bought two fresh Cuban ponies, and one morning the little cavalcade clattered down a narrow street, the big mule in the lead with a veritable mountain of stuff packed upon its broad back. All that could be seen of the ponies were their heads and tails. The grass-woven baskets slung across them were large enough to hold as much as half a dozen saddlebags. Cox and Cathard trudged cheerfully in sturdy army shoes and behind them came the two Cuban strikers, also well clad and in the most exuberant spirits.

Yet, even at the best, it was a pathetic departure when the young men turned their backs on the shipping in the harbor, with the troops cheering madly on the crowded decks and the regimental bands playing "Home Again, Home Again, From a Foreign Shore." It seemed like a forlorn hope, this toilsome journey of three hundred and thirty miles, the fever and the jungle and the blazing heat, and their comrade, DeVinne, perhaps dead ere they reached him.

And how young Cox did yearn to go home! The dumb hunger of it was written on his face. But in his soul was something more compelling, that divine constraint called duty which lights the humblest shrines.

General Adna R. Chaffee, as fine a soldier as could be found in that intrepid little regular army, one of the conspicuously gallant brigade commanders in the battle of Santiago, had shown a lively interest in these two heroic young men. After they had gone, he sat meditating at a table in the club. Then he looked up to say, with a quizzical smile on the brown, resolute visage:

"If I had been in their place, after getting this far, and I heard a transport blow her whistle — well, boys, I don't know but what I might have weakened. There is more than one kind of courage. That was twenty-four karats fine, the real thing!"

XXVIII

JAILED WITH EVERY COURTESY

Louis Seibold and Ralph Paine had begun to discuss attempting to reach Havana. It was a sealed port to Americans, they surmised, but the chance seemed worth taking. Technically a state of war still existed. An armistice was in force, as defined by the terms of the protocol or preliminary articles of surrender and negotiation. The Spanish flag still floated over Havana, and a Spanish Captain-General ruled undisturbed in his palace. That American visitors would be welcomed with open arms seemed unlikely, what with the graves of those thousands of Spanish soldiers so freshly dug on the battle-field of Santiago and Cervera's shattered cruisers rusting on the beach.

But there would be something to write about in Havana, this large and stately city, the capital of the island, which had been closely blockaded for three months and which American correspondents had been forbidden to enter. How had the population fared during this long period of deprivation, shut in by sea and denied access to food supplies inland by the ravaging bands of Cuban insurgents? What were the defenses and the military forces, which had been vastly increased to withstand the expected attack by an American fleet and army?

Havana had the elements of an attractive mystery. It was concealed behind a curtain, you understand.

How could we get there? This was a problem awkward to solve. For lack of a railway the overland journey was impossible. By sea no steamers plied up and down the coast. Havana was isolated and remote from Santiago. However, there wandered one day into a harbor a rusty, wall-sided, disreputable little Norwegian tramp called the Bratsberg, in quest of coal for her bunkers. She was a sort of salt-water orphan. Formerly in the live-cattle trade between Cuba and Florida, she was poking about to take a look at the situation, now that active hostilities had ceased.

The skipper was of a mind to jog along to Havana on the chance of picking up a few stray dollars. He was a leathery, brine-pickled curmudgeon of a Norwegian mariner, with a heart as hard as flint. Passengers? He never bothered with 'em. They were a nuisance. He had no accommodations.

A lengthy parley, and he consented to take the two correspondents aboard, as so much freight, mind you. He would give them nothing to eat, not even drinking-water, and they could sleep on the soft side of a plank. He treated the live cattle better than this, but why be captious? The dirty little hooker was bound to Havana. This was the point. Incidentally this thrifty Scandinavian demanded passage-money on the scale of a first-class liner with an orchestra and your own bath. He needed funds.

It was necessary to ration ourselves for the voyage. Canned meat was obtainable from the Army commissary, roast beef and corned beef. Unfortunately we received the variety of meat which later became a national scandal as "embalmed beef" upon which the Army in Cuba had been compelled largely to subsist. An official investigation whitewashed the packing-house interests responsible for this sordid deed. The gentlemen in question should have been thrust into cells and compelled to subsist on the abominable stuff, or to make the voyage to Havana in the Norwegian tramp with Seibold and Paine.

Other canned provender was hastily garnered from the almost empty shelves of the shops of Santiago; a variety curious and indigestible, canned plum pudding and *pâté de foie gras*, for instance, which nobody else would buy. Our good friend, Julien Cendoya, agent of the Ward Line, contributed a demijohn of native rum. It was excess baggage, for only a man with a copper plumbing system could have used it without risk of fatal corrosion.

For Ralph Paine there was an errand at the Red Cross headquarters to beg clothing as a worthy person in dire want. This was the month of August, and he had been afield and afloat since January with a wardrobe which had become extremely sketchy. It seemed, at last, to go all at once, like the famous one-hoss shay. The Red Cross mercifully handed him a pair of cast-off golf breeches, fished out of a barrel. The pattern was a plaid check so blatant that you could hear it shriek. There was a cap to match, and it was no less obstreperous. Between the baggy folds of the breeches and the tops of the battered riding-boots was a considerable gap. The effect was really strange. The decorous Louis Seibold swore when he beheld his shipmate.

The little tramp steamer moved out of Santiago harbor with her engines groaning and hammering. They were evidently unwell. It was inferred that sudden exertion might make her drop dead, like a person with a weak heart. At six knots she crawled along the coast, smelling like a cattle-boat, while the two passengers looked for shady spots.

There was no pity in the soul of that square-head of a skipper. We did find a tiny, spare stateroom filled with paint-pots, cordage, and other junk, and cleared one bunk in spite of the mariner's spluttering protests. Thrice daily we chewed on the tasteless strings and shreds of embalmed beef, washed it down with tepid water, and perhaps fought a round with a can of plum pudding.

For men more or less knocked out by malarial fever and what the doctors call badly "run down," it was a dismal voyage. And there was so infernally much of it! Seven or eight hundred miles to run, and that evil little tramp crept over the blazing ocean like a fly in a saucer of molasses, six knots when she felt a flurry of health, four or five when there came a relapse.

The ship's cook was bribed to give us, now and then, a cup of the hot bilgewater he called coffee, but the skipper used to come prowling into the galley to stop anything like that. As for food, his crew fared no better than the two passengers on deck. They were even grateful for a few cans of that army beef. We urged the skipper to try it for dinner, and prayed it might poison him.

There was one sublime comfort and consolation. In the cool of the velvet nights, under a sky all spattered with stars, the two argonauts stretched themselves on deck and indulged in such beguiling fancies as these:

"And when we reach Havana, Ralph, if we ever do, it's me for the Pasajé Café as fast as a *cochero* can whirl me from the Machina wharf. Then, listen to me address the *muchacho* — consommé, a roast chicken, a mixed salad, iced sherbet, a melon, real coffee, and one of Señor Bock's well-known cigars. And after that a BED, with springs and sheets and two fat pillows."

"Order the same for me, Louie, while I stop at the first gents' furnishing store. I don't want to be thrown out of the Pasajé Café. These golf breeches! *Oiga!* They have split already, and the idea of making myself so conspicuous in Havana just now — well, it's not tactful. It would be like the impulsive populace to play it was a bull-fight, with me as the *toro*, and stick me full of *banderillas*. Remember, I am no Fitzhugh Lee."

"But supposing the Spanish officials won't let us go ashore," uneasily suggested Seibold. "This stinking ship may lie in the harbor a month."

"God forbid! Don't think of it! Your mind will give way. We should have to kill the skipper, overpower the crew, and sail her to Key West ourselves. Two desperate men can stir up quite a brisk little mutiny if they are goaded far enough."

Early one morning the Norwegian tramp feebly kicked her way into the harbor of Havana and found a mooring buoy where she rode alone. The port was almost bare of shipping, only a few Spanish steamers tied up in idleness and some small sailing craft. Above the muddy surface of the water rose the ghastly, twisted débris of the battleship Maine, now red with rust and infinitely tragic. Those dead bluejackets had been avenged. Their countrymen had remembered the Maine!

The city of Havana, beautiful, foreign, picturesque, revealed itself as sloping from the water-front. It conveyed visions of hotels, of the opera, of the band playing on the Prado, of the comforts and the luxuries which had been so long denied the two grimy, wretched correspondents who gazed rapturously from the deck of that rotten little cattle-boat. They had their luggage ready. One of them yelled to a harbor boatman.

Just then there came alongside a launch and out of it clambered a Spanish military officer in an ornate uniform. He was the Chief of the Harbor Police, a man of frowning mien and peremptory speech. With a gesture he pinned the Norwegian skipper to the side of the deck-house and demanded to know, in the name of the Twelve Apostles, what these *Americanos*, these detestable *corresponsales*, were doing on board. The situation explained, the brass-bound dignitary declared himself in this wise:

"His Excellency, the Captain-General, has given no permission for Americans to land. There has come no official decree from Madrid that the war is finished. Least of all does His Excellency desire to admit *corresponsales* to Havana. They were most troublesome liars before the war began, an accursed pest! They made incredible vexation for us. Therefore the Captain-General will not allow these two *Americanos* to set foot in Havana. They will remain in this ship."

This was an edict so calamitous that you could have

knocked us down with the smallest feather that ever sprouted
on an incubator chicken. For much less, strong men have
burst into an agony of weeping. The Chief of the Harbor
Police twiddled his needle-pointed *mostachios*, turned on his
heel, and beckoned two swarthy *soldados* in uniforms of bed-
ticking. They were lavishly draped with side-arms. Sternly
these were commanded to stand guard until further notice.

They were two sturdy Spanish privates of the harbor police, and their swords had a nasty look. To assault and tie
them up with lengths of a heaving-line was dismissed as im-
practicable. A passing boatman was hailed and sent ashore
to buy food, but the thought of having it cooked in the ship's
galley was very depressing. It was the cook's habit to serve
at least one cockroach in every dish. He could n't help it.
They were too many for him.

In this stagnant and breathless harbor, rank with sewage,
the forenoon dragged interminably for the two prisoners
aboard the cattle-boat. They watched the cabs pass along the
seaward boulevard. A flag above the distant roofs marked a
large and comfortable hotel.

The pair of Spanish soldiers took their duties calmly.
They slung their hammocks beneath the awning upon the
bridge and took turns sauntering about to scowl at the marooned and drooping correspondents. Louis Seibold per-
spired, brooding, in the bunk among the paint-pots. He was
never a loquacious man and just now his emotions were beyond words. In this emergency he could be trusted to employ
an intelligence that was canny and diplomatic. If he had been
able to speak Spanish well enough, he would have whispered in the ear of the Chief of the Harbor Police who, no
doubt, had his price.

You could pretty well prognosticate what Seibold's forth-
coming strategy would be like — a dignified protest in writing
to the Spanish Government of Havana — the request for a
personal interview — a cable to the State Department in

Washington — adroit manipulation all along the line — and ultimate success.

This was, of course, the sensible procedure. Anything else would be asinine. This, I presume, is why Ralph Paine decided to attempt something else. He craved action more direct.

The opportunity was offered him during the afternoon. To the two Spanish soldiers had been freely given what was left of the embalmed beef and the untouched demijohn of Santiago rum. Possibly this was done with malice aforethought. If the beef did n't get them, the rum might. They had tough constitutions, these two peasant conscripts, and it was an enjoyable fête under the awning. After a time, however, they became afflicted with drowsiness. One rolled into his hammock, the other sat nodding, his back to a stanchion, his sword across his knees.

Louis Seibold still brooded in the bunk. There was nothing else to do. The skipper and his crew were likewise snoring, those of them who had not gone ashore to get drunk. The ship was wrapped in a profound peace.

Ralph Paine wandered aft, with no particular purpose in mind. Unfathomable *ennui* pressed down upon his soul. Presently a small rowboat moved out from the Regla shore of the harbor and skittered over the glassy surface like a lazy water-bug. A black Cuban was at the oars. A tattered shirt hung in patches from his brawny shoulders. It was perceived that this craft would pass close to the stern of the Norwegian tramp.

The present writer glanced forward. Not a soul of the ship's company was visible. The chart-room and wheel-house intercepted the view of the two Spanish soldiers. Heaven had sent this chance to slide into Havana and explore the situation in person. It was forbidden, but perhaps one might learn something to his advantage. Anything was preferable to the ship in which we were confined.

There was no time to consult Seibold. I would return anon and tell him all about it. Warily crawling over the steamer's turtle-back, I made eloquent signals to the black oarsman in the bathtub of a skiff. He changed his course, but hesitantly, until his vision caught the glint of a Spanish gold piece. Then he almost broke his back in pulling under the vessel's stern.

It was easy enough to descend by a handy rope. I plopped into the boat, almost upsetting it, and told the Cuban to row for the Regla shore as he had come. This kept us astern of the steamer and hidden from the observation of the two Spanish soldiers at the forward end. The ship still seemed to be in a comatose condition, as though prostrated by the heat. There was no alarm. Soon it was possible to make a cautious détour and pull for the Havana side of the harbor and a convenient wharf.

This far the escape had been conducted with success. For an amateur fugitive from armed sentries, you might say it was done with *aplomb*.

To the superficial eye the Havana streets appeared much as usual, but after walking well into the city it was seen that the shops did little business and the whole tone of things was pitched in a quiet, subdued key which conveyed an impression of melancholy. There was concrete manifestation of suffering in the masses of shabby, dejected people in the poorer quarters of the city who crowded in long processions to the public soup kitchens to be fed.

A clothing store supplied the errant correspondent with a white linen suit, underwear, socks, shirts, a Panama hat. Joyfully he flung away those fearful golf breeches which were so like a public disturbance. He even acquired a bamboo cane and a flower in his button-hole. Next he found a barber-shop with a bathroom annexed. He felt much more like looking Havana in the eye. He was ready to take it to pieces to see what made it tick.

Wandering into a café to order a frosty claret lemonade, he

encountered a group of Spanish army officers seated around a table. To the greeting, "*Buenos dias, Señores,*" they arose, bowed, and returned the salutation with grave politeness. Whatever hostility they felt toward this American visitor was masked by an inherent courtesy of demeanor, even though he was of the race of the enemy, the first they had seen in Havana since that day when Fitzhugh Lee, the Consul-General, had hauled down the Stars and Stripes and made his exit as the final ceremony before the declaration of war.

Perhaps the people in the street mistook the correspondent for an Englishman or a German. At any rate, there was no overt sign of resentment and he strolled into the Prado with his feelings unruffled. It was strange to enter the Hotel Inglaterra and find it empty of Americans. Spanish officers loafed at the long windows, or sipped their cognac in the large barroom, or drove away in dilapidated little victorias. A glee club of students from the University of Havana halted to sing *La Paloma* and collect money for the Spanish Red Cross. They sang melodiously, thrumming guitars and mandolins. It was memorably romantic.

American affairs were nominally in the hands of the British Consulate, and it seemed worth while to ask Her Majesty's representative to lay the case before the Spanish officials. There was no sensible reason why these two correspondents should be treated like criminals. But it was a bootless errand to the consulate, where a dapper secretary or something declared that it would serve me jolly well right to be thrown into prison for daring to show myself in Havana after being ordered to stay aboard the ship. And if I did get in trouble for it, there would be not the slightest use in appealing to the British Consulate and all that silly rot, what?

There was not a tuppence worth of sympathy or humanity in this starched young diplomat, so I thanked him and gently faded out, twirling the bamboo cane.

It was enjoyable to roam about the city until early evening, finding many things to interest a journalist. Then came the supreme event, ordering such a dinner as had been dreamed of aboard the Norwegian tramp. In the best restaurants there was no specter of starvation. And yet it was not the happy event which had been anticipated. It did n't seem quite fair to my shipmate, Louis Seibold, still a brooding captive among the smells and cockroaches. And yet, had I invited him, he would not have slid down the rope and eluded the Spanish soldiers. His dignity would have prevented, likewise his habit of looking before he leaped. Ought I to have remained and shared his fate?

The ethical problem was a trifle befogged. I lingered in the restaurant, inwardly debating the point, while a band played in the plaza. It was an alluring environment, leading one to forget that he was a fugitive. Leisurely enjoying another cigar, I noticed by chance that two Spanish officers stood on the pavement, just outside the long open window with its iron grill-work. They were of no importance, however, until they glanced in several times and conferred with their heads together. After some time they stalked into the restaurant and approached the table.

It was done with the utmost consideration. They had waited until the American señor had finished his dinner — a colonel of the military police of Havana and his aide. Urbane gentlemen, it was their unpleasant duty to place the señor under arrest. He would be good enough to accompany them to the palace of the Captain-General in the Plaza de Armas.

The colonel displayed the slightest irritation only when he explained that he had pursued the American Señor Ralph Paine rapidly, from place to place, in Havana and, *Madre de Dios!* he had set them a pace of the swiftest.

The señor expressed his deep regrets that he should have so fatigued and inconvenienced the esteemed colonel of the military police. Confidentially it may be imparted that, although the señor tried to carry it off in the grand manner, he was privately shaking in his shoes.

With a party at another table in the restaurant was a most attractive girl, black-eyed, vivacious, a rose in her dusky hair. The American señor had found her exceedingly easy to look at. She was kind enough to feel pity for him in his plight. She talked excitedly in Spanish to her companions. There was sympathy in her frightened gaze. Alas, the poor young *Americano* was to be placed in a dungeon of the Cabañas and shot at sunrise against the bullet-pitted wall in the dry moat! Thus it had befallen so many prisoners of the military police during the insurrection!

Her companions addressed her as Lolita. The American let a sad, grateful smile wander in that direction. *Adios, adios para siempre,* la belle Lolita! Farewell, farewell forever, beautiful Lolita! You made the situation a little easier to bear.

The stately colonel and his aide conducted the señor to the pavement and invited him to enter a waiting *coche,* one of those innumerable, shabby little victorias, drawn by rats of ponies, which plied for hire. The prisoner wrapped himself in a gloomy silence. He felt far from chatty. Louis Seibold had displayed sagacity, as usual, and Ralph Paine's procedure had been asinine, also as usual.

The sound of those words, "the palace of the Captain-General," had been bleak and forbidding. They were too suggestive of the reign of Weyler, "The Butcher," with his lantern jaw and his mutton-chop whiskers. Such contemplations were interrupted when the victoria drew up at the curb of the Hotel Inglaterra. The colonel asked the señor to alight. Needless to say, the señor offered no comment. The trio — one prisoner, two officers — walked into the hotel café and joined a group of five other Spanish military officers at a round table. The welcome was most cordial.

I maintain that this incident was out of the ordinary. The

American fugitive, who had led the colonel such a devil of a chase, was introduced to these other officers as a friend, *mi amigo*, and not a hint was let fall that he was an enemy of Spain in a disgraceful fix. They begged him to be seated, to join the group. It transpired that the Chief of the Military Police was enjoying the opera and therefore there would be an interval of waiting for his personal decision with respect to the señor. This was confided by the colonel. Meanwhile here was congenial company to pass the hour in an agreeable manner.

Tiny glasses of cognac were ordered, first by one Spanish officer, then by another. The American señor was not permitted to beckon the waiter. There had been a war with his country, *si*, but at the table he was the guest. Such was the custom among officers and gentlemen of Spain. When the parting came, they wished the señor the best of fortune. They had been honored by his acquaintance.

The journey in the victoria was resumed. It ended at the great, white-walled palace which was the seat of Spanish government in Cuba. The colonel was thoughtful enough to inform his prisoner that the matter would be referred, not to the Captain-General's staff, but to the jurisdiction of the Governor of Havana. This was reassuring. One might faintly hope for further civility and not a revival of the Spanish Inquisition.

The destination was a reception-room of the Chief of the Military Police. A sleepy interpreter was dragged out of bed. Conversation moved more fluently thereafter. The American culprit was raked fore and aft with such annoyed interrogations as these:

"Why do you wish to be in Havana?"

"Why did you not stay on your ship?"

"Do you know how much trouble you have made?"

"It is a very serious offense, do you know that, to defy and hurl contempt at the commands of this royal government?"

These were awkward questions, but the señor managed to stand up under them fairly well until the interpreter went on to say, with increased vehemence:

"The Chief of the Military Police himself will be compelled to give you his attention, after the opera. It is his wish to go at once from the opera to a magnificent supper to be given at his own house. He has invited many friends. *This is the feast day of his brother-in-law!*"

Now, indeed, was the señor greatly moved and with shame and contrition. To cloud and interfere with the feast day of the brother-in-law of the Chief of the Military Police of Havana! This was heinous. It was to apologize with heart-felt emotion. The colonel found a box of very good cigars. We smoked pensively, awaiting the conclusion of the opera. The interpreter took a nap in his chair. He awoke to harrow the señor's feelings once again.

"Ah, the two poor soldiers, the guards who were left on the ship to keep you from running away! They did not know you had escaped from them. No, they did not know at all until you were seen in Havana and the news was taken to the Chief of the Harbor Police. He it was who went out to the ship and told those two poor soldiers that you had vamoosed!

"They are very much surprised. They weep. They beg for mercy. *Carramba,* they are put in jail by the Chief of the Harbor Police. They will suffer the court-martial. Their dear sweethearts and wives in Spain! They will be widows, *quien sabe?* Their hearts are busted. You have been an affliction to these two soldiers, Señor Ralph Paine."

This was lamentable and unforeseen. Something would have to be done about it. It made one feel enormously guilty and base. The hasty act of a thoughtless young man had played hob generally. In his wake followed one tragedy after another!

The colonel politely changed the subject, referring to the events of the war and defending the policies of the Spanish

Government in Cuba. The rebellion would have been easily crushed, said he, thus averting hostile collision with the United States, had it not been for the flagrant violation of the laws of neutrality — the aid and comfort so freely given the *insurrectos* in '95 and '96. It had been most unfair of a friendly power to permit it. The American señor coughed and nervously rubbed his chin. Almost word for word he could remember certain phrases of a legal document, to wit:

That the said vessel Three Friends, on or about the 21st day of December, while upon the high seas, in or about the neighborhood of the waters at the entrance of the San Juan River, in the island of Cuba, was then and there by certain persons, to wit, John O'Brien, William T. Lewis, John Dunn, Henry P. Fritot, August Arnao, Michael Walsh, Ralph D. Paine and divers other persons to the said attorneys unknown, furnished, fitted out and armed with wilful intent to commit piratical aggressions and depredations, and that said persons did then and there discharge the Hotchkiss gun or cannon mounted in the bow of the said vessel, on a certain Spanish gunboat, and that the persons being on the said vessel also discharged their rifles on the said Spanish gunboat, all of which was done wilfully and with intent to injure, and without legal authority of lawful excuse, the subjects, citizens and property of the king of Spain in the island of Cuba.

It was difficult for the American señor to join with the colonel in any extended discussion of the unfriendly filibustering industry as conducted during the revolution in the island of Cuba. It was a personal matter which had its awkward aspects. And it was to be devoutly hoped that this present investigation would not delve too thoroughly into the official records on file in the palace. Even Spanish courtesy might have its limitations. There had been casualties among the crew of that certain gunboat.

The arrival of the Chief of the Military Police put an end to these disquieting reflections. He was a tall man, saturnine, immaculate, and of a vexed demeanor. He could not be blamed for this. The feast day of his brother-in-law was demanding his presence. With the zeal of a bureaucrat, however, he announced that the matter must be looked into. He would go with us to the office of the Chief of the Harbor Police who was directly responsible for the escape of this inexpressibly troublesome American correspondent.

A victoria was found and we rode down to the harbor-side where the official in question was hauled out of bed. He yawned and sputtered and was in a bad temper. His reputation had suffered. He was in the shadow of displeasure. It was his desire, said he, to put the *Americano* in the Cabañas fortress and leave him there until Spain and the United States should have signed the treaty of peace.

There followed a long discussion. The hour was past midnight, yet the whole affair had to be thrashed over from the beginning. The courteous colonel who had made the arrest was opposed to inflicting harsh punishment, for reasons of policy. Another impatient glance at his watch, and the Chief of the Military Police told the colonel to hold the señor as a prisoner until morning. It was a case quite complicated.

Then the Chief of the Harbor Police was possessed of a brilliant idea. He grinned as he announced it to the colonel.

"It will be a bigger punishment to put him on his ship and keep him there. I myself have seen the ship."

The colonel rushed after the Chief of the Military Police to tell him this. He caught that icy gentleman just before he rattled away in the victoria to celebrate the feast day of his brother-in-law. It was received as a happy suggestion. The *Americano* would be carried out to the Norwegian cattle-boat early in the morning and there kept *incomunicado*. In this manner would the account be squared for all the tribulation he had caused.

It was not an uncomfortable night — a small room with barred windows — to call it a cell would brand one as a jail-bird — and there was a cot with a mattress and a pillow, and a box of cigars left by the colonel. Compared with the dirty little hooker anchored in the harbor, it was a palatial night.

The Chief of the Harbor Police was confidentially interviewed in the morning. The first estimate of him had been correct. There was cupidity in his eye and he had an itching palm. Those two poor Spanish soldiers, could he not be persuaded to deal less severely with them? Their wives and sweethearts in Spain, consider that! His fingers closed and he put something in his pocket. Yes, his anger had cooled, said he. It was not their fault, after all, only two of them to guard a whole ship, and who would have imagined the wicked audacity of a man, to slide down a rope from the stern of the ship where he could not be seen at all! The verdict would be lenient.

But there was no soothing Louis Seibold as easily as this. I dreaded facing him. When I was carried off to the ship, escorted by a formidable guard of soldiers, he met me at the gangway and spoke in terms of bitter accusation:

"You big loafer! I was framing things to get ashore in a day or so and you went and messed it all up. I hope they threw a scare into you."

"Suspend judgment, Louie," said I. "I stirred things up a bit while you were still considering them. They know all about us in Havana. Something may come of it. I think I made a hit. And I never spent a pleasanter night in jail."

Later in this same day the officials of the Government of Havana relented. Word was sent off to the ship that the two correspondents would be permitted to land, on parole. This was explained to mean that they were to give their word of honor in writing that they would attempt to send no news to the United States either by mail or cable. In short, they would be received as visitors, but not as correspondents. This was a solution very much in the Spanish manner.

The parole was promptly signed. For two weary newspaper men, much in need of a vacation, it was no hardship to loaf a little while in civilized Havana, bound in honor to do no work and well aware that their salaries and expense accounts would not be interrupted. And this was how they saw the finish of the war with Spain in the summer of 1898.

Time and distance have softened Louis Seibold's memories of that distressing reunion on board of the Norwegian hooker in Havana Harbor. Under date of April 20, 1922, he writes from the Washington Bureau of "The New York Herald":

Harking back to the voyage of the infamous Bratsberg, I recall with joy and gratitude how you bullied the villainous old thief of a skipper when I was too sick to lift my head. I may have called you a loafer for not having taken me ashore with you, but no insults were intended. How could I, when you came back with real ice and champagne and a lot of medicine I needed, and a pair of shoes to take the place of those which had been stolen by one of the pirates in the forecastle.

I shall never forget the tumult caused by your forcible return to the ship under escort of most of the Spanish army and navy. I could hear the noise and see the boats from the time you left the Machina wharf until they bundled you up on deck. You had a gunny sack over your shoulder filled with stuff for me. You had insisted upon waking up sleepy shop-keepers in order to dig up stuff for me. This aroused great indignation among your captors. They lined you up in front of me on deck and accused you of breaking every law and committing every crime on the Spanish calendar. Then they left us to our feasting. We could forget the smells and the cockroaches. Come to think of it, perhaps I did call you a few hard names, old man, but after you emptied the gunny sack, I'm sure I apologized with tears in my eyes.

XXIX

A LITTLE JOURNEY ON THE PEI-HO

THE tragedy of the foreign legations besieged by hordes of Boxer fanatics and Chinese Imperial troops, in the summer of 1900; their fate darkly obscured for many weeks; the forced march of a mixed army of the soldiers of all nations to Peking; the arrival in the nick of time; the orgy of loot and bloodshed which disgraced the name of civilization, the collapse of the proud and ancient Manchu dynasty, and the long-drawn-out intrigues of European diplomats — this was one of the most fantastic adventures in all modern history.

Against a lurid background mankind displayed its best and its worst traits, chivalry soiled by unspeakable cruelties, heroism clouded by insensate greed, self-sacrifice marred by a barbaric lust for vengeance. One of the greatest and richest cities of the world was given over to wholesale pillage. There had been nothing like it since the wars of the Middle Ages, since the Spanish Fury in the Netherlands.

It was not to be wondered that the hapless Chinese people, confronted by such exemplars as these, should have more than ever preferred Confucius to Jesus of Nazareth. By their fruits ye shall know them.

It was a long journey for a correspondent ordered to China, a slow mail-boat across the Pacific to Shanghai and thence a slower little Chinese coasting steamer northward to the Gulf of Pechili and the war-swept port of Tientsin, six weeks out from home. Much had happened in that time. After many futile attempts a message had made it known to the outer world that the legations and the refugees within their walls were still fighting for their lives and praying for rescue.

A small column of bluejackets and marines, British,

American, Russian, German, Japanese, Italian, French, and Austrian, hastily assembled from the fleet of warships off Taku Bar, had endeavored to storm its way inland, more than a hundred miles to Peking, but had been driven back with heavy losses.

Then came an interval of breathless preparation while an army was hurled together, American regulars from the Philippines, regiments of Bengal Lancers, Rajputs, Gurkhas, Sikhs, from India, French colonial infantry from Saigon, impetuous Cossacks from Manchuria, efficient divisions of Japanese from across the Yellow Sea, and odds and ends from elsewhere. Such an army as might have poured out of the tower of Babel! Haughty generals delayed the advance to wrangle over rank and precedence. There were jealousies, diplomatic complications, the old, old distrust among nations.

A brusque American major-general, grizzled, with deep-set eyes and a heavy jaw, who had lived most of his life in a cavalry saddle, broke into the foolish altercations of this allied council of war by announcing:

"I am ordered to go to the relief of the United States Legation in Peking. I shall leave for that city at once. If you do not care to move your commands at once, gentlemen, I will go alone with my American force."

This was Adna R. Chaffee who continued to rasp the feelings of some of his European associates because he was naught else than a hard-hitting, single-minded soldier.

Its disagreements patched up after a fashion, the variegated relief expedition had raced across the North China plain twenty thousand strong and the devil take the hindmost, the summer heat slaying men by hundreds, bloody skirmishing with bands of Boxers in red aprons and sashes, fiercer fighting with bodies of Imperial troops, burning the villages and laying waste the country, sweeping up to the great walls of Peking and battering down the gates, and storming into the wreckage of the fortified legation com-

pounds to find the defenders alive and still gallantly carrying
on!

It was like a tapestry of pageantry and melodrama shot
through with threads of crimson.

By a few days I missed the grand climax, this relief of the
legations. To journey ten thousand miles and arrive just a
bit too late was a keen disappointment, but the course of
events could not have been foreseen. It was merely a bit of
hard luck incidental to the trade of journalism. Tientsin had
suffered siege and battle before the allied forces could gain
a foothold and a base. Defended by picked Chinese troops
trained by German officers and drill sergeants, it had been a
hard nut to crack. In danger of being swept back into the
sea, the allies, while awaiting reënforcements, had fought
with stubborn valor, and no regiment had suffered so griev-
ously, in dead and wounded, as the famous old Ninth Infantry, U.S.A.

The native city of Tientsin, in which almost a million
Chinese had dwelt, was a desolation of ruins, of looted shops
and temples and yamens, of festering corpses and prowling
dogs. The handsomely built European quarter had survived,
although many buildings were shattered by Chinese artillery. The streets were filled with troops of many races,
with pitiable missionary refugees from inland stations, with
all the human débris that eddies in the wake of fighting
armies. Peking had fallen, but the embers of conflict blazed
or smouldered far and wide.

On the long piazza of the German hotel, curiously called
the Astor House Hotel, which had been struck by shells
but not demolished, smartly uniformed officers swaggered
and talked many languages, or clicked their heels and saluted
with precise gestures. It was a queer place in which to find,
all alone, an American girl of gentle breeding, like a castaway
on a tempestuous reef. She inspired curiosity and appealed
to one's sympathy, this girl of twenty with the troubled

eyes and the brave yet tremulous smile. She was rather small and slight, but conveying an air of trim competency and un-faltering resolution.

The anxious girl in the khaki skirt, white shirt-waist, and brown army hat was a bride, it became known, and her husband was Captain "Jack" Meyers, of the Marine Corps, who had been sent to China shortly after the wedding in Seattle. This Captain Meyers had been in command of the American marines of the legation guard through all the desperate fighting of the siege of Peking. And when the fate of the defenders had been for so long enshrouded in mystery, young Mrs. Meyers had been unable to endure it. From the Pacific coast she had sailed alone on her dear pilgrimage, to endeavor to reach North China and to get tidings of her husband, to venture as near to him as might be possible.

At Nagasaki she had persuaded the quartermaster officer of an American transport to grant her passage over the China Sea to Tientsin. It was against regulations, but true love breaks through many a barrier. In this manner the girlish Mrs. Meyers had reached the last stage of the journey and was within a hundred miles of Peking.

From the American troops who had fought their way into the city, the word came back that Captain Meyers had been seriously wounded by a thrust from a Chinese spear while holding the city wall behind the American Legation with his company of marines. Still suffering from this injury, he had been stricken down with typhoid fever. This was the news that made his wife so pitifully eager to go on to Peking, no matter how hazardous the way might be.

The obstacles appeared to be insurmountable. The ranking American officer in Tientsin was deaf to her pleadings. It was no trip for a woman to undertake, with bands of Boxers still roaming the countryside like hungry wolves, and the glow of burning villages on the horizon all night long. The American cavalry detachments and wagon-trains could not be bothered with a woman. It was out of the question. The overland journey was frightfully rough, at best, the railway totally wrecked by the enemy, and the highways worse than none at all. Yes, the army was sending junks laden with supplies up the Pei-ho, but there was no room for Mrs. Meyers. It was absurd of her to make such a request. This was what she was told, with emphasis.

There was no better fortune when she petitioned the British transport officers. Under no circumstances would they be responsible for sending a woman to Peking. In this motley crowd at the Astor House Hotel was an American civil engineer, C. D. Jamieson, who had escaped from the remote interior no more than two jumps ahead of the murderous Boxers. He had urgent business in Peking and valuable property there, and he was not a man to be daunted by difficulties.

Jamieson's scheme was to hire a junk and proceed up the river. He was good enough to invite me to join him and, naturally enough, we bethought ourselves of the valiant girl whose one thought was to reach the bedside of Captain "Jack" Meyers in the improvised hospital of the shattered American Legation compound.

Her gratitude was very moving, nor did she hesitate an instant to risk the discomforts and possible danger of the voyage. And now there came breezing into Tientsin two impetuous young naval officers, ensigns from the cruiser Brooklyn which flew the two-starred pennant of Rear Admiral Remey off Taku Bar. One of these young men carried dispatches for the American Legation and the other had begged leave of absence on the chance of mixing up with an armed rumpus of some sort. They were, of course, in haste to be starting for Peking nor were they at all fussy about the manner of getting there. Ride, walk, or swim, it was all the same.

They made the acquaintance of the civil engineer and the

correspondent, and then there were four of us to man the quarter-deck of the junk and gladly escort young Mrs. Meyers on the turbid Pei-ho.

"You bet we'll trail along," said Ensign Tardy, "and it's an honor to be aboard with the lady."

"I wish her the best of luck," said Ensign Tarrant, "but it will make it a heap more interesting if a few stray Boxers try to hop the junk."

It was a clumsy, squalid craft, this Chinese river-boat, with a little cabin or shelter contrived of bamboo poles and grass matting. Most of this space we curtained off for the lady passenger and we men found space to stow ourselves on the after-deck where a huge, carven beam, slung with rope tackles, served for a tiller. On the forward deck were crowded the fifteen half-naked coolies whose toilsome task it was to scramble along the muddy bank at the end of a tow-rope and haul the junk against the current by main strength.

Ruffianly beggars these were, of the stalwart northern race, swarthy and scowling, pates unshaven, queues unbraided, and some of them, no doubt, had worn the flaming Boxer girdles and turbans and had yelled the ferocious incantations presumed to make them bullet-proof against the guns of the foreign devils.

However, they were docile coolies now, and there were things to remind them to be good. No sooner had the junk floated away from Tientsin on that sultry summer afternoon than the bodies of dead Chinese came drifting down the yellow tide. They bobbed grotesquely in the current or were stranded on the sandbars and in the shallows, some identified as Boxers by the sodden streamers of regalia, others in the blue cotton blouse and breeches of the peasants of the Great Plain or the dwellers in the mud-walled towns which had been obliterated by the hurricane blasts of war and pillage.

The coolies straining at the towline jabbered and jested

among themselves at sight of these repulsive relics. Their
sense of humor was peculiar.

Until twilight the junk moved very slowly in this winding
stream which threaded a landscape infinitely sad and monotonous, trampled fields of corn and millet, a treeless, brown
expanse varied now and then by a glimpse of a distant grove
shading a temple or the roofless walls of a little village whose
people had fled before the path of the allied invasion.

The river was lively with traffic, junks plodding upstream
with the fluttering flags of Japan or England or Russia and
swimming deep with stores and munitions, soldiers sprawled
on deck or loafing along the bank with rifles on their shoulders. Junks came down-river more rapidly, coolies plying
the long sweeps, huge battened sails hoisted to catch the
favoring breeze, and perhaps you perceived under an awning
of matting a group of haggard, weary men and women in
garments curiously nondescript, survivors of missionary set-
tlements which had seen and suffered horrors indescribable.
For these the trip down the Pei-ho must have seemed commonplace. They were dulled to all sense of peril.

Every few miles there was a military outpost to protect
this flowing road to Peking, perhaps a troop of Bengal Lancers, black-bearded, turbaned men of splendid appearance;
or a body of hard-riding Cossacks, white tunics, long boots,
tough little ponies; or lean, tanned Americans of the Sixth
Cavalry, swinging along on patrol with an easy nonchalance.

It was the intention of the junk with the lady passenger to
tie up for the night at one of these outposts, but after stranding on a bar and losing an hour or more, the darkness closed
down over the lonely fields, and the coolies, all smeared with
mud, swarmed on board to quarrel over the ration of boiled
rice and morsels of dried fish. The push-poles were driven
into the ooze to hold the junk against the bank as a lodging
for the night.

In the tiny cabin young Mrs. Meyers was an admirable

hostess at a frugal supper served upon a packing-box. It was one of the eternal feminine miracles to see her sitting there, so fresh and sweet and cool, in that cramped and filthy old junk, not in the least perturbed by her unusual surroundings. Presently the four men crawled out to the after-deck and contorted themselves to find space to stretch their kinked muscles without tumbling overboard. They arranged to stand watch, two hours each.

It was not a notable or a valorous adventure for the civil engineer, the two young ensigns, or the correspondent — this trip up the Pei-ho. They took it as a matter of course, as an incident in their several vocations. It is here recalled as a tribute to the pluck and devotion of a thoroughbred American girl. In these various memories, as they are written, it is not always easy to decide which stories to tell. There were bound to be many of them, in the years of roaming hither and yon with a lively interest in one's fellow mortals. The choice resolves itself into those scenes, events, or persons that stamped impressions the most vivid and enduring. This was one of them.

It was disquieting, I must confess, to stand your night watch with carbine and pistol, the junk snuggled against a field of tall, tangled millet through which the breeze rustled with sinister implications, as though stirred by creeping men. The feeling of anxiety was greatly accentuated by the thought of the girl asleep in the cabin. For Ralph Paine his turn at sentry duty was conducive to what his old shipmate McCready would have diagnosed as the yips and the fantods.

In the distance there was more or less rifle-firing all night, skirmishing patrols, or Chinese slaying one another, Boxers and native Christians fighting a private war of extermination. The western sky flared in a sudden conflagration. Some luckless village was blazing like a torch. It was surmised to be beyond the destructive swath of the allied advance. Like far-off thunder came the sullen rumble of artillery fire. And, now and then, the night air bore very faintly the rattle of musketry fusillades. It was curiously fascinating to sit and gaze at this incarnadined sky and to listen to the echoes of the savage uproar, and to wonder what kind of men were at one another's throats, and why.

The long night passed without disaster to the junk and the precious passenger in the sty of a cabin. At dawn the noisy coolies scrambled to the bank and, with grunts and a shrill, cadenced working song, heaved ahead on the towline. In the débris of a hamlet at a bend of the stream, several Chinese prowled and poked about. One of them unslung a rifle and dropped upon his knees, shooting wildly at the junk. The bullets flew high. A few shots in reply and he scampered from sight, a stubborn-minded son of Satan who refused to be pacified and was waging hostilities on his own account.

Later in the day young Mrs. Meyers, tired of the cramped confines of the cabin, sauntered on the towpath and unless cautioned she might have walked right on to Peking without an escort. The civil engineer, the two energetic ensigns, and the correspondent swore to finish the river trip in two days more or massacre the fifteen coolies. A Mexican dollar was promised every one of the rugged scoundrels if he would hang to that towline until midnight instead of quitting at sundown.

They squatted and slid and fell heels-over-head in black darkness, but the sluggish junk continued to creep against the current and Peking was by that much nearer. By daylight an occasional bullet twittered over the junk as some stray sniper fired from a hiding-place in the millet stalks. At the foreign military outpost of Ho-si-wu two of the men jumped ashore and hastened to where the Stars and Stripes flew above a half-demolished dwelling in which a capable sergeant clicked a telegraph key.

Mrs. Meyers had been yearning to send a message of inquiry over this army field wire to Peking. But it was unnecessary. A message from Peking was waiting for her, and the correspondent almost broke his neck in racing back to the junk with it. Captain "Jack" Meyers was alive and convalescing.

And now who cared whether the rest of the journey was unpleasant or not! By the gods, it was a mere holiday excursion! The blessed old junk shoved her nose along, a mile or two an hour, and nudged the floating corpses aside, and so came to Tung-Chow which was at the head of river navigation. Thence it was a distance of thirteen miles by land to Peking. An American army ambulance was waiting, and a pair of good Kentucky mules. General Chaffee himself had sent it to Tung-Chow to spare a weary American girl the torture of riding in a springless Chinese cart at a snail's pace.

Over the frightfully rutted road we rattled and bounced until from the monotonous plain loomed the endless walls of Peking and the impressive crenellated towers and gateways— Peking the most incredible and surprising city in the world, a fortified capital of Central Asia preserved intact from the thirteenth century, now conquered, ravaged, humiliated, in the ruthless grip of a little army of twenty thousand despised foreign troops.

Soon there were outspread acres and acres of ruins, leveled by shell-fire, by the torch, streets crowded with every army uniform under the sun, soldiers burdened with armfuls of plunder, gorgeous furs, priceless brocades and embroideries, sacks of jade or silver bullion — halting to quarrel while the stronger snatched the spoils from the weaker.

Then we came to the area of the defenses which had been so magnificently held by those few hundred allied marines, bluejackets, legation clerks, secretaries, and missionaries — gaunt, ragged walls, countless barricades of brick, and breastworks of sand-bags.

These ramparts of sand-bags were gorgeous to behold, thousands of sacks made of silk fabrics snatched from Chinese shops, crimson and yellow and blue and white. They had been cut and stitched together by the women gathered within the beleaguered walls, the wives of diplomats, the white-faced fugitives from distant mission stations, the native Christian girls — all these women mobilized in one building and stitching for their lives. They had glorified the prosaic sewing machine, purring its song by night and day while an inferno raged outside and the men fell dying at the loopholes or were fetched back bleeding from the desperate sortie.

Wide-eyed, amazed, the American bride who had dared so much to find her husband read in one swift glance after another some realization of what he had done and suffered. The ambulance clattered into the enclosure of the American Legation where the fighting had been fiercest. Just beyond it towered the great grim wall of the Tartar City and the rude barricade upon its wide summit where Captain "Jack" Meyers and his marines had held a position vital to the safety of the whole system of defense.

The wife of Captain Meyers was out of that ambulance before it stopped at the doorway. A natty young diplomat, impeccable in his white linen suit, stiff collar, Panama hat, stood in his tracks to admire this charming vision. He seemed most incongruous amid this welter of devastation and the clash of arms. For once his perfections failed to intrigue. The girl flew past him, asking a breathless question of a strapping marine on orderly duty.

He told her where to go. Then he said to the wide world, with the smile of a man who had a sweetheart of his own:

"Huh, I know one captain of marines that's due to get well in a hell of a hurry!"

Ensign Tardy, U.S.N., confided to his comrade: "Hanged if it does n't make me feel sort of sentimental and all churned up inside. That girl is certainly a peach, a perfect wonder. I would n't mind having a Chinese spear stuck into me — not too far —"

"Shut up, you poor ass," chided Ensign Tarrant, U.S.N. "Go deliver your dispatches and then we'll give this town a ramble. There is some shooting going on somewhere I just now heard it."

"Bully! And a few souvenirs," brightly suggested Ensign Tardy. "No looting, understand, for we are in uniform, but some trinkets to send the girl back home."

The civil engineer dolefully observed: "I owned a good house in Peking, rather comfortably furnished. I guess I had better go and try to find the site of it."

The correspondent, very much adrift and night coming on, was moved to remark: "There being no hotels, nor anything else left standing as far as I can see, please watch me rustle a place to sleep."

He found it with a battalion of American marines encamped in the enormous palace of one of the Seven Hereditary Princes, and the officer who produced a canvas hammock to sling between two gilded pillars was one of the lot who had held the hill in Guantanamo Bay.

Kipling said it for them in the lines:

"'An' after I met 'im all over the world, a-doin' all kinds of things,
Like landin' 'isself with a Gatlin' gun to talk to them 'eathen kings . . .'"

XXX

THE DISPERSION OF HENRY BECKINGHAM

THE problem of living quarters turned out to be difficult. Where everything was so frightfully unsettled, it seemed absurd to talk of getting settled. Peking was a city of magnificent distances and it was advisable to be somewhere near the legations and the diplomats. These would be the chief sources of news and information now that the troops had achieved their purpose. The Chinese people had paid for their folly, in blood and tears and beggary, but for many months the foreign ministers would be wagging their heads around the council table, matching wits, stacking the cards against each other, demanding punishments, indemnities, decapitations, oblivious of the fact that the anti-foreign uprising, called the Boxer Rebellion, had been caused by the shameless greed of England, France, Russia, in gobbling huge slices of Chinese territory with one flimsy pretext after another.

Peking was a city in which there were no accommodations for visitors. Mile after mile of shops, dwellings, warehouses had been burned or looted by the Boxer bandits before the allied invasion had begun to plunder. The Chinese population, in a frenzy of terror, had taken to its heels as soon as the foreign columns had approached the outer walls. It was a depopulation unprecedented in modern times. This vast and teeming city had been deserted by the living. Only the dead remained, and there were many of them. There were no markets, no street booths, no processions of peddlers stridently chanting their wares. Money could buy almost nothing to eat.

General Chaffee's regiments were encamped in the great park of the Temple of Agriculture which for centuries had been held sacred and inviolate against all intrusion. Before its marble altars the Emperors of China had made annual sacrifices and oblations to the spirits of the earth and the rain and the fruition of harvests, a worship of the Supreme Deity and a rite more ancient than Confucian or Taoist or Buddhist doctrines had exemplified.

This walled park was three miles from the legation quarter where it was much more convenient to try one's luck at housekeeping amid the ruins. Therefore you might have seen Ralph Paine and Martin Egan, of the Associated Press, in search of a building that could be inhabited. It was discovered in the region which had been most savagely and persistently fought over, the modest compound of some Chinese merchant or official who had vanished with his household.

By a twist of chance the tiled roofs and the brick walls had escaped destruction. They stood in the midst of a woeful expanse of rubbish, of heaps of tumbled brick and mortar, charred timbers, smashed furniture and carts, an oasis in an appalling desert of destruction.

The rooms faced the inner courtyard and these inside walls were mostly of lattice-work covered with oiled paper. There was an outer surrounding wall, of brick, of course, with a gateway heavily timbered as a protection against marauders even in time of peace. The place had been thoroughly stripped. It was an empty shell, but, after all, there was no place like home to the pair of derelict correspondents. They were not in a critical mood. Two doors were pulled down and propped upon bricks to serve as beds. A teakwood table was borrowed from elsewhere, to use a polite phrase, and tin cups and plates, of the campaign kits, equipped the pantry.

The kitchen was a sooty, greasy, most unpleasant den, but it had a charcoal cooking stove of brick and a battered pot and pan or two. Life was largely a struggle for existence, a

WHERE MARTIN EGAN AND THE AUTHOR FOUND A HAPPY HOME
AMID THE RUINS OF PEKING

ANXIOUS PARENTS LOOK ON WHILE THE CHINESE "ARMY" LEARNS
THE YALE CHEER, "LAH, LAH, LAH!"

daily trip to the American camp to beg a little bacon and bread, a couple of cans of tomatoes, a few potatoes, from the commissary sergeant. Perhaps long exploration might yield a dozen native eggs or a scrawny fowl, but such luxuries were rare. It really preyed on one's mind and sapped his energies, this foraging for enough to eat.

Martin Egan was a suave, resourceful young man with a dignity that was seldom rumpled. To-day he holds an important position in the great banking house of J. P. Morgan & Co., and during the Great War he was borrowed first by Henry P. Davison when he was directing the vast activities of the American Red Cross, and later by General Pershing for service at the Army Headquarters in France; but Martin Egan was no less dignified and impressive, twenty-odd years ago, when he took his turn as pot-wrestler in that smoky, vile Chinese kitchen and evolved the next meal. It was a victory of personality over circumstances.

He would emerge sniffing the frying-pan as if wondering what the concoction really was, and blandly murmur to his comrade:

"My boy, dinner is served. I cannot vouch for it. Everything I cook seems to absorb several centuries of flavor from the kitchen, and as fast as you scrub off one layer of grease you uncover another stratum. This is a very old country."

However, it was a happy home until, in a moment of misguided altruism, we invited a third man to join the mess. An excellent word, that! It was so obviously a mess. Let us call this interesting person Henry Beckingham. For once in this narrative I am reluctant to give a man his real name. The reason will appear later.

We found this Beckingham wandering along the Chienmen Road in the Chinese City. He was a stranger and we took him in. One of the London illustrated weeklies had told Henry Beckingham to take his large and cumbersome camera and go to China with it. He could make excellent photographs, you could say that much for him. When discovered in the midst of the swirling military traffic of the Chien-men Road, Henry Beckingham was dodging from under a Russian artillery team while the bell-camel of a Mongolian pack-train was trying to eat his hat. On his long, thin face (Beckingham's, not the camel's) was an expression of intense dislike and bewilderment, as if to say that things were done much better in Tottenham Court Road.

He had come out to Tientsin in a British army transport and from there the good-natured staff of the Indian Field Post organization had forwarded him to Peking, at parcel rates or something like that. It was incredible that Henry Beckingham could have made the journey unassisted, without being lost, strayed, or stolen. As a campaigner he moved in an aura of pathos. You simply could n't help feeling sorry for him. His lanky figure drooped, likewise his yellow mustache, and his voice was always bewildered and sorrowful. A world in which you could not find a respectable restaurant or tea-shop, or a tall policeman in a chin-strapped helmet, was beyond his comprehension.

"I have been looking for a hotel all over the bally place," explained Henry Beckingham, "but I can't seem to find any. Wretched, is n't it!"

"Very poor service," gravely replied Martin Egan. "I must speak to the management about it. Better trot along with us, old man."

Beckingham was very grateful. In this rough-and-tumble game he failed somehow to fit, like a curate in a riot. And now there were three of us in the Chinese home among the ruins. It was soon made manifest, however, that we had welcomed a guest and not a fellow toiler. Beckingham failed to do his share, probably because he did not know how. Moreover, he was an individualist, mostly absorbed in the welfare of Henry Beckingham. It was the wrong attitude toward life.

With unconcern he beheld Egan and Paine spend half a day in trudging about to find something in the way of provender and then cooking the stuff, for Beckingham. His friends of the Indian Field Post loaned him a folding cot and he set it up in an empty room, with a gloating air that was a trifle irritating. His comrades twain were still sleeping upon hardwood doors. And it pricked the admirable dispositions of Martin Egan and Ralph Paine, when the dinner was on the table after prodigious exertion, to watch Henry disdainfully finger his yellow mustache and to hear him drawl:

"I say, old chaps, have n't you any buttah? I really can't live without buttah, don't you know. It's absurd to have no buttah on the table, really."

Paine was for braining Henry with a bronze image of Buddha which reposed in the courtyard, but Egan stayed his hand. A crisis was averted by the capture of a Chinese youth who was persuaded to serve in the kitchen. He was very unhappy, but it was any port in a storm and he felt grateful for foreign protection. He was no coolie, but a young man of some position and refinement. His finger-nails curled like tendrils, as symbols of gentility, and he wept when he broke one of them on the pots and kettles. It was like lopping a branch from the family tree of a Colonial Dame.

He spoke some English, and when you smoothed it out the story ran like this:

"My father was a wealthy seller of cloth in Peking and he intended that I should be a seller of cloth and succeed to his business. But my father discovered that I did not have brains enough to be a seller of cloth, so he sent me as a student to the Peking University."

This was illuminating. It explained why a certain number of young men in America spend four years on a college campus. Martin Egan listened to his confession and innocently remarked to Beckingham:

"You are a university man, I believe. Now I can understand."

The shot missed the target. Henry smiled in a superior manner. He was not quick-witted. It was the same when we poked fun at that enormous camera, advising him to cut a door in it and use it as a portable house.

"Oh, it is n't large enough for that. Yes, it is a bit awkward to get about with. They make 'em much lighter now, but I have lugged this one about with me for twenty years or so, and I am rather used to the feel of it."

The question of finances obtruded itself. At intervals Henry flourished a five-pound note and complained that nobody would change it for him. Ridiculous! No banking facilities in a city like Peking! A Bank of England note was respected anywhere in the world! Of course Henry had never thought of bringing a bag of Mexican silver dollars up the coast with him. This was the only money recognized in distracted Peking whose one foreign bank was not to be distinguished from a dust-heap.

Meanwhile the two American correspondents paid the mess bills and other expenses. And Henry Beckingham continued to make useless gestures with the five-pound note. It was all right, of course, and there was no thought of dunning him. After a fortnight, however, a British acquaintance was kind enough to crack the five-pound note for Beckingham who rambled in to announce it and then walked out again.

"Ah, our star boarder from dear old London will now blow us to all the delicacies he can lay his hands on," hopefully exclaimed Martin Egan. "Maybe we have misjudged the poor old blighter."

When Beckingham returned, it was with ten cents' worth of Chinese apples. There were eight apples in the bag and he took six of them. The other apples — two, count them, two — were his splendid contribution to the household commissary. And that night he plaintively criticized the supper.

Egan wiped large flakes of soot from his nose and regarded a blistered thumb. He had been assisting the Chinese sophomore in the kitchen. Homicide was averted by the narrowest of margins. We were fond of dear old Beckingham. but there was such a thing as crowding us too far. This was no garden of the Hesperides, but the apple of discord had been tossed in our midst.

Henry Beckingham was a nervous person — built that way. As he viewed Peking it was a place of frightful disorder, very poorly policed. In the suburbs and the countryside there was still more or less fighting, clearing out nests of Boxers with their frenzied war-cry of "*Sha! Sha! Sha!*" (Kill! Kill! Kill!) This Chinese house of ours had an isolated aspect in the wilderness of ruins, and the nearest French and Japanese sentry posts were on Legation Road, several hundred yards distant. To Beckingham it seemed not impossible that a bunch of pig-tailed outlaws might come swarming over our wall some dark night. He mentioned it now and then, in his sad, resigned manner. Martin Egan told him not to worry. All he had to do was to crawl into his camera and keep perfectly quiet. No Chinese would touch a camera. They thought it possessed by evil spirits.

The two correspondents sat at the table in the courtyard one evening. By the light of candles stuck in bottles they were writing many pages of manuscript to be sent home by mail. Only the actual news of the day was transmitted by cable at a cost of $1.72 a word. It might have surprised the American reader to know that a column dispatch which was hastily scanned had cost more than a thousand dollars merely to send it from Peking. Description, impressions, anecdotes, the color and movement of the campaign were forwarded in the mails.

We were writing the story of our trip through the Forbidden City, that sacrosanct and gorgeous assemblage of palaces, throne-rooms, parks, and pagodas hidden behind massive and towering walls which, for many centuries, had inspired prodigal conjecture, romance, mystery, and baffled curiosity. Until this allied invasion, no foreigner had ever passed inside the gates of the Forbidden City. It was one of the world's last great secrets which had defied exploration.

For diplomatic reasons the allied army had spared this Purple City, the seat of the Son of Heaven, denying admission, guarding every gate, protecting its priceless loot. The Empress Dowager, that wonderful old lady who had ruled China with an iron hand, had fled the Sacred City, with her train of officials and the helpless young Emperor, barely in time to avoid capture, leaving the vast household, several thousand trembling servants, eunuchs, and concubines who expected to be slaughtered by the foreign soldiers. They were unmolested.

The Forbidden City was still sealed against intrusion, but the Russian admiral, Alexiev, had journeyed arduously from Taku for the sole purpose of visiting it, and permission was granted him by the allied diplomats. A few days later a similar request was made by Lieutenant-General Osaka, inspector-general of the Japanese armies and chief aidè of the Emperor. He could not be denied without treading on the toes of international amity. It became known that General James Grant Wilson, U.S.A., was to escort the distinguished Japanese party through the Forbidden City.

No correspondents were invited. In fact, they were told to waste no breath on the matter. It was profoundly secretive and exclusive. However, Ralph Paine and Martin Egan were waiting at the north gateway of the Forbidden City at the hour appointed for the entrance of the official cavalcade. When General Wilson rode through with Generals Osaka and Yamaguichi, followed by their staffs, the two correspondents were close behind them. And there they stayed through many hours of sight-seeing memorable and unique. Said General Wilson, very sternly:

"Remember, now, I gave you no permission whatever. You have disobeyed orders and defied authority, but now that you are in here I won't put you out, in the face of these Japanese officers. There are times when we Americans must hang together."

I have no intention of describing that day in the Forbidden City. It is an old story now. But it was fresh and new and entrancing when Egan and I toiled to set it down on paper that night, with the candles flaring and sputtering in the bottles. It was a long, hard task, for we wrote columns of it, hard-driven newspaper men who could not wait for moods and inspirations. Perhaps the stuff was better for it. And I must say, reading it twenty years after, that the story was n't half bad.

It was after midnight when we finished writing, two tired men, eyes aching, heads feeling fuzzy, nerves a bit rasped. Behind the lattice-work, a few feet distant, Henry Beckingham snored loudly upon his cot. On the morrow we should have to rustle grub for him and listen to his dissatisfied remarks about it.

There is one last straw that will break the back of the stoutest Mongolian camel, one final provocation to make the meekest worm turn. If Beckingham had not been snoring away like a gigantic bumble-bee, the thing might not have happened. It symbolized the whole situation. The rest of the world could jolly well go hang as long as Henry was snug and comfortable and provided for.

The florid, amiable countenance of Martin Egan was overcast with deep thought. Smoking a pipe, he sat meditating until some sudden conclusion made him exclaim:

"Henry wears on us both. And we are not impatient men. We ought to get rid of him, really we ought, but we can't tell him so. It is awkward — very — he has friends in the British camp — they might be glad to take him on for a while — sort of pass him along."

"You tell him, Martin," said I. "Being so soft-hearted, I—"

"Coward!" cried Egan. "You have been a pirate on the high seas. Brutal work is right in your line.'

"If Henry should leave us of his own accord —" I reflected aloud.

"No such luck," my comrade grunted. "Pry him loose from his meal ticket, of his own free will? Never, my boy, never!"

"But I think it can be done, Martin. Diplomacy, finesse! Have n't we been absorbing it through our pores? Henry Beckingham suspects that this villa of ours is not quite safe. He worries about a midnight attack. If something like that should happen, he would leave us rapidly, spontaneously. *Qui qui, chop, chop!*"

Martin Egan grinned. You did not have to hammer an idea into his wise noddle with a club.

"Can-do," he said, with animation. "If we can stage one-piecee attack and make it lively, the star boarder may be last seen galloping down the pike. *Maskee!* All right. Let us proceed to go to it. For the love of Mike, will you listen to him snore? That last blast lifted the tiles off the roof."

There were many details to be carefully arranged. They were executed with seriousness. This was no childish entertainment. Two war correspondents viewed it as a necessity. Their morale had been already impaired. Another month of Henry Beckingham and they would be ordering themselves home as invalids.

A few feet inside the gate of the wall stood a monstrous wooden screen elaborately carved and painted. It was perhaps ten feet high. Placed athwart the entrance of the courtyard, this screen or barrier permitted a détour to be made around either side of it. The purpose was to head off or circumvent the Chinese evil spirits. To invade the compound they would have to tack or double around this screen instead of moving straight ahead. It is well known that Chinese devils can travel only in straight lines. The habit of the bad spirits of other races is quite the reverse, of course, for their paths are proverbially crooked. For lack of the Chinese name of this contrivance, we called the picturesque fabric of painted wood "the devil-stopper."

In a shed of the collection of low buildings we stabled our two ponies. It was easy, therefore, to carry bundles of straw and fodder across the yard and heap them around the huge screen, so old and dry and richly painted, so very inflammable. As souvenirs there had been picked up several carbines and rifles, heavy swords, the crimson aprons and sashes and turbans worn by the Boxer troops.

The Chinese sophomore was rudely aroused from his pallet in the kitchen. By this time another boy had been accumulated, as hostler and chambermaid. He was firmly hauled out of the shed. These two servitors were commanded to array themselves in the terrifying Boxer regalia and to clutch the long, bright swords. The American conspirators armed themselves with rifles and filled their pockets with cartridge clips.

As a final touch, bundles of straw were laid against the brick walls and tossed upon the tile roofs. There have been stage managers less competent drawing salaries in the theatrical business. We were proud of our handiwork. It indicated a certain versatility.

The brace of sleepy Chinese youths were instructed, at the signal, to scamper around and around in the courtyard, making themselves as numerous as possible, yelling "*Sha! Sha! Sha!*" They promised to obey, exhibiting no astonishment. This was merely another freak of the insane foreigners who always behaved without wit or reason. You might have thought they had been told to have breakfast ready a little earlier than usual. If they perceived any humor in the situation it was inscrutably masked.

"All set," said Martin Egan. "Where is that box of matches? I have an intuition that something will occur very shortly."

It did. We ran to touch off the pile of straw at the devil-stopper and the bundles placed elsewhere. They blazed up instantly, grandly. The courtyard was all yellow glare and smoke. The flames greedily licked that elaborate wooden screen at the gateway and it began to snap and crackle. Tongues of fire were licking along the walls and up on the roofs.

Around and around flew the two Chinese youths, emitting screeches, the swords wildly gleaming, their make-up amazingly effective. As they dashed through the smoke, I could have sworn there were a dozen of them.

Martin Egan was making a gallant stand in one corner of the yard, shooting off rifles so fast that he was a human bunch of fire-crackers. He was dying hard, brave old Egan, shouting hoarsely for help before he was overpowered, but never yielding an inch.

Paine was defending the gateway, now and then prodding the Chinese chorus, as you might call it, when the two youths galloped past for another circuit, felt shoes twinkling, queues whipping out behind, mouths wide open in ear-splitting yells.

I tell you, as seen through that infernal glare and drifting smoke, it was a mighty realistic performance. Henry Beckingham thought so, too. He must have awakened suddenly, nor could you blame him for a confused and startled state of mind. This was apparent when he neglected to use the door of his room as an exit. Instead of this, he ploughed through the flimsy wall of lattice-work and oiled paper, emerging into the courtyard as though he had been catapulted from the cot.

Henry could be more agile and animated than we had dreamed possible. It was queer to see him pop through that wall amid the flying splinters and fragments.

The circumstances were such that it was difficult for him to pull himself together, to know whether this was a nightmare or a reality. There was no doubt that we had achieved the ambition of every true artist, to create a perfect illusion. Henry Beckingham was convinced. For a moment he stood rubbing the sleep from his eyes, and then he broke for the gateway. It was barred by a raging conflagration. With a low moan he turned in another direction, but two infuriated Boxers ran at him. He doubled toward the kitchen, and rifles were dinning in his ears.

What else was there for Henry Beckingham to do but run around and around, hemmed in, hopeless, his mentality in a stew, and as he sprinted he was heard to gasp:

"*My word! My word! My word! How very extra'nary!*"

Sooner or later he was bound to bolt from this orbit, for fiends in scarlet garments were at his heels. The flaming wooden screen soon began to collapse, being a flimsy structure. In the middle of it appeared a gap. Henry Beckingham never delayed to make the détour and so win a passage out of the gateway. He went through that tall devil-stopper precisely like a circus rider through a blazing hoop. It was immensely spectacular, an impromptu bit, but quite the best thing on the bill.

It was later learned that he checked those flying feet of his only when he reached the grounds of the British Legation where he was securely surrounded by the Australian Naval Brigade and three batteries of Royal Field Artillery

The friends he had left behind him proceeded to demobilize the forces and to extinguish the conflagration with buckets of water. They were talking it over when in trotted an alert squad of Japanese infantry at the double-quick. They had turned out to quell the attack! This was a complication unforeseen by the stage managers. The Japanese captain demanded to know.

The explanation required some quick thinking. It was a

false alarm, an accidental fire, a panic brewed by silly Chinese servants. The little captain was shrewd and skeptical. He demanded to know some more. We took him arm-in-arm between us and marched him off to a Japanese canteen which was open late at night. We became fast friends.

Henry Beckingham never came back to live with us. He considered it unsafe. Several years later I was writing in London, and Beckingham got wind of my whereabouts. He invited me out to Hackney for supper and was most cordial and hospitable. And a motherly Mrs. Henry welcomed me, and seven young Beckinghams arranged in a row, all sizes of them.

And then was I filled with remorse and contrition and shame! Poor old Henry! He had been careful of his money in Peking because compelled to be — the small salary for his job with the camera and probably a scrimped expense account — and this populous household in Hackney to carry on his back. In the sight of Mrs. Henry and all the young Beckinghams, he was a hero beyond compare, with his tales of the China campaign.

He lived it over again while they listened entranced, that wild night when his bully chums, Martin Egan and Ralph Paine, had stood off a Boxer attack and saved his life.

"My word, children!" said Henry. "Those frightful beggars almost did us in."

The wretched Ralph Paine sat and squirmed through Henry Beckingham's thrilling narrative. Now you will understand why he has avoided using Henry's real name. It is the stern mandate of conscience. The one desire, during supper in that little house in Hackney, was that Martin Egan might have been there to take his share of punishment.

XXXI

THE WRITHING DRAGONS ON THE RAFTERS

IT was a rugged, shaggy Manchurian pony with a warped disposition and a rampant anti-foreign spirit. After pitching Ralph Paine off upon his head in the dust of the Hat-a-men Road, it proceeded to kick him with malice aforethought. The foolish young man had wagered five dollars that he could stay with this four-legged package of iniquity. He lost. The stone pavement was hard and the pony's heels high-powered and well-aimed. Consequently there was a bruised correspondent who walked with a limp. The skin had been knocked from one knee. This was a trifling hurt, but the infection of the filthy Peking dust made trouble after a little while.

The field hospital of the American Army was one of the many buildings of brick and stone in the park of the sacred Temple of Agriculture. The curving roof was ornamented with green and yellow tiles, the timbers curiously carved and gilded. It was like an immense warehouse with the adornments of a temple, standing close by the terraced marble altars where Emperors had come to worship beneath the open sky. The interior of the building was shadowy and lofty, and a regiment could have been drilled on its marble floor. Huge columns soared in aisles to the roof-beams which were ablaze with monstrous dragons, painted in vermilion and gold, and they seemed to writhe and twist in the dusky obscurity.

It was in this strange hospital that Ralph Paine had to spend several weeks of the autumn, upon a cot among a hundred sick and wounded American soldiers. Three years later he was making an attempt to write fiction, to break into the magazines with the natural diffidence of a newspaper man. The first short story he wrote was called "The Jade Teapot," and the hero was a homesick lad of the Ninth Infantry, wasted by illness and lying in this bizarre field hospital in Peking. The story was sent to "Scribner's Magazine" and cordially accepted by the editor, Mr. E. L. Burlingame.

The background of the slight plot was true to the facts, as I had experienced them, and such bits as these were of the very texture of reality.

Private Saunders was gazing up into the gloom of the distant rafters and trying to count the racing gilded dragons which would not be still. They made his head ache intolerably. When lanterns were lighted at the ends of each aisle of cots, the shadows danced worse than before, and, to his fevered eyes, the great temple was populous with glittering shapes in terrifying agitation. . . .

Between flights of delirium he heard the groans and restless mutterings of many men and his fancy magnified them into an army. There were neither screens nor walls to divide the wards, only the rows of cots between the pillars which marched across the temple floor, so that all individual suffering and the tenacious struggle of dying became common property. The soldiers who passed away in the night did not trouble their comrades so much as when death came in daylight and the end was a struggle thrust upon those in surrounding cots. . . .

It happened almost daily that the Ninth Regiment band trailed through the hospital compound, playing a dead march. There was always a halt in front of the great marble staircase outside, and after a few moments the dragging music sounded fainter and farther away. A little later those in the temple could barely hear the silvery wail of "Taps" floating from a corner of the outer wall where a line of mounds was growing longer week by week. Then the band returned, playing a Sousa march or a rag-time melody. . . .

A little after midnight the tramp of stretcher-bearers punctuated a thin, wailing outcry coming from that which they bore between them, and the temple floor awoke with weary curses. Those near the doorway learned that a Chinese coolie, caught in the act of stealing coal from the quartermaster's corral, had been tumbled off a wall by a sentry's shot. The lamentations of the victim rasped sick nerves beyond endurance, and the hospital held no sympathy in its smallest crevice. The coolie was an old man and badly hurt. Opium had made him impervious to customary doses of morphine, and after he had been drugged in quantities to kill four men he was no nearer quiet. From a far corner of the temple the wounded coolie wailed an unending:

"Ai, oh!" — "Ai, oh!" — "Ai, oh!"

Soldiers rose in their gray blankets and made uproar with cries of:

"Kill him!"

"Smother the beast!"

"Wring his fool neck!"

"Give him an overdose of dope, Doc."

"Ain't this an outrage!"

"Hi, there, One Lung, give us a chance to sleep!"

"Throw him out in the yard!"

Daylight brought to Private Saunders infinitely grateful respite from a world through which he had fled pursued by flaming dragons that shrieked, as though in torment:

"Ai, oh!" — "Ai, oh!" — "Ai, oh!"

This hospital lacked many things to make it adequate and comfortable, and when the biting autumn winds swept down from the Mongolian deserts and presaged the North China winter, so hard and clear and cold, the vast barn of a temple chilled these sick soldiers to their very souls. The American forces were ten thousand miles from home and they had been very hurriedly thrown into China. Transportation was slow and difficult, and it was a long time before the necessary supplies reached the front.

The army hospital system was still crude, at best, and although the campaigns in Cuba and the Philippines had taught the War Department something, you could not have called it overcrowded with energy and intelligence. For instance, after two months of occupation no competently trained nurses had been sent to Peking. The hospital stewards and orderlies were faithful men, God bless them, but they were fairly worked off their feet, and they simply did not know how to give the serious cases the proper care.

The operating-table was in a corner of the temple, behind a screen, and the surgeons were parsimonious in the use of chloroform or ether, either because of a limited supply or because a buck private was presumed to stand the gaff without flinching, unless they were cutting him up in an important manner. It was one of the few diversions that helped to pass the time, to listen and pass on the merits of a comrade when he went under the knife. If he set his teeth and took it without whimpering, he was a "sandy guy." If he yelled, the comments were disparaging. "The trouble with that bird is that he has a streak of yellow."

It therefore befell that when the surgeon decided to use his tools on Ralph Paine and remove a bunch of infected glands, it was obligatory to try to grin and bear it. The most reluctant coward would have braced himself for the ordeal, with this critical audience that surrounded the cot before and after — hairy convalescents wrapped in blankets who were all kindness and affection and sympathy, forgetting their own woes.

These were regulars of the old Army, and sensitive persons of a coddled refinement might have thought them a rough and horrid lot. They gambled and they swore and some of them got drunk every pay-day, but when the bugles blew they fought like heroes, and through thick and thin they stood by their pals. And after all, are not these shining attributes and to be named among the essentials of worthy manhood?

Men of this pattern, as I knew and loved them in my youth, helped to build an abiding faith in the intrinsic nobility of humanity. The flame may flicker dim and low, but the spark is unquenchable. In the tale of "The Jade Teapot" I tried to offer a glimpse of the goodness of these soldier friends of mine.

"Shorty" Blake and "Bat" Jenkins of D Company strove to make Private Saunders take some interest in life, and they would have been cheered if he had even sworn at the rations and the lack of hospital comforts. They brought him jam and condensed milk from the commissary sergeant; they assembled around his cot the most vivacious convalescents, selecting as entertainers those valiant in poker and campaign stories.

. While Ralph Paine lay stretched upon a cot, and the days dragged into weeks, he was often reminded of an experience in his father's career, Samuel Delahaye Paine, the British lad who had run away from home in his teens to serve through the Crimean War against Russia in the Royal Field Artillery. He too had been in hospital, as well as in the trenches, and he had kissed the shadow of Florence Nightingale when it fell athwart his cot as she had passed through the wards.

Out of his comradeship with the rank and file had come his own unswerving allegiance to the gospel of faith, hope, and charity. This is the story as he used to tell it, and as it came back to mind in that dreary, remote field hospital in Peking:

"After the capture of Sevastopol, my siege train went into winter quarters on the heights of Balaclava, overlooking the Black Sea. There was little diversion, the fighting was over, and many young soldiers were gripped by the homesickness which swept the camps like a blighting epidemic. Soon all the hospitals were filled with worn-out men and I was one of them, men whose malady was mostly homesickness.

"I shall never forget the last night I spent on the Crimean Peninsula. In the evening I walked to the ruins of an old Genoese fort and sat down and looked across the Black Sea and wondered if I should ever see the England that lay beyond those waters. A gun boomed the signal to return to the hospital. The bugles called 'Lights Out' and the nurses and sisters of mercy said good-night through the wards. We tried to sleep.

"Sometime during that restless night an orderly from the front aroused us with the news that an English steamer had arrived at Balaclava with a momentous message. An armistice had been arranged between Russia and the Allied Powers. The orderly was mauled by frantic invalids in a sheer frenzy of delight. And presently the order came that all men of the siege train then in hospital, who could parade next morning in heavy marching order, would be immediately embarked in ships bound to England.

"There was no more sleep in the wards. We spent the rest of the night in singing, shouting, cleaning uniforms and accouterments. Mental healing worked miracles. Men who had been given up to die were scrambling from their cots and struggling to get into their boots.

"In the convalescent ward, to which I had been assigned, all the patients were able to stand and walk to parade excepting one lad. The surgeon refused to pass him as fit to embark. His name was Joe Benton and he had enlisted with me at Woolwich, and we had been chums in the trenches. On the second night of the last great bombardment of Sevastopol he had been hit in the leg by a fragment of shell. It was a bad wound and we thought he could not live through the night. We had carried him to the ambulance station in a ravine near the trenches, putting him in a chair on the back of a mule while I sat on the other side to balance the weight.

"When Joe was almost cured of his wound he was transferred to the hospital at Balaclava. There he went into a decline, from homesickness and a low fever. When the surgeon told him he could not go with us to England, he turned his face to the wall and cried like a little child.

"'Don't leave me here, boys,' he quavered. 'I shall die here after you are gone. I'll take my chances. If I must die, I want to die with my comrades.'

"We held a consultation and decided that Joe Benton must go with us. Early in the morning we took the kit out of his knapsack and stuffed it with paper. Then we dressed Joe in his old uniform of the red and blue of the Royal Artillery

and got him on his feet. He swayed and could not stand
alone, but two of the tallest men of the company stood at his
elbows and pressed close and held him up while they moved
very slowly to the parade ground. The major of our company, a rough, profane old war-dog, was not burdened with
sympathy, as a rule, but he wiped his eyes when he saw the
pale face of Joe Benton in the rear rank.

"The bands struck up 'The British Grenadiers,' and
'Cheer, Boys, Cheer, No More of Idle Sorrow,' and we
marched downhill to the transport in Balaclava harbor while
Joe Benton's toes dragged between the tall artillerymen who
supported him. We put him in a hammock between decks
and did not expect him to live through the first week. When
the captain of the ship gave the order to weigh anchor, we
invalids shoved the sailors aside and manned the capstan
bars. Then we steamed across the Black Sea, through the
Bosphorus, and anchored in the Golden Horn.

"Joe Benton was no worse for the voyage. After coaling,
the transport steered down the Dardanelles, past the isles of
Greece, and entered the harbor of Malta. Joe was feeling
stronger every day. We went ashore and bought him figs
and fresh milk and eggs, and the color began to show in his
cheeks. Through the Bay of Biscay we passed and on up
the Thames to Woolwich where we were to go ashore. In the
distance we could see the royal standards of England, Ireland, and Scotland, and by this token we knew that the good
Queen Victoria was there to welcome the vanguard of her
soldiers returning from the Crimea.

"Our band played 'Home, Sweet Home' — the first time
we had heard that tune since leaving England, for it was
never played in the Crimea, by special order. Veterans of
the old Royal Artillery who had fought England's battles in
many parts of the world were shedding tears as they formed
on deck and gazed at home once more. We marched ashore
and were paraded past the royal reviewing stand where the

Queen stood, with the royal family and many of the nobility of England.

"Joe Benton was at my elbow, straight and strong and active. As we tramped abreast of the reviewing stand, a little woman in black was in the crowd held back by the troopers of the Household Brigade. Her face was very sad, for she had heard that her boy had been killed in the trenches of Sevastopol, and she had come to join the great throng of welcoming people and to try to find some of her boy's comrades and ask them what they could tell her.

"When she caught sight of Joe Benton, she broke through the cordon of cavalry and rushed to throw her arms around her boy's neck, he that had been dead and was alive again, and brought safely home to her. The good Queen Victoria noticed the break in the column and the momentary halt, and inquired the reason. When she was told of the glad reunion, she commanded that Joe and his mother be escorted to the reviewing stand. And there the Queen kissed the cheek of the little woman in black and then pinned on the breast of Joe Benton's faded tunic the Crimean medal with the clasps of Inkerman, Alma, and Sevastopol."

XXXII

"HOCH DER KAISER" IN CHINA

WHEN, at length, Ralph Paine was able to leave the army hospital in Peking, he still limped and felt far from strong. Martin Egan, his best friend among the correspondents, had been ordered to Manila in charge of the Associated Press service in the Philippines, and was ready to go down the Pei-ho in a junk. There was a fairly decent hotel in Tientsin, and better hospital facilities, and so Paine went along to recuperate for a fortnight or so.

By this time, in November, the German army had arrived in North China, twenty-five thousand invincible, goose-stepping, gray-clad warriors in command of the high and puissant Field Marshal Count von Waldersee. They were considerably belated, Peking having been captured in August, but it was a long journey from the Fatherland. There was no more fighting and the allied military leaders were making every effort to pacify and reassure the Chinese people, to restore order, and to repopulate the cities and villages.

Not so with the tardy columns of the Kaiser. He had made them a farewell address, the famous gesture of the mailed fist.

You know very well that you are to fight against the cunning, brave, well-armed, and terrible enemy. If you come to grips with him, be assured quarter will not be given, no prisoners will be taken. Use your weapons in such a way that for a thousand years no Chinese shall dare to look upon a German askance.

All the allied generals, excepting Major-General Adna R. Chaffee, U.S.A., agreed to recognize Field Marshal Count von Waldersee as the commander-in-chief. The blunt, independent American soldier perceived that the German purpose was to wreak mischief and raise a bloody disturbance, and he promptly told the Prussian commander-in-chief:

"Under my instructions, I cannot take part in any movement which, in my judgment, has a tendency to promote rather than allay hostilities in the surrounding country. I shall not place my forces under the orders of the Field Marshal for the reason that the United States does not wish its troops to engage in offensive work."

Watching a regiment of German infantry pass in review, every hobnailed boot smiting the pavement with a resounding thump, General Chaffee made this shrewd comment:

"One could read on the face of every man, 'I am a German soldier. Hurrah for the Emperor and the Fatherland! The world is looking on, and I am proud to show it what I can do.'"

This spirit was conspicuous in Tientsin, even before the German army had begun its advance to Peking. With a truly Prussian lack of humor, it made no difference that the campaign had long since been finished. There were to be powerful German expeditions against the Chinese, nevertheless — deeds of bright and shining valor. It was to be observed that this so-splendid army was all snarled up for lack of transport organization and equipment. It was rigid, inelastic, unresourceful, adapted only for movements on a European terrain with a network of military railways and so on.

The Field Marshal rode overland to Peking in an American quartermaster's wagon courteously offered for this purpose. The glittering officers ran about aimlessly and stole all the native carts, mules, ponies, junks that could be found. It was an amusing display of the boasted efficiency which had so bedazzled civilization.

The Astor House Hotel in Tientsin had become an impossible place, so Egan and I discovered. The manager was a German, Herr Ritter, and his backbone must have ached with so much bowing and scraping to the haughty officers of the legions of the All-Highest. It was the servile, worshipful attitude of the German civilian, as natural to the plump Herr Ritter as breathing.

The staff of the Field Marshal monopolized the hotel. He had not yet borrowed a wagon for the ride to Peking. A few officers of other nations were tolerated as guests, but civilian insects, such as correspondents, were received with coldness. If there happened to be rooms to spare, they were permitted. It was at this time that Martin Egan and Ralph Paine, who were previously without prejudice because of a training fairly cosmopolitan, conceived a dislike for the Prussian military caste and all its works.

There was concrete provocation, a specific incident. In the hotel dining-room was a long table at which sat such outcasts as wore civilian garb. This would include consular officials, secretaries, correspondents, and occasionally British officers in mufti. At the other tables were German officers who, of course, flocked by themselves. Fierce and stiff and martial they were, to see them thus assembled, tremendously impressive, barring such a detail as their table manners.

Egan and I walked in for luncheon one day, feeling not quite so amiable as normally. Some fiend in human guise had stolen the trunk which Egan had left in the hotel for safe-keeping when he had advanced to Peking, and he was left with the raiment he stood in. I was still limping and there was the prospect of another sojourn in a hospital.

We took our accustomed seats at the civilian's table, so called, before other guests arrived, and were engaged with the soup when two young German officers entered the dining-room, a captain and a lieutenant. Ceremoniously they clicked their heels and bowed to the room.

At their own small table there chanced to be no vacant chairs. Their fellow officers had invited two friends for luncheon. Therefore they stalked over to our table and found seats directly facing us. Something annoyed them. This was quite evident. Their faces crimsoned and they twisted the ends of the neat little mustaches. They glared, muttered to each other with a shrug and a toss of the chin. Martin Egan looked up from his soup and whispered:

"Watch out, my boy! You'll see some fun presently. Our presence, so close to them, insults the Hoch-der-Kaisers. Do you get it?"

The taller of the two officers, the captain, clattered to his feet and leaned forward to address us in precise English:

"*You will find seats at another table!*"

It was his expectation that meek obedience would promptly follow this edict. This would have been the result in Berlin, but such things were not done with us. Martin Egan forsook his soup and Ralph Paine did likewise, but it was not their intention to seek another table. They stood up, suddenly, and their weight averaged two hundred pounds and their height better than six feet, nor was either one a fat man. The German lieutenant bobbed up beside the captain. Each of them laid a hand upon the hilt of his sword. It was an interesting tableau.

This was the customary procedure, according to what we had heard and read of the Kaiser's officers in the good old German Fatherland. If a civilian talked back or refused to be jostled off the sidewalk, honor required that an officer should run him through with a sword. Cripples were especially good hunting.

I felt uneasy myself, with a wary eye on those sabers just across the table and these indignant Prussians fingering the hilts. There would be no fair chance in an honest rough-and-tumble rumpus. While you swung for the jaw of one of these human arsenals, what would he be doing with his sword?

This also occurred to Martin Egan who grasped his chair by the back and was ready to use it right handily. I had hastily mobilized the crockery within reach. It was heavy ware and I fancied the sugar bowl and milk pitcher. This ammunition conveniently arranged, I laid hold of my own chair. Elsewhere I had seen a wooden chair, well served, mow a considerable swath. In Key West, for instance, it had caused the sudden subsidence of "John J. McCarthy, E-S-Q with a period."

All this had occurred quicker than it takes to tell it. Egan had promptly and vehemently spoken his reply to the command that we find seats at another table. It is superfluous to tell you where he told the German officers they could go. The destination was hotter than Tientsin in July. They were amazed! The incredible insolence of it!

And while they were recovering from the shock I echoed my comrade's crisp remarks. It was a pleasure to unburden one's mind, with no ladies present. Our frankness dumbfounded those two officers, I give you my word it did. They were almost as bedazed as if the sugar bowl and milk pitcher had been bounced off their frowning visages. Civilians, and of no official position whatever, mere scribblers, telling a captain and a lieutenant of the Field Marshal's staff to go to — er — to go to blazes, and worse than that, oh, much worse!

This verbal assault granted us a moment's respite during which the ranking German officer in the dining-room, a staff colonel, came rushing over to the table. Uncertain whether he meant to join the battle or to intervene, the two correspondents swung their chairs on the defensive. And now Herr Ritter appeared, a hotel manager in great distress. Leaning his stomach against the end of the table where he could paw the air between the combatants, he implored them to refrain from violence. His chief concern was for the crockery and the chairs, I suspect.

There ensued a conference, the German staff colonel and the two grossly offended young officers with their heads together while Herr Ritter argued with the correspondents.

Several other resplendent heroes of His Imperial Majesty's China Expeditionary Force clanked from their tables to join the group. It was a most serious affair. The honor of the uniform had been besmirched. Never had he heard of such behavior in civilians, boomed the purple-jowled staff colonel.

Herr Ritter was babbling something about an apology from the two Americans. It was the least that could be expected of them. In consideration of the fact that the German and American military forces were brothers-in-arms, leniency would be exercised. A full apology was awaited. It would be enough.

Martin Egan looked apoplectic. The Irish in him was very near the exploding point. Turning to Herr Ritter, he exclaimed:

"As guests of yours, we have a right to expect protection from insults. What the devil do you mean by insisting that we apologize? Why don't you ask these two German asses to apologize to us? Now shut up and go sit down somewhere."

"But you will *have* to make the apology," faltered the hotel manager.

"You will listen for it a long while," thundered Egan, who was now at the top of his form. "And you can tell this whole Prussian outfit that if the Kaiser himself should waltz in and tell us to go find another table, we'd be all set and ready to soak *him*."

"Me, too, Martin," echoed Ralph Paine, who had once more edged toward the heavy sugar bowl.

Presently the altercation talked itself out, simmering down in a most astonishing manner. Perhaps the staff colonel comprehended that this small ruction might have the aspect of an international affair and that Tientsin was not German soil. At any rate, it was reluctantly agreed to by Herr Ritter that the correspondents should remain at their own table, nor was anything more heard of the foolish demand for an apology.

The two correspondents demobilized the crockery and finished the luncheon unmolested, while the two young German officers, whose sensitive feelings had been so mortally offended, sat across the table and glowered and grumbled.

From the German military point of view it was a dilemma, an awkward *impasse* unprovided for in the code. The stain could not be wiped out by challenging the Americans to fight duels, because they were mere civilians, declassed, beyond the pale. This was the ludicrous angle of it.

"We called their bluff," said Martin Egan. "But I felt squeamish, did n't you?"

"Marked loss of appetite," I confessed. "From the soup on, nothing had any taste to it — a most uncomfortable meal. I must tell General Chaffee about it when I go back to Peking. He loves this German Expeditionary Force."

It may have been a little absurd, but when Egan and I went about in Tientsin, after this episode, we were careful to carry revolvers. There was the chance of encountering one or more of our German friends in a dark or lonely street and having a quarrel forced on us. We had roamed about Peking at all hours without weapons, but it seemed advisable to be armed because of the Kaiser's officers and gentlemen. Nothing happened, however, beyond black looks and disdainful hauteur when we took our accustomed seats in the dining-room of the Astor House Hotel.

In itself this brawl amounted to nothing. Any other Americans in the same circumstances would have behaved precisely as we did. But the collision with Prussian military arrogance was more significant than we were aware. It was typical of the behavior of the German army in North China from start to finish, and the spirit of it foreshadowed the cataclysm in Europe fourteen years later when the hobnailed boots went trampling across Belgium and France.

XXXIII

A DINNER GUEST WHO MISBEHAVED

MARTIN EGAN sailed for Manila in an army transport, still peevish over his lost wardrobe and the purloined trunk. He knew who the culprit was, an American beach-comber who posed as a journalist, and they were likely to meet again in some port of the Far East. In that event the guilty party would bitterly regret stealing the clothes of Martin Egan. This was a sure prediction. I felt forlorn when this good chum left me in Tientsin. It was in his mind that the odds were against me, with another stay in hospital necessary. Although he would n't say so, his face betrayed the doubt of ever seeing me again.

"You ought to chuck it and go home," said he. "This is no game for a man with a leg that refuses to mend. Go as far as Japan, anyhow, where you can get first-class care, and stay there awhile."

"Oh, I 'll be fit after another operation, Martin. If you were in my place, you 'd stick it out until spring. You know you would. In our business a man hates like the deuce to quit the job."

It was not a wise decision, but the fear of being a quitter haunts any normal young man. And I had been fortunate in having comrades who never knew when to quit. Such examples could not be ignored. And so I hunted up an American army surgeon in Tientsin and, oh, but he was a rough man with the knife, brutal and thorough. It was his opinion that the patient would get well. If not, come back and he would be glad to saw the leg off. The hospital was small and unexpectedly comfortable, with a fine young contract doctor in charge, and the ten days spent there were like finding a snug haven after stormy weather.

Anxious to return to Peking, I found a junk and a crew of coolies who, after much argument, consented to undertake the trip. Winter was setting in and they were afraid of the river freezing and trapping them *en route*. A servant of some kind was essential, and, by luck, I discovered a treasure of a portly, middle-aged Chinese who had been cook and number-one boy in a European household of Tientsin. He was called John, for short. He waddled off with a list of supplies and equipment and "squeezed" no more than ten per cent of the bills as his legitimate graft.

What he called the kitchen in the junk was a box just big enough for him to squat over his earthen fire-pot in which he burned balls of coal dust mixed with clay. And while the shivering, ragged coolies pulled the junk upstream, John served the lone passenger with dinners of five and six courses, setting a little table upon the sleeping-platform in the cabin where the blankets were spread at night. A cheerful figure was John, a smile on his broad face, giggling over small jokes of his own devising, his unfailing doctrine, "*Can-do, Master*," busily moving about in his baggy white breeches and wadded blue coat, and in his leisure moments singing little Chinese love-songs in a high falsetto key.

It was a cold, uncomfortable voyage made endurable by the companionship of John. The passenger was too lame to walk along the bank and so keep warm, and an earthen fire-pot in the flimsy cabin was merely an illusion of heat. The river was freezing along the edges at night, but the channel held open. It was rather humiliating to contemplate that, by now, the only danger of molestation was not from the Chinese, but from the riff-raff of Christian nations, army deserters and stragglers, camp followers of all races who had flocked from Shanghai, Hongkong, even from San Francisco, to take their dirty toll from the soldiers with rum and painted women, with cards and dice.

My junk had tied up to the bank at sunset, and a few

hundred yards ahead of it was another river-boat, also moored in the mud, which flew an American flag. John was getting dinner ready in his magical and ceremonious fashion which made one feel that he really ought to dress for the event. Along the towpath came tramping a solitary American doughboy in blue, heading toward Tientsin. The lone correspondent hailed this fellow countryman and invited him aboard for dinner. A guest was more than welcome.

The soldier was glad to accept. He had no kit on his back, and it was disclosed that he belonged to no escort outfit with the river traffic. He was not a prepossessing guest, a long, loose-jointed fellow with a truculent manner, a shifty eye, and a bad mouth. He had the marks of a tough *hombre*. The recruiting net of the Regular Army sweeps them in now and then, particularly when they are wanted elsewhere. However, any American was good company for the ailing correspondent who was down on his luck and condemned, for this voyage, to no other conversation than John's very scanty pidgin English.

The dinner passed pleasantly enough. The soldier wolfed it down as though he had not eaten a square meal in days. He was an entertaining rascal, but when it came to his army career in China he was taciturn. It was plausible to guess that he had been presented with a bob-tailed, or dishonorable, discharge.

After dinner he proposed a little whirl at two-handed poker. For the correspondent it was anything to pass the time. We sat cross-legged upon the sleeping-platform with the low table between us, while John kept the candles lighted or squatted watchfully upon his haunches, like a big Chinese idol in the shadows. He did not like this stray soldier, but with the gambling fervor of his race he was fascinated by the poker game, the pit-pat of the cards on the table, the clink of the Mexican dollars.

I had no desire to win the soldier's money. It was pastime,

nothing more, but perhaps John was a mascot. The cards ran in a manner uncanny. Whenever a jack-pot justified real action, the soldier had to shove more of his silver across the table. He was growing surly and would not listen to stopping the game. It was an awkward situation. And still the luck drifted all one way until, with an oath, the soldier fished in his tunic and withdrew a rumpled pay-check for sixty-odd dollars.

By this time Chinese John must have been invoking the spirits of his ancestors and they were rooting for his American "master." Playing against the pay-check, with matches for chips, the correspondent continued to ruin the soldier's finances. The cards were indubitably bewitched.

A crisis was inevitable. The soldier would not hear of quitting. He was talking from a corner of his mouth and his voice had a snarling note. The other player was anxious to push the silver and the pay-check across the table, as a gift, and bid this visitor good-night. The trouble began when the sullen soldier broke out: "Playin' with your own deck, hey, bo? I fell for it, all right. Pretty soft, this graft of junkin' up and down the river all by your lonesome and layin' for marks with easy money in their jeans."

He reached over to grab the pay-check, but the quick movement tilted the table. The slip of paper and the heap of silver coin slid to the floor. The candles slid off at the same time. One of them was extinguished, but John snatched up the other and shielded the flame with his coat. It was difficult to see in the gloomy little cabin.

Ralph Paine hastily concluded that he had added another idiotic episode to a list already lengthy. To be accused by this tramp of a soldier of cheating at cards was provoking, but it was reasonable to assume that he might have a gun or something concealed about his person. He was distinctly that kind of a dinner guest. On the correspondent's part, therefore, there was a prudent moment of hesitation.

It was John, roly-poly, middle-aged, good-humored, who rose to the occasion. He did not understand the language, but he grasped the implication. With a high-voiced, sputtering curse in Tientsin Chinese, he hurled the heavy brass candlestick at the base vagabond who had insulted his master's hospitality. This left the cabin in darkness, but the candlestick had found its target, for the soldier yelped with pain and amazement.

There followed a brief scrimmage during which the soldier somehow went out of the door. He had acquired a momentum which was further assisted on deck in the starlight. There was much muscle in John's well-cushioned body. The soldier leaped for the bank, but missed his footing and tumbled into the mud and water. John laughed loudly. Then he toddled into the cabin and returned with a rifle, but his master forbade using it.

Either the soldier was unarmed, after all, or he had lost his pistol during the exit from the junk. He was hailed and told to wait for his pay-check. But he stood in the obscurity of the river-bank and hurled obscene threats. There was an American junk a little way up the river, he shouted, and maybe some guys from his regiment were aboard, and he'd go rouse 'em out and come back to clean up the tin-horn sport that had trimmed him and then booted him into the mud.

It was most unpleasant. The correspondent resolved to play no more poker. His intentions had been thoroughly harmless, but now look at him! The dinner party was menaced by still another sequel. It was conveyed to John, by means of words and signs, that a boarding party might be expected. A grin bisected his round features as he chirruped:

"*Can-do, Master! Maskee!* Plenty soldiers come, *chop-chop* — me kill 'um."

We waited. There was nothing else to do. But no sounds of commotion came from the junk moored a few hundred yards up the river. The better part of an hour passed, and John still squatted on deck, a rifle in his lap. Then the figure of one man became dimly visible on the bank. It was the soldier's voice that called out:

"Say, bo, no rough stuff, savvy? I done quit bein' hostile. What about a truce?"

"Sure thing," was the answer. "What happened to you? Come aboard and get your cash and the pay-check, if you like, but no monkey business."

"It's on the level, pardner," insisted the rough-neck soldier, and his accents were curiously mild. "The trouble is all off. I guess I got off on the wrong foot when I called you a crook."

Here was a mystery. John was persuaded to lay aside the rifle, and the soldier jumped to the deck. There was no false pretense. He was quite a different man. With a kind of sheepish chagrin he explained:

"That ain't no army junk yonder. I went bustin' into it with a whoop, figgerin' I could drag out a bunch of fightin' buddies, same as I said. Say, I played the wrong card. Guess what I crashed into — a *Y.M.C.A. boat bound for little old Peking!* There was several men an' three women — *ladies*, by God! I stood battin' my eyes and sayin' excuse me. And there they set, readin' books and sewin' fancy-work around a table with a red cover on it, same as we used to have at home. And they asked me, so cussed sweet and polite, to set down an' what could they do for me? I says will they please let me just be quiet and look at 'em. *Young ladies*, bo, and they had come out from my country. Why, one of 'em rode through my town in a train not two months ago!"

The soldier had found a perch upon the long timber tiller and was swinging his legs as he continued the wonderful tale.

"They sure did talk pretty to me. American soldiers is their one best bet. Call me a liar, but they fished out a stone crock an' handed me *three doughnuts!* They aim to cook 'em by the bushel in Peking. Here's a doughnut I saved to show you. Naw, they did n't spiel religion to me — but one young lady, the blonde-headed one, she sees I was wet an' muddy, and she makes me dry off some by the kerosene stove and asks me where my outfit is, and I can crawl in the junk if I ain't got no place else to go. Now what do you think o' that, bo? Could you beat it?"

He moved to the cabin door and gravely exhibited the doughnut by the light of a candle.

"I think you had better stay aboard this junk until morning," affirmed the correspondent. "John can rustle you a pair of blankets. And here is your pay-check, while I think of it. And you had better take back your Mexican dollars."

"But I lost 'em fair and square," protested the vagabond doughboy, and this was an apology handsome enough.

"The game was more for fun than for money," he was told. "You will have to take it, or start another ruction."

"Once was enough," smiled the soldier. "I might bust the doughnut."

After breakfast he resumed his long march to Tientsin and the coast, an army outcast bound he knew not whither. But we shook hands at parting. He was not such a disgraceful guest, after all. I had never written any fiction at this time, and had no idea of attempting it, but here was the raw stuff for a short story, complete from introduction to climax. And was n't it really better fun living a short story like this than writing it? I think so.

Six days it took to drag that junk to Tung-Chow, and John and I were heartily sick of the Pei-ho in November. On the fourth day the river froze in broad, brittle sheets of ice which so dismayed the crew of coolies that they talked of turning back to hasten down with the current to Tientsin. In fact, they decided so to do, and it was only after strenuous coaxing that they laid hold of the towrope and push-poles and forced the junk out into the channel which still ran clear of ice.

Some of the coaxing had to be done by means of the butt of a Colt revolver, and John valiantly yelled "Can-do, Master," and waddled out of the cabin with his trusty rifle, the sight of which exerted much moral suasion. It did seem unfortunate, this whole trip down to Tientsin to recuperate one's health and find rest and comfort. A man with a game leg had bumped into one disturbance after another, unreasonable German officers in the hotel dining-room, hectic poker on the Pei-ho, and the dozen wild river coolies who wanted to go in the wrong direction.

At Tung-Chow was found an American quartermaster's wagon-train almost ready to hit the trail for Peking. John and I bunked overnight with the wagon-master, and the four-mule outfits pulled out at daybreak. It was a slow, hard journey, but greatly enlivened by the companionship of these mule-skinners and packers who had come straight from the vanishing American frontier, from the desert and the mountains where the isolated army posts, built to protect the settlers against hostile Indians, were still scattered far and wide.

Every other army in China gave these wagon-trains a wide berth. The big mules, the massive, canvas-covered vehicles, went ploughing through a press of traffic like an armored cruiser in a fleet of fishing smacks. And these lanky, dusty men with the wide Stetson hats and the lazy drawl were bad medicine. For some reason their particular aversion was the French force of colonial infantry from Saigon, sloppy little chaps in uniforms a mile too big for them.

"Funny, but whenever these boys of mine get a night off," said my friend, the wagon-master, "they lick a few Frenchies. It appears to amuse 'em a whole lot. Seems like us two republics ought to be fraternizin', according to Lafayette and all that stuff. But I find myself gettin' the same hankering as the rest of the boys. I dunno as when I enjoyed myself more than mussin' a half a dozen of these yere parley-voos about a week ago. One of 'em hit my off lead mule on the nose with a gun when he stepped on a squad that would n't get out of the road. So I had to learn 'em something."

When the wagon-train creaked into the quartermaster's corral in the grounds of the Temple of Agriculture, Ralph Paine was a weary pilgrim. He had made certain plans concerning living quarters, but these seem to have been delayed. All he can find in his diary to cover the three days of November 27–30 is the entry:

"Hospital tent in Peking."

Curious, but there is no recollection of that hospital tent, where it was situated or who took care of him. His mind is a blank. He must have crawled down from that tall freight wagon and sought immediate refuge, with the recurrent fever muddling his wits. Faithful John was in attendance, of this there can be no doubt.

Memory clears after that, and it was a transfer from the tent to U.S. Peking Hospital No. 2, a smaller building than the vast, chilly temple with the gilded dragons writhing on the rafters, and made snug and warm for the winter. There was good nursing, competent young women sent out from the United States, and a fortnight was more than endurable. It was even pleasant, a blessed interlude. The correspondent went out of this hospital able to mount a pony and make the rounds after news, to the American Legation, the various army headquarters, the telegraph office, riding through the dusty, swarming streets in bleak, bright weather.

XXXIV

AN ARMY THAT CHEERED FOR YALE

THIS is for the purpose of correcting an error. In matters of biography one cannot be too particular. The "Bookman" magazine of March, 1904, contained an article describing the work of various war correspondents. Beneath a snap-shot photograph of a tall, heavily built young man in khaki clothes, standing in a Peking doorway, were the words:

RALPH D. PAINE IN CHINA

It is said that at the time of the invasion of China by the Allies, after the Boxer uprising, Mr. Paine taught the Yale "Boola" football song to the Japanese soldiers and that they sang it as a battle hymn.

It is a pity that the correspondent never thought of this. It might have been one of his bright ideas. The little fighting men of Nippon would have made a stirring war chant of "Boola." However, the tale was not entirely fictitious. There was a very small grain of fact which must have sprouted as the wind of rumor blew it along.

Late in the winter, after leading the existence of a transient guest in various army hospitals, Ralph Paine had resumed housekeeping, down in the Chinese City, remote from the legation district, among the native people who had flocked back to crowd the streets and alleys and follow their incredibly industrious and noisy manner of life. The Chinese children were delightful. For warmth they were bundled in layers of little wadded blue coats, and the colder the weather the more numerous the coats because of the lack of heat in the dwellings. These swarms of small boys and girls were like balls of blue cotton and fur from which came piping shouts and giggles and laughter.

They were quick to imitate the ways of the wonderful foreign soldiers, and their games in the streets took a military turn. The band of infant marauders which made its headquarters outside my gateway organized an army of its own amid a tumult like a flight of sparrows. When I first encountered this force at drill, it was like stumbling into a miniature Boxer outbreak. In age the officers and privates must have averaged six or seven years, all boys, for they had scorned to recruit their little sisters. A row of shaven heads and sprouting pigtails the size of a lead-pencil bobbed excitedly along one side of the alley, and the blue cotton puffballs were enough alike to make it look as though the army was uniformed for the occasion.

Every pair of chubby brown fists grasped a bit of stick, as a gun, and when I rode past, the soldiers presented arms as solemnly as a dress parade. I wheeled my pony and saluted with the utmost gravity. The soldiers lost their dignity and broke ranks with shrill shouts of "*Bean Lao Yet!*" "*Bean Lao Yet!*" This was to address me by name, *Bean* being as near as they could come to pronouncing *Paine*, while the *Lao Yet* signified plain "Mister" without honorary titles.

The next time the army turned out to be reviewed, I was given warning. Reining my pony into the alley in which these troops maneuvered, I saw small scouts scampering on ahead and yelling "*Bean Lao Yet!*" The company toddled and tumbled out of doorways and courtyards and was formally in line, guns at the present, when I passed and acknowledged the honor with a most punctilious salute. Happening to have a pocket full of copper cash, these trifling coins were tossed to the army, which became instantly a scrambled mob. This deed of prodigality won prompt promotion. The customary greeting was changed into an ear-piercing clamor of: "*Bean-Da-Rin!*" "*Bean-Da-Rin!*" "*Bean-Da-Rin!*"

At an outlay of four cents in American money, I was now The Most Honorable and Exalted One. It was buying titles at a bargain price. This promotion had placed me on a level of rank with a *Man-Da-Rin*.

Weeks after the contest had been played at New Haven, there filtered up the China coast to the frozen north country the news that the great Yale eleven of 1900 had trounced fair Harvard to the tune of 28–0. It was a glorious victory for the blue. And it caused a homesick correspondent to rejoice. A celebration was in order, but there was no satisfaction in celebrating alone.

In the foreign armies of occupation had previously been found two Yale men, one a lieutenant of the Ninth Infantry, U.S.A., the other a Japanese officer on the staff of General Yamaguichi. Their camps were five miles apart, but I ordered a pony saddled and set forth to find the comrades who had once lived beneath the campus elms. Alas, after riding a dozen miles, it was impossible to find either man.

Sorrowfully turning into the alley nearest my gateway, it was observed that the ever-vigilant army of Chinese was rushing out to parade, piping *"Bean-Da-Rin,"* as they scampered. Here was my celebration, ready and eager. The troops were beckoned into the courtyard. They obeyed with trepidation, but bravely tried to dissemble it. It was a novel procedure in their military career. They did not comprehend what the friendly big foreign devil proposed doing with them. Several anxious mothers and fathers followed timidly, but were comforted with a tray of canned peaches, tea, and cakes. From the sweetmeat-seller's at the corner, one of the servants fetched enough sugar balls to give the army one vast, ecstatic stomach-ache.

And then this foolish, homesick correspondent in exile forgot his loneliness while he wasted the best part of that afternoon in teaching all these jolly puff-balls the Yale cheer. They had not the remotest notion of what all the fuss was about, but they dutifully yelled until their wadded little bodies fairly bounced from the pavement and their shoe-button black eyes snapped with delicious excitement.

A long session of assiduous coaching produced encouraging results. When the signal was given, twoscore piping voices screamed with frantic enthusiasm and in splendid unison:

" Lah-lah-lah! Lah-lah-lah! Lah-lah-lah! Ylale! Ylale! Ylale! Bean-Da-Rin! Bean-Da-Rin! Bean-Da-Rin!"

XXXV

DESTINY AND THE SPIDER FARMER

THIS chapter includes a confession of guilt. Already having boasted of committing piracy upon the high seas, lesser crimes can be paraded without a blush. In my youthful years as a reporter, the Sunday editor once asked me to go forth and find what he called a lively news feature for the magazine section. It was a roving commission. After several hopeful trails had ended in disappointment, a chance clue led me to an old stone farmhouse with a mossy roof among the green hills near the Pennsylvania town of Wayne. Here lived alone a white-bearded Irishman, robust and active in spite of his threescore years. In top boots and blue jumper he was vigorously splitting fence rails when I sauntered into the yard.

This was John Quigley. His claim to distinction was that he had been hit three times by locomotives; and the total number of yards they had bounced him off the right of way would have carried him well across an acre lot if covered in one flight. In my opinion he deserved a Sunday newspaper story, with spirited illustrations by an artist with a reckless pencil.

Some men have survived one encounter with a locomotive. A few, of exceptionally hardy constitutions, have lived to tell of a second bout with a cow-catcher, but old John Quigley was unique in that he had made a habit of it, a sort of favorite outdoor pastime. Having raised a family of fifteen children, he was now enjoying the well-earned repose of old age by working all day long on his farm.

"Yes, sorr," said John Quigley, "they seemed to have a grudge ag'in' me when I was section boss on the railroad.

They tried to kill me about often enough, so they did, and if iver I git hit ag'in I think I 'll be layin' for the engineer an' learnin' him a lesson. I was a young man the first time. It was in the old Glassly Cut near Devon where I was repairin' a bit of track. Around the curve come the Columbia express, goin' like blue blazes, without no warnin' at all. I did n't have time to wink me eye before she hit me. The cow-catcher caught me square, an' I wint up high as the smoke-stack. I was wearin' an old army overcoat, one of thim blue wans, and with the cape flyin' about me head I sailed away, grabbin' for a holt in the air.

"Down I lit in a field by the track, smashin' three rails of a fence to bits. When I come to, they was luggin' me home. The doctor found me jaw broke in two places an' all me teeth jolted loose, wid a shakin' up inside an' all over that was sure to be fatal in twenty-four hours. So sure was the doctor man that I would turn up me toes that he niver come back next day.

"So I took off the bandages meself an' got around ag'in without none of the doctor's help nor hindrance. This time I was kept away from me job eight weeks, an' it was in the winter-time, I remimber, because the cow-catcher was covered wid sheet-iron. 'T was this that saved me legs from bein' broke.

"It was ten years after that when I got hit ag'in, sorr. I was standin' at the Devon station talkin' to a friend. I stepped on the track and was sayin' good-bye when a local passenger train that had no business there at all come rollin' down. The engine struck me hard an' throwed me across the station platform. This time I landed ag'in' something that would n't break, so I broke. Four of me ribs was smashed, not to mintion a crack on the head that knocked me stupid for a while. The doctor tied me all up wid bandages an' I wint back to bossin' me section gang the next week or mebbe 't was the week after that.

"It was about five years after this whack that I got hit ag'in. It was below the Strafford station, close by where the old Spread Eagle Tavern used to be. Since the time whin that first engine hit me, I would have terrible cramps in me legs now an' thin. I was tampin' ties wid me gang whin these cramps caught me cruel, an' I sat down on the rail to take off me boot and rub me swelled muscles. It hurted so bad that I paid no attintion to an express that come hellin' along without whistle nor bell.

"I was stoopin' over whin the engine butted me from behind and I left the track sudden. Away I wint through the air, me boot in me hand, wid me whiskers stickin' out straight in front from the shock. This trip I did n't sail very high, but kept on a level, as ye might say, movin' like a bullet. The fence I wint through was old an' rotten, bless the saints for that!

"I did n't faint away nor nothin', but I was mighty well dazed, sorr, an' whin I picked meself up an' start walkin' for home, I dropped frequint an' had to stick me head in th' puddles of water to brace me up a little. This time I was laid off a month, for I was shook up bad, an' the doctor found me breast-bone cracked where I had cracked it before as a lad.

"Did n't I tell ye about that? I was workin' a dump car outside a mine in Allegheny County. A gang of us was diggin' out a cut, an' I was fillin' me car. A whoppin' big rock caved in from the bank. It knocked me car flyin' across the cut, an' me all mixed up wid it. I was pinned ag'in' the wall of the cut by the big rock and the dump car. There was another time whin a load of lumber spilled on top of me . . ."

So much by way of an excerpt from the true tale of the ironclad John Quigley as he told it and as Ralph Paine wrote it for the Sunday editor. Straightway came the demand for more news stories, of real life, to help fill that insatiable magazine section. Gazing idly from a car window during the return trip from John Quigley's farm, an idea had popped from a clear sky. It was pure invention, but harmless enough to present as the actual fact. And surely the average sense of humor could be trusted to perceive the innocent foolery of it.

John Quigley existed, but I proceeded to create the interesting Frenchman, Pierre Grantaire, who had the only spider farm in the world. The situation of his farm, as I described it, was a trifle vague — on the old Lancaster Pike. There this Pierre Grantaire bred his spiders in profusion, selling them at so much per hundred to the wine merchants and the *nouveaux riches* who were thereby enabled to stock their cellars with tiers of bottled vintages and, a few weeks later, behold them veiled in filmy cobwebs. Blowing dust into the bins was an easy matter, of course, but cobwebs — ah, that was different — cobwebs spun from cork to cork, draping the slender necks of the bottles like delicate lace, sealing them with the testimony of years of priceless and mellow maturity.

It was not difficult to describe in detail this unique spider farm, how the curious live-stock was nurtured and marketed — walls covered with wire frames for the webs — cracks and knot-holes for the parent spiders to live in — the nursery for the infants — the lively emotions of the reporter when he was escorted in among thousands of the industrious arachnids. And the courteous Frenchman, Monsieur Grantaire, with the soul of an artist, explaining his singular enterprise!

"You desire to know first the facts of the business? Before you make the acquaintance of my pets? This is like the Americans — money first, then the sentiment! In this room are four thousand spiders — spinning the webs, producing families, minding their own affairs. Is that not a lesson? When the infants are big enough, I put them in another room, for they are great cannibals, my pets, and they devour their little ones, and the children eat each other. They are of the species of the Nephila Plumipes which the entomologist will inform you spins the finest webs.

"But what money is there in it, you insist to know! *Mon dieu,* money, always money! Well, monsieur, a customer comes to me. He is a wine merchant who has stocked his cellar with recent vintages, champagnes, clarets, port, Burgundy. In shipping, the bottles have been brushed clean. They look new, vulgar, of a cheapness. They will not sell at high prices for old wines. He tells me how many hundred bottles. I make the estimates — how many of my pets will soon cover his bins with the finest cobwebs. He pays me two francs, something like that, for every spider. I send them to him in little paper boxes, so many dozen in each crate. Wonderful! In two months you will suppose his cellar has not been disturbed in fifty years.

"The wine merchant leads the rich parvenu into the dark cellar. By the light of the candle he sees the rows of dusty bottles adorned with the cobwebs of Pierre Grantaire, *mon ami!* It is easy to pull the leg, to charge the tremendous prices for the rare old wines.

"Then you will find my other customers — the so-quick millionaires of Chicago, of Denver, of Pittsburgh. They wish the grand establishment, the dignity. The wines must have the tone, the air, the age, the vast expense. I send my pets. They do the work. The millionaire takes his rich friends into the cellar. 'Ah,' they say, 'this is superb. It is magnificent. We give you congratulations, my boy.'

"Then my spiders, they stop spinning in that cellar and they wink the other eye."

. . . Pierre Grantaire led the way to a glass dome in a corner of the room, in which was an immense web of very beautiful pattern. The Frenchman touched one of the filaments and a huge, black spider danced nimbly out of its downy nest and ran up the vibrating thread to the old man's finger. He gave it a fly to eat and the startling pet tripped back indoors with the booty.

"That is Sara," said Monsieur Grantaire. "She has the grace, the *chic,* the slender beauty of the divine Bernhardt. She is the pride of my establishment. And, behold, Zola is gazing at you."

A hideous, hairy monster had crawled up the fine wire netting which kept it within bounds, and was staring sardonically a few inches from the reporter's nose. A frightened exclamation was unavoidable, but Pierre seemed grieved.

"I do not blame you so much," said he, "but this Zola is of a kind nature and will not hurt you, although he has the horrible appearance. His temper is uncertain sometimes, but only when he is approached with unkindness. Permit him, and he would eat or kill all my little pets in one day. He is the bird-hunting spider of Surinam, king of them all, *le grand monarque.* Therefore I name him Zola, a compliment to the grandest of writers."

It was in this manner that fancy wove the description of the spider farm, with a certain persuasive color and verisimilitude which modesty forbids me to emphasize. When printed, it made something like two columns and the author's conscience was serene. Like any other self-respecting reporter, he would not have dreamed of faking or inventing a story of real news value or significance. He had no expectation that the spider farm would be taken seriously.

Soon, however, the scissors of the exchange editor were snipping this yarn from newspapers far and wide. It carried matter-of-fact captions to inform the reader of a new and peculiar industry. Then letters began to come in, written by earnest souls who had wearied of seeking fortunes in raising squabs or rabbits or broilers. They were anxious to visit the spider farm of Pierre Grantaire on the Lancaster Pike, or to correspond with him, if the editor would be kind enough to direct them.

After making the newspaper rounds the story began to appear, condensed as a paragraph, in the popular and religious journals, under the heading of "Scientific Notes," or "Nuggets of Fact." And then the innocent instigator, Ralph Paine, went off to report a war, and so forgot the web of deception which he had never intended to weave. He had learned another lesson in the school of experience, always to label his facts and his fancies unmistakably as such.

Five years later he was on the staff of the "New York Herald." During a dull afternoon in the city room, a voice from the desk suggested: "Hey, Paine! There's a man outside with some kind of a story to sell. Go see what he's got."

In the reception room stood a young man who had seen better days. His manners were pleasing, his speech that of a gentleman, but his clothes were perceptibly shabby, his shoes broken. One's sympathy was stirred by the first impressions. Presumably this was a newspaper man in hard luck who had failed to find, or hold, a job in the whirlpool of New York daily journalism. With more than perfunctory courtesy I asked him to sit down. From a pocket he extracted a typewritten manuscript and nervously fumbled it while he explained:

"I dug up a good story the other day. It's real news stuff. I went out to his place on the Lancaster Pike, near Philadelphia, and spent an afternoon with the old codger. He runs the only spider farm in the world."

This was an announcement calculated to create a feeling of bewilderment. Scrutinizing the young man, I inquired:

"What is the old codger's name and what does he do with his spider farm?"

"Pierre Grantaire," was the glib reply. "He is a veteran of the French Army and fought against the Prussians in '70. He has thousands of these spiders and —"

"Ah, yes, he fought against the Prussians," I murmured absent-mindedly. "I had forgotten that detail. Pardon me, you were about to say —"

The young man displayed traces of self-consciousness as he resumed:

"He sells these spiders to spin cobwebs to cover wine bottles, fake 'em to look like rare old vintages. Get the idea? He does a big business with Pittsburgh millionaires and so on. It's an exclusive story. If I leave the stuff with you, could you look it over and give me a decision to-night? Regular space rates will be all right. I'm up against it, and —"

"You need n't bother to leave it. The 'Herald' is not interested in buying the story," said I, more in sorrow than in anger.

"But is n't it a corker?" exclaimed the nervous young man.

"It is all of that. It was when I wrote it five years ago.

I happen to be the man who invented old Pierre Grantaire and his confounded spider farm."

The unhappy young man stared dumbly, dropped his manuscript, picked it up, and was about to fade from the "Herald" building when I detained him. His face was so haggard and hunted and pitiful that the only thing to tell him was:

"Better cut out this burglary stuff. You can't get away with it. You must be down and out, to steal an old story from the files. If a couple of dollars will do any good — "

He called it a loan, muttering his thanks with a hang-dog air, and passed down the marble staircase in his sodden, broken shoes. It was an odd coincidence, this reincarnation of the mythical spider farmer who had long since passed from the mind of the original culprit. In fact, I had preferred to forget it, what with all the bother the guileless readers had caused. Now, however, recalled in this curious manner, it set in motion a novel train of thought.

Up to this time, in 1902, it had never occurred to me to write fiction or to seek any other means of livelihood than as a reporter and correspondent in daily journalism. But this tale of the spider farmer was a piece of fiction, and certainly it had been successful. The idea persisted. Why not try to write fiction undisguised and see what could be done with it in the magazine and book markets?

But the relentless pressure of the newspaper game left neither the time nor the energy to attempt anything else. I had enjoyed an unusual variety of experiences and adventures for a young man seven years out of college, but it so happened that after a few months on the "Herald" staff I became conscious of a distaste for newspaper work. One finds his own road of destiny as trifles turn him this way or that. In my own case the resurrection of the spider farmer was like meeting a chance wayfarer who suggested journeying in a new direction.

Another incident conspired to point the same way. This was the tragedy of the gold button.

It was the pleasure of James Gordon Bennett, ruling his great newspaper by cable from Paris, to pose as a dictator, absolute and arbitrary, who might descend at any moment and throw the entire staff out of the window. This legend was artfully fostered. His desk in a sumptuous private office was kept ready for instant use. It was believed that in his New York house dinner was ready to serve every night while the butler stood in majestic and expectant dignity.

For reasons of his own, the self-exiled autocrat of the "New York Herald" seldom revisited his native land, but it gratified his vanity to have his employees regard him as a perpetual threat. On one occasion, after an absence of several years, he strolled into the "Herald" building late at night, immaculate in evening dress, tarried an hour, and sailed for Paris the next day. There was no cataclysm, but robust men shivered at the recollection. It was like discussing a narrow escape. More than ever they felt as though they were working for a mysterious bogey-man.

It was the duty of one of the "Herald" desk-men to mark copies of the various daily editions to be forwarded to James Gordon Bennett in Paris or to his yacht in the Mediterranean. These notations, by means of a code of numbers, indicated the writer of every story or paragraph, as well as the copy-reader who had edited it. By this method the owner was enabled to fix responsibility and to cable praise or censure if it so pleased his royal whim.

Now the thing most dreaded by a "Herald" reporter was to be assigned to a news story which in any manner pertained to yachts or yachting. It was known that James Gordon Bennett would search every sentence for the smallest flaw in technical accuracy. It was one of his obsessions.

At this time Prince Henry of Prussia was touring the United States, and while in New York he was given a reception at the residence of Cornelius Vanderbilt. It was a tremendously exclusive and swagger affair, and the "Herald" sent an excellent reporter to describe it. Let us call him Higginson.

Prince Henry was an enthusiastic yachtsman and sailor, and the courtesies, or the formalities, required that Mr. Vanderbilt, as host, should wear the evening dress of the New York Yacht Club, including a coat with silver buttons or gold buttons, I forget which. The zealous "Herald" reporter, mindful of the long-range but baleful scrutiny of Mr. James Gordon Bennett, assembled his facts and wrote them with the most scrupulous care. He was complimented by the city editor.

A week passed. Then came the cable message from Paris:

Fire Higginson.

No explanation accompanied the fatal mandate. On Friday afternoon poor Higginson found a blue envelope in his office mail-box, while the emotions of the staff were aptly reflected in Tennyson's lines:

> "Was there a man dismayed?
> Not though the soldier knew
>   Some one had blundered:
> Theirs not to make reply,
> Theirs not to reason why,
> Theirs but to do and die."

Higginson put on his hat and walked out to look for another job. A few days later came an enlightening letter from Paris. The wretched reporter had escaped with more mercy than he deserved. On the evening coat of Cornelius Vanderbilt he had placed gold buttons when they should have been silver, or *vice versa*. The point is immaterial now, but it meant much to Higginson at the time.

Gold or silver buttons, whichever they were, the offense was heinous. His keen eye detecting this momentous and unpardonable blunder, the indignant James Gordon Bennett had consulted his code of numbers. The "17" scrawled on the story in blue pencil was found to be a slave named Higginson. Off with his head!

Thereafter when a member of the "Herald" staff discovered a blue envelope in his mail-box, the manner of his exit was figuratively designated among his fellows as "getting the gold button."

The misfortune of Higginson accentuated my own feeling that this was an unhappy and uncongenial shop in which to work. Men who dwell with the fear of losing their jobs not only hamper their efficiency, but, in time, tarnish their self-respect. The best service can never be obtained from a newspaper staff which reports for duty with a sense of uneasiness and departs at night with a sigh of relief.

Absurd, but true, that an elderly spider farmer named Pierre Grantaire, who never existed, and the gleaming buttons on the evening coat of Cornelius Vanderbilt should have influenced a young man to seek a change of occupation. Life often speaks from behind the jester's mask. It seemed best to go while the going was good. If I lingered with the "New York Herald," I might some day be assigned to cover a yachting story. The fate of Higginson had left a deep impression.

Instead of making a connection with another newspaper, I concluded to burn all bridges and attempt an invasion of the magazine field. It was, perhaps, adventurous for a man on the very brink of matrimony, to separate himself from a first-class newspaper income. There were kind friends who called it another attack of *damfoolitis*, but at thirty-one it is still permissible to shake dice with fortune. Prudence is waiting around a turn of the road and she will caution you soon enough. It is worth much to be one's own master. And there is a grain of wisdom in the reflection of a fine old gentleman of my acquaintance:

"I can't say that my career has made much of a dent in the

general scheme of things, but I have been most infernally interesting to myself."

The assets for the experimental encounters with magazine editors and book publishers were a certain facility for writing gained by means of arduous training in journalism and a small degree of talent which would never set literature agog. Included also in the equipment was the knowledge, gained by experience, that there was still romance in the world, and an abiding belief in the nobility of the simple virtues of plain people. Of such had been the friends I had made by land and sea.[1]

The equipment was enough to bring success, as measured by contentment, freedom, money, and the enjoyment of work for its own sake. After a while the road led to a broad New Hampshire farm beside a tidal river as a permanent home, but this did not interfere with roaming the world now and then among interesting people and places. And it was much pleasanter and more profitable than being tethered to a managing editor's office by telegraph wire or cable.

---

[1] The first attempt at a novel was called *The Story of Martin Coe*. It dropped into the ocean of printed fiction without making a perceptible splash, but the author was encouraged to try it again when the following letter was received:

THE WHITE HOUSE
WASHINGTON
Sept. 25, 1906

MY DEAR PAINE:

I am not a competent critic, but for my own satisfaction I must tell you how genuinely I have enjoyed *Martin Coe*. I read it all thru without being able to put it down; and I hold it against you that you did not add a hundred pages to describe Martin's ultimate home-coming, and especially to have him meet the old sundowner, Judah Haines, again. It is the kind of story of manliness and adventure and good-heartedness that appeals to me very strongly, and I congratulate you on having written it.

Sincerely yours

⟨   THEODORE ROOSEVELT

XXXVI

THE OLD TRAIL OUTWARD-BOUND

FOR Ralph Paine the years slipped by like a current flowing swiftly but without turbulence, bringing many blessings and few regrets. Fortune had always been much kinder to him than he deserved. Occasionally he felt a twinge that his impulsive, irresponsible youth had fled and that middle-age was overtaking him, but any poignant emotion of this kind was deferred until the United States entered the Great War in the spring of 1917.

Then he realized that he had long since dropped out of the active ranks of the newspaper correspondents, and there came no summons to pack his kit and sail overseas. As for service with the flag, at the age of forty-six he seemed to fit in nowhere at all. It seemed a wretchedly futile business to sit at home on the farm and half-heartedly grind out indifferent fiction while the world was one vast hell of darkness and destruction and slaughter.

After a few months there came a letter from George Creel's Committee on Public Information. Would Ralph Paine be willing to undertake some special work in the Navy Department? It had been decided to lift one corner of the curtain of secrecy and permit the country to know a little of what its naval forces were doing on active service against the enemy. Many merchant steamers were sailing with naval gun crews on board, and the records of the Bureau of Navigation already contained numerous reports of the heroism of the Armed Guard and the engagements it had fought with hostile submarines.

As a very willing volunteer I worked for several weeks at this task, under the competent direction of Commander Louis

Farley, and the naval story, as put together in a series of articles, was distributed to the Sunday newspapers of the country by the Committee on Public Information. But the operations of the destroyer flotilla based on Queenstown were still enshrouded in mystery. All was romance, conjecture, curiosity, so far as the public was concerned. The American Army was not ready to cross in force to France, and a long training period was still ahead of it. The first thrilling war story of large dimensions was that of the dashing destroyers.

In the opinion of many officers in the Navy Department, it was time to reveal the exploits of the Queenstown Flotilla, within the limits of military discretion. In matters of naval publicity, however, George Creel asserted an authority which was upheld by Secretary Daniels. This was against the wishes of the regular naval organization within the Department which considered itself competent to conduct its own affairs and resented the interference of George Creel. It was a pretty quarrel while it lasted.

While in Washington and caught up in the swirl of events, I resolved to join those alluring destroyers that cruised the Irish Sea and the rough Atlantic. It was the great opportunity to follow once more the old trail outward-bound, to harken to the call of high adventure as I had done in my youth. A telegram was sent to Mr. George Horace Lorimer, of the "Saturday Evening Post," and he replied that he would be glad to take a series of articles if official permission could be obtained to get afloat with the destroyer force.

The Navy Department was cordially anxious to have this mission undertaken. In the final issue, however, it was necessary to have the consent and sanction of George Creel, Chairman of the Committee on Public Information. It was difficult to arrange the requisite interview. Mr. Creel was, by all odds, the busiest man in Washington. This was the impression he conveyed.

When we met he talked most solemnly about what he

called "the Queenstown permit." The inference was that only one could be granted. The problem was whether to confer it upon Ralph Paine or some other person. The decision was favorable. This phrase, "the Queenstown permit," had a large, important sound. It was like firing a gun.

"What does this permit look like, and when do I get it, Mr. Creel?" was my earnest question.

"I will advise Secretary Daniels to give you a letter to Admiral Sims. That is all you will need."

"And this letter, with your O.K., will enable me to visit the Queenstown base and go to sea in our destroyers?"

"Why, of course," almost testily answered George Creel. "I have also talked with Mr. Lorimer over the 'phone about your series of articles for the 'Saturday Evening Post.' As a correspondent, you are agreeable to him and to me. You will make your own financial arrangements with him, of course. This kind of publicity ought to please the Navy and appeal to a wide audience. You say you want to write a book later. That does not interest me." [1]

This seemed auspicious enough, and from the serious presence of Mr. George Creel I betook myself to the office of the Secretary of the Navy. It was the noon hour, and at his desk Josephus Daniels was eating a luncheon of milk, pie, and sandwiches in company with Thomas A. Edison. Stately admirals came in and awaited their turn for consultation. During a momentary lull the Secretary exclaimed, with his affably informal manner and broad smile:

"Hello, Paine. What can I do for you?"

"George Creel told me to ask you for the Queenstown permit, Mr. Daniels."

"What the dickens does he mean by that? He spoke to me

---

[1] The book was *The Fighting Fleets* (Houghton Mifflin Company, 1918). This publishing house cordially coöperated with the author's plans. It is a pleasure to mention it. Although the adventure was uncertain of results, funds were cheerfully advanced as well as sympathy. In the opinion of Ferris Greenslet, with whom the author had a hurried chat before sailing, it was helping to get on with the war.

about your going across. All you want is a letter to Sims, I reckon. I'll be glad to give it to you. Those destroyers of ours are doing great work. Go sit down and write the kind of a letter you wish me to sign. Then let me look it over."

This method of doing business seemed both expeditious and satisfactory. At a typewriter in the little side-room, with the aid of my friend Wilbur Jenkins, who was a sort of unofficial and indispensable private secretary to Mr. Daniels, I prepared my own credentials, to wit:

MY DEAR ADMIRAL SIMS:

This will introduce to you Mr. Ralph D. Paine, the author, who has prepared for the Committee on Public Information a series of articles on our armed merchantmen and now wishes to get some material for some articles for the Committee and for the "Saturday Evening Post," regarding the work of the destroyer flotilla.

Any courtesies you may show Mr. Paine will be appreciated by me. He is undertaking this work with my cordial approval.

Sincerely yours

VICE-ADMIRAL WM. S. SIMS, U.S.N.
   Commanding United States Naval
      Forces Operating in European Waters

The Secretary of the Navy scanned this letter, nodded approval, and affixed the signature of Josephus Daniels. With this precious document in my pocket, all obstacles appeared to have been removed. Rear Admiral Leigh Palmer, Chief of the Bureau of Navigation, was kind enough to write a personal letter to Admiral Sims which said, in part:

As you may know, the publicity which the Navy has been getting is not altogether satisfactory and we are most anxious to get some of the proper kind. I think that Mr. Paine, with his previous associations with the Navy and his good standing as an author, can be counted on to deliver the kind of stuff we want. By necessity, of course, he is working nominally under the auspices of the Committee on Public Information. Any courtesies you can extend to Mr. Paine to facilitate his gathering the necessary material will be greatly appreciated by me and will, I am sure, redound to the credit of the service.

A hasty trip home and it was good-bye and fare-ye-well. The voyage across was made in the brave old American Line steamer St. Louis and the few passengers were those who had some special business abroad. London in October of 1917 was found to be a city of gloom and distress — darkened streets, frequent German air raids, short rations, and a grim realization that the war might be lost unless America made haste.

As soon as possible I presented myself at the mansion in Grosvenor Gardens which flew the flag of the United States Naval Headquarters. A spruce marine orderly summoned a messenger who carried my various letters upstairs, leaving me standing in the entrance hall. Presently the word came back that Admiral Sims was in Paris, attending a meeting of the Allied Naval Council. This was disappointing, but not serious, in my opinion. Without doubt the Chief-of-Staff would pay courteous heed to the credentials. Did they not include what George Creel had so impressively designated as "the Queenstown permit"? In a placid frame of mind I sat and cooled my heels upon a bench in the hall.

After some delay there came briskly down the staircase an officer wearing the sleeve-stripes of a commander. In his right hand were clutched my treasured documents which he waved in an impatient manner. Curtly introducing himself as Commander Babcock, personal aide to Admiral Sims, he exclaimed:

"My God, another letter from Josephus Daniels!"

This was a reception so unexpected that it had the effect of an explosion. The annoyed officer handed back the letters which I had intended leaving for Admiral Sims, and indignantly announced:

"How do you suppose we can get on with the war, with interruptions like this? I can't do a thing for you. Correspondents are a nuisance. I have no time to be pestered with them."

There ensued an argument. It was not pacific, but on my part it was tempered by the presence of the marine orderly. In time of war tact is always essential in dealing with a military organization. Just why Commander Babcock should have lost his temper was perplexing and in other circumstances it might have been entertaining, but I was vitally concerned with getting on with the war on my own account. My credentials and personal letters of introduction had been flung back at me, a novel procedure, to say the least, and the thing was to discover the reason why. The riddle was partly solved when Commander Babcock emitted this information:

"Queenstown is a British base controlled by the Admiralty. Our destroyer flotilla is operated by a British admiral. You will have to have his permission to go to Queenstown, and I doubt if he gives it. However, I'll drive you over to the Admiralty and leave you there."

Here was news, indeed! There was more to this situation than had been learned in Washington. A sense of humor stirred faintly. George Creel also had something to learn. And he assumed to control all matters of naval publicity! "The Queenstown permit!" Its dimensions were shrinking with startling rapidity.

In a staff car Commander Babcock escorted me to the vast, gray old warren of the Admiralty Building in Whitehall. It was mellowed by tradition and filled with historic associations. There was no bustling haste in the shadowy halls and passages which seemed to wander at random, up and down stone stairways deeply worn. Wherever the salt water was deep enough to float a keel, from the Orkneys to the South Seas, British ships of war were moving in obedience to commands transmitted from these quiet and dingy rooms.

We entered the office of the Chief Censor of the Admiralty. A coal fire blazed in a small grate. At a long table heaped with papers sat several diligent officers, in uniform or in civilian garb, and in one corner a lone stenographer who was like an anachronism. At the head of the table was a heavily built, ruddy man with a straight, grim mouth and a trick of scowling over his glasses. This was the Chief Censor, Commodore Sir Douglas Brownrigg, Bart., C.B.

Commander Babcock dumped the credentials on the table and explained:

"This is Mr. Ralph Paine, an American correspondent. He has letters from the Secretary of the Navy and other people. Admiral Sims will be glad to have you do what you can for him."

Still quite upset about it Commander Babcock took his departure, for he had to get on with the war. The American correspondent, friendless and in a mood of deep dejection, was left to the tender mercies of the British Admiralty. Commodore Sir Douglas Brownrigg, Bart., read the credentials with deliberate care. Once he was interrupted by the stenographer who timorously informed him:

"Lord —— is in the hall and anxious to see you, sir."

"Tell the silly old rotter to wait," growled the Chief Censor.

If this was the way he dealt with lords, the prospect looked dismal for a mere correspondent. At length the naval arbiter of fate looked up to say:

"These letters appear to give you a sort of official status — this Committee on Public Information and all that, although I don't know what the devil it amounts to. Never heard of it! Of course I will do anything I can to oblige your Secretary of the Navy and your Admiral Sims. A bully old boy, that!"

"What about permission to visit Queenstown?" I ventured. "Commander Babcock was rubbed the wrong way, and I couldn't get much out of him.'

"Oh, he is overworked and nervous and worn to the bone. You mustn't mind Babcock's manner. He is a fine chap, quite all right. Sims thinks the world of him. You were a sort of bally last straw, do you see? This may be one of his off days, and possibly he did n't like your face, or something like that. Now about Queenstown, I can't give you permission. That's not my say-so."

"Then where do I go from here?" I implored.

"Sit tight and wait," rumbled this bulldog of a British commodore. "It's doubtful, but there is a sporting chance. I shall have to send a signal to our Commander-in-Chief at Queenstown, Admiral Sir Lewis Bayly. I will send you word at your hotel, possibly to-morrow. Don't feel too confident about it. If there is one thing old Bayly hates with a mortal hatred, it is correspondents and publicity of every description. I have had a hard time getting anybody down there at all."

Commodore Sir Douglas Brownrigg, again absorbed in a wire basket filled with cable and radio messages and other memoranda, said a gruff, "Good-bye, Mr. Paine." In from the hall tiptoed the "silly old rotter" of a lord. Out into the rain and the gloom wandered a correspondent who wished he had never left home. That night the German raiders dropped bombs freely. Inasmuch as they had hit the hotel once before, the odds were against their doing it again.

On the following day I had an engagement for luncheon at the Ritz with Senator Kenyon of Iowa, Senator Kendrick of Wyoming, and Judson Welliver, London correspondent of the "New York Sun." Such good company should have been cheering, but the party was joined by an American Associated Press manager who discovered my sorrows and consoled them as follows:

"This Admiral Bayly is one of the ablest officers in the British Navy, and I have heard it said more than once that he should have commanded the Grand Fleet instead of Jellicoe. But he is rated a hard man — they call him 'Black Bayly' in his own service, and the younger officers shiver in their shoes when you mention him."

"Um-m, it sounds like a genial welcome," said I. "What is this I hear about his detesting correspondents?"

"A mild word for it," answered the comforting informant. "Listen! I sent an Associated Press man down there to stay on the job and cover what news the censors would let through. Admiral Bayly would n't stand for him, and he had to leave Queenstown so fast that his coat-tails caught on fire from atmospheric friction. The allied naval forces, British and American, work together splendidly, with Bayly as the senior officer in command. It is the best arrangement possible, but —"

"But a correspondent is liable to be a casualty of war?" I murmured, quite pensively.

"I don't envy you the least little bit," observed this in-spiriting acquaintance.

After another unhappy night in London, a telephone message summoned Ralph Paine to the Admiralty. The Chief Censor was busy and brief, as usual, but there was something like a twinkle of sympathy in his eye as he said:

"The C.-in-C. directs me to send you along to Queenstown. You will go through to-night, in the train to Holyhead. Good luck to you."

He shoved across the table an Admiralty permit to be signed. It was an imposing document, bearing a red seal, and read as follows:

OFFICE OF CHIEF CENSOR
ROOM 37, OLD BUILDING
31 *October*, 1917

It is essential that you have your Identity Book on you

Mr. Ralph Paine of American Department of Information *is hereby authorized* to visit Queenstown subject to the discretion of the Commander-in-Chief, H.M. Ships and Vessels, Queenstown. He will report to the Commander-in-Chief, Queenstown, and Commanding Officer U.S.S. Melville on arrival in that area.

It is requested that every facility may be given him to mix freely with officers and men of the United States Flotillas in order to obtain material for articles for American Department of Information *without revealing any technical matters.*

All articles are to be submitted to the inspection of the Commanding Officer U.S.S. Melville, the Commander-in-Chief, Queenstown, and the Chief Censor, Admiralty, and nothing will be published without their sanction, and their decisions shall be final and binding.

D. BROWNRIGG
Chief Censor, Admiralty

I agree to the above conditions
RALPH D. PAINE

Unable to obtain a sleeping-car berth at such short notice, I found it was a wearisome journey which ended at noon the next day. Heavy-eyed, bedraggled, and dirty, I was met at the station in Queenstown by a dapper young British naval officer who introduced himself as an aide on the Admiral's staff. Most politely he suggested:

"I think we had better go up the hill at once. Admiral Bayly wishes to see you."

"Not until I feel fairly clean and respectable, my dear young man," was the firm rejoinder, "and there will be a square meal under my waistcoat."

My escort was visibly perturbed at this rebellion and gently requested haste as we trudged through the mud to the Queen's Hotel on the harbor-side. I halted to gaze long at a flock of Yankee destroyers riding at the mooring buoys, their lean flanks fantastically streaked with dazzle paint, the funnels white with salt. A division of them was steaming seaward, bound out to buck the Atlantic gales a thousand miles offshore and find the groping troop convoys and guard them safe to France. Ah, it was the finest game in the world, enough to make the pulse leap in any man who loved ships and the sea.

The boyish British aide plucked at my sleeve. It would never do to delay the visit to Admiralty House a minute longer than necessary. He was, oh, so courteous, but as firm as adamant. Therefore matters were rushed in the dingy, damp Queen's Hotel which was depressing enough in itself to make a low-spirited stranger leave all hope behind.

Climbing the narrow, cobbled streets of that Queenstown hill was a breathless performance for middle-age whose athletic prowess was a far-off memory. The town appeared to be set on edge. The sad autumn sky was weeping an habitual drizzle of rain. This made the footing slippery. The limber young British aide fairly strode up that hill, with wind to spare for an easy flow of conversation. It would have been humiliating, of course, to suggest that he slacken speed by a few knots.

We passed, at length, through the gateway of the spacious grounds and gardens of Admiralty House while the blue-jacket sentries saluted. The white ensign floated from a tall mast beyond the stone mansion with its wing in which were the offices of the staff.

The agile aide convoyed me to the door of a large square room and there bowed his adieu. It was the only flaw in his deportment, thus to desert a man who, if ever in his life, needed a friend. Fagged by the overnight journey and dead for sleep, panting for air after being towed up that wicked hill under forced draft, it could fairly be said that Ralph Paine was not in his best form to wrestle with an emergency.

He entered the room, which was cold and bare. Upon the walls were huge charts of the Irish Sea and the Western Ocean, dotted with tiny flags to indicate the positions of troop and cargo convoys and the courses of the divisions of far-flung American and British destroyer escorts.

There was no other furniture than the flat-topped desk and the chair behind it in which sat a grizzled, elderly man in a well-worn blue uniform. His features were serene and austere, like the profile on a Roman coin. It was perceived at a glance that he possessed the qualities of leadership, an unusual intelligence, and an inflexible tenacity of purpose. This was Admiral Sir Lewis Bayly, K.C.B., K.C.M.G., C.V.O., Commander-in-Chief of the Coasts of Ireland.

At the entrance of the American correspondent he did not

look up from his desk, but finished writing a letter. There was an odd illusion, that the temperature of the room was falling. Soon it reached the freezing point. The visitor felt like rubbing his ears or blowing on his fingers. After several years Admiral Sir Lewis Bayly raised his eyes and said in a voice from which the icicles hung:

"What can I do for you, Mr. Paine?"

"My errand is to describe the work of the American destroyers, sir, and I was instructed to report to you."

"Oh, indeed!" was the utterly bored and indifferent comment. "Your Admiralty permit allows you to 'mingle freely' with the officers and ratings, I believe. That means in port, of course. I have no objection to that."

"But that is not at all what I came from the United States for," I protested. "It will not be worth while staying in Queenstown, merely to meet the crews on shore."

"That is precisely what you have my permission to do," was the verdict, in accents hard and final.

"But I am expecting to cruise at sea in these vessels of ours, sir. Do I understand you to say there is no chance of that?"

Admiral Sir Lewis Bayly picked up his pen and signed a document or two before he said:

"*This war is not a pastime, Mr. Paine.* Good-afternoon. Oh, by the way, you will report your arrival to the American Chief-of-Staff, Captain Pringle, aboard the flagship Melville."

Such a man seemed impervious to arguments. They would have glanced off his chilled-steel surface like a shell-burst from a turret. I found myself outside the room and absently moving past the sentries at the gate to descend the hill to that forlorn refuge, the Queen's Hotel. In the conduct of a stupendous war my personal fortunes were, of course, entirely negligible, but they were of considerable importance to me and also to a large and adorable family at home on a New Hampshire farm. Youth may laugh at failure and ignore disappointments, but middle-age cannot afford to fail.

ADMIRAL SIR LEWIS BAYLY, K.C.B., K.C.M.G., C.V.O., LATE COM-
MANDER-IN-CHIEF OF THE COASTS OF IRELAND

In that shabby, sodden Irish hotel beside the harbor there was one cheerful spot, an alcove near the bar with an open fire flanked by cushioned settles. There I sat and pondered and recalled to mind a story which Richard Harding Davis used to tell of the Russo-Japanese War. For many tiresome weeks the drove of correspondents was politely marooned in Tokio by the adroit Japanese officials who kept them from going to the front. Finally it was announced that a certain number of them would be allowed to embark for Korea.

They were advised to take horses with them, as none would be found in the field. There was a great scurrying about to buy Japanese ponies, but Dinwiddie, the news photographer, remained indifferent and aloof from the scramble. He was taken to task by his agitated comrades who foresaw him stranded afoot in Korea. Sublimely confident and untroubled was his demeanor as he answered:

"There is always a horse for Dinwiddie!"

It became a famous slogan in hard places and tough crises. And it seemed to fit most admirably the situation of Ralph Paine in Queenstown. Why be downhearted? There was always a horse for Dinwiddie! In a brighter mood I murmured aloud:

"There is always a destroyer for Paine."

The pretty, blonde barmaid set down the glass she was polishing and leaned over to say:

"A destroyer for pain, is it you need, sir? Some of the gentlemen would be taking a drop of Irish whiskey for that."

"Thank you, Miss McMurray," said I, "but whiskey is not the proper treatment for my case. It seems to require prayer."

XXXVII

QUEENSTOWN IMPROVES ON ACQUAINTANCE

I⊤ was necessary to become acquainted with Admiral Bayly to discover how far astray had been the first impressions of him. The American destroyer captains had learned to like and admire him tremendously and were as loyal to his leadership as to that of their own force commander, Admiral Sims. There was much more to it than the confidence inspired by distinguished ability and fifty years of experience in the British Navy. The ice once thawed, this stern admiral was found to be a man of very human sympathies and a genuine affection for the bold sailormen whose flag was the Stars and Stripes.

My first interview had been so brief and disconcerting that it had seemed to forecast an ignominious retreat from Queenstown. Twenty years earlier there had been a meeting with another austere admiral, on the quarter-deck of the American cruiser New York when a certain abashed correspondent had said to himself that it was a long swim to Key West. Apparently he was not destined to be fortunate with admirals.

The formality of reporting to Captain J. R. P. Pringle, the American Chief-of-Staff, aboard the flagship Melville was more agreeable than expected. It led to an invitation to luncheon in his cabin. There was a rift in the clouds. He was an officer of unusual professional accomplishments and rare tact, competently carrying on a task both novel and difficult. For the first time in history American and British ships and sailors were operating together as one force. All the ancient quarrels on blue water had been forgotten.

Thanks to the intercession of Captain Pringle there came

an invitation to dine at Admiralty House. He called for me at the melancholy Queen's Hotel and we went bumping up the hill on the hurricane deck of an Irish jaunting car. There were several other guests, commanders of American destroyers in from sea for a brief respite before sailing on other hazardous voyages.

The mistress of Admiralty House was Miss Violet Voysey, the niece of Sir Lewis Bayly, and I can do no better than echo the tribute paid her by Admiral Sims:

> Miss Voysey was a young woman of great personal charm and cultivation; probably she was the influence that most contributed to the happiness and comfort of our officers at Queenstown. From the day of their arrival she entered into the closest comradeship with the Americans. She kept open house for them; she was always on hand to serve tea in the afternoon, and she never overlooked an opportunity to add to their well-being. As a result of her delightful hospitality, Admiralty House really became a home for our officers. The dignity with which she presided over the Admiral's house, and the success with which she looked after his comfort, also inspired their respect. Miss Voysey was the leader in all the war charities at Queenstown and she and the Admiral made it their personal duty to look out for the victims of torpedoed ships. At whatever hour these survivors arrived they were sure of the most warm-hearted attention from headquarters. . . .

At the dinner-table, brought together in this sociable and unofficial manner, it was soon apparent that Admiral Bayly might possibly consent to overlook the crime of being a correspondent. Let any two men hit upon topics of mutual interest and the barriers begin to crumble. As a youngster in the naval service, Captain Pringle had admired the exploits of Captain "Dynamite Johnny" O'Brien in the Three Friends and the Dauntless. A question was asked concerning my own previous acquaintance with the Navy. It came out, naturally enough, that the Navy had pursued the acquaintance, in gunboats and cruisers, from Fernandina to the Dry Tortugas.

The attitude of Admiral Sir Lewis Bayly became friendly. He could be said to thaw before your eyes. He had always been fond of pirates. In fact, he admired them, but he had assumed the race to be extinct. That this Ralph Paine had been stained with piracy of a sort was vastly in his favor. As a correspondent he belonged to an objectionable profession. As an outlaw of the Caribbean it was proper that he should be warmly welcomed to Admiralty House. The ice was broken.

By way of an avocation Admiral Bayly was an enthusiastic gardener — flowers, fruits, and vegetables. In this he was like the great old Admiral Benbow of the vanished days of tall spars and wooden walls, who had puttered among his posies at Deptford when he was not blockading the French fleet off Dunkirk or blowing their frigates out of water. Here was another theme of discussion mutually congenial in which an amateur farmer from New Hampshire had many facts and theories to air. Given two men who genuinely love the soil and no urging is required to set them going.

It was suggested that the visitor might like to see the gardens of Admiralty House. This was arranged for the next morning. Up the hill he tramped to keep this pleasant engagement in a mood much brighter than when the polite young aide of the Royal Navy had towed him into the presence of the awesome Commander-in-Chief of the Coasts of Ireland. While inspecting the gardens a cruise in an American destroyer was mentioned as permissible.

Two days later the correspondent went to sea in the destroyer O'Brien, Commander Charles A. Blakely. So little had then been told of the operations of these dashing, hard-driven vessels that it proved to be a most fascinating and enjoyable experience — something new and different — plunging through November gales with decks awash, alert to find and pursue the hostile submarine and as vigilant to avoid attack, the hunter and the hunted, sighting the convoy of three huge transports crammed with fourteen thousand Yankee troops who roared with delight and relief when they saw the division of six destroyers come reeling out of a spray-swept horizon to wheel and circle them at twenty-five knots.

Only one incident occurred to mar the cruise, and this was when an infantile bluejacket of some seventeen years was overheard to remark to a mate:

"That's Paine up on the bridge, the man that writes stories. They say he's a pretty good guy, but don't you think he's too blamed old to be bangin' around out here in a destroyer?"

Having returned to Queenstown in the O'Brien, this gracious and unexpected message was received from Admiral Bayly.

"The niece and I agree that the hotel is a most disagreeable place for you, quite impossible to write in with any comfort. Please pack your traps and come up to Admiralty House. We want you to make it your home while you stay in Queenstown."

The fortunate sojourn at Admiralty House permitted the guest to enjoy an intimate acquaintance with the direction and events of the naval warfare. It was a unique privilege. The trouble was that the best stories could not be written, stories which, in the sight of a correspondent, were like priceless jewels. It was enough to afflict Ralph Paine with nervous prostration, the fact that what he was permitted to write was so tame and flat compared with the forbidden epics of the war zone.[1]

---

[1] Some of these personal impressions were later woven into fiction material. Before sailing from New York I had called to say good-bye to my friend, Charles Agnew MacLean, editor of *The Popular Magazine*.

"There ought to be some good short stories in it, some day, Mac," said I. "Do you want to take a sporting chance and advance a thousand dollars on it?"

"Sure thing," answered MacLean. "Shall I send the check to your home address?"

After magazine publication, the series of stories appeared as a book, *Ships Across the Sea*. (Houghton Mifflin Company, 1920.)

Admiral Bayly was rather amused by this predicament and made it even more tantalizing. He would saunter into the living-room from his office adjoining, wearing a shabby blue coat with the gold stripes of his exalted naval rank running halfway to the elbow, knock his short, black pipe against the grate, and turn to say with a quizzical smile and a most sardonic glint in his eye:

"Come along to my desk, Buccaneer, and I will let you read a full report of the most sensational Q-boat, or mystery ship, exploits. The Admiralty has just sent me down a copy of the latest compilation. It is really ripping. A good many of these ships have been fitted out at Queenstown, you know. And, oh, I have asked Captain Gordon Campbell for dinner to-night. He is the most famous Q-boat skipper of the lot. You will like to talk to him, I'm sure."

My reply was a groan of despair. In truth, it would have been worth losing a leg to have been able to write and publish the story of Captain Gordon Campbell, awarded a mysterious Victoria Cross, by all odds the most sensational and heroic figure in the whole British naval service. In the annals of modern sea warfare there had been nothing to match it. Ranging the high seas in what appeared to be slovenly tramp merchantmen, he and his picked crews had destroyed four enemy submarines, fighting until their Q-boats were sunk or blown up under their feet. During the war it could not be told, and after the war great deeds found an indifferent audience.

When Captain Gordon Campbell came to dine at Admiralty House, he turned out to be as stolid and quiet and bashful a British hero as you might have expected to find him. He had been removed from the mystery ship service to command the light cruiser Active which Admiral Bayly used as a flagship whenever he went to sea. This was against the wishes of Gordon Campbell, but in the opinion of the Admiralty he had earned the right to live a while longer. There was a reluctance to lose him, as would probably happen if he should tempt fate again. But this man of hairbreadth escapes and incredible adventures was fairly eating his heart out in the enforced security of the cruiser Active. Sad and restless, he was eager to have another try at stalking the ambushed and elusive foe.

Admiral Bayly happened to be inspecting a mystery ship in Queenstown harbor before she sailed on one of those profoundly secretive voyages. His keen eye could detect no flaws in the ingenious and elaborate disguise of the vessel and her people. As a final touch the imaginative naval skipper had devised two passengers, an elderly man with gray whiskers, a battered tall hat, and seedy black coat, and his motherly wife Maria who wore a straw bonnet and green veil and carried a parasol. Sedately they strolled on the upper deck, Maria leaning on the arm of her solicitous husband.

The severely critical Sir Lewis Bayly was about to compliment the skipper when he chanced to see the amiable Maria step to the rail, lift her veil with a large hand encased in a white cotton glove, and deposit her quid of tobacco over the side.

"Very unladylike, my man," chided the Admiral. "Better swallow it next time and risk the consequences."

If there was an interesting ship in the harbor to visit, perhaps a torpedoed steamer which had come limping in with a shattered cavern in her side, this thoughtful host would place at the correspondent's disposal the Admiral's barge, a cabin steam launch with a brass funnel, a four-starred pennant, and a smart coxswain in command. On one occasion this privilege proved to be acutely embarrassing. A German crew had been captured alive from a submarine depth-bombed and sunk by the destroyer Fanning. The prisoners were brought into Queenstown and transferred to the flagship Melville. The happy crew of the Fanning was mustered on deck the next morning to hear their feat commended, including a congratulatory signal from Admiral Sims in London.

Ralph Paine went grandly off alone in the Admiral's barge to witness the ceremony. Approaching the destroyer some commotion was noted on deck, the crew rapidly assembling, the officers drawing up in line. In a twinkling the ship was taut and ready to receive the Commander-in-Chief, Admiral Sir Lewis Bayly. When the barge sheered alongside and there was visible only one blushing and unimportant correspondent, the bluejackets grinned from ear to ear, and one godless young scamp was heard to remark:

"This bird Paine certainly hung one on Captain Pringle and the rest of 'em this time. All hands thought Uncle Lewis Bayly was coming off, and I was scared to death. I got a loose button on my reefer, and if he spotted it I guess I'd do thirty days in the brig or something."

The Admiral's work-room, or office, was the focal point of momentous information uncannily conveyed by radio messages from perilous waters near and distant. American troops were moving across the sea in rapidly increasing numbers and, in a large measure, the Queenstown destroyer fleet was responsible for the safety of these precious argosies. It was also Admiral Bayly's heavy task to guard the Irish Sea and the plodding cargo-boats which were so vital to an England that was close to the shadow of starvation. Under his direction moved a fleet of British destroyers, mine-sweepers, trawlers, and cruisers. In brief signals the news of tragic losses came to Admiralty House, a faithful trawler blown up with all hands, a foundering merchantman, or such a moving farewell as this, faintly whispered by radio:

"*Good-bye. We are sinking.*"

All day long and far into the night the Admiral was on duty, the brief diversion a stroll in the gardens after breakfast when we used to discuss celery and cauliflower and triumphantly loot the hen-house of one egg. One afternoon a week he tramped over the hills of Queenstown harbor, five or six miles across a stiff country, while the two ladies of the household, Miss Voysey and Lady Pinhey, a cousin from India, and Captain Pringle and Ralph Paine found abundant exercise in following the pace of this active leader who was sixty years old.

At the dinner-table it pleased his whimsical fancy to enter-tain British naval guests with strange tales of the habits and customs of the extraordinary Americans as he had observed them while serving as a naval attaché in Washington. He had once wandered into Portland, Maine, on some official errand, and was unfortunate enough to find himself inter-mingled with an Old Home Week celebration. The hotels and restaurants were jammed to the guards with visitors and the British stranger had an unhappy time of it.

"As you know," was the way he put it, "all rational per-sons are jolly well glad to get rid of their relatives, and it usually requires a lot of maneuvering and all that sort of thing. Cousins once removed are supposed to stay there, what? But I give you my word, these curious Americans, having once got comfortably rid of their relatives, proceed to organize, quite deliberately, *and get them all back again.* And they call it Old Home Week!"

He had learned to fathom what he called the broad or exaggerated style of American humor and it was his delight to try the effect upon some bewildered British admiral or commodore who might be a guest. One of these test stories had been passed along by Admiral Sims. It went like this:

"It was a winter day in a Western mining camp, a bliz-zard raging, temperature below zero. In the saloon cow-boys ordered hot whiskey punches with a dash of red pepper. A stranger entered and said to the bartender:

" 'Will you be good enough to give me a long, cool lemon-ade, with plenty of cracked ice in it?'

" 'Hell, no,' snorted the bartender. 'I can't give you no lemonade, but I can lend you a pair of white duck pants!' "

It was almost pathetic to have a hale and ruddy British naval guest turn to ask in a confidential and imploring aside:

"I say, Mr. Paine, you are an American, don't you know. You can probably make it clear. *Why* did it occur to the bartender person to offer the stranger a pair of white duck trousers in such beastly cold weather?"

When the professional task of the correspondent was finished, to write his articles describing the work of the American destroyers for the "Saturday Evening Post," Admiral Bayly personally censored the manuscript instead of turning it over to an officer of his staff. To sit and watch him reading it after dinner was as anxious an ordeal as I can remember experiencing. His judgments were merciful, however, and the only erasures were those paragraphs which mentioned his own career or his superbly efficient and loyal coöperation with the naval forces of the United States. He ran his pencil through every word of this. His self-effacement was consistent and complete.

Reluctantly and with abounding gratitude, I bade adieu to the hospitality of Admiralty House and to the companionship of one of the ablest, noblest, and, beneath the surface, one of the kindliest men I have ever known. Admiral Sims was at his headquarters when I returned to London. News of the adventure at Queenstown had reached him and he was pleased, of course, that an American correspondent should have found so cordial a welcome. His organization was expanding day by day and Washington had begun to recognize its importance. Later in the war it was to include almost four hundred vessels of war and a hundred thousand men operating from the North Sea to the Mediterranean.

Energetic, straight as a lance, with the color of a boy in his cheek and the trim white beard close-cropped, William S.

Sims appeared to carry his complex responsibilities easily and cheerily. Like his friend and ally, Admiral Bayly, he had always devoted himself to the work in hand, oblivious of criticism, undaunted by obstacles, indifferent to rewards. The two men were also alike in that it had been their habit to speak out with the courage of their convictions, regardless of personal consequences, wherefore the one had, from time to time, set the United States Navy Department by the ears, while the other had made himself equally unpopular among the barnacles of the British Admiralty.

Of Sims it may be said that he wears official reprimands with as much credit as other men wear medals. It is a disgrace to the American Nation that he has received no official recognition or promotion for his splendid service in the war. He has paid the penalty for courageously telling the truth.

In chatting about naval affairs at Queenstown he became indignant when the attitude of the Sinn-Fein element of the Irish was mentioned. Pacing the floor he expressed his own opinions of this faction which had displayed open hostility to the American naval forces and was secretly aiding Germany. His profanity was crisp and righteous. I had been in a position to know and hear these things myself. Admiralty House was the headquarters of naval intelligence.

"True, of course it's all true!" gustily exclaimed the American Admiral. "What makes me hot is that there is a political element in the United States that will defend what I call the treason of these Queenstown Sinn-Feiners and deny their guilt. I intend to tell them what I think when I go home."

"And you will have the politicians in Congress on your back," said I, "and they will try to block every effort to give you proper credit for your part in the war."

"That does n't bother me a little bit." And this was Sims speaking, straight from the shoulder, always willing to hit a head if he thought it deserved hitting. "There is no reason why the Government of the United States, or any department of it, should truckle to a certain element of Irish vote or to any other fifty-per-cent-American vote."

Commander Babcock joined the conversation. There was no reference to the first interview in which the intrusion of Ralph Paine had been so excessively annoying. He beamed as friendly a greeting as could have been desired. All's well that ends well is a sensible maxim. It fitted this situation. And what mattered it if a correspondent's feelings had been a bit ruffled, when Commander Babcock handsomely deserved such praise as this, as written by Admiral Sims:

Many men have made vital contributions to our success in the war of whom the public scarcely ever hears the names. A large part of the initiative and thinking which finds expression in successful military action originates with officers of this type. They labor day after day and night after night, usually in subordinate positions, unselfishly doing work which is necessarily credited to other names than their own, daily lightening the burdens of their chiefs, and constantly making suggestions which may control military operations or affect national policy. Commander Babcock is a striking representative of this type. My personal obligations to him are incalculable; and I am indebted to him not only for his definite services, but for the sympathy, the encouragement, and the kindly and calculated pessimism which served so well to counterbalance my own temperamental optimism.

In this last sentence is a phrase which throws a certain light on the woes of an American correspondent. He had happened to encounter Commander Babcock when he was in one of those moods of "calculated pessimism."

XXXVIII

ADMIRALS OF THE ALLIED FLAGS

"Why not have a look at the British Navy?" suggested the Chief Censor of the Admiralty. "Your chaps and ours are all in the one service together. You seem to have got on well at Queenstown, after a ragged start. Lewis Bayly has asked me to do what I can for you. We shall be glad to show you everything we've got."

Commodore Sir Douglas Brownrigg was as good as his word. By way of preliminary information he was asked if it would be permissible to look over the confidential reports of the British submarine flotilla which cruised against the German submarines in the North Sea. There they stalked each other, hunting in ambush, lying in wait, a perilous and desperate enterprise which had been waged so secretly that the world was almost unaware of it. Submarine against submarine!

At the request for these documents the Chief Censor glowered over his glasses, but nodded assent and heaved himself out of his chair to go and fetch the material. He came back with an armful of papers and gruffly exclaimed, as he laid them upon the table:

"That heap of junk ought to keep you quiet for a while. When you want more, let me know."

Great tales were briefly, simply told in these Admiralty documents. Here was recorded the toll of tragic disaster which it was not permitted to reveal. Twenty-five British submarines vanished with all hands and no man knew what their fate had been! Their grave was the gray North Sea. Those that survived to lurk off the German coast faced odds far greater than the soldiers risked in the trenches of France and Flanders. But in losses inflicted on the enemy it was worth the price it cost, and therefore the Harwich Flotilla. grimly, gallantly carried on.

Here and there from these concise Admiralty reports one was able to glean material for an article which might possibly pass the scrutiny of the Chief Censor. It was taking a sporting chance. The manuscript was duly submitted, and after reading it he replied to a question:

"Yes, it got past me, Mr. Ralph Paine, but by a blooming close squeak. Better not try to run it quite so fine again."

It was at his suggestion that the next fortnight was spent at the great North Sea naval base of Harwich, as the guest of Rear Admiral Cuthbert Cayley. This genial and breezy host made it convenient to cruise the wintry North Sea in various kinds of fighting craft, under the surface in a submarine of the dauntless flotilla which had dared and suffered so much, a mile above the sea in a huge flying boat of the bombing patrol, up and down the war channels in minesweeping vessels, or in a swift destroyer which ventured over into enemy waters to search for several miles of anti-submarine nets that had been blown adrift in a gale.

Commodore Sir Reginald Tyrwhitt, commanding the famous light cruiser division, who had gained high renown in the brilliant action called the Battle of the Bight, was good enough to send the following note from his flagship Concord:

DEAR MR. PAINE:

I hear you are in the port and are anxious to see something of the ships. Will you give me the pleasure of your company to dinner to-night at eight o'clock? We will discuss the best way of showing you all there is to be seen. Do not dress. If you can come, just make a signal or telephone.

Such courtesies as these are recalled to show how wholeheartedly sincere was the war-time alliance of the British and American naval forces, how these officers of high rank and grave responsibilities were never too weary or too occupied to be kind to a guest from overseas. And how weary they must have been, after three years of unbroken vigilance, of incessant readiness to engage the enemy!

Admiral Cayley's residence was in a quaint old village four miles back from the coast, a rambling Tudor house in a bit of Tudor England removed from the haunts of tourists. Mary Boleyn, the sister of Anne, had once dwelt within the ivied walls of this mansion, and her initials, scratched with a diamond, were to be seen on one of the small leaden panes of a window in the oaken hall. The Admiral lived and slept in his office quarters down by the harbor of Harwich, motoring home to dine and departing at ten o'clock. During this brief glimpse of his family, the favorite card game was what he called "the jolly American game of coon-can."

Once or twice the vicar's two daughters came in to join this exciting revel at coon-can which the Admiral played with the gusto and noise of a man who never tolerated halfway measures. And during a lull, one of the vicar's charming daughters looked up to say, with an air of engaging interest:

"Do you know, Mr. Paine, you are the first American my sister and I have ever met."

Admiral Cayley waged war as he played cards, with zest and sporting spirit. Amusement flickered on his lean, brown face and softened its harsh outlines when he spun such yarns as this:

"One of our lightships was anchored about halfway across the North Sea and we had not removed it because our destroyers found it handy for taking their bearings while on patrol. The German submarines also used the lightship, we discovered, as a mark by which to turn when they were bound north to pass around Scotland and so into the Atlantic. It occurred to me that Fritz was a methodical blighter, do you see, his mind running in a groove, what? The lightship was there, and there it would remain, thought he.

"So I sent a destroyer out one night with orders to take

the lightship in tow, move it a mile or so and anchor it on the tail of a shoal with two fathoms of water. My diagnosis was correct, by Jove. A few mornings after that we found *two* big, fat, seagoing submarines tidily stranded on the tail of the shoal. A very good haul! I had out-guessed old Fritz, as you say, by moving the lightship a bit."

This unquenchable sporting spirit was displayed by the officers of the British submarine flotilla. One afternoon I played golf with three of these commanders, wind-reddened, frost-bitten young men just in from six days of cruising or resting on the sea bottom, off the mine fields and war channels of the German coast. Did they mention their perils and hardships? Not a solitary word. The war was studiously ignored. It might have been a foursome playing at any country club prior to 1914. They were golfers, nothing else, for a fleeting hour, with a complete absorption in every stroke. It meant nothing to them that the next cruise might be the last. They were splendid.

The correspondent's tour extended to Lowestoft and Grimsby, those ancient North Sea fishing ports whose noble mariners manned the fleets of the Trawler Naval Reserve; dour, booted men with gold rings in their ears, who sailed and fought and died like their fathers before them.

It was the Commodore at Lowestoft who had leased several thousand acres of shooting preserves by way of keeping his hand in, for he was one of the finest shots in England. A man would be frightfully bored by such a stupid war as this, said he, unless one could knock off for a day now and then. He invited the correspondent to go along. Forty bluejackets were ordered off their ships to serve as beaters. It would buck them up and stretch their legs. A member of Parliament and a staff captain joined the party. It was quite like a novel of English country life — the gaudy pheasants rocketing out of the coverts as the sailors flushed them with shouts of "Starboard she goes" and "Sail ho" — the guns bringing them down with methodical accuracy — luncheon at the gamekeeper's cottage.

From the North Sea coast the Chief Censor of the Admiralty sent the American visitor down to Dover where Vice-Admiral Sir Reginald Bacon kept the flowing road across the Channel open and secure for the passage of millions of British troops and their supplies and munitions, a command second in importance to that of the Grand Fleet. With what solicitous care the Admiralty arranged these personal excursions is indicated in this letter from the Chief Censor:

DEAR MR. PAINE.

Vice-Admiral Sir Reginald Bacon, in command at Dover, will be very glad to see you on Friday, the 28th December, and you can stay several days there. He will send you out in a destroyer and tells me he thinks he can fix you a visit to Dunkirk and an aerial trip as well. Anyway, I think he will look after you all right. When you get down to Dover I should be glad if you would report yourself at the Vice-Admiral's office and make his acquaintance, and probably he will send some one to meet your train. I want to know what train you expect to take. Perhaps you will call me up on the telephone and let me know this. I send you herewith your permit. Please let me know that you get it safely.

Yours faithfully

D. BROWNRIGG

Cruising with the Dover Patrol was a varied and interesting experience and it led, at length, to the French port of Dunkirk which was the base of the huge British monitors engaged in bombarding Ostend. Dunkirk had been incessantly bombed and shattered by land and sea and air, ever since 1914, a wreck of a city with a spirit unconquerably magnificent. There was a feeling among the heroic citizens of this tormented seaport, which clung so tenaciously to life, that it had been somehow overlooked and ignored. Visitors seldom tarried to acquaint themselves with the proud story of the courage of Dunkirk.

That an American correspondent should care to linger with

them, to sit and chat across the table with the mayor and the military officials and the naval officers, to express a profound admiration and sympathy, appeared to inspire the friendliest gratitude. It created an intimacy quite unusual. One felt that Dunkirk had adopted him. You might have concluded that some tangible benefits, instead of mere sympathy, had been conferred.

Some time after this visit, the mayor of Dunkirk, Commandant Terquem, sent a staff officer to London with a letter of thanks and a beautifully painted copy of the coat of arms of the city, together with the Dunkirk Medal. The inscription was "To an American Friend of France." A souvenir highly valued, this message from Dunkirk, and to be remembered also as another bit of proof, along the rough highway of life, that kindliness eases many a hurt.

Among the fine figures of the war was my host at Dunkirk, the British Commodore, Hubert Lynes. An unterrified bantam of a sailor, he would step to a window and cock his eye at the weather and chirrup:

"A clear sky and little wind. A perfectly splendid night for them to come over. We shall be bombed without fail. Dunkirk is only ten minutes from the enemy's lines by the air route, so near that his machines can go back and load up again — dump two or three lots of bombs on us the same night. Let me see, I have been bombed in Dunkirk one hundred and forty-nine nights. Really, this looks like the most favorable night in weeks. You could n't have hit it more opportunely, upon my word. It is rather a nuisance to have to leg it into a dugout almost every evening. And so many of these poor people of Dunkirk have been killed or had their houses knocked about their ears. It is very distressing."

The salt-water pilgrimage now veered back to the American naval forces and the Bay of Biscay where Vice-Admiral Henry B. Wilson directed his fleet of yachts and destroyers

and was rapidly building a vast organization extending coastwise from Brest to Bordeaux. Admiral Sims was gracious
enough to furnish the following letter, by way of an open sesame wherever the American ensign was flown in European
waters:

To whom it may concern:
The bearer of this letter, Mr. Ralph D. Paine, has, with the permission of the United States Navy Department and with my full
approval, visited the bases of our U.S. Naval Forces operating in
British waters, and also numerous bases of British Forces in connection with publicity questions in the United States.
Mr. Paine has my full confidence as well as that of the United
States Naval authorities in Washington, and his discretion and
good judgment may be fully trusted.
I desire that any officers of this command, to whom Mr. Paine
may present himself, extend him every facility in visiting our ships
and bases in European waters, and in acquainting himself with the
nature of our operations and the existing condition and morale of
our forces.
There is no objection to his actually going to sea on our vessels,
as he has done both in British and American vessels in British
waters.
The work that Mr. Paine is performing I consider of great value
to the Naval Service and hence to the Allied Cause, and any facilities which may be extended to him by the Allied Services will be
greatly appreciated.

> (Signed) WM. S. SIMS
> *Vice-Admiral U.S. Navy*
> *Commanding U.S. Naval*
> *Forces in European Waters*

This was a letter which it was just as well to keep safely
tucked in an inside pocket and to be careful lest it fall into
the wrong hands. Admiral Sims exclaimed, as he signed it:
"There, you can't say that the British Navy has treated
you any better than that. Show it to Sir Douglas Brownrigg
the next time you drop in at the Admiralty. He may loosen
up with another batch of secret documents. Well, you ap-

pear to be equipped to investigate the whole works, so go to it." [1]

I sailed out of the port of Brest a week later in an untamed, coal-burning destroyer named the Reid. January in the Bay of Biscay was rougher and colder than the North Sea had been. In all manner of war vessels my sea-legs had fairly well stood the test and the appetite for three meals a day had been seldom impaired, even in other bucking, twisting, cavorting destroyers. But this offshore cruise in the Reid was a personal calamity, and the result was total ruin.

Stretched in the skipper's bunk, for he never used it while at sea, I reflected that the sagacious young bluejacket of Queenstown had been correct in surmising that this guy Paine was too old to be bangin' around out here in a destroyer. For months I had been uneasily afraid of being torpedoed and now I was afraid it would n't happen. The crew of the Reid included many brisk college lads, one of whom was unfeeling enough to compose this ribald epitaph:

> "Grim Father Neptune has his throne
> In the Bay of Biscay all alone,
> And on the day of which we speak,
> He served out weather rough and bleak;
> He sent us wind and he sent us rain,
> And 't was not long ere Ralph D. Paine
> Did hie himself to the skipper's bunk
> And swear the writing game was punk."

However, the unhappy correspondent survived the voyage and was soon afloat again, in the naval yacht Wanderer which convoyed the cargo steamers that passed along the

[1] In view of the confidence shown by Admiral Sims, and the assistance so unreservedly offered, it was most gratifying to receive the following telegram from the Secretary of the Navy, several months later:

"I wish to express my own appreciation and that of the Navy for the services you have rendered in acquainting the country, through your book *The Fighting Fleets*, and your other writings, with the work of the naval forces in the War Zone. Admiral Sims and all our officers across the water feel as I do, that you have rendered a real service.

"Josephus Daniels"

Britanny coast, bound to and from the Channel ports. Wonderful youngsters they were who manned this fleet of yachts, zealous greenhorns whom the vicissitudes of the sea and the traditions of the service had hammered into competent officers and smart sailors within a few months. The yachts were unfit for the heavy duties assigned them, but, in all weathers, they were driven as long as they held together.

And when the war was over and these young men had returned to the campus or the Wall Street office or the business house, you may be sure that memory would hark back with a certain proud affection to some battered yacht which they had kept afloat in the stormy Bay of Biscay-O. For a ship which has faithfully withstood the manifold ordeals of the ocean becomes something more than a mere artifice of wood and steel. She seems almost sentient, like a living thing, to those who have shared her fortunes, and therein is the eternal romance of blue water.

Mr. J. P. Morgan felt a sentiment akin to this when his stately yacht Corsair was returned to him by the Navy Department after two years of racking war service in foreign waters. The staunch vessel was still fit to be overhauled and made ready for the peaceful and leisurely employment of former days. But when, trim and immaculate, the Corsair once more flew the Commodore's flag of the New York Yacht Club, the wooden plugs were left in the spotless decks to mark the half-circles where the gun-mounts had been bolted, and the pine planking was scarred where cases of shells had been dragged to be ready for the swift team-work of the agile gun crews.

These were marks of honor which it seemed a pity to obliterate. They signified that the Corsair had been something more than a yacht.

A cruise in the Wanderer from Brest to Quiberon and back again, and then Ralph Paine spent some time ashore with Admiral Wilson. When the Queenstown destroyers came into Brest for fuel oil, and the officers found time to go ashore, you might have heard them boast, in the most gentlemanly terms, of the splendid efficiency of their own base and the extraordinary ability of Admiral Sir Lewis Bayly who directed their operations.

At this, the officers from the yachts were likely to fling back that the Queenstown outfit ought to get on, with the vast resources of the British Admiralty at its disposal, and a mere fleet of destroyers to be looked after. The whole French coast was cluttered up with transports and cargo-boats, said they, and it was some job to keep them moving, not to mention chasing Fritz. As for Admiral Sir Lewis Bayly, K.C.B., he was said to be a very fine old boy, but he was n't the only iron-bellied, two-fisted admiral in the war zone, and the doctrine of the Breton Patrol was "Wilson, That's All."

In such manner was voiced the keen but friendly rivalry between the American naval men of Brest and Queenstown, and it was the kind of loyalty which might have been expected.

XXXIX

GOOD–BYE AND FARE–YE–WELL!

FAR up in the North Sea, in the gloom and mist of the Ork-
ney Islands, was a squadron of American battleships under
Rear Admiral Hugh Rodman, which had joined the Grand
Fleet. Thither the correspondent journeyed from the Bay
of Biscay and found a welcome aboard the mighty flagship
New York. Another slant of good fortune so arranged it
that in the middle of the night the Grand Fleet moved out
to sea in battle formation, hoping and expecting to find the
German High Sea Fleet which was known to be cruising off
its own coasts.

Thick weather and a roaring gale of wind made it impossible to come in contact with the enemy, but through the
night and all the next day more than two hundred ships of
war, flying the white ensign and the Stars and Stripes,
crashed through the surges of the North Sea as one stupendous fleet responsive to the orders of Admiral Sir David Beatty
in his flagship Queen Elizabeth.

Never again, in all probability, will there be such a magnificent pageant of a fighting fleet on active service. This was
the chief significance of it, unrealized then. The battleship
as the dominant weapon of naval warfare will soon be obsolete. Already Jutland is studied by naval experts, not for
its lessons in strategy and tactics, but as an episode in history, like the defeat of the Spanish Armada. The salty traditions of centuries are in process of obliteration, although
the conservative influences of Admiralties and Navy De-
partments may cling a while longer to the doctrine that the
ship-of-the-line is the backbone of the fleet. Swarms of air-
craft and their shattering bombs will make blue water un-

tenable for the most powerful battleships afloat or building.

And so it is something to remember, to have stood all day upon the bridge of the New York with burly Admiral Rodman, in the stinging spray and rain of the North Sea while, in faultless formation, the squadron of American battleships, splendidly handled, steamed in the position of honor behind the Queen Elizabeth, eager for a fight to a finish with the enemy's fleet.

There was one more American force which I was anxious to visit. This was the submarine flotilla that had daringly crossed the Atlantic in mid-winter and was operating at the secret base of Bantry Bay on the coast of Ireland. This quest led to Queenstown and another delightful visit at Admiralty House. Admiral Bayly concluded that he ought to go and make the personal acquaintance of these intrepid Yankee submarines. Therefore we motored together across a wild region of southeastern Ireland and so came to the bleak and lofty shores of Bantry Bay.

It had the aspect of a sporting pilgrimage. The American submarines were in training for the stern business of hunting the enemy's undersea boats. With them was a veteran British submarine squadron which had played this game of stalking Fritz in the North Sea. Daily the Britishers and the Yanks hunted each other in the deep waters of Bantry Bay by way of practice. It pleased Admiral Bayly to go out in a submarine of his own navy while I jammed myself down through the conning-tower hatch of an American boat.

For hours these two craft dived and came up for a glimpse through a periscope, and shot torpedoes with dummy heads at each other. The fact that the British Commander-in-Chief was a passenger and observer inspired all hands with zeal to the nth power. It so happened that the American skipper gave the order for a "crash dive," to show the Admiral how rapidly the boat could submerge. Watch in hand, the executive officer counted the seconds as soon as the commander had screwed fast the hatch-plate above his head. The boat was sealed and tight to vanish from the surface.

The propulsive power had been shifted from surface engines to the purring electric motors. Gently, patiently the sensitive craft was nursed until properly trimmed. Water was forced out of one of many ballast-tank compartments or admitted somewhere else. In a small cleared space of the brilliantly lighted interior and its complexity of machinery, two petty officers sedately sat upon stools in front of the large dials of the depth gauges. They twirled the handles which controlled the horizontal diving rudders at bow and stern.

It was the commander's intention to dive to a depth of thirty feet and hold her there. This was sufficient to submerge the two periscopes. But the praiseworthy ambition of making the "crash dive" in record time had caused the submarine to slant downward with a trifle too much zeal. She failed to recover her poise as soon as expected.

The depth gauges showed that she had dropped to fifty feet below the surface — then to sixty feet, and was still going down, placidly but stubbornly. The crew showed not the slightest agitation, but several of them were twisting valves and crouching over pumps in a manner very intent. Like two statues the petty officers upon the stools stared at the faces of the depth gauges and solemnly twirled the handles of the diving-rudder gear.

And still the boat dropped lower and lower, swimming so lightly in the fluid element — to seventy feet, to eighty feet. It was obvious to Ralph Paine that something had gone wrong with the programme of the "crash dive." There was too much of it. He gazed at the dials of those depth gauges with fascinated interest. It was with reluctance that he took his eyes off them for an instant. They were extremely eloquent. Every additional foot of depth they showed was as important to him as increasing the length of his nose by an inch.

Nobody else seemed to be indulging in foolish conversation, wherefore he wiped the sweat from his brow and held his peace. More than ever he admired the courage and calmness of the men who habitually go down in the ticklish and temperamental submarine.

The telltale needles of the gauges still moved on the dials and the boat was still sinking in the direction of the bottom. The commander was now heard to say in accents mildly surprised:

"We don't seem to catch her, Bill. Something ails this fool boat."

"It sure does," heartily agreed the navigator. "Gee, I wish I could smoke a cigarette. There is deep water here, and if she keeps on behaving this way, the pressure will start something, and we'll be out of luck."

"Oh, I guess we can catch her before long."

They did. The submarine had concluded to behave herself. The only scared man was a correspondent named Paine who had been filled with — he almost said divers emotions. Otherwise the ship's company discussed it as a passing incident of their trade. Presently the boat blew her ballast tanks and slowly rose to the surface, poking up a dripping bridge while the water gushed from the openings in the false deck. A British submarine riding on the surface signaled the Admiral's compliments. The "crash dive" had been immensely well done! Our youthful skipper grinned for joy and danced a jig on the tiny box of a bridge to warm his freezing toes.

That night the Admiral and the correspondent dined aboard the British mother ship as the guests of Captain Nasmith who commanded the submarines in Bantry Bay during the training period. He was another sailor who had won the Victoria Cross and for a most spectacular achievement. This was the man who had taken a British submarine through the maze of nets and mines in the Dardanelles and played about in the Sea of Marmora and the Black Sea for many weeks, shelling Constantinople with his popguns by way of diversion, sinking a Turkish battleship right under the heaviest guns of the forts, shooting torpedoes into transports, and enjoying himself most gorgeously.

Much against his inclination Captain Nasmith was persuaded by Admiral Bayly to spin a few yarns after dinner, and the best of them all, because it revealed the spirit of a chivalrous fighting sailor, went something like this:

"While barging about in the Black Sea I sighted a Turkish steamer laden with supplies and so on, and decided to slip a torpedo into her. Running on the surface my boat headed her off and I hailed the bridge, giving them time to get the boats out and all hands away. There was a mad scramble, the devil of a mess, but the crew tumbled into the boats and pulled off, and I was about to let drive at the ship.

"Just then there came boiling up from below a passenger who had been overlooked in the excitement. I rather fancy he had been asleep in his berth. He was a fat man — oh, very fat — and he was clad in a pink undershirt, nothing more. We yelled at him to wait for a boat to turn back, but he had lost his wits. With a tremendous bellow he plopped overboard. The Turkish boats were legging it away for dear life and paid no attention to his yells. I had to move my submarine close enough to fish him out myself.

"There he sat, on my forward deck, like a dripping walrus in a pink undershirt. I was for chasing after one of the boats and chucking him in, but first we had to torpedo the steamer and make sure she went down. This job out of the way, I was about to put after a boat and get rid of this bothersome beggar, but just then a Turkish gunboat came bustling along and I had to dodge her.

"I was anxious to submerge, of course, so we sung out to the pink walrus to climb the conning-tower and we'd poke him down the hatch. He answered in German, being a manager of some branch bank out that way. The Turkish gunboat was coming up unpleasantly fast, so we hauled this corpulent castaway up by main strength and the slack of his pink undershirt, and tried to get him below.

"My word, the round conning-tower hatch was n't big enough to squeeze him through! His midship section stuck hard and fast, like a cork in a bottle. A brawny quartermaster was hammering him from on top, like a pile-driver, and down inside the sub a machinist and the torpedo lieutenant were hauling at his legs. But it simply could not be done. It was most awkward, I give you my word, for if we did n't submerge in a jiffy that hostile gunboat might pot us.

"We had to heave the pink walrus out again and dump him on deck, with a blanket to keep him warm. And there he sat, confound him, while we hooked up and ran on the surface, the gunboat tossing shells at us. We could n't submerge and drown the poor rotter, although he was a frightful nuisance as you can very well understand. Night was coming on and we managed to give the gunboat the slip.

"But for the next two days it was out of the frying-pan into the fire. This objectionable pink ruffian was carried on deck — he had to be — and we gave him a drink now and then. As luck would have it, every Turkish gunboat in that part of the Black Sea seemed to be getting after us. We were quite fed up with it. It was the deuce of a job to go clear of them, running on the surface as we had to, do you see — could n't submerge and hide, for there was that animated pink hogshead on the forward deck, and he could n't be shoved down through the hatch unless you whittled him a lot.

"To cut it short, I finally overhauled a Turkish sailing vessel and put my passenger aboard. Hanged if he even thanked me, after I had been to all that trouble on his account. It was thoroughly sporting, the whole show — to be frisking about between the devil and the deep sea with this absurd derelict decorating the top-side of your submarine."

This trip to Bantry Bay was the last of the correspondent's excursions with the Allied Naval Forces. He had been permitted to see a wonderful diversity of activities afloat and ashore. It was time to go home and write a book about it. As in his youth there had been many enjoyable experiences along the roads of adventure.

Some time after the war he happened to be reading, with lively interest, a volume called "Indiscretions of the Naval Censor," by Rear Admiral Sir Douglas Brownrigg, R.N. It is the desire of all men to be thought well of by their neighbors, whether they deserve it or not. And at the conclusion of these random reminiscences, the author feels an anxiety to leave as favorable an impression as possible.

He has confessed to many follies in his younger days and it is no more than fair to let him try to improve his average by calling to your attention this opinion of the Chief Censor of the Admiralty:

Another writer who came over here in the autumn of 1917 was Mr. Ralph Paine. Wherever he went he won friends. His first trip was to Queenstown to see the American destroyers. He went for ten days and stayed with our Commander-in-Chief six weeks, and Sir Lewis Bayly, in returning him to me, said, "If you have any more like him, send them along." That was pretty good testimony as to his tact and popularity, combined with his discretion in han dling facts. He saw everything there was to see in the life of that gallant flotilla, and I never had to censor or delete a word from anything he wrote.

He subsequently went to Harwich where he was equally appreciated, and also visited several other of our naval bases. Later I sent him up to the Grand Fleet where he spent a few days with the American Battle Squadron under Admiral Hugh Rodman. He then began to talk about going home and was actually on the point of getting off when I told him that if he went without seeing the Western Front he should never be forgiven, as he would miss one of the greatest educational sights of all time.

The time was short, but under the auspices of our Army men, who ran these Western Front trips so extraordinarily successfully and smoothly during the last three years of the War, I arranged a five days' trip for him. He came back really grateful to me for having forced him to go. I hope that Peace will not keep him from returning here and renewing the many friendships he made whilst in this country.

.   .   .   .

The pile of manuscript on my desk had been steadily growing in bulk, but I was wondering whether it ought not to include such stories as "The Spinster Ladies in Search of Pirates' Gold," and "How Jordan was Kidnaped in Nagasaki," and "Why Jack Teal Bit off the Sheep-Herder's Ear." Providentially one of my twin sons, aged eleven, sauntered to the desk and inquired, in a skeptical manner:

"Do you expect people to read all that?"

"Well, my son, we are always hoping for the improbable to happen."

"Um-m-m! Won't they feel very tired?"

"I had n't thought of that. You inherit your sagacity from your mother, young man. It is time for me to stop."

THE END